Harvard Business Review
On Human Relations

Harvard
Business Review

On Human
Relations

Harper & Row, Publishers

New York, Hagerstown, San Francisco, London

ABR 3611
m-698

Grateful acknowledgment is extended to Holt, Rinehart & Winston, Inc. for permission to reprint lines from "What Fifty Said" from *The Poetry of Robert Frost,* edited by Robert Connery Lathem. Copyright 1928, © 1969 by Holt, Rinehart and Winston. Copyright © 1956 by Robert Frost.

FIRST EDITION

Designer: C. Linda Dingler

Library of Congress Cataloging in Publication Data
Main entry under title:

Harvard business review—on human relations.
Articles originally published in the Harvard business review.
  Includes index.
  1. Organizational behavior—Addresses, essays, lectures. 2. Management—Addresses, essays, lectures.
I. Harvard business review. II. Title: On human relations.
HD58.7.H37   658.4   78-20166
ISBN 0-06-011789-3

RECEIVED

79 80 81 82 83 10 9 8 7 6 5 4 3 2 1

Contents

PART IV

Intuitive Ways of Relating to People

PART V

Being an Effective Leader

Foreword

Over the years many of the articles on general business strategies and philosophies that have appeared in the *Harvard Business Review* have been based on a scientific, medical model. Using this model a manager does investigative work to see if he or she has a problem, then diagnoses it, then solves it, the solution being to install a system of some sort. However, also during these years, the editors, sometimes wittingly sometimes not, were selecting articles that were out of the mainstream of business practice in that they hinted at an area of management concern that science and analysis, no matter how elegant, cannot define.

This is not to say that the management sciences do not have a legitimate role to play in organizations. Obviously, they do; each year new management texts continuing the search for the ultimate management model proliferate and do well. But management science cannot map all the terrain that managers must cross to do their jobs; much of the landscape does not lend itself to rational analysis, to Cartesian quests for the straight line between thinking and reality.

These stubborn areas of resistance to science are human motivations and needs. They are also, however, managers themselves, who cannot be rationalized any more than their employees can be. For a long time the main aim of many behavioral scientists has been to rationalize management systems, among them motivation and appraisal systems. With these attempts ride the unquestioned assumption that good managers are themselves rational and consistent, with their emotions and intuitions in check.

The authors of the articles in this book question whether the effort to rationalize organizations and managerial work isn't itself a form of tilting at windmills. Challenging the assumption that to be rational is to be right, these authors assert that certain things cannot or ought not be rationalized and that the attempt actually limits organizations and the people who manage them. Emotion, intuition, judgment, creativity, spontaneity, and faith ought not to be merely legitimate in organizations; they are necessary to managerial excellence.

In other words, sometimes a manager has to be a scientist, but sometimes he or she must be an artist.

As science can be appreciated secondhand (we don't have to see Einstein's original conception of the theory of relativity to understand it), so can rational systems work in organizations apart from their creators. But as art cannot be appreciated second hand, any more than a good meal can be, so managers influence people through what they perceive the manager to be.

But this way of thinking raises many questions for managers and teachers of managers. If management of people is an art, requiring spontaneous, nonrational creation, how does one teach it? How do organizations develop young managers? If, in some situations, intuition or judgment is worth more than rational systems, how do we know when one and not the other should apply?

If people and managers themselves cannot be completely rationalized, how do we appraise them? And how can we begin to understand what goes on between people if we cannot systematize it? Should managers accept ambiguity and uncertainty as a fact of life? If so, how can they work with them? Finally, how ought managers to lead people?

The linking premise of the articles in the book is not that rationality is right or wrong but that sometimes it is inappropriate, that sometimes other aspects of people, managers as well as their employees, are more important. These authors encourage the reader to explore the nonrational aspects of managing, developing managerial talent, relating to people, and being a leader or person in authority.

The Editors
Harvard Business Review

Part I
The Limits of
the Rational Approach

Preface

Ever since Plato determined that opinion is no more reliable than a shadow show and that truth is universal, Western society has had a bias for the products of reason, and one against the insights of intuition. In most U.S. schools and universities one is not considered intelligent unless one is verbally adept and can show on paper the products of one's thought processes. In U.S. business, the well-reasoned argument and proof positive usually win out over judgment. And sometimes this is as it should be.

But there is more to intelligence than the spoken word can reveal. In the section that follows, Henry Mintzberg points out in "Planning on the Left Side and Managing on the Right" how recent experiments have shown that the two hemispheres of the brain both process information, but in very different ways. The left hemisphere is the domain of reason, which involves analysis of singular elements linked in a sequence. The right hemisphere works holistically, perceiving simultaneously the relations between individual parts. An intuitive insight, for instance, a composer's "hearing" a whole symphonic movement or a poet's "seeing" a whole poem, is the product of the right hemisphere.

The two hemispheres have different functions, but they are not discrete, and no person is "all left" or "all right." People are, however, usually dominated by one side or the other. In the words of James McKenney and Peter Keen, in "How Managers' Minds Work," people have different cognitive styles.

Because intelligence is not a product of the left hemisphere only, it would seem that the emphasis on reason is misplaced. Reason cannot solve all management problems any more than intuition can. Neither, however, is adequate on its own. In the articles that follow the authors discuss what can and what cannot be rationalized in organizations and how managers can go about closing the gap between the management scientists and the management artists, the operating managers.

1. Planning on the Left Side and Managing on the Right

Henry Mintzberg

Did you ever wonder why some things come so easily and others seem so difficult, why sometimes you just cannot get your brain to work? Maybe the problem is not that you are stupid or tired, but that you are tackling a problem that taxes the less-developed hemisphere of your brain. Recent scientific research shows that the human brain is specialized, the logical, linear functions occurring in the left hemisphere, and the holistic, relational ones occurring in the right. The author of this article maintains that this finding has great implications for both the science and the art of management. For instance, in an organization, the author suggests that the top managers should have well-developed right-hemispheric processes, and the planners well-developed left-hemispheric processes. Perhaps the most important conclusion he arrives at is that the functions and capacities of the two hemispheres should both be respected, but that one should not be confused or applied where the other is better suited.

In the folklore of the Middle East, the story is told about a man named Nasrudin, who was searching for something on the ground. A friend came by and asked, "What have you lost, Nasrudin?"

"My key," said Nasrudin.

So the friend went down on his knees, too, and they both looked for it. After a time, the friend asked, "Where exactly did you drop it?"

"In my house," answered Nasrudin.

"Then why are you looking here, Nasrudin?"

"There is more light here than inside my house."

This "light" little story is old and worn, yet it has some timeless, mysterious appeal, one that has much to do with the article that follows. But let me leave the story momentarily while I pose some questions—also simple yet mysterious—that have always puzzled me.

First: Why are some people so smart and so dull at the same time, so capable of mastering certain mental activities and so incapable of mastering others? Why is it that some of the most creative thinkers cannot comprehend a balance sheet, and that some accountants have no sense of product design? Why do some brilliant management scientists have no ability to handle organizational politics, while some of the most politically adept individuals seem unable to understand the simplest elements of management science?

Second: Why do people sometimes express such surprise when they read or learn the obvious, something they already must have known? Why is a manager so delighted, for example, when he reads a new article on decision making, every part of which must be patently obvious to him even though he had never before seen it in print?

Third: Why is there such a discrepancy in organizations, at least at the policy level, between the science and planning of management on the one hand, and managing on the other? Why have none of the techniques of planning and analysis really had much effect on how top managers function?

What I plan to do in this article is weave together some tentative answers to these three questions with the story of Nasrudin around a central theme— namely, that of the specialization of the hemispheres of the human brain and what that specialization means for management.

The Two Hemispheres of the Human Brain

Let us first try to answer the three questions by looking at what is known about the hemispheres of the brain.

QUESTION ONE

Scientists—in particular, neurologists, neurosurgeons, and psychologists—have known for a long time that the brain has two distinct hemispheres. They have known, further, that the left hemisphere controls movements on the body's right side and that the right hemisphere controls movements on the left. What they have discovered more recently, however, is that these two hemispheres are specialized in more fundamental ways.

In the left hemisphere of most people's brains (left-handers largely excepted) the logical thinking processes are found. It seems that the mode of operation of the brain's left hemisphere is linear; it processes information sequentially, one bit after another, in an ordered way. Perhaps the most obvious linear faculty is language. In sharp contrast, the right hemisphere is specialized for simulta- neous processing; that is, it operates in a more holistic, relational way. Perhaps its most obvious faculty is comprehension of visual images.

Although relatively few specific mental activities have yet been associated with one hemisphere or the other, research is proceeding very quickly. For example, a recent article in the *New York Times* cites research that suggests that emotion may be a right-hemispheric function.[1] This notion is based on the finding that victims of right-hemispheric strokes are often comparatively untroubled about their incapacity, while those with strokes of the left hemisphere often suffer profound mental anguish.

What does this specialization of the brain mean for the way people function? Speech, being linear, is a left-hemispheric activity, but other forms of human communication, such as gesturing, are relational rather than sequential and tend to be associated with the right hemisphere. Imagine what would happen if the two sides of a human brain were detached so that, for example, in reacting to a stimulus, a person's words would be separate from his gestures. In other words, the person would have two separate brains—one specialized for verbal communication, and the other for gestures—that would react to the same stimulus.

This "imagining," in fact, describes how the main breakthrough in the recent research on the human brain took place. In trying to treat certain cases of epilepsy, neurosurgeons found that by severing the corpus callosum, which joins the two hemispheres of the brain, they could "split the brain," isolating the epilepsy. A number of experiments run on these "split-brain" patients produced some fascinating results.

In one experiment doctors showed a woman epileptic's right hemisphere a photograph of a nude woman. (This is done by showing it to the left half of each eye.) The patient said she saw nothing, but almost simultaneously blushed and seemed confused and uncomfortable. Her "conscious" left hemisphere, including her verbal apparatus, was aware only that something had happened to her body, but not of what had caused the emotional turmoil. Only her "unconscious" right hemisphere knew. Here neurosurgeons observed a clear split between the two independent consciousnesses that are normally in communication and collaboration.[2]

Now scientists have further found that some common human tasks activate one side of the brain while leaving the other largely at rest. For example, a person's learning a mathematical proof might evoke activity in the left hemisphere of his brain, while his conceiving a piece of sculpture or assessing a political opponent might evoke activity in his right.

So now we seem to have the answer to the first question. An individual can be

1. Richard Restak, "The Hemispheres of the Brain Have Minds of Their Own," *New York Times*, January 25, 1976.

2. Robert Ornstein, *The Psychology of Consciousness* (San Francisco: W. H. Freeman, 1975), p. 60.

smart and dull at the same time simply because one side of his or her brain is more developed than the other. Some people—probably most lawyers, accountants, and planners—have better developed left-hemispheric thinking processes, while others—artists, sculptors and perhaps politicians—have better developed right-hemispheric processes. Thus an artist may be incapable of expressing his feelings in words, while a lawyer may have no facility for painting. Or a politician may not be able to learn mathematics, while a management scientist may constantly be manipulated in political situations.

Eye movement is apparently a convenient indicator of hemispheric development. When asked to count the letters in a complex word such as *Mississippi* in their heads, most people will gaze off to the side opposite their most developed hemisphere. (Be careful of lefties, however.) But if the question is a specialized one—for example, if it is emotionally laden, spatial, or purely mathematical—the number of people gazing one way or another will change substantially.

QUESTION TWO

A number of word opposites have been proposed to distinguish the two hemispheric modes of "consciousness," for example: explicit versus implicit; verbal versus spatial; argument versus experience; intellectual versus intuitive; and analytic versus gestalt.

I should interject at this point that these words, as well as much of the evidence for these conclusions, can be found in the remarkable book entitled *The Psychology of Consciousness*, by Robert Ornstein, a research psychologist in California. Ornstein uses the story of Nasrudin to further the points he is making. Specifically, he refers to the linear left hemisphere as synonymous with lightness, with thought processes that we know in an explicit sense. We can *articulate* them. He associates the right hemisphere with darkness, with thought processes that are mysterious to us, at least "us" in the Western world.

Ornstein also points out how the "esoteric psychologies" of the East (Zen, yoga, Sufism, and so on) have focused on right-hemispheric consciousness (for example, altering pulse rate through meditation). In sharp contrast, Western psychology has been concerned almost exclusively with left-hemispheric consciousness, with logical thought. Ornstein suggests that we might find an important key to human consciousness in the right hemisphere, in what to us in the West is the darkness. To quote him:

Since these experiences [transcendence of time, control of the nervous system, paranormal communication, and so on] are, by their very mode of operation, not readily accessible to causal explanation or even to linguistic exploration, many have been tempted to ignore them or even to deny their existence. These traditional psychologies have been relegated to the "esoteric" or the "occult," the realm of the mysterious—the word most often employed is "mysticism." It is a taboo area of inquiry, which has been symbolized by the Dark, the Left side [the right hemisphere] of ourselves, the Night.[3]

Now, reflect on this for a moment. (Should I say meditate?) There is a set of thought processes—linear, sequential, analytical—that scientists as well as the rest of us know a lot about. And there is another set—simultaneous, relational, holistic—that we know little about. More importantly, here we do not "know" what we "know" or, more exactly, our left hemispheres cannot articulate explicitly what our right hemispheres know implicitly.

So here is, seemingly, the answer to the second question as well. The feeling of revelation about learning the obvious can be explained with the suggestion that the "obvious" knowledge was implicit, apparently restricted to the right hemisphere. The left hemisphere never "knew." Thus it seems to be a revelation to the left hemisphere when it learns explicitly what the right hemisphere knew all along implicitly.

Now only the third question—the discrepancy between planning and managing—remains.

QUESTION THREE

By now, it should be obvious where my discussion is leading (obvious, at least, to the reader's right hemisphere and, now that I write it, to the reader's left hemisphere as well). It may be that management researchers have been looking for the key to management in the lightness of logical analysis whereas perhaps it has always been lost in the darkness of intuition.

Specifically, I propose that there may be a fundamental difference between formal planning and informal managing, a difference akin to that between the two hemispheres of the human brain. The techniques of planning and management science are sequential and systematic; above all, articulated. Planners and management scientists are expected to proceed in their work through a series of logical, ordered steps, each one involving explicit analysis. (The argument that the successful application of these techniques requires considerable intuition does not really change my point. The occurrence of intuition simply means that the analyst is departing from his science, as it is articulated, and is behaving more like a manager.)

Formal planning, then, seems to use processes akin to those identified with the brain's left hemisphere. Furthermore, planners and management scientists

3. Ibid., p. 97.

seem to revel in a systematic, well-ordered world, and many show little appreciation for the more relational, holistic processes.

What about managing? More exactly, what about the processes used by top managers? (Let me emphasize here that I am focusing this discussion at the policy level of organizations, where I believe the dichotomy between planning and managing is most sharp.) Managers plan in some ways, too (that is, they think ahead), and they engage in their share of logical analysis. But I believe there is more than that to the effective managing of an organization. I hypothesize, therefore, that *the important policy processes of managing an organization rely to a considerable extent on the faculties identified with the brain's right hemisphere.* Effective managers seem to revel in ambiguity; in complex, mysterious systems with relatively little order.

If true, this hypothesis would answer the third question about the discrepancy between planning and managing. It would help to explain why each of the new analytic techniques of planning and analysis has, one after the other, had so little success at the policy level. PPBS, strategic planning, "management" (or "total") information systems, and models of the company—all have been greeted with great enthusiasm; then, in many instances, a few years later have been quietly ushered out the corporate back door. Apparently none served the needs of decision making at the policy level in organizations; at that level other processes may function better.

Managing from the Right Hemisphere

Because research has so far told us little about the right hemisphere, I cannot support with evidence my claim that a key to managing lies there. I can only present to the reader a "feel" for the situation, not a reading of concrete data. A number of findings from my own research on policy-level processes do, however, suggest that they possess characteristics of right-hemispheric thinking.

One fact recurs repeatedly in all of this research: the key managerial processes are enormously complex and mysterious (to me as a researcher, as well as to the managers who carry them out), drawing on the vaguest of information and using the least articulated of mental processes. These processes seem to be more relational and holistic than ordered and sequential, and more intuitive than intellectual; they seem to be most characteristic of right-hemispheric activity.

Here are ten general findings:

1. The five chief executives I observed strongly favored the verbal media of communication, especially meetings, over the written forms, namely reading and

writing. (The same result has been found in virtually every study of managers, no matter what their level in the organization or the function they supervised.) Of course verbal communication is linear, too, but it is more than that. Managers seem to favor it for two fundamental reasons that suggest a relational mode of operation.

First, verbal communication enables the manager to "read" facial expressions, tones of voice, and gestures. As I mentioned earlier, these stimuli seem to be processed in the right hemisphere of the brain. Second, and perhaps more important, verbal communication enables the manager to engage in the "real-time" exchange of information. Managers' concentration on the verbal media, therefore, suggests that they desire relational, simultaneous methods of acquiring information, rather than the ordered and sequential ones.

2. In addition to noting the media managers use, it is interesting to look at the content of managers' information, and at what they do with it. The evidence here is that a great deal of the manager's inputs are soft and speculative—impressions and feelings about other people, hearsay, gossip, and so on. Furthermore, the very analytical inputs—reports, documents, and hard data in general—seem to be of relatively little importance to many managers. (After a steady diet of soft information, one chief executive came across the first piece of hard data he had seen all week—an accounting report—and put it aside with the comment, "I never look at this.")

What can managers do with this soft, speculative information? They "synthesize" rather than "analyze" it, I should think. (How do you analyze the mood of a friend or the grimace someone makes in response to a suggestion?) A great deal of this information helps the manager understand implicitly his organization and its environment, to "see the big picture." This very expression, so common in management, implies a relational, holistic use of information. In effect, managers (like everyone else) use their information to build mental "models" of their world, which are implicit synthesized apprehensions of how their organizations and environments function. Then, whenever an action is contemplated, the manager can simulate the outcome using his implicit models.

There can be little doubt that this kind of activity goes on all the time in the world of management. A number of words managers commonly use suggest this kind of mental process. For example, the word *hunch* seems to refer to the thought that results from such an implicit simulation. "I don't know why, but I have a hunch that if we do x, then they will respond with y." Managers also use the word *judgment* to refer to thought processes that work but are unknown to them. *Judgment* seems to be the word that the verbal intellect has given to the thought processes that it cannot articulate. Maybe "he has good judgment" simply means "he has good right-hemispheric models."

3. Another consequence of the verbal nature of the manager's information is of interest here. The manager tends to be the best-informed member of his organization, but he has difficulty disseminating his information to his employees. Therefore, when a manager overloaded with work finds a new task that needs doing, he faces a dilemma: he must either delegate the task without the background information or simply do the task himself, neither of which is satisfactory.

When I first encountered this dilemma of delegation, I described it in terms of time and of the nature of the manager's information; because so much of a manager's information is verbal (and stored in his head), the dissemination of it consumes much of his time. But now the split-brain research suggests that a second, perhaps more significant, reason for the dilemma of delegation exists. The manager may simply be incapable of disseminating some relevant information because it is removed from his verbal consciousness. (This suggests that we might need a kind of managerial psychoanalyst to coax it out of him!)

4. Earlier in this article I wrote that managers revel in ambiguity, in complex, mysterious systems without much order. Let us look at evidence of this. What I have discussed so far about the manager's use of information suggests that their work is geared to action, not reflection. We see further evidence for this in the pace of their work ("Breaks are rare. It's one damn thing after another"); the brevity of their activities (half of the chief executives' activities I observed were completed in less than 9 minutes); the variety of their activities (the chief executives had no evident patterns in their workdays); the fact that they actively exhibit a preference for interruption in their work (stopping meetings, leaving their doors open); and the lack of routine in their work (only 7% of 368 verbal contacts I observed were regularly scheduled, only 1% dealt with a general issue that was in any way related to general planning).

Clearly, the manager does not operate in a systematic, orderly, and intellectual way, puffing his pipe up in a mountain retreat, as he analyzes his problems. Rather, he deals with issues in the context of daily activities—the cigarette in his mouth, one hand on the telephone, and the other shaking hands with a departing guest. The manager is involved, plugged in; his mode of operating is relational, simultaneous, experiential—that is, encompassing all the characteristics of the right hemisphere.

5. If the most important managerial roles of the ten described in the research were to be isolated, *leader, liaison,* and *disturbance handler* would certainly be among them. (The other seven are *figurehead, monitor, disseminator, spokesman, negotiator, entrepreneur,* and *resource allocator,* and the last two are also among the most important roles.) Yet these three are the roles least "known" about. *Leader* describes how the manager deals with his own employees. It is

ironic that despite an immense amount of research, managers and researchers still know virtually nothing about the essence of leadership, about why some people follow and others lead. Leadership remains a mysterious chemistry; catchall words such as *charisma* proclaim our ignorance.

In the *liaison* role, the manager builds up a network of outside contacts, which serve as his or her personal information system. Again, the activities of this role remain almost completely outside the realm of articulated knowledge. And as a *disturbance handler* the manager handles problems and crises in his organization. Here again, despite an extensive literature on analytical decision making, virtually nothing is written about decision making under pressure. These activities remain outside the realm of management science, inside the realm of intuition and experience.

6. Let us turn now to strategic decision-making processes. There are seven "routines" that seem to describe the steps involved in such decision making. These are *recognition, diagnosis, search, design, screening, evaluation/choice,* and *authorization.* Two of these routines stand out above the rest—the *diagnosis* of decision situations and the *design* of custom-made solutions—in that almost nothing is known of them. Yet these two stand out for another reason as well: they are probably the most important of the seven. In particular, diagnosis seems to be *the* crucial step in strategic decision making, for it is in that routine that the whole course of decision making is set.

It is a surprising fact, therefore, that diagnosis goes virtually without mention in the literature of planning or management science. (Almost all of the later literature deals with the formal evaluation of given alternatives, yet this is often a kind of trimming on the process, insignificant in terms of determining actual outcomes.) In the study of the decision processes themselves, the managers making the decisions mentioned taking an explicit diagnostic step in only 14 of the 25 decision processes. But all the managers must have made some diagnosis; it is difficult to imagine a decision-making process with no diagnosis at all, no assessment of the situation. The question is, therefore, *where* did diagnosis take place?

7. Another point that emerges from studying strategic decision-making processes is the existence and profound influence of what can be called the *dynamic factors.* Strategic decision-making processes are stopped by interruptions, delayed and speeded up by timing factors, and forced repeatedly to branch and cycle. These processes are, therefore, dynamic ones of importance. Yet it is the dynamic factors that the ordered, sequential techniques of analysis are least able to handle. Thus, despite their importance, the dynamic factors go virtually without mention in the literature of management science.

Let's look at timing, for example. It is evident that timing is crucial in virtually everything the manager does. No manager takes action without considering the effect of moving more or less quickly, of seizing the initiative, or of delaying to avoid complications. Yet in one review of the literature of management, the authors found fewer than 10 books in 183 that refer directly to the subject of timing.[4] Essentially, managers are left on their own to deal with the dynamic factors, which involve simultaneous, relational modes of thinking.

8. When managers do have to make serious choices from among options, how do they in fact make them? Three fundamental modes of selection can be distinguished—analysis, judgment, and bargaining. The first involves the systematic evaluation of options in terms of their consequences on stated organizational goals; the second is a process in the mind of a single decision maker; and the third involves negotiations between different decision makers.

One of the most surprising facts about how managers made the 25 strategic decisions studied is that so few reported using explicit analysis; only in 18 out of 83 choices made did managers mention using it. There was considerable bargaining, but in general the selection mode most commonly used was judgment. Typically, the options and all kinds of data associated with them were pumped into the mind of a manager, and somehow a choice later came out. *How* was never explained. *How* is never explained in any of the literature either. Yehezkel Dror, a leading figure in the study of public policy making, is one of the few thinkers to face the issue squarely. He writes:

> Experienced policy makers, who usually explain their own decisions largely in terms of subconscious processes such as "intuition" and "judgment," unanimously agree, and even emphasize, that extrarational processes play a positive and essential role in policymaking. Observations of policymaking behavior in both small and large systems, indeed, all available description of decisional behavior, especially that of leaders such as Bismarck, Churchill, DeGaulle, and Kennedy, seem to confirm that policy makers' opinion.[5]

9. Finally, in the area of strategy formulation, I can offer only a "feel" for the results since my research is still in progress. However, some ideas have emerged. Strategy formulation does not turn out to be the regular, continuous, systematic process depicted in so much of the planning literature. It is most often an irregular, discontinuous process, proceeding in fits and starts. There are periods of stability in strategy development, but also there are periods of flux, of groping, of piecemeal change, and of global change. To my mind, a "strategy" represents the mediating force between a dynamic environment and a stable operating system. Strategy is the organization's "conception" of how to deal with its environment for a while.

Now, the environment does not change in any set pattern. For example, the

4. Clyde T. Hardwick and Bernard F. Landuyt, *Administrative Strategy and Decision Making,* 2nd ed. (Cincinnati: South Western, 1966).
5. Yehezkel Dror, *Public Policymaking Re-Examined* (Scranton: Chandler, 1968), p. 149.

environment does not run on planners' five-year schedules; it may be stable for thirteen years, and then suddenly blow all to hell in the fourteenth. And even if change were steady, the human brain does not generally perceive it that way. People tend to underreact to mild stimuli and overreact to strong ones. It stands to reason, therefore, that strategies that mediate between environments and organizational operations do not change in regular patterns, but rather, as I observed earlier, in fits and starts.

How does strategic planning account for fits and starts? The fact is that it does not (as planners were made so painfully aware of during the energy crisis). So again, the burden to cope falls on the manager, specifically on his mental processes—intuitional and experiential—that can deal with the irregular inputs from the environment.

10. Let me probe more deeply into the concept of strategy. Consider the organization that has no strategy, no way to deal consistently with its environment; it simply reacts to each new pressure as it comes along. This is typical behavior for an organization in a very difficult situation, where the old strategy has broken down beyond repair but no new strategy has yet emerged. Now, if the organization wishes to formulate a new strategy, how does it do so (assuming that the environment has stabilized sufficiently to allow a new strategy to be formulated)?

Let me suggest two ways (based on still tentative results). If the organization goes the route of systematic planning, I suggest that it will probably come up with what can be called a "main-line" strategy. In effect, it will do what is generally expected of organizations in its situation; where possible, for example, it will copy the established strategies of other organizations. If it is in the automobile business, for instance, it might use the basic General Motors strategy, as Chrysler and Ford have so repeatedly done.

Alternatively, if the organization wishes to have a creative, integrated strategy which can be called a "gestalt strategy," such as Volkswagen's strategy in the 1950s, then I suggest the organization will rely largely on one individual to conceptualize its strategy, to synthesize a "vision" of how the organization will respond to its environment. In other words, scratch an interesting strategy, and you will probably find a single strategy formulator beneath it. Creative, integrated strategies seem to be the products of single brains, perhaps of single right hemispheres.

A strategy can be made explicit, can be announced as what the organization intends to do in the future, only when the vision is fully worked out, if it ever is. Often, of course, it is never felt to be fully worked out, hence the strategy is never made explicit and remains the private vision of the chief executive. (Of course, in some situations the formulator need not be the manager. There is no reason why a manager cannot have a creative right-hand man—really a left-hand man—who works out his gestalt strategy for him, and then articulates it to him.) No management process is more demanding of holistic, relational, gestalt thinking than the formulation of a creative, integrated strategy to deal with a complex, intertwined environment.

How can sequential analysis (under the label *strategic planning*) possibly lead to a gestalt strategy?

Another "famous old story" has relevance here. It is the one about the blind men trying to identify an elephant by touch. One grabs the trunk and says the elephant is long and soft; another holds the leg and says it is massive and cylindrical; a third touches the skin and says it is rough and scaly. What the story points out is that

> Each person standing at one part of the elephant can make his own limited, analytic assessment of the situation, but we do not obtain an elephant by adding "scaly," "long and soft," "massive and cylindrical" together in any conceivable proportion. Without the development of an overall perspective, we remain lost in our individual investigations. Such a perspective is a province of another mode of knowledge, and cannot be achieved in the same way that individual parts are explored. It does not arise out of a linear sum of independent observations.[6]

What can we conclude from these ten findings? I must first reemphasize that everything I wrote about the two hemispheres of the brain falls into the realm of speculation. Researchers have yet to formally relate any management process to the functioning of the human brain. Nevertheless, the ten points do seem to support the hypothesis stated earlier: *the important policy-level processes required to manage an organization rely to a considerable extent on the faculties identified with the brain's right hemisphere.*

This conclusion does not imply that the left hemisphere is unimportant for policy makers. I have overstated my case here to emphasize the importance of the right. The faculties identified with the left hemisphere are obviously important as well for effective management. Every manager engages in considerable explicit calculation when he or she acts, and all intuitive thinking must be translated into the linear order of the left if it is to be articulated and eventually put to use. The great powers that appear to be associated with the right hemisphere are obviously useless without the faculties of the left. The artist can create without verbalizing; the manager cannot.

Truly outstanding managers are no doubt the ones who can couple effective right-hemispheric processes (hunch, judgment, synthesis, and so on) with effective processes of the left (articulateness, logic, analysis, and so on). But

6. Ornstein, p. 10.

there will be little headway in the field of management if managers and researchers continue to search for the key to managing in the lightness of ordered analysis. Too much will stay unexplained in the darkness of intuition.

Before I go on to discuss the implications for management science and planning, I want to stress again that throughout this article I have been focusing on processes that managers employ at the policy level of the organization. It seems that the faculties identified with the right-hemispheric activities are most important in the higher levels of an organization, at least in those with "top-down" policy-making systems.

In a sense, the coupling of the holistic and the sequential reflects how bureaucratic organizations themselves work. The policy maker conceives the strategy in holistic terms, and the rest of the hierarchy—the functional departments, branches, and shops—implement it in sequence. Whereas the right-hemispheric faculties may be more important at the top of an organization, the left-hemispheric ones may dominate lower down.

Implications for the Left Hemisphere

Let us return to practical reality for a final word. What does all I've discussed mean for those associated with management?

FOR PLANNERS AND MANAGEMENT SCIENTISTS

No, I do not suggest that planners and management scientists pack up their bags of techniques and leave the field of management, or that they take up basket weaving or meditation in their spare time. (I haven't—at least not yet!) It seems to me that the left hemisphere is alive and well; the analytic community is firmly established, and indispensable, at the operating and middle levels of most organizations. Its real problems occur at the policy level. Here analysis must coexist with—perhaps even take its lead from—intuition, a fact that many analysts and planners have been slow to accept. To my mind, organizational effectiveness does not lie in that narrow-minded concept called "rationality"; it lies in a blend of clear-headed logic *and* powerful intuition. Let me illustrate this with two points.

☐ *First, only under special circumstances should planners try to plan.* When an organization is in a stable environment and has no use for a very creative strategy—the telephone industry may be the best example—then the development of formal, systematic strategic plans (and main-line strategies) may be in order. But when the environment is unstable or the organization needs a creative strategy, then strategic planning may not be the best approach to strategy formulation, and planners have no business pushing the organization to use it.

☐ *Second, effective decision making at the policy level requires good analytical input; it is the job of the planner and management scientist to ensure that top management gets it.* Managers are very effective at securing soft information; but they tend to underemphasize analytical input that is often important as well. The planners and management scientists can serve their organizations effectively by carrying out ad hoc analyses and feeding the results to top management (need I say verbally?), ensuring that the very best of analysis is brought to bear on policy making. But at the same time, planners need to recognize that these inputs cannot be the only ones used in policy making, that soft information is crucial as well.

FOR THE TEACHER OF MANAGERS

If the suggestions in this article turn out to be valid, then educators had better revise drastically some of their notions about management education, because the revolution in that sphere over the last fifteen years—while it has brought so much of use—has virtually consecrated the modern management school to the worship of the left hemisphere.

Should educators be surprised that so many of their graduates end up in staff positions, with no intention of ever managing anything? Some of the best-known management schools have become virtual closed systems in which professors with little interest in the reality of organizational life teach inexperienced students the theories of mathematics, economics, and psychology as ends in themselves. In these management schools, management is accorded little place.

I am not preaching a return to the management school of the 1950s. That age of fuzzy thinking has passed, thankfully. Rather, I am calling for a new balance in our schools, the balance that the best of human brains can achieve, between the analytic and the intuitive. In particular, greater use should be made of the powerful new skill-development techniques that are experiential and creative in nature, such as role playing, the use of video tape, behavior laboratories, and so on. Educators need to put students into situations, whether in the field or in the simulated experience of the laboratory, where they can practice managerial skills, not only interpersonal but also informational and decisional. Then specialists would follow up with feedback on the students' behavior and performance.

FOR MANAGERS

The first conclusion for managers should be a call for caution. The findings of the cognitive psychologists should not be taken as license to shroud activities in darkness. The mystification of conscious behavior is a favorite ploy of those seeking to protect a power base (or to hide their intentions of creating one); this behavior helps no organization, and neither does forcing to the realm of intuition activities that can be handled effectively by analysis.

A major thrust of development in our organizations, ever since Frederick Taylor began experimenting in factories late in the last century, has been to shift activities out of the realm of intuition, toward conscious analysis. That trend will continue. But managers, and those who work with them, need to be careful to distinguish that which is best handled analytically from that which must remain in the realm of intuition, where, in the meantime, we should be looking for the lost keys to management.

2. Fallacy of the One Big Brain

Pearson Hunt

If things in business were completely rational, all problems would be analyzed and solved by one person or brain having complete access to information from all over the organization. The decisions would be objective, well defined, and timely. Because people often design things according to a rational ideal, it is understandable that business executives would try to design decision-making systems in organizations as if there were one big brain at the top or center that could solve all problems. The author of this article exhorts business people to consider how decisions are actually made, that in reality business decisions are not made instantly by one big brain or computer but by many little brains over time. He argues that by eliciting the opinions and ideas of other people, executives elicit their commitment and involvement as well.

As managers change their ways in response to the opportunities offered by computerization, simulation, linear programming, and the other valuable procedures stemming from recent developments in the quantitative sciences, they may lose sight of equally important contributions offered by recent findings in the behavorial sciences. If they do neglect this side, they can easily fall victim to the fallacy of the one big brain.

I refer to the neglect, in the study and practice of business management, of proper organizational assignment of the work to be done. This neglect is seen whenever people act as if business problems were solved by a single entity having one big brain. All too often, we design schemes of analysis that assume that problems can be recognized, defined, analyzed, and solved by one brain of enormous capacity, which operates in a completely objective manner, searching for and comparing all possible alternatives in one thinking process (lasting perhaps only a few seconds if we have the aid of a computer) to arrive at the

AUTHOR'S NOTE: I should like to acknowledge the major contribution of Edna Homa in the preparation of this article.

best possible answers. For example, take the capital budgeting procedures of many companies:

"Projects" are submitted to a planning and analysis group, which accumulates them until an annual or other predetermined review date, and then—in one fell swoop—ranks them in an order of priority. Unfortunately, the criteria the group uses normally reflect only financial factors. Such an episodic review, performed outside the ongoing work of the going concern, is evidence of the idea of one big brain. And it produces some weird decisions.

A corollary of the proposition that there is one big brain, of course, is that all the lesser brains in the organization need not concern themselves with the big questions, so it matters very little how the work of decision making in the company is organized. Nothing could be further from the truth. The manager of any business faces the unavoidable problem of shaping the organization so that brains of human scale will reach necessary decisions efficiently.

This article is really a plea for business executives to take a close look at the organizations they manage to see who is making what decisions, and to consider whether some of the findings about the process of decision making that I shall describe indicate any desirable changes in their company's organizational assignments.

Erroneous Abstraction

It is amazing how often one sees evidence of the assumption that all the heavy thinking in an organization can be left to some specialized group. This assumption not only lies behind the way theorists reason; it also affects the way managers act. To illustrate:

The widespread use of the words "management" and "administration" is evidence of the fallacious abstraction. Management doesn't make decisions, but managers do. We must talk, not about an abstraction—management—but about the *behavior of managers* as they do their work. It is of supreme importance to recognize that it is the behavior of people as they make decisions that makes up management—and nothing more abstract than this.

Yet we hear the word "management" instead of "managers" in conversations, we see it in publications, we listen to it in speeches of politicians, and we use it ourselves when we talk. All of this reflects the fallacy of the one big brain.

How often does one see in an organization evidence of the idea that problems are solved by selecting a procedure to solve them? How often does one see, when reading books—even recent books—on finance, marketing, or some other business function, a problem-oriented description that handles with great skill the important things which have to be done, showing how new analytical techniques can be used, and yet forgetting in its coverage that this work must be done by a group of people in an organization?

SALIENT DIFFERENCES

In fact, business decisions are not made in a few moments by one big brain, but by a lot of smaller brains. (Let it be understood I did not say "small" brains; rather, I am referring here to brains of human scale, and we all know that such brains often have great ability.) These brains, in dealing with business problems, must act in coordination with each other, *often* over a considerable period of time, *usually* in a situation that has ways of shifting one's attention from one problem to another, and *always* in a situation in which an individual's position in the total structure has great influence both on the work and thinking that he does and on the way his conclusions are received and used.

Fortunately, some worthwhile work in the study of decision making is being done. In my view, one of the great contributions of recent study about decision making is the opportunity offered to managers to reorganize the assignment of work in ways that can produce more effective results for their companies. More and more, we are able to describe the salient differences between the way one brain might attack a problem and the kind of thinking that takes place when many brains are working on it.

The differences are not simple ones, for when the whole problem is broken down into parts, the parts change their nature and one can never put them back to make the picture of the operation of one big brain.

Decision Process

To elaborate on this point, I shall present the two key features of decision making—(1) sequential breakdown of the problem, and (2) hierarchical assignment of the work—which have been made more clear by behavioral studies in recent years.

SEQUENTIAL BREAKDOWN

When a manager faces a major decision, he must subdivide it into a number of smaller problems and assign these to various persons. Thus, it inevitably follows from the fact of subdivision that the work is going to be done in separate places at different times. That is to say, the sections of the work will become *sequential* in the sense that some portions must wait for and use the results of prior portions.

Since this is so, it follows that decisions made in earlier portions of the sequence become constraints on or prescriptions for the later decisions to a degree that is not always recognized. Recent studies show very clearly that as the sequence progresses, the "best estimates" (always representing someone's judgment) become the "facts" for subsequent analysis. Sales forecasts, for example, are best estimates—the forecaster never insists that he is absolutely right; he is only helping as best he can. And yet time after time subsequent decision makers respond to these sales forecasts as if they were factual.

HIERARCHICAL ASSIGNMENT

Just as sequence is inevitable, the assignment of the work in parts inevitably becomes *hierarchical*. That is to say, persons doing different levels of work have positions with different levels of authority, and they deal with one another with reference to these levels.

The varying significance of the word "advice" serves to emphasize the importance of considering the organizational position of a decision maker. Thus:

The organizational manual of a certain company states flatly that the treasurer selects the banks in which the company's deposit accounts will be placed. It would appear from this that he is a pretty important officer! But then, in an adjacent column, "advice from the president" is mentioned. Suddenly the scope of the treasurer's job changes. Surely, you will agree that advice from one's boss has a force quite like that of an instruction!

Suppose, instead, that the notation had read "advice from the cashier." Here the treasurer's decision-making authority is certainly very different! But before we leave the example, it is interesting to look also at the responsibility of the cashier. Although he will not select the bank, surely he is expected to give advice only after due consideration. Actually, the content of upward-moving advice represents a responsible decision within the level of authority occupied by the subordinate, and he will be held accountable for its quality.

One of the outmoded ideas about organization is the description of a "staff" person as distinguished from one in the "line." According to this scheme, a staff man has no authority; he merely advises some manager in the line, who may choose to ignore him. In fact, even though the line executive need not accept such advice when it is offered, no experienced manager can say that staff advice has no force.

The point that I wish to make is that there is no such thing as irresponsible advice in either direction between superior and subordinate, or between staff and line personnel. *But one must know where in the organizational level the giver of advice is placed in order to understand the force of his advice.*

An obvious conclusion that arises from such observations of sequence and levels of authority is that the order in which the parts of a task are to be done may have a significant effect on the final answer. It would be desirable, then, to arrange that the decisions having the least uncertainty be made first, thus building on the most stable foundation.

"Uncommitted State"

What can a manager do about the fact that the best estimates made at lower levels tend to be treated as facts as the decision process moves upward? I used to feel (and I know that others still feel) that a way must be found for top-level decision makers to restore, before the final decision is made, the warnings and uncertainties that will have been lost in the sequential process. Indeed, there are experiments going on now that have to do with the ways in which organizations can maintain what is referred to as the "uncommitted state" during an entire decision-making procedure. As I have thought about this, however, I have come to feel that maintaining the uncommitted state is likely to land the top manager on a psychiatrist's couch, full of anxiety and unable to make decisions at all.

I propose that the last-minute review is, in fact, both impossible to perform objectively and undesirable. The subdivision and assignment of work inevitably causes judgment to be used by each person in the organization with reference to his part of the process. The upper levels in a decision-making process accept estimated findings from lower levels, not only because they must, but also because great advantage is gained in the process by using the judgment of people at levels where they have the capacity to exercise this judgment. The rare quality of high capacity may thus be concentrated where it is really needed; judgments of lesser importance can be made at lower levels.

If one wishes to suggest that sometimes some of the lesser judgments that are accepted will be wrong, and therefore the big judgments will also be wrong, he will obviously be correct. But I suggest that perhaps the best thing any business can hope for in an ongoing decision-making situation is a good batting average.

TIMELY SUBDECISIONS

In contrast to the idea of the uncommitted state, I offer frequent inquiry and the timely obtaining of subdecisions from responsible persons. An example of the consequences of not following such a procedure may serve as an illustration:

The planning staff of a large chemical manufacturer was assigned the task of studying the desirability of building a new plant for the manufacture of resins that were coming from the development division of the company. The expenditure of many millions of dollars was in prospect, and the study was therefore an important one.

The habitual procedure of this planning staff, in the words of one observer, was that "once they have received a problem they shut the door, and the only way to communicate with them is by slipping notes under it."

The results of this isolation were unfortunate. The planning staff analysts worked diligently to label all the important variables; those that were significant were estimated at five levels of possibility, and probabilities were assigned to the various levels. The staff then came up with its best estimate of net funds flows. This estimate, regarded as factual at this stage in the sequence, was used to calculate a promised return on the investment, and a recommendation to approve the project was handed up to the president of the company.

All this work, which took several analysts many weeks (and drew on their best judgmental efforts), was rejected within an hour by the president. *Why?* Because the president could not accept the pattern of probabilities that had been selected by the analysts.

One may ask, whose probabilities were better? Frankly, so far as I could tell, the analysts' were better than the president's. But looking at the matter from an organizational perspective, I would like to point out something else. The analysts were wrong in not finding out what the president's estimates of probability were long before they made their final presentation. *Again why?* Because, if they had, it might have helped in the success of their recommendation; and, after all, the president of the company was the one who bore the responsibility for this decision.

I believe that the real test of the appropriateness of organizational assignments occurs when something goes wrong. When people are working together smoothly, it is not really important who is responsible for what. But if something goes wrong, then it becomes important to know the organizational position of the individual who should bear the responsibility. And since it is the chief operating executive of any company who bears the ultimate responsibility, his judgment should prevail. His subordinates can argue with him and try to help him change his mind, but if the executive is firm in his convictions, he should win. He is the accountable officer, and accountability and authority must sit in the same chair.

Let me suggest an organizational principle that I think comes out of this discussion: a process involving many people is one that requires that (a) work be properly sequenced, and (b) people be authorized (indeed, *instructed*) to communicate with one another—up the organization, down the organization, and across the organization—as necessary. If not, matters which require the making of certain judgments are either handled by persons at an undesirable level of the organization, or they are decided according to a subordinate's conception, which may well be misinformed, of a superior's likely conclusion.

In other words, a multibrain process is a sequential process that calls for a host of subdecisions. And wherever a person requires information or judgment from another level in the organization, it should be specified that he is expected to get promptly what is needed from the responsible officer, and not wait until a project is completed. It is part of the judgment of a person making a study to know when to ask questions.

Personal Commitment

Another most important finding about a multibrain decision process is that as each person completes his portion of a study—knowing he is accountable for the judgments he has exercised—he becomes *committed* to the support of his conclusions, and thus his subsequent behavior becomes in part that of an advocate. There is nothing like a commitment to make a person feel involved. People who have a commitment argue with a different kind of emotional base than they do when they have not made their position known in advance. Commitment changes the nature of the argument and one's feelings about it.

RATIONALIZATION FACTOR

For the reason of commitment, it is not by chance that a report often becomes known as a "presentation." It is no longer a full statement of the doubts and uncertainties that surround the conclusions. It may not be all on one side—like a lawyer's brief—but it is often closer to it than most of us willingly admit. After people become committed to a conclusion they have reached, their judgment can never again be as open as it was before. Take this actual example from a company operating in a country whose currency was facing possible devaluation:

Many of the managers of this company had decided that they must finance their planned expansion program by borrowing from abroad, promising payment in the currency of the lender's country. Yet when I asked one manager, "What are your plans or thoughts about the situation if your currency is devaluated and you have to pay dollars?" his answer was, "We can't think about that, or we'll never make an investment."

As this response shows, one of the aspects of commitment is that if a person is really committed, he usually rules out of consideration what I call the preemptive possibility which might force a reversal from his committed position. He seems to say, "We'll assume it won't happen," or (as this particular firm did), "The government will take care of us; we don't know how, but it must," or something of the kind.

Commitment grows from the accumulation of little decisions—even from continued familiarity with a situation. We have all experienced it, in business and in our private lives. Therefore, when I put myself in the place of a manager who awaits his opportunity to make a final decision, I do not recommend that he attempt to maintain an "uncommitted state."

Instead, I suggest that he keep in touch with a project as it develops, so that the key subdecisions can be reviewed by him at a time well before the commitment of his subordinates becomes too strong. In so doing, of course, the manager builds up his own commitment, but it is easier to handle his own prejudices than those of others.

Nevertheless, a manager must train himself to recognize those apparently small commitments which, in fact, so precondition later work that one final course of action—unless unusually great negative forces arise—is inevitable. The gathering force of commitment is very much like momentum; it keeps getting harder and harder to stop.

IRREVERSIBLE COMMITMENT

The final decision is seldom, if ever, the last step in an analytical process where everyone remains uncommitted until the eleventh hour. Major decisions are usually found, on investigation, to have emerged at some earlier time in the multibrain decision process. *Imperceptibly, the "minor" decisions taken all along the line have made the conclusion inevitable.* The case is even more clear when major resources as well as people have been committed as the work went along. Thus, it is hardly a surprise to hear so often that top-level approval will be a formality.

Though it seldom can be determined exactly, there comes a time when it is inevitable that an important decision is going to be made in a certain way. There is a point when it would not be too costly to change to another course, but there is also a point when commitment has, in fact, taken place. I vividly remember the request of an executive involved in a major planning operation of which I was in charge. "Please be sure," he wrote me, "to let me know when you come to the brief moment between 'too soon' and 'too late' so that my suggestions will be heard."

Finally, it must be remembered that the process of human-scale decision making is carried out in an organizational environment where the brains involved are doing other things at the same time. In other words, decisions are made by people who have become committed to certain policies, who are in the process of becoming committed to other policies at the same time, and who cannot avoid the effects of those other commitments on the decisions they now face.

Let me summarize these points by paraphrasing the words of another author:

We view the decision making in complex organizations as emerging from a continuous social process, composed of many small acts, and carried out by different people at divergent points of time. We reject the notion that one specific decision can be made the focus of analysis. Instead we suggest concentration on the dynamic social process in which activities are carried out. We must depict the system instead of looking for a logical process that can be isolated from it.[1]

Managerial Implications

Let me now draw some conclusions from my observations about the salient differences between a single-brain and a multibrain process.

The manager who wants to get the best possible results from the multibrain process finds himself face to face with a prerequisite. He must be sure that he heads an organization where work is accomplished with the least possible friction and waste. Such an organization is one that is capable of *evolving major decisions as a normal part of its whole system of doing work*. The idea of a planning staff operating independently of the rest of the organization is dangerous. A planning staff can be very useful, but only if it is integrated with the operating executives so that there is free interaction, and the judgments that define policy are actually made by persons who later will be accountable for results. For example:

One rapidly expanding company has established branch manufacturing operations and new sales outlets in two new areas in recent years. In each case, the preliminary studies were made by a vice president, who enlisted the help of the sales manager, chief engineer, and personnel director (as well as the usual staff of junior financial and economic analysts). These senior officers, while not working continuously on the study, were in touch with it from beginning to end, so that there could be no unhappy ending, as in the chemical company I referred to earlier.

ORGANIZATIONAL REQUIREMENTS

The first requirement in reforming an organization is for the manager to recognize one undeniable fact: if a group of people have been working together, there is already an organization. This is a certainty, for work cannot be done by

1. See Yair Aharoni, *The Foreign Investment Decision Process* (Boston, Division of Research, Harvard Business School, 1966).

more than one person without division and allocation. The organization may be "good" or it may be "bad," but it *exists*.

The second requirement is to be explicit in formulating organizational assignments. As an acute observer has said:

> Most, if not all, members of organizations are only dimly aware of the pattern of tasks which are being allocated day in and day out—the tasks which constitute not some peripheral frill but the very function which the organization has been set up to fulfill. The members of the organizations are of course unconsciously aware of all the tasks— and do carry them out. But there is a shying away from explicit formulation. Why we are so anxious about the explicit recognition of tasks and work is not a subject for discussion [at this point], but shy we certainly are, and [progress cannot be made] until this recoil away from looking at the realities of allocated tasks has been overcome.[2]

The most important thing for a manager to consider is neither the formality nor informality of his organization, but its capacity to do the work that is to be carried out. The study of the work to be done is important in organizational design—more important in my view than the personality interactions of those who will occupy posts in the organization. Many of us are coming to recognize that the great pacemaking work of the human relations school of management needs now to be supplemented by considerations that take into account more strongly the nature of the work to be done.

WORK-ROLE BOUNDARIES

A few basic insights concerning work assignments are already finding confirmation in recent studies. The essential property of a job is not defined by whether it is skilled or unskilled, line or staff, but rather by the nature of the judgments that the job calls for. A field hand may work himself to the point of exhaustion, but he does not have important judgments to make and his job is not highly rated. Others may lead physically easy lives, but their work is regarded highly, because the judgments they make strain their capacity and create a great deal of anxiety. They have to bear the burden of making decisions and implementing them despite a long time of uncertainty as to whether these decisions are right or wrong. In business, a person is evaluated in his work primarily by the way he utilizes his judgment.

There are several dimensions to be considered if a complete job description is to be made, but nothing is so important as the sentences which contain the words *he decides*. The knowledge needed and the technical skills required constitute prerequisites that supply boundaries to the work role, but the all-

2. Elliott Jaques, *Time Span Handook* (London, Heineman, 1964), p. 5.

important thing that happens within these boundaries is the exercise of discretion. And may I point out that wherever judgment is, there accountability should also be found. By the same token, no one should be held accountable for a decision unless he is given the authority to commit the resources to carry it out.

PLANNING DIMENSIONS

As soon as it is recognized that decision making is inevitably performed by many persons in an organization, each one exercising his own judgment and committing resources within the boundaries of his job, it will be clear that the responsibility to do part of the company's planning has also been subdivided. *Planning and creative thinking cannot be made the exclusive responsibility of a chosen few within a business organization.* The janitor is responsible for planning his work, and for ideas to improve it. The middle manager is equally responsible for planning his work, and for obtaining desirable changes within the bounds of his particular authority. The chief executive himself will not have fulfilled his own planning responsibility unless he has made it clear to members of his organization at all levels that each one has planning to do, and unless he has also provided the time and resources that are necessary to permit the fulfillment of this dimension of each person's work.

If it is true, as I am sure it is, that "one learns by doing," it must be recognized that one only learns what one does. A company that denies the planning dimension of work to the lower levels of management obtains what it deserves—men who, when promoted, are not able to plan ahead. *A company whose organizational scheme requires planning at every level finds men who have learned how to look ahead because they have been doing it.* They will have learned how to plan, just as they have learned the other things that justify their promotion.

Unfortunately, planning is not so treated in many businesses—where the fallacy of the one big brain still denies the lower-level managers this part of their work.

To those who would avoid the fallacy of the one big brain, I would urge a more thorough study of the nature of the work assignments which exist in their organization. One cannot, through centralization, computerization, or otherwise, create one big brain. The facts of human scale require that decision making be subdivided, and new findings in organizational research are available to managers to guide them in creating work assignments that will vastly improve the processes of decision making.

3. How Managers' Minds Work

James L. McKenney and Peter G. W. Keen

A number of researchers have pointed to particular aspects of thinking and personality that differ between the people who build models and those who use them. Obviously, management scientists and general managers think differently. In an effort to narrow this gap, the authors discuss their recent research on cognitive style, which provides a means of developing strategies of action for the management scientist and a useful way of focusing on the implementation of analytic models for the general manager.

A common topic in management literature over the past few years has been the difference between managers and management scientists, usually in relation to the argument that their association has not been a productive one. For example, an article by C. Jackson Grayson, Jr., compares the situation with C. P. Snow's famous notion of the two cultures of science and humanities: "Managers and management scientists are operating as two separate cultures, each with its own goals, languages, and methods. Effective cooperation—and even communication—between the two is just about minimal."[1] Perhaps this is an overpessimistic viewpoint, but it is one that is expressed often and by individuals who have substantial experience with the use of analytic methods in management.

Management science techniques have been very successful in such areas of business as logistics planning, resource allocation, and financial forecasting. It appears that, on the whole, these techniques have found the applications for which they are best suited, and managers make substantial and continued use of them.

However, in other areas of business they have been unable to gain any real foothold. Most obviously, they have had little impact on areas of decision making where the management problems do not lend themselves to explicit formulation, where there are ambiguous or overlapping criteria for action, and where the manager operates through intuition.

---

1. "Management Science and Business Practice," HBR July-August 1973, p. 41.

The major issue for management science as a discipline now seems to be to get managers in such situations to make use of the formal techniques that can clearly be so helpful to them but have not yet been so in practice. There seem to be two main factors affecting this problem.

One concerns the actual techniques available. Obviously, process chemists use linear programming because it suits the constraints and natures of the problems they deal with.

The primary factor, however, is the differences in approach and behavior between the two cultures. A feature under little control by either manager or scientist is that each has a distinctive style of thinking and problem solving. In its own context, each style is highly effective but not easily communicated to the other. The differences in thinking are neither "good" nor "bad"; they simply exist.

In a way, it is platitudinous to state that managers and scientists are different, but a reason for focusing explicitly on this factor is to examine the argument, maintained by management writers, that to bridge the gap between the two groups each should become a little more like the other. In this view, the differences themselves are the problem, and education is generally recommended as the solution: the manager should be trained in elementary quantitative techniques, and the scientist, in interpersonal and managerial skills.

Yet it is this very differentiation of thinking style that makes each of them successful in his chosen specialization. But the cost of differentiation is the increased difficulty it presents in integration. Therefore, the issue for both manager and scientist is complex: how to communicate with each other; how to complement each other's strengths without sacrificing too much of one's own.

In this article, we are explicitly concerned with these differences in thinking between the two cultures. We shall offer suggestions as to how the manager and the scientist can best work together in the development and use of analytic models and decision aids.

We suggest that such aids must be designed to amplify the user's problem-solving strategies. Thus it seems that the central factor determining whether a manager will use a model to reach a decision is the extent to which it "fits" his style of thinking. The main body of this paper largely defines what we mean by "fit."

Over the past four years, we have developed and tested a model of cognitive style, drawing on the developmental psychology that has in recent years reinvigorated the whole study of thinking and problem solving.[2] Our main aim has been to better understand the cognitive aspects of the decision-making process.

2. See Jerome S. Bruner, Jacqueline J. Goodnow, and George A. Austin, *A Study of Thinking* (New York, John Wiley & Sons, 1956).

Exhibit I Model of cognitive style

	Information gathering		
	Preceptive		
Information evaluation			
Systematic			**Intuitive**
	Receptive		

In the first section of this article, we shall provide a statement of our model in terms applicable to problem solving and decision making in general, rather than just to analytic techniques. Next, we shall discuss the experimental data we have gathered in validating the model. Finally, we shall extend our findings to the implications of cognitive style for implementing formal analytic models.

Model of Cognitive Style

We view problem solving and decision making in terms of the processes through which individuals organize the information they perceive in their environment, bringing to bear habits and strategies of thinking. Our model is based on the dual premise that consistent modes of thought develop through training and experience and that these modes can be classified along two dimensions, information gathering and information evaluation, as shown in *Exhibit I*.

Information gathering relates to the essentially perceptual processes by which the mind organizes the diffuse verbal and visual stimuli it encounters. The resultant "information" is the outcome of a complex coding that is heavily dependent on mental set, memory capacity, and strategies—often unconscious ones—that serve to ease "cognitive strain." Of necessity, information gathering involves rejecting some of the data encountered, and summarizing and categorizing the rest.

Preceptive individuals bring to bear concepts to filter data; they focus on relationships between items and look for deviations from or conformities with their expectations. Their precepts act as cues for both gathering and cataloging the data they find.

Receptive thinkers are more sensitive to the stimulus itself. They focus on detail rather than relationships and try to derive the attributes of the information from direct examination of it instead of from fitting it to their precepts.

Each mode of information gathering has its advantages in specific situations; equally, each includes risks of overlooking the potential meaning of data. The preceptive individual too easily ignores relevant detail, while the receptive thinker may fail to shape detail into a coherent whole. In management positions, the former will be most successful in many marketing or planning roles, and the latter in tasks such as auditing.

Information evaluation refers to processes commonly classified under problem solving. Individuals differ not only in their method of gathering data but also in their sequence of analysis of that data. These differences are most pronounced in relation to formal planning.

Systematic individuals tend to approach a problem by structuring it in terms of some method which, if followed through, leads to a likely solution.

Intuitive thinkers usually avoid committing themselves in this way. Their strategy is more one of solution testing and trial-and-error. They are much more willing to jump from one method to another, to discard information, and to be sensitive to cues that they may not be able to identify verbally.

Here again, each mode of information evaluation has advantages and risks. In tasks such as production management, the systematic thinker can develop a method of procedure that utilizes all his experience and economizes on effort. An intuitive thinker often reinvents the wheel each time he deals with a particular problem. However, the intuitive person is better able to approach ill-structured problems where the volume of data, the criteria for solution, or the nature of the problem itself does not allow the use of any predetermined method.

FOCUS ON PROBLEM FINDING

Most modern theories of the decision process stress "rationality." Mathematical decision theory and game theory, for example, are both mainly concerned with defining the basics of rational behavior. Accounting for the discrepancies between it and observed behavior is only a secondary aim. Other theories, particularly those concerning organizational decision making, include factors of motivation, personality, and social forces but still treat decision making as essentially equivalent to problem solving.

In our model of cognitive style, we focus on problem solving, but our central argument is that decision making is above all situational and, therefore, includes problem finding. The manager scans his environment and organizes what he perceives. His efforts are as much geared to clarifying his values and intents as to dealing with predefined problems.

Obviously, some problems do force themselves on his awareness; this is particularly true in crisis situations. Nonetheless, he generally has some discretion in the selection of problems to deal with and in the level of aspiration he sets for himself. (His aspiration often determines the extent to which he involves himself in terms of effort and risk.)

The manager's activities are bounded not only by the formal constraints of his job but also by the more informal traditions and expectations implicit in his role. Because of this, the decision-making activity is strongly influenced by his perception of his position. A decision "situation" exists when he sees some event or cue in his environment that activates him into a search-analyze-evaluate sequence that results in a decision. This sequence is initiated by and depends on his environment assessment.

Our cognitive-style model provides some explanation of the processes affecting the manager's assessment of his environment. It thus includes an important aspect of behavior omitted in most theories on decision making—namely, that of problem finding, problem recognition, and problem definition. Generally, other theories assume that the situation has already been defined; the manager is presented with a neatly packaged problem and instructions on what he should try to do.

Implicit in the focus on problem finding is the concept that particular modes of cognition are better suited to certain contexts than others. As we mentioned earlier, the central argument of our study is that there needs to be a fit between the decision maker's cognitive style and the information-processing constraints of his task. Given this fit, the manager is more likely to gather environmental information that leads to successful (or at least comfortable) problem finding. He should also be able to evaluate that information in a way that facilitates successful problem solving. Perhaps the implications of a misfit are easier to indicate.

We mentioned earlier than a receptive thinker focuses on detail rather than pattern. But a receptive field sales manager who receives a wide range of information may well be flooded by it. He probably cannot examine all the sales reports, orders, phone calls, and so on. Instead, he should try to filter his information and be alert to trends and discrepancies. Thus a combination of the sales pattern in a particular region and a recent salesman's report of several customers' comments may lead him to recognize signs of change in consumer taste.

The preceptive individual is particularly suited to those tasks where he must have a concept of his environment. A preceptive manager would not be very successful in a task such as editing.

Similarly, it is easy to envisage tasks in which the intuitive thinker cannot come to terms with the data that are required in his decision making because he is unable to think in terms of a methodical sequence of analysis.

We have chosen the term *style* rather than the more common one of *structure* to stress the fact that modes of thinking relate more to propensity than to capacity. An individual's style develops out of his experience. For example, there is a tendency, particularly in late high school and college for a student to increasingly choose courses that build on his strengths. This reinforcing pattern further develops those strengths and perhaps atrophies the skills in which he is less confident.

This suggests not only that tasks exist that are suited to particular cognitive styles, but also that the capable individual will *search out* those tasks that are compatible with his cognitive propensities. In addition, he will generally approach tasks and problems using his most comfortable mode of thinking.

Our model indicates some important differences in the ways in which individuals of particular styles approach problems and data. The accompanying list summarizes the main characteristics of each style:

Systematic thinkers tend to
- ☐ look for a method and make a plan for solving a problem.
- ☐ be very conscious of their approach.
- ☐ defend the quality of a solution largely in terms of the method.
- ☐ define the specific constraints of the problem early in the process.
- ☐ discard alternatives quickly.
- ☐ move through a process of increasing refinement of analysis.
- ☐ conduct an ordered search for additional information.
- ☐ complete any discrete step in analysis that they begin.

Intuitive thinkers tend to
- ☐ keep the overall problem continuously in mind.
- ☐ redefine the problem frequently as they proceed.
- ☐ rely on unverbalized cues, even hunches.
- ☐ defend a solution in terms of fit.
- ☐ consider a number of alternatives and options simultaneously.
- ☐ jump from one step in analysis or search to another and back again.
- ☐ explore and abandon alternatives very quickly.

Receptive thinkers tend to
- ☐ suspend judgment and avoid preconceptions.
- ☐ be attentive to detail and to the exact attributes of data.
- ☐ insist on a complete examination of a data set before deriving conclusions.

Preceptive thinkers tend to
- ☐ look for cues in a data set.
- ☐ focus on relationships.
- ☐ jump from one section of a data set to another, building a set of explanatory precepts.

Exhibit II Tasks and roles compatible with each cognitive style

	Preceptive	
Production & logistics manager Statistician Financial analyst		Marketing manager Psychologist Historian
Systematic		Intuitive
Auditor Clinical diagnostician	Receptive	Architect Bond Salesman

Our research supports the concept that particular tasks and roles are more suited to one cognitive style than to another. *Exhibit II* shows careers that seem to be especially compatible with the skills and predispositions implicit in each of the cognitive modes of style.

Experimental Results

We have carried out a range of experiments over the past four years aimed at validating the assertions made in the preceding statements.[3] The main effort in the experiments has been to identify and measure cognitive style. In the spring of 1972, a set of 12 standard reference tests for cognitive factors, developed by the Educational Testing Service, was administered to 107 MBA students. Each test was specifically chosen to fit one particular mode of style. The results confirmed most of the main characteristics of each style summarized earlier.

INITIAL TESTS

In our first set of experiments, 70% of the sample showed distinct differences in performance level between the systematic and the intuitive tests or between the receptive and the preceptive. This supports our basic contention that individuals tend to have a definite style.

We chose a conservative approach for our tests, classifying a subject as "intuitive," "systematic," and so on, only when the scores on tests requiring, say, an intuitive response were substantially different from those measuring capacity for the other mode of style along the same dimension. The comparisons

---

3. These experiments are described in detail in Peter G. W. Keen, "The Implications of Cognitive Style for Individual Decision Making," unpublished doctoral dissertation, Harvard Business School, 1973.

focused on relative, not absolute, performance. The numeric scores were converted to a 1 to 7 scale, with a "1" indicating that the subject scored in the lowest seventh of the sample and a "7" corresponding to the top seventh.

From our main sample of 107 MBA students, we selected 20 whose test results indicated a distinct cognitive style for a follow-up experiment. This made use of a "cafeteria" set of 16 problems from which the subjects were asked to choose any 5 to answer. In individual sessions, which were tape recorded, the subjects were invited, though not required, to talk aloud as they dealt with each problem. The results pointed to distinct differences in the ways in which individuals of particular styles respond to problems.

As expected, the systematic subjects tended to be very concerned with getting into a problem by defining how to solve it. They were conscious of their planning and often commented on the fact that there were other specific ways of answering the problem.

In contrast, the intuitive subjects tended to jump in, try something, and see where it led them. They generally showed a pattern of rapid solution testing, abandoning lines of exploration that did not seem profitable.

More important, each mode of response was effective in solving different kinds of problems. In one instance, which required the decoding of a ciphered message, the intuitive subjects solved the problem—sometimes in a dazzling fashion—while none of the systematics were able to do so. In this particular case, there seemed to be a pattern among the intuitives: a random testing of ideas, followed by a necessary incubation period in which the implications of these tests were assimilated, and then a sudden jump to the answer.

There were often unexplained shifts in the reasoning of the intuitives, who were also much more likely to answer the problems orally. The latter tendency provided some confirmation for the idea that intuitive individuals use their own talking aloud to cue their activities and to alert themselves to possible lines of analysis.

There were distinct differences in the problems chosen by each of the groups, and their ratings of which problems they enjoyed most were remarkably consistent. The systematics preferred program-type problems, while the intuitives liked open-ended ones, especially those that required ingenuity or opinion.

The overall results of the initial experiments provided definite evidence to support both our model of cognitive style and the classification methods we developed through the main-sample test scores. The verbal answers in particular highlighted the degree to which these subjects consistently and distinctively respond to problems. There seems little doubt that, in these extreme cases at least, the individual maps himself onto the problem, rather than matching his behavior to the constraints and demands of the particular task.

SECONDARY SAMPLING

In another set of tests, again using the main sample of 107 subjects, we examined the relationship between cognitive style and personality. We did this through comparisons of our test results with the Myers-Briggs scales used to classify individuals in relation to Jungian theories of psychological type.[4]

The most striking result of our experiment was that, while the scores on the Myers-Briggs scales showed virtually no correlation with absolute performance on our tests, there was a relationship between cognitive style and those scales. In particular, the systematic subjects were very likely to be of the "thinking" type and the intuitives much more likely to be at the other end of the scale, "feeling." R. O. Mason and I. I. Mitroff provide a useful summary of the difference between the thinking-feeling types:

A Thinking individual is the type who relies primarily on cognitive processes. His evaluations tend to run along the lines of abstract true/false judgments and are based on formal systems of reasoning. A preference for Feeling, on the other hand, implies the type of individual who relies primarily on affective processes. His evaluations tend to run along personalistic lines of good/bad, pleasant/unpleasant, and like/dislike. Thinking types systematize; feeling types take moral stands and are interested in and concerned with moral judgments.[5]

We found a more modest relationship between systematic style and "introversion" and, similarly, between intuitive style and "extroversion." Thus our findings mesh well with Mason and Mitroff's predictions (they did not report any experimental data) about psychological type and information systems.

FINAL STUDY

A year after the first two sets of experiments, we examined the relationship between style and career choice, using a sample of 82 MBA students. The results showed consistent differentiations between systematic and intuitive subjects. We compared the career preferences of the two groups and also looked at the test scores of those individuals who showed strong preference for particular careers.

In this experiment, the systematic students were attracted to administrative careers, to the military, and to occupations involving production, planning,

---

4. See Isabel Briggs Myers and Katharine C. Briggs, "The Myers-Briggs Type Indicator," Educational Testing Service, Princeton, New Jersey, 1957.
5. "A Program for Research on Management Information Systems," *Management Science*, January 1973, p. 475.

control, and supervision. The intuitive group's choices centered around the more open-ended business functions; they preferred careers in psychology, advertising, library science, teaching, and the arts.

The overall result of the three sets of student experiments supports the validity of our conceptual model as a useful and insightful framework for examining the role of cognitive processes in decision making. More important, now that we have established such proof, we plan to extend our research to the study of business managers and especially to model builders and model users.

Analytic Models

One of our major conjectures, which partly underlay the whole development of our model, has been that computer systems in general are designed by systematic individuals for systematic users. Although management science has lost its early tones of missionary zeal, of bringing "right" thinking to the ignorant, the implementation of analytic techniques not unreasonably reflects the scientist's own distinctive approach to problem solving.

Model building, from the viewpoint of the management scientist, involves making the causal relationships in a particular situation explicit and articulating the problem until he gets a reasonably predictive model; he will then generally refine that model. He has a faith in his own plan and process, and his specialized style of thinking enables him to literally build a model, shaping ideas and concepts into a methodological whole, and above all articulating relationships that the manager may understand but may not be able to make explicit.

The management scientist's skill is indeed a specialized one; the powerful organizing and systematizing capacity he brings to model building is his special contribution. But, obviously, that can be a vice rather than a virtue in specific situations. What Donald F. Heany calls the "have technique, will travel"[6] banner really amounts to the rigorously systematic individual's preference for a methodical approach to all problems in all contexts.

Fortunately, there are many systematic managers. Our assumption is that most general managers who use management science techniques are likely to be systematic in style. The techniques match their own innate approach to problems, and they gravitate to occupations that are suited to their style.

For example, since inventory control is a task that can be systematized, it will attract systematic managers, and it will therefore be an area in which management science techniques will find fruitful ground.

6. See "Is TIMS Talking to Itself?" *Management Science*, December 1965, p. B-156.

Exhibit III Classification of tasks and problems

| | | Information acquisition, perceptual process | |
		Known	Unknown
Information manipulation, conceptual process	Known	Planning, Type 1	Intelligence-search, Type 2
	Unknown	Invention, Type 3	Research, Type 4

However, there are just as many management positions not filled by systematic thinkers. For example, advertising, which is not so easily systematized, will attract intuitive people. If management scientists want their techniques used in these more loosely structured business areas, they must try both to make their models less awesome to the intuitive managers they will be working with and to support the managers in their decision-making processes.

This requires understanding the intuitive approach to problem solving in general and developing models that will amplify and complement that approach.

CLASSES OF PROBLEMS

We have found it useful to categorize tasks—and problems in general—in terms of the problem solver's assessment of his ability to first recognize and then act on relevant information.[7] This process provides four basic classes of problems, as in *Exhibit III*.

The classes are easily illustrated. If, for example, a manager encounters a problem of inventory control in which he feels that he knows both what data are relevant and what mental operations and analysis are required to deal with that data, the problem is one of planning (Type I in *Exhibit III*). His whole effort then involves merely arranging the data into a form that can be used as input to a defined sequence of evaluation.

Another class of problem (Type 2) exists when the required operations and

7. See James L. McKenney, "A Taxonomy of Problem Solving," working paper, Harvard Business School, 1973.

methods are known, but the data involved are not. Price forecasting in complex markets is an example of this situation. Before a forecast can be made, a mass of data on economic, price, and market variables must be organized and sifted. Once this has been done, the forecasting procedure is simple.

A very different state of affairs exists when the individual understands the data but does not know how to manipulate them. Many production-scheduling problems fall into this class, invention (Type 3). The relevant data are known and the problem consists of finding a way to achieve the desired end.

The last class of problem, research (Type 4), exists when both information and operations are unknown. In this situation, there is a conscious search for cues and a generation of explanatory concepts, together with the development of a method for manipulating the data thus organized. The development of new products is a typical research problem.

SPECIALIZED STYLES

Many management science projects start as research. For example, modeling a complex environment such as the housing market in order to make industry or demand forecasts generally requires a complicated first step in which two areas of the problem are worked on in parallel: (1) the generation of concepts to "explain" reality and identify the most relevant variables, and (2) the definition of the outputs, aims, and implementation of the model.

Systematic individual

In our cafeteria experiment, the one problem rated most enjoyable by well over half the systematic group was a basic planning task. The systematic management scientist can often take a research problem and shift it to one of planning. The methodological formalization he provides helps translate unknown states of perception and conception into known ones.

However, there is sometimes the danger that he will force the translation; he may insist on some objective function that does not really fit the situation, partly because his preference for planning leaves him unwilling to accept "unknown" states. He needs to make the implicit explicit.

Intuitive manager

Just as the systematic management scientist's specialized style of thinking provides very definite strengths in specialized tasks, so too does the intuitive manager's. It is important to again stress that the intuitive mode is not sloppy or loose; it seems to have an underlying discipline at least as coherent as the systematic mode, but is less apparent because it is largely unverbalized.

There are many situations where the volume of information, the lack of structure in the task, and the uncertainty of the environment defy planning and programming. In such situations the intuitive manager's style can be highly effective.

For example, there is no way for any manager to systematically forecast consumer tastes for furniture styles. He can, however, build a set of cues and flexible premises that may alert him to shifts in taste. He may also use the rapid scanning and testing (the main characteristic of the intuitive) for a sense of fit among disparate items of information. More important, he need never make his concepts and methods explicit.

Unlike the model builder, the intuitive manager can act without making any conscious articulation of his premises. An amusing instance of this fact occurred in many of the early efforts to use process-control computers in paper making. The computer experts "knew" that paper makers knew how to make paper; the experts' only problem was articulating the decision processes that the paper makers used, which turned out to depend mainly upon the operators' "tasting the broth" and controlling the paper flow.

For a long time, this well-established and highly effective human decision process defied conversion into formal and explicit terms. The operators were not too helpful. They "knew" what worked; they had built up out of their experience a clear but not conscious sense of the process, but this sense often varied with the individual. Thus, when a shift changed, the new crew chief, for example, might reset the valves and modify the whole operation, asserting that the changes were needed because of the time of day. There was no articulated set of concepts or methods by which this assertion could even be tested.

The decision makers here—and they merit the term, since controlling the paper-making process is a constant series of evaluations, assessments, and actions—were able to act efficiently even though they could not articulate their own procedures. This lack of articulation became a problem only when it was necessary for the computer experts to build a model of that process.

APPROACH DIFFERENCES

Systematic and intuitive individuals often treat the same project as two entirely different problems. The systematic management scientist may try to structure the problem to reduce the unknowns and to define very explicitly all the constraints in the situation. He aims at a model that is complete and has predictive power, which he can then improve and refine. That, essentially, is how he regards problem solving.

However, consciously or not, the intuitive manager is most concerned with using the model to give him a better sense of the problem. He focuses on and enjoys playing with the unknowns until he gets a feeling for the necessary steps for completion. Then he is ready to delegate the process of dealing with the problem to some individual in his organization who can systematically handle it in a more routine fashion.

The intuitive manager may also approach a task for which a model is to be built not with a need to understand the analytic process but with a desire to discover what he can trust in order to make useful predictions. This can be of value to the systematic scientist, in that, if he can build a model which "works," the manager may well be ready to use it even though he does not understand it.

The central issue, however, is the validation of the model. The scientist validates his model formally and methodologically; he can test it in relation to known inputs and outputs. In general, he will have faith in his plan and in his own systematic process. The manager will validate the model experientially and test it against some of his own concepts and expectations. He places much less faith in external "authority."

Recommendations for Action

If our line of argument is valid, it is clear that the solution to the difficulties intuitive managers and systematic management scientists have in working together will not be obtained by trying to blur the differences. The intuitive manager may learn what network optimization is, but that is unlikely to make him think in the same systematic mode as the management scientist, who, in turn, is unlikely to develop intuitive responses through any form of education.

(This is not to assert that cognitive style is fixed, but to reinforce the point that individuals with very distinctive styles in specialized areas of activity have strengths that are directly related to their styles. It seems unlikely that the cognitive specialist will change easily—or that he should do so in any case.)

The real solution seems to lie in two areas: (1) in defining the model's role within the larger decision-making process of the particular situation, and (2) in determining how to validate the model.

From this, the manager and scientist together can better control both the process of building the model structure and their mutual expectations and actions. At the root of both these areas of concern is the whole question of trust and communication, less in the interpersonal than in the cognitive sense.

ROLE DEFINITION

The management scientist's role can be one of either product or service. It is important that he decide which it is in a particular situation.

On the one hand, if his model will mainly help clarify a manager's sense of the issues and options, then there is no point in the scientist's trying to provide a meticulous and complex simulation. The manager does not intend to use the model as the basis for any decision. In fact, the model may simply help him decide what the problem is and can then be thrown away.

On the other hand, the manager may need a product rather than a service; for example, a financial forecasting model, once validated, may be used by a manager as the main basis for ongoing decisions.

The degree and direction of the scientist's efforts will be very different, depending on how he perceives the manager's needs in the situation. The scientist can only identify those needs by asking questions: How does this manager approach problems? How does he define his problem, given the four different classifications in *Exhibit III*? Does he want the model to further his own learning or to help him make a specific decision?

The answer to each question has distinct consequences. For example, if the manager's response to problems is systematic, the model should explicitly reflect this fact. The scientist should explain to him the underlying assumptions as to method; the two can afford to invest substantial time and discussion on how to deal with the problem. Here, the manager is essentially looking for a technique and the scientist is the expert, with a catalog of methods.

However, if the manager is intuitive in style, the scientist should recognize that the model must allow the manager to range over alternatives and test solutions in the fashion that fits his natural mode of problem solving.

In this context, J. W. Botkin has used the paradigm of cognitive style in designing an interactive computer system for intuitive subjects.[8] He has identified five necessary features for such a model:

1. The user should have the ability to create an arbitrary order of processing; the system should not impose a "logical" or step-by-step sequence on him. In Botkin's words, "This lack of set sequence allows the intuitive user to follow his instinct for developing his ill-defined information plan directly from environmental cues."

2. The user should be able to define, explore, and play out "scenarios" that may either generate cues or test solutions.

3. The user should be able to shift between levels of detail and generality.

8."An Intuitive Computer System: A Cognitive Approach to the Management Learning Process," unpublished doctoral dissertation, Harvard Business School, 1973.

4. The user should have some control over the forms of output and should be able to choose visual, verbal, and numeric displays at varying levels of detail.

5. The user should be able to extend his programming, providing input in an irregular and unspecific form (i.e., he should be able to provide commands such as, "Repeat the last step, increasing X by 10%").

Botkin's experiment showed fairly clearly that intuitive and systematic subjects used his model in greatly differing ways. The differences corresponded on the whole to those found in our cafeteria experiment. The intuitive group seemed to learn from the system and to enjoy using it as much as the systematic group.

Even though Botkin's model was a special case, his results suggest that an effort on the part of the model builder to consider how the manager will use the model—in terms of process rather than output—will provide large dividends.

Here again, there is a distinction between service and product. Where the manager is most concerned with the recommendations he can derive from the model, the sort of cognitive amplifiers Botkin provides are unnecessary. However, where the manager wants the model to help him clarify his own understanding of the situation, it may well be essential to build them into the formal structure of the model.

Thus the management scientist needs to consider what a "good" model is. For himself, goodness is largely a quality of predictive power and technical elegance. For the manager, it is more a concern of compatibility and comfort—that is, the fit between how he approaches the problem and how the model allows him to do so.

MODEL VALIDATION

Perhaps even more important than either recognizing the relevance of the user's own problem-solving process or determining how that person will use the model is the whole question of trust. Often, the manager does not get involved in the model itself; he simply asks for the outputs. He may well wish to validate the model by testing out some scenarios for which he has some expectations of the outcome.

However, John S. Hammond suggests that the model builder should recognize that in a large and complex model the user will have neither the desire nor the ability to understand its mechanics. The designer must, therefore, provide the user with some other way of testing out—of building trust in—the model. Hammond recommends, therefore, that the management scientist should aim

... to get something simple and useful up and running as soon as possible. By skillfully manipulating the resultant model, the management scientist should be able to obtain results that will give great insights about the problem, its nature, and its alternatives to the manager. These insights should cue the mind of the manager and cause him to perceive the problems and alternatives differently, which will in turn affect the priorities and direction of the management science effort. . . .

Thus the management scientist, too, will learn about the nature of the problem and also about the nature of the manager's perception of it.[9]

This recommendation seems particularly relevant in cases where the manager's cognitive style is highly intuitive. For relatively little effort and minimal commitment to a particular definition and design, the manager can obtain the initial exploration and trial testing that may enable him to articulate his assessments of the problem—or, better, that may enable the scientist to deduce them for him.

Our recommendations are fairly modest. Essentially, they argue that if both manager and scientist alike will look at the process instead of the output the techniques will look after themselves. It seems of central importance for the manager and scientist to recognize that each has a distinctive style of problem solving, and that each should accept the other's difference.

If the management scientist can anticipate the fact that the manager may not use in his decision-making process the conscious planning that is so natural for the scientist himself, he will be less likely to assume that the manager's reluctantly given statement of what the problem is has any permanent force. The intuitive manager can recognize a good plan, if he can validate it at some point on his own terms; the scientist's responsibility is to provide the plan and also the validation.

The manager's responsibility is to make very clear, first to himself and then to the scientist, what he wants the model to do and to be. If he asks for an optimization program for a facilities planning project, he should decide well in advance what he will do with the results. If he knows that he will not make his decision on the basis of the model's output, he should make sure that the design process and the model structure allow him to use the model to amplify his own thinking.

The intuitive manager is very happy to relinquish the mechanics of formal analytic techniques to the expert, but only after he has developed confidence and trust in that expert. It is in this sense that the common recommendation of educating the manager in quantitative skills seems so inadequate. The intuitive manager will learn to make use of these skills supplied by others; but this learning is internal, experiential, and informal.

More than anything, the manager needs to learn how to tell a good model from a bad one. For him, a good model is one that he can, by testing his own

9. "The Roles of the Manager and Analyst in Successful Implementation," paper presented to the XX International Meeting of the Institute of Management Sciences, Tel Aviv, Israel, 1973.

scenarios, make sense of. However sloppy this may seem to the systematic scientist, his model will be used only if it allows the manager to make such tests or if the process of designing it has done so on a more ongoing basis.

Concluding Note

People in general tend to assume that there is some "right" way of solving problems. Formal logic, for example, is regarded as a correct approach to thinking, but thinking is always a compromise between the demands of comprehensiveness, speed, and accuracy. There is no best way of thinking. If the manager and the management scientist can recognize first that each has a different cognitive style, and thus a different way of solving the same problem, then their dialogue seems more likely to bear fruit.

Our model of cognitive style is not necessarily either complete or precise. We suggest, however, that it does provide a useful way of focusing on the implementation of analytic models for decision making and of developing strategies of action that are much more likely to succeed than those based on concepts of technique, education, and salesmanship.

4. The Fateful Process of Mr. A Talking to Mr. B

Wendell Johnson

Just as many successful executives adopt Murphy's law and assume that if something can go wrong it will, so the author of this article suggests wise managers will expect to be misunderstood. A manager's success in anticipating what misunderstandings will arise has much to do with his success in working with people. From this revealing analysis of the process of communication—and the difficulties and disorders that beset it—businessmen will derive many ideas that should be of help not only in speaking with subordinates but in drafting letters, press releases, directions, and so forth. A key part of the process is an acceptance that speaking and listening is a deceptively simple affair, that few of us do well.

It is a source of never-ending astonishment to me that there are so few men who possess in high degree the peculiar pattern of abilities required for administrative success. There are hundreds who can "meet people well" for every one who can gain the confidence, goodwill, and deep esteem of his fellows. There are thousands who can speak fluently and pleasantly for every one who can make statements of clear significance. There are tens of thousands who are cunning and clever for every one who is wise and creative.

Why is this so? The two stock answers which I have heard so often in so many different contexts are: (1) administrators are born, and (2) administrators are made.

The trouble with the first explanation—entirely apart from the fact that it contradicts the second—is that those who insist that only God can make a chairman of the board usually think themselves into unimaginative acceptance of men as they find them. Hence any attempt at improving men for leadership is automatically ruled out.

Meanwhile, those who contend that administrators can be tailor-made are far from omniscient in their varied approaches to the practical job of transforming bright young men into the inspired leaders without which our national economy could not long survive. Nevertheless, it is in the self-acknowledged but earnest fumblings of those who would seek out and train our future executives and administrators that we may find our finest hopes and possibilities.

This article does not propose to wrap up the problem of what will make men better administrators. Such an attempt would be presumptuous and foolhardy on anyone's part; there are too many side issues, too many far-reaching ramifications. Rather, this is simply an exploration into one of the relatively uncharted areas of the subject, made with the thought that the observations presented may help others to find their way a little better. At the same time, the objective of our exploration can perhaps be described as an oasis of insight in what otherwise is a rather frightening expanse of doubt and confusion.

The ability to respond to and with symbols would seem to be the single most important attribute of great administrators. Adroitness in reading and listening, in speaking and writing, in figuring, in drawing designs and diagrams, in smoothing the skin to conceal and wrinkling it to express inner feelings, and in making the pictures inside the head by means of which thinking, imagining, pondering, and evaluating are carried on—these are the fundamental skills without which no man may adequately exercise administrative responsibilities.

Many of the more significant aspects of these administrative prerequisites may be brought into focus by means of a consideration of what is probably the most fateful of all human functions, and certainly the one function indispensable to our economic life: communication. So let us go on, now, to look at the process of communication and to try to understand the difficulties and disorders that beset us in our efforts to communicate with one another.

The Process Diagrammed

Several years ago I spent five weeks as a member of a group of university professors who had the job of setting up a project concerned with the study of speech. In the course of this academic exploring party we spent a major part of our time talking—or at least making noises—about "communication." By the second or third day it had become plain, and each day thereafter it became plainer, that we had no common and clear notion of just what the word "communication" meant.

After several days of deepening bewilderment, I recalled an old saying: "If you can't diagram it, you don't understand it." The next day I made a modest attempt to bring order out of the chaos—for myself, at least—by drawing on the blackboard a simple diagram representing what seemed to me to be the main steps in the curious process of Mr. A talking to Mr. B. Then I tried to discuss

Exhibit I The process of communication

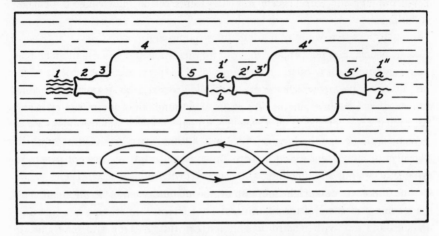

Key: Stage 1, event, or source of stimulation, external to the sensory end organs of the speaker; Stage 2, sensory stimulation; Stage 3, preverbal neurophysiological state; Stage 4, transformation of preverbal into symbolic forms; Stage 5, verbal formulations in "final draft" for overt expression; Stage 1′, transformation of verbal formulations into (a) air waves and (b) light waves, which serve as sources of stimulation for the listener (who may be either the speaker himself or another person); Stages 2′ through 1″ correspond, in the listener, to Stages 2 through 1′. The arrowed loops represent the functional interrelationships of the stages in the process as a whole.

communication by describing what goes on at each step—and what might go wrong. Since sketching that first diagram on the blackboard eight or nine years ago, I have refined and elaborated it, and I have tried from time to time, as I shall again here, to discuss the process of communication in terms of it (see *Exhibit I*).[1]

Inside Mr. A

What appears to take place when Mr. A talks to Mr. B is that first of all, at Stage 1, some event occurs which is external to Mr. A's eyes, ears, taste buds, or other sensory organs. This event arouses the sensory stimulation that occurs at Stage 2. The broken lines are intended to represent the fact that the process of communication takes place in a "field of reality," a context of energy manifestations external to the communication process and in major part external to both the speaker and the listener.

The importance of this fact is evident in relation to Stage 2 (or Stage 2′). The small size of the "opening" to Stage 2 in relation to the magnitude of the "channel" of Stage 1 represents the fact that our sensory receptors are capable

1. The diagram reproduced here is reproduced from my article "The Spoken Word and the Great Unsaid," *Quarterly Journal of Speech*, December 1951, pp. 419–429. Used by permission.

of responding only to relatively small segments of the total ranges of energy radiations.

SENSORY LIMITATIONS

The wave lengths to which the eye responds are but a small part of the total spectrum of such wave lengths. We register as sound only a narrow band of the full range of air vibrations. Noiseless dog whistles, "electronic eyes," and radar mechanisms—to say nothing of homing pigeons—underscore the primitive character of man's sensory equipment. Indeed, we seem little more than barely capable of tasting and smelling, and the narrowness of the temperature range we can tolerate is downright sobering to anyone dispassionately concerned with the efficiency of survival mechanisms.

The situation with regard to the normal individual may appear to be sufficiently dismal; let us not forget, however, how few of us are wholly normal in sensory acuity. We are familiar with the blind and partially sighted, the deaf and hard of hearing; we notice less the equally if not more numerous individuals who cannot taste the difference between peaches and strawberries, who cannot smell a distraught civet cat or feel a fly bite.

All in all, the degree to which we can know directly, through sensory avenues, the world outside (and this includes the world outside the sensory receptors but inside the body) is impressively restricted.

Any speaker is correspondingly limited in his physical ability to know what he is talking about. Relatively sophisticated listeners are likely to judge a speaker's dependability as a communicating agent by the degree to which he discloses his awareness of this limitation. The executive who demonstrates a realistic awareness of his own ignorance will in the long run acquire among his peers and subordinates a far better reputation for good judgment than the one who reveals his limitations by refusing to acknowledge them.

PREVERBAL STATE

Once a sensory receptor has been stimulated, nerve currents travel quickly into the spinal cord and normally up through the base of the brain to the higher reaches of the cortex, out again along return tracts to the muscles and glands. The contractions and secretions they cause bring about new sensory stimulations, which are "fed back" into the cord and brain and effect still further changes. The resulting reverberations of stimulation and response define what we may call a preverbal state of affairs within the organism. This state is represented at Stage 3 of the diagram.

Two statements about this preverbal state are fundamental: (1) we need to realize that our direct knowledge of this state is slight; (2) at the same time we are justified in assuming that it does occur.

No one has ever trudged through the spinal cord and brain with gun and camera, at least not while the owner of those organs was alive. Nevertheless, we are reasonably sure of certain facts about the nervous system. Observations have been reported by neurosurgeons, electroencephalographers, nerve physiologists, and anatomists. Thousands of laboratory animals have been sacrificed on the altars of scientific inquiry. We know that there are nerve currents and that they travel at known rates of speed, exhibit certain electrical properties, and are functionally related to specified kinds and loci of stimulation and to specified kinds and loci of response.

Thus, though our factual information is meager as yet, certainly it is sufficient to demonstrate that the nervous system is not merely a hypothetical construct. We can say with practical assurance that stimulation of our sensory end organs is normally followed by the transmission of nerve currents into the central nervous system, with a consequent reverberation effect, as described above, and the resulting state of affairs within the organism.

Two specific observations about this state of affairs are crucial: (1) it is truly preverbal, or silent; (2) it is this noiseless bodily state that gets transformed into words (or other symbols). Therefore—and these next few words should be read at a snail's pace and pondered long and fretfully—besides talking always to ourselves (although others may be listening more or less too), and whatever else we may also be striving to symbolize, *we inevitably talk about ourselves.*

THE INDIVIDUAL'S FILTER

What the speaker—whether he be a junior executive or the general manager—directly symbolizes, *what he turns into words,* are physiological or electrochemical goings-on inside his own body. His organism, in this sense, operates constantly as a kind of filter through which facts (in the sense of things that arouse sensory impulses) must pass before they can become known to him and before they can be *communicated* by him to others in some symbolic form, such as standard English speech.

It follows, to present a single, seemingly trivial, but quite representative example, that when the junior executive says to the general manager, "It's certainly a fine day," he is exhibiting an elaborate variety of confusion; indeed, he appears literally not to know what he is talking about. In the meantime, he is talking about himself—or at least about the weather only as "filtered" by himself. He is symbolizing an inner state, first of all. In this he is the brother of all of us who speak.

I do not mean to imply that we talk solely about our inner states. We often talk about the world outside; but when we do, we filter it through our inner states. To the degree that our individual filters are standardized and alike, we will agree in the statements we make about the world outside—allowing, of course, for differences in time, place, observational set, equipment, sensory acuity, perceptive skill, and manner of making verbal reports.

The existence of the filter at Stage 3 of the process of communication is the basic fact. We may differ in our manner of appreciating and interpreting the significance of the filter, and in so doing make ourselves interesting to each other. But when the administrator—when anyone at all—simply never learns that the filter is there, or forgets or disregards it, he becomes, as a speaker, a threat to his own sanity and a potential or actual menace in a public sense.

SELF-PROJECTION

Because the filter is there in each of us, self-projection is a basic bodily process that operates not only in all our speaking but in other kinds of communicative behavior. To claim to speak literally, then, a person must always say "as I see it," or "as I interpret the facts," or "as I filter the world" if you please, or simply "to me."

An administrator whose language becomes too "is"-y tends to persuade himself that what he says the facts are is the same thing as the facts, and under the numbing spell of this illusion he may become quite incapable of evaluating his own judgments. If he is aware of projection, he must make clear, first of all to himself, that he is not speaking about reality in some utterly impersonal or disembodied and "revealed" sense, but only about reality as the prism of his own nervous system projects it upon the gray screen of his own language—and he must realize that this projection, however trustworthy or untrustworthy, must still be received, filtered, and reprojected by each of his listeners.

Sufficient contemplation of this curious engineering scheme renders one sensitive to the hazards involved in its use. As with any other possibility of miracle, one is well advised not to expect too much of it.

PATTERNS AND SYMBOLS

Stage 4, the first stage of symbolization, is represented in our diagram as a great enlargement in the tunnel through which "the world" passes from Stage 1 to Stage 1'. The words ultimately selected for utterance (at Stage 5) are a very small part of the lush abundance of possible verbalizations from which they are abstracted. Moreover, the bulge is intended to suggest that the state of affairs at

Stage 3 becomes in a peculiarly human way much more significant by virtue of its symbolization at Stage 4.

At Stage 4 the individual's symbolic system and the pattern of evaluation reflected in its use come into play. The evaluative processes represented at this stage have been the object of much and varied study and speculation:

Freud Here, it would appear, was the location of Freud's chief preoccupations, as he attempted to explain them in terms of the so-called unconscious depths of the person, the struggle between the Id and the Super-Ego from which the Ego evolves, the ceaseless brewing of dreamstuff, wish and counterwish, the fabulous symbolism of the drama that we call the human personality.[2] Indeed, at this stage there is more than meets the eye—incredibly more so far as we may dimly but compellingly surmise.

Korzybski Here, too, were the major preoccupations of the founder of general semantics, Alfred Korzybski: the symbol; the creation of symbols and of systems of symbols; the appalling distortions of experience wrought by the culturally imposed semantic crippling of the young through the witless and artful indoctrination of each new generation by the fateful words of the elders—the words which are the carriers of prejudice, unreasoning aspiration, delusional absolutes, and the resulting attitudes of self-abandonment. But also here we find the unencompassable promise of all that *human* can suggest, and this Korzybski called upon all men to see, to cherish, and to cultivate with fierce tenderness.[3]

Pavlov The father of the modern science of behavior, Pavlov, also busied himself with ingenious explanations of occurrences at what we have called Stage 4.[4] In human beings, at least, the learning processes, as well as the drives and goals that power and direct them, appear to function at this stage of incipient symbolization.

It seems useful to conjecture that perhaps the general *patterns* of symbolic conditioning are formed at Stage 4, in contrast to the conditioning of specific symbolic responses (i.e., particular statements) produced at Stage 5. We may put it this way: at Stage 4 the syllogism, for example, as a *pattern* or *form* of possible symbolic response, is laid down, while at Stage 5 there occur the specific verbal responses patterned in this syllogistic mold.

Again, at Stage 4 we find the general form, "X affects Y"; at Stage 5 we see its specific progeny in such statements as "John loves Mary," "germs cause disease," and "clothes make the man." In this relationship between general forms or patterns at Stage 4, and the corresponding specific utterances at Stage 5, we find the substantial sense of the proposition that our language does our thinking for us.

2. Sigmund Freud, *A General Introduction to Psychoanalysis,* translated by Joan Riviere (New York, Liveright Publishing Corporation, 1935).

3. Alfred Korzybski, *Science and Sanity: An Introduction to Non-Aristotelian Systems and General Semantics* (Lancaster, Pennsylvania, Science Press, 3rd ed. 1948).

4. I. P. Pavlov, *Conditioned Reflexes: An Investigation of the Physiological Activity of the Cerebral Cortex,* translated and edited by G. V. Anrep (London, Oxford University Press, 1927).

In fact, one of the grave disorders that we may usefully locate at Stage 4 consists in a lack of awareness of the influence on one's overt speech of the general symbolic forms operating at Stage 4. The more the individual knows about these forms, the more different forms he knows—or originates—and the more adroit he is in the selective and systematic use of them in patterning specific statements at Stage 5, the more control he exercises over "the language that does his thinking for him." The degree of such control exercised over the verbal responses at Stage 5 represents one of the important dimensions along which speakers range themselves, all the way from the naïveté of the irresponsible robot—or compulsive schizophrenic patient—to the culture-shaping symbolic sophistication of the creative genius.

(Generally speaking, most of the disorders of abstracting described and emphasized by the general semanticists are to be most usefully thought of as operating chiefly at Stage 4. These disorders include those involving identification or lack of effective discrimination for purposes of sound evaluation.[5])

THE FINAL DRAFT

The fact has been mentioned, and should be emphasized, that the "final draft" formulated at Stage 5, the words that come to be spoken, represents as a rule a highly condensed abstract of all that might have been spoken. What enters into this final draft is determined, in a positive sense, by the speaker's available knowledge of fact and relationship, his vocabulary, and his flexibility in using it, his purposes, and (to use the term in a broad sense) his habits. What enters into it is determined negatively by the repressions, inhibitions, taboos, semantic blockages, and ignorances, as well as the limiting symbolic forms, operating at Stage 4.

Mr. A to Mr. B

As the communication process moves from Stage 5 to Stage 1′, it undergoes another of the incredible transformations that give it a unique and altogether remarkable character: the words, phrases, and sentences at Stage 5 are changed into air waves (and light waves) at Stage 1′. At close quarters, Mr. A may at times pat the listener's shoulder, tug at his coat lapels, or in some other way try to inject his meaning into Mr. B by hand, as it were, but this transmission of meaning through mechanical pressure may be disregarded for present purposes.

5. See Alfred Korzybski, op. cit., and Wendell Johnson, *People in Quandaries,* particularly chaps. 5 through 10.

INEFFICIENCY OF AIR WAVES

In general, it seems a valid observation that we place an unwarranted trust in spoken words, partly because we disregard, or do not appreciate, the inefficiency of air waves as carriers of information and evaluation. The reasons for this inefficiency lie both in the speaker and in the listener, of course, as well as in the air waves themselves. What the listener ends up with is necessarily a highly abstracted version of what the speaker intends to convey.

The speaker who sufficiently understands this—the wise administrator—expects to be misunderstood and, as a matter of fact, predicts quite well the particular misunderstandings with which he will need to contend. Consequently, he is able not only to forestall confusion to some extent but also to give himself a chance to meet misunderstanding with the poise essential to an intelligent handling of the relationships arising out of it. A minimal requirement for the handling of such relationships is that either the speaker or the listener (or, better, both) recognize that the fault lies not so much in either one of them as in the process of communication itself—including particularly the fragile and tenuous air waves, whose cargo of meaning, whether too light to be retained or too heavy to be borne, is so often lost in transit.

Such an executive takes sufficiently into account the fact that words, whether spoken or written, are not foolproof. He will do all he can, within reason, to find out how his statements, his letters and press releases, his instructions to subordinates, and so on are received and interpreted. He will not take for granted that anyone else thinks he means what he himself thinks he means. And when he discovers the misunderstandings and confusions he has learned to expect, he reacts with disarming and constructive forbearance to the resentments and disturbed human relationships that he recognizes as being due, not to men, but to the far from perfect communications by means of which men try to work and live together.

Inside Mr. B

The air waves (and light waves) that arrive at Stage 2′—that is, at the ears and eyes of the listener—serve to trigger the complex abstracting process which we have just examined, except that now it moves from 2′ through 5′ instead of 2 through 5. That is, the various stages sketched in the speaker are now repeated in the listener. To understand speech, or the communication process in general, is to be aware of the various functions and the disorders operating at each stage in the process—and to be conscious of the complex pattern of relationships among the various stages, as represented schematically by the double-arrowed loops in the diagram.

EFFECT OF FEEDBACK

Always important, these relationships become particularly significant when the speaker and listener are one and the same individual. And this, of course, is always the case, even when there are other listeners. The speaker is always affected by "feedback": he hears himself. What is significant is precisely the degree to which he is affected by feedback. It may, in fact, be ventured as a basic principle that the speaker's responsiveness to feedback—or, particularly important, the *administrator's* responsiveness to feedback—is crucial in determining the soundness of his spoken evaluations. It is crucial, also, in determining his effectiveness in maintaining good working relationships with his associates.

Application to Problems

This view of the process of Mr. A speaking to Mr. B may be applied to any one of a great many specific problems and purposes. The diagram can be used especially well as a means of directing attention to the disorders of communication, such as those encountered daily in the world of trade and industry.

PREVENTING TROUBLES

In this connection, let me call attention to the fact that Professor Irving Lee of the School of Speech at Northwestern University has written a book called *How to Talk with People*,[6] which is of particular interest to anyone concerned with such disorders. Its subtitle describes it as "a program for preventing troubles that come when people talk together." The sorts of troubles with which Professor Lee is concerned in this book are among those of greatest interest and importance to personnel managers and business administrators and executives generally, and there would seem to be no better way to make my diagram take on a very practical kind of meaning than to sketch briefly what Professor Lee did and what he found in his studies of men in the world of business trying to communicate with one another.

Over a period of nearly ten years Professor Lee listened to the deliberations of

6. New York, Harper & Brothers, 1952.

more than 200 boards of directors, committees, organization staffs, and other similar groups. He made notes of the troubles he observed, and in some cases he was able to get the groups to try out his suggestions for reducing such troubles as they were having; and as they tried out his suggestions, he observed what happened and took more notes.

Among the many problems he describes in *How to Talk with People* there are three of special interest, which can be summarized thus:

1. First of all, misunderstanding results when one man assumes that another uses words just as he does. Professor Quine of Harvard once referred to this as "the uncritical assumption of mutual understanding." It is, beyond question, one of our most serious obstacles to effective thinking and communication. Professor Lee suggests a remedy, deceptively simple but profoundly revolutionary: better habits of listening. We must learn, he says, not only how to define our own terms but also how to ask others what they are talking about. He is advising us to pay as much attention to the right-hand side of our diagram as to the left-hand side of it.

2. Another problem is represented by the person who takes it for granted that anyone who does not feel the way he does about something is a fool. "What is important here," says Lee, "is not that men disagree, but that they become disagreeable about it." The fact is, of course, that the very disagreeable disagreer is more or less sick, from a psychological and semantic point of view. Such a person is indulging in "unconscious projection." As we observed in considering the amazing transformation of the physiological goings-on at Stage 3 into words or other symbols at Stage 4, the only way we can talk about the world outside is to filter it through our private inner states. The disagreeable disagreer is one who has never learned that he possesses such a filter, or has forgotten it, or is so desperate, demoralized, drunk, or distracted as not to care about it.

A trained consciousness of the projection process would seem to be essential in any very effective approach to this problem. The kind of training called for may be indicated by the suggestion to any administrator who is inclined to try it out that he qualify any important statements he makes, with which others may disagree, by such phrases as "to my way of thinking," "to one with my particular background," and "as I see it."

3. One more source of trouble is found in the executive who thinks a meeting should be "as workmanlike as a belt line." He has such a business-only attitude that he simply leaves out of account the fact that "people like to get things off their chests almost as much as they like to solve problems." Professor Lee's sensible recommendation is this: "If people in a group want to interrupt serious discussion with some diversion or personal expression—let them. Then bring

them back to the agenda. Committees work best when the talk swings between the personal and the purposeful."

CONSTRUCTIVE FACTORS

Professor Lee saw something, however, in addition to the "troubles that come when people talk together." He has this heartening and important observation to report:

In sixteen groups we saw illustrations of men and women talking together, spontaneously, cooperatively, constructively. There was team-play and team-work. We tried to isolate some of the factors we found there: (1) The leader did not try to tell the others what to do or how to think; he was thinking along with them. (2) No one presumed to know it all; one might be eager and vigorous in his manner of talking, but he was amenable and attentive when others spoke. (3) The people thought of the accomplishments of the group rather than of their individual exploits.

This can happen—and where it does not happen, something is amiss. The diagram presented in *Exhibit I,* along with the description of the process of communication fashioned in terms of it, is designed to help us figure out what might be at fault when such harmony is not to be found. And it is intended to provide essential leads to better and more fruitful communication in business and industry, and under all other circumstances as well.

Conclusion

Mr. A talking to Mr. B is a deceptively simple affair, and we take it for granted to a fantastic and tragic degree. It would surely be true that our lives would be longer and richer if only we were to spend a greater share of them in the tranquil hush of thoughtful listening. We are a noisy lot; and of what gets said among us, far more goes unheard and unheeded than seems possible. We have yet to learn on a grand scale how to use the wonders of speaking and listening in our own best interests and for the good of all our fellows. It is the finest art still to be mastered by men.

5. Management Science and Business Practice

C. Jackson Grayson, Jr.

Management science has grown so remote from and unmindful of the conditions of "live" management that it has abdicated its usability. Managers, for their part, have become disillusioned by management science, and are now frequently unwilling to consider it seriously as a working tool for important problems. The author believes that management science can make a contribution to management; and in this article he suggests how a bridge between the two groups can be constructed. He also makes it clear that the scientists must be the ones to start construction.

"What we need to do is humanize the scientist and simonize the humanist." This dictum is a popularization of C. P. Snow's view of science and the humanities as two distinct cultures, and it is all too true when applied to management. Managers and management scientists are operating as two separate cultures, each with its own goals, languages, and methods. Effective cooperation—and even communication—between the two is just about minimal. And this is a shame.

Each has much to learn from the other, and much to teach the other. Yet, despite all kinds of efforts over the years, it seems to me that the cultural and operating gap which exists between the two is not being closed. Why?

I can offer some explanations, based on my years as an academician, consultant, businessman, and most recently, head of an organization with control over a large part of our economy—the Price Commission. I can also suggest a way to build the bridge so badly needed between the two cultures and the people who make them up. This bridge must span the gap between two quite different types:

☐ *The management scientists.* As people, they want to help managers make decision making more explicit, more systematic, and *better* by using scientific methodology, principally mathematics and statistics. They can be found largely in universities and in staff operations of enterprises. They may belong to any of a number of professional associations, such as the Institute of Management Sciences (TIMS), Operations Research Society of America (ORSA), and the American Institute for Decision Sciences (AIDS).

□ *The managers.* They make and implement decisions, largely by rough rules of thumb and intuition. They are the operating executives, found principally in the line.

The lines of distinction are never so pure, but most people, I believe, understand what I mean.

What I have to offer to the management scientists is a few bouquets and then a load of bricks. First, the bouquets:

□ Management scientists have had *some* impact on real-world operations and managers.

□ Some management science tools have been successfully applied in accounting, finance, production, distribution, and weapons systems.

□ Managers do tend to give a little more conscious thought to their decision making than in previous years—but still precious little.

□ By indicating how abysmal our knowledge is about decision making, management scientists have highlighted areas for further research.

□ Both the faculty and the students at business schools have gained some added prestige in the business and academic communities for being more "scientific."

And now the bricks. The total impact of management science has been extremely small. Its contribution looks even smaller than it is if one compares it to the revolution promised for management offices in the early years. And the "wait-until-next-generation" theme is wearing thinner and thinner.

Let me quickly acknowledge that there are *some* management scientists who operate effectively in both cultures. But they are rare birds. Most management scientists are still thinking, writing, and operating in a world that is far removed from the real world in which most managers operate (and in which I personally have been operating). They often describe and structure nonexistent management problems, tackle relatively minor problems with overkill tools, omit real variables from messy problems, and build elegant models comprehensible to only their colleagues. And when managers seem confused or dissatisfied with the results of their activities and reject them, these scientists seem almost to take satisfaction in this confirmation of the crudity and inelegance of the managerial world.

Have I overdrawn the picture? Only very slightly.

Why the Gulf?

I do not mean to say that management scientists have purposefully created this cultural gap. Most of them feel that much of what they are doing today is really helpful to managers. But I'm afraid it simply isn't so. Others argue that much of what they are doing is "pure research," which will be useful one day. I do not discount the value of pure research; some of it is needed. But the fact remains that only a small fraction of management science "results" are being used.

Those management scientists who do acknowledge a gap often excuse it by one of two reasons:

☐ "The manager doesn't understand the power of the tools."

☐ "He isn't sympathetic to systematic decision making and would rather fly by the seat of his pants because this is safer for his ego."

I myself am a counterexample to both these excuses. I have had some fairly good training in management science. I have done research in the area and written a book urging the use of more explicit decision tools in a specific industry—oil well drilling.[1] I have taught various courses in the area, for example, in statistics, management control systems, and quantitative analysis.

And yet, in the most challenging assignment of my life—putting together the Price Commission—I used absolutely *none* of the management science tools explicitly. One might think that in the task of developing an organization of 600 people (mostly professionals), creating a program to control prices in a trillion-dollar economy, and making decisions that involve costs, volume, prices, productivity, resource allocations, elasticities, multiple goals, trade-offs, predictions, politics, and risk values, an expert would have found ways to use his familiarity with management science to advantage. I did not.

A defender of the faith will quickly say that, although I did not use them explicitly, I probably used them *implicitly,* and that they helped to discipline my approach to decision making. I agree that this is probably true. But I nevertheless think it is a damning indictment that I can identify *no* incident of a conscious, explicit use of a single management science tool in my activities as head of the Price Commission.

Further, my conscience is clear. To my mind there are five very valid reasons for my rejecting the idea of using management science.

SHORTAGE OF TIME

Although I thought about using management science tools on many occasions, I consistently decided against it because of the shortage of time. Management

1. *Decisions Under Uncertainty* (Boston, Division of Research, Harvard Business School, 1960).

scientists simply do not sufficiently understand the constraint of time on decision making, and particularly on decisions that count; and the techniques they develop reflect that fact. They may write about time as a limitation. They may admonish managers for letting time push them into a "crisis" mode. They may recognize the constraint of time with a few words and comment on its influence. They may say that they, too, experience time constraints. But their techniques are so time-consuming to use that managers pass them by.

Does this mean that all management science work ought to be thrown into shredders? No, it simply means that management scientists (a) need to get out of their relatively unpressured worlds and *experience* the impact of time on the decision-making process, and (b) need to build the time factor into models instead of leaving it as an exogenous variable.

INACCESSIBILITY OF DATA

The second reason for ignoring management science in practice is related to the time problem. A manager will ordinarily use data or a management science tool only if both are conveniently, speedily accessible. If he is told that the needed data are buried in another part of the organization, or that they must be compiled, or that the model must be created, nine times out of ten he will say, "Skip it." I did, ten times out of ten.

True, many management scientists would say that I must have developed "trade-offs" in my mind, weighing the cost of obtaining data or building a model against the probable opportunity payoff, and that my mental calculator ground out negative responses on each occasion. This is perfectly plausible. Unconsciously I probably did build a number of such informal investment-payoff models.

But where does this leave us? It leaves us with management scientists continuing to construct models that call for substantial investments in design and data collection and managers discarding them. The statement is made ad nauseam that most data are not in the forms that most models call for, or that they are not complete; yet the management scientists go right on calling for inaccessible, nonexistent, or uncompiled data to suit "theoretically correct" models. And hence managers continue to say, "Skip it."

Instead of asking a manager to lie in the Procrustean bed of the theoretically correct model, why shouldn't the management scientist design a realistic model, or a realistic part of a model, or come up with a realistic data prescription? The result might be extremely crude; it might embarrass a theoretician; it might be shot down by the purist and the theoretician. But it just might be *used*.

RESISTANCE TO CHANGE

The third reason that I did not use management science tools explicitly is that educating others in the organization who are not familiar with the tools, and who would resist using them if they were, is just too difficult a task. Management scientists typically regard this problem as outside the scope of their jobs—at most, they remark on the need to educate more people and to change organizations so they become more scientific. Or, if they *do* recognize the problem, they grossly underestimate the time and organizational effort needed to "educate and change." I suggest that management scientists do two things:

1. They should build into their models some explicit recognition of the financial and emotional cost of change of this kind and make explicit allowance for the drag of change resistance. I am quite aware that some change techniques are being used: sensitivity training, Esalen-type devices, management by objectives, quantitative analysis courses for managers, and so on. I have used them myself, and I know that they help. But the magnitude of time and energy required to install them is not generally appreciated—certainly not by management scientists—and their impact is highly overrated.

2. They should get themselves some education and direct experience in the power, politics, and change-resistance factors in the real world of management so they can better incorporate the imperfect human variables in their work.

LONG RESPONSE TIME

Fourth, few management science people are geared up to respond to significant management problems in "real time." Management science people in universities live largely by the school calendar, and if they receive a request for help, they are likely to respond in terms of next semester, next September, or after exams. And once again the manager is likely to say, "Skip it." Even most management science personnel in staff positions of live organizations operate in a time frame that is slower than that of the line managers. It is their nature to approach a problem in a methodical, thorough way, even when the required response time dictates that they come up with a "quick and dirty" solution.

INVALIDATING SIMPLIFICATIONS

Fifth, and finally, it is standard operating procedure for most management science people to strip away so much of a real problem with "simplifying assumptions" that the remaining carcass of the problem and its attendant solution bear little resemblance to the reality with which the manager must deal. The time constraints, the data-availability questions, the people problems, the power structures, and the political pressures—all the important, nasty areas that lie close to the essence of management—are simplified out of existence so that a technically beautiful, and useless, resolution may be achieved.

This is somewhat paradoxical, since management science originated in wartime Britain, when many interdisciplinary talents were forced into combination to grapple with the problems of total mobilization. That situation tolerated no fooling around. But in subsequent years management science has retreated from the immediate demands for workable results. It has increased its use of the hard sciences of mathematics and statistics, hardening itself with methodological complexity, weakening its own reliance on the softer sciences of psychology, sociology, and political science, and losing the plain, hardheaded pragmatism with which it started out.

Realizing this, many managers think it pointless to turn the really important problems over to management science. Their experience has shown them the impotence of emasculated solutions.

At the risk of repeating a tired joke, let me recall the story of the man who said he had a way to destroy all the enemy submarines in the Atlantic during World War II: "Boil the ocean." Asked next how he would do this, he replied, "That's your problem." Similarly, when managers ask management scientists how to solve a problem, they too often say, in effect, "Boil the company." They leave it to the manager to worry about shortages of time, inaccessibility of data, resistance to change, slow response times, and oversimplified solutions.

Firing the Furnace

At the Price Commission we operated, I think fairly successfully, without getting the data we "should" have had, without using any explicit decision tools, without once formally consulting a management scientist, and without building models of our decision-making processes. I am not especially proud of these facts; I am a member, and an intellectually loyal member, of ORSA, TIMS, and AIDS. I believe in the general direction in which these organizations want to go. But I also have a personal dedication to action, a sense of the urgency and immediacy of real problems, and a disbelief in the genuine responsiveness of management science models to my managerial needs.

I have asked myself the question whether we might have done better by using some management science models, and my honest answer is *no*. Using models would have slowed decision making. It would have frustrated most of our personnel. Given the fact that most models omit the factors of time, data accessibility, people, power, and politics, they simply would not have provided sufficient predictive or prescriptive payoff for the required investment of energy.

Consider the severity of the demands that were made. Establishment of the Price Commission required fulfillment of seemingly impossible tasks and directives:

☐ Create and staff a fully competent organization.

☐ Work out regulations worthy to bear the force of law.

☐ Keep the program consistent with policies established in Phase I and the current state of the economy.

☐ Work in conjunction with the Pay Board, the Internal Revenue Service, and the Cost of Living Council.

☐ Control the prices of hundreds of millions of articles and commodities in the world's largest economy.

☐ Do not inhibit the recovery of the economy.

☐ Do not build a postcontrol bubble.

☐ Do all of this with a regulatory staff of 600.

☐ Have the entire operation functioning in 16 days.

A natural first reaction to such demands might well have been General McAuliffe's famous one-word response: "Nuts!" It would have been very easy to point out, for example, that:

☐ Nobody could begin to do the job of price control with 600 people, even with the services of 3,000 Internal Revenue Service agents to help with enforcement. It had taken 60,000 people to handle the assignment in World War II and 17,000 in the Korean War.

☐ To do the job right would require a thoroughgoing study of what was involved—the resources and kinds of personnel required, the most efficient way of actually controlling prices, the optimum method of working in concert with other federal agencies—as well as the accumulation of data about the economy and the testing of various models.

☐ The 16-day period was too short. There was not enough time to get the Price Commission appointed, let alone to build, organize, and house the right kind of staff, promulgate regulations, and get it all functioning.

I might have pointed out these things and many others. I did not. I simply started bringing in staff, renting quarters, creating an organization, framing regulations, and developing a modus operandi. In 16 days the organization was accepting requests for price increases from U.S. business; the staff was at work—in some cases eight to an office, four to a telephone, and a good many spending up to 20 hours a day on the job.

I cite this record not to boast. Our achievement did not grow out of extraordinary capability. It was simply a matter of orientation and intuition—

orientation and intuition toward action. But just as managers incline toward intuition and action, management scientists incline toward reflective thinking. They tend to be scholarly, less action-oriented, and averse to taking risks—even risk of criticism from their peers. They dissect and analyze, they are individualistic, and they are prone to trace ideas much as one can trace power flows in a mechanical system, from gear to belt to gear. They have not cared much about firing the furnace that makes the steam that drives the gear in the first place.

The manager offers an almost complete contrast. He integrates and synthesizes; he sees situations as mosaics; his thoughts and decision processes are like electrical circuits so complex you can never be sure how much current is flowing where. At the core of his value system are depth and breadth of experience, which he may even permit to outweigh facts where the whole picture seems to justify it.

For his part, the management scientist tends to optimize the precision of a tool at the expense of the health and performance of the whole. He has faith in some day building ultimate tools and devising ultimate measurements, and this lies at the foundation of his values and beliefs.

The problem, then, boils down to two cultures—the managers' and the management scientists'—and not enough bridges between them. Somebody has to build the bridges.

Who Shall Build the Bridges?

Closing any gap requires that one or both cultures change. It is my strong belief that the management scientist must move first, and most. *The end product is supposed to be management, after all, not management science.* Further, as a philosophical point, I think science has greater relevance to our world if it moves constantly toward art (in this case the management art) than the other way around. Then, instead of moving toward increased and separated specialization, both evolve toward a mature symbiosis, a working and dynamic unity of the kind found in successful marriages, détentes, and mergers.

The management scientist is not going to find it easy or comfortable to change, and yet it is he who must change most in attitude, action, and life style. He is going to have to think in terms of the *manager's* perceptions, the *manager's* needs, the *manager's* expectations, and the *manager's* pressures— that is, if he wants to have impact in the real world of the manager. If not, he will go on missing the mark.

What, concretely, can be done? Let me offer a few suggestions to the management science people and the managers they are supposed to be helping.

First, top management should not isolate the management science people but sprinkle them throughout the organization in situations where they can really go to work. It should give them *line* responsibility for results. Their natural tendencies will cause them to flock together at night or on weekends to compare and refine tools, and that, again, is as it should be; but their prime responsibility should be to the line unit, not to a management science group. To put the matter another way: management should not think of having an operating person on a management science team—it should think of having a management scientist on an operating team.

Second, managers should demand implementation by management scientists; they should not tolerate "package" solutions that leave out the complicating factors. In that way, managers can avoid simplistic, unworkable solutions that ignore the factors of time, data accessibility, unwillingness of people to change, power, and so on.

Third, even when professional management scientists are brought into companies as consultants, they are often given the easy, old problems, for the reasons that I have named. This expectational cycle has to be broken.

AT THE UNIVERSITY

The same general approach is valid within universities.

First, both management science faculty and students have to get out of the isolated, insulated world of academe. They must go beyond structured cases and lectures and become directly involved in real-world, real-time, live projects, not as a way of applying what they know, but as a way of learning.

It is a mistake to teach the student linear programming or decision theory and then search for a problem to which the tool can be applied. That creates the classic academic situation from which managers are revolting—the tool in search of a problem. Instead, tackle the *real* problem. This will be frustrating, but the frustration of trying to reach a *workable* solution can be used to teach the management scientist or student in a way that is useful both to him and to the business or government unit. The solutions thus derived may not be so elegant as they might be, but they may be used. The student who wants to reach for higher, more sophisticated theories should be treated as a special case, not the general case.

Second, management science people should stop tackling the neat, simple problems, or refining approaches to problems already solved. These projects may be easier, but working and reworking them will not help bridge the cultural gap I am talking about. Instead, tackle the *tough* problem. The management of time pressure and the use of the persuasion and negotiation required by a real, tough problem will give both the faculty member and the student some salutary discipline in convincing others to follow a strange idea, to cooperate, and to listen.

The best example of what I am describing occurred at Case Institute in the early days of Russell L. Ackoff, E. L. Arnoff, and C. West Churchman. There, faculty and student teams worked on real problems in real time in real business settings. That example does not seem to have caught on at other universities, partly because of the difficulty of doing it, and partly because it flies against the nature of the management science personality that I have described. The process is messy, people-populated, schedule-disrupting, time-demanding, and complicated by power and politics. That is exactly as it should be.

Third, faculty members should plan to get out of the university, physically and completely, for meaningful periods of time. They should plan their careers so that they schedule at least a year, periodically, in which they get direct real-world experience in business, nonprofit organizations, or the government.

One helpful device with which I am familiar is the Presidential Personnel Interchange Program of the federal government, now in its third year. So far this year it has brought 60 business executives into government work and 18 federal government managers into business. These numbers should be expanded tremendously, and the organizations involved should include universities. The universities could well join in a three-way interchange, or start their own program with business.

Finally, universities should bring in real managers and involve them directly in problem-solving and joint-learning sessions. Doctors expect to return to medical school as part of their normal development; so should managers. The universities can offer managers an update in science; corporate managers can offer universities an update in management.

These are some of the ways to build bridges. There are other ways to tear them down, or to maintain the gap. Jargon, for example, will drive away managers. So will intellectual snobbery toward "intuitive" decision making. Management scientists should dispense with both. Managers can maintain the gap by continuing to refer to past disillusionments and never allowing management science people to tackle executive-suite programs. Managers should recognize that. In fact, defensive behavior on the part of either group can block reconciliation and progress.

People *do* exist who effectively bridge the two cultures. Such people do not always bear an identifying brand; one cannot distinguish them by their degrees, university course credits, titles, experience, or even home base. But they do have one strong, overriding characteristic—they are *problem- and action-oriented.* They are essentially unicultural; they employ a healthy mix of science and intuition in their decision making.

Words to the Wise

I am not suggesting that the two specializations—management science and management—be destroyed. Primary bases and modes of operation can be preserved, provided that both groups are receptive to and understanding of the other's basic orientation, and that they work together in harmony, not in dissonance. And all should remember that the problem is the thing, not the methodology; the function, not the form.

My slings and arrows have been directed mostly toward management science—rightly so, I think. But managers must assist in the bridge-building process:

☐ They should stop recounting tales of how "they never laid a glove on me" in encounters with management scientists. They should make it a point of future pride to use management science.

☐ They should make available the real nasty, complicated decisions to management scientists.

☐ They should not expect a lot.

☐ They should not deride small gains.

☐ They should hold any management science approach or individual accountable for producing *results,* not recommendations.

The management science people must play their part, too:

☐ Get out of the monasteries, whether these are universities or staff departments.

☐ Submerge the paraphernalia (journal articles, computer programs, cookbooks) and rituals ("sounds like a linear programming program to me" or "we need to get the facts first").

☐ Put people, time, power, data accessibility, and response times into models and create crude, workable solutions.

☐ Learn to live with and in the real world of managers.

Again, I submit it is the management science people who will have to change most. They should take the first step toward closing the gap between the two cultures. The consequences can only be better for managers, for management science, and for the problem itself.

Part II
Putting Judgment Back into the Manager's Job

Preface

It may be well to assert that judgment and intuition are important aspects of intelligence. It is another thing to assert that that kind of intelligence is important in managerial work. Aren't there some aspects of intelligence that simply are not appropriate at work?

As long as one conceives of the manager's job as being orderly, controlled, and systematic, one would be hard pressed to show that greater use of judgment, for instance, would make a manager perform better. But managerial work is not orderly. The view that it is is probably more a product of wishful thinking than careful study of managers' jobs.

Perhaps because it's easier to understand things that are orderly, behavioral scientists have been trying for years to organize the manager's job. Recent studies show, however, that the manager's job defies organization; it simply is not systematic. Because of this lack of order, judgment, flexibility, and an ability to tolerate ambiguity may be more important in general managerial jobs than the ability to systematize, analyze, and control. In "Good Managers Don't Make Policy Decisions," for instance, H. Edward Wrapp discusses how in his experience the successful executive is the one that can muddle through, exploiting his or her sense of opportunism, resisting temptation to conceptualize long-range plans.

The articles in this section focus on the manager's job, what he or she actually does and how so often the job requires a person to be flexible, to be able to ride with ambiguity, to be able to juggle, and finally, to come up with an assessment, a judgment.

Suddenly, the intuitive part of a manager can be seen to be an effective management asset rather than a quality that needs to be quashed in the name of efficiency, objectivity, and clarity.

6. Good Managers Don't Make Policy Decisions

H. Edward Wrapp

The successful general manager does not spell out detailed objectives for his organization, the author believes; nor does he make master plans. He seldom makes forthright statements of policy. He is an opportunist, and he tends to muddle through problems— although he muddles with a purpose. He enmeshes himself in many operating matters and does not limit himself to "the big picture."

The upper reaches of management are a land of mystery and intrigue. Very few people have ever been there, and the present inhabitants frequently send back messages that are incoherent both to other levels of management and to the world in general. This may account for the myths, illusions, and caricatures that permeate the literature of management—for example, such widely held notions as these:

☐ Life gets less complicated as a manager reaches the top of the pyramid.

☐ The manager at the top level knows everything that's going on in the organization, can command whatever resources he may need, and therefore can be more decisive.

☐ The general manager's day is taken up with making broad policy decisions and formulating precise objectives.

☐ The top executive's primary activity is conceptualizing long-range plans.

☐ In a large company, the top executive may be seen meditating about the role of his organization in society.

I suggest that none of these versions alone, or in combination, is an accurate portrayal of what a general manager does. Perhaps students of the management process have been overly eager to develop a theory and a discipline. As one executive I know puts it, "I guess I do some of the things described in the books and articles, but the descriptions are lifeless, and my job isn't."

What common characteristics, then, do successful executives exhibit *in reality?* I shall identify five skills or talents which, in my experience, seem especially significant. (For details on the method used in reaching these conclusions, see the Appendix on page 88.)

Keeping Well Informed

First, each of my heroes has a special talent for keeping himself informed about a wide range of operating decisions being made at different levels in the company. As he moves up the ladder, he develops a network of information sources in many different departments. He cultivates these sources and keeps them open no matter how high he climbs in the organization. When the need arises, he bypasses the lines on the organization chart to seek more than one version of a situation.

In some instances, especially when they suspect he would not be in total agreement with their decision, his subordinates will elect to inform him in advance, before they announce a decision. In these circumstances, he is in a position to defer the decision, or redirect it, or even block further action. However, he does not insist on this procedure. Ordinarily he leaves it up to the members of his organization to decide at what stage they inform him.

Top-level managers are frequently criticized by writers, consultants, and lower levels of management for continuing to enmesh themselves in operating problems, after promotion to the top, rather than withdrawing to the "big picture." Without any doubt, some managers do get lost in a welter of detail and insist on making too many decisions. Superficially, the good manager may seem to make the same mistake—but his purposes are different. He knows that only by keeping well informed about the decisions being made can he avoid the sterility so often found in those who isolate themselves from operations. If he follows the advice to free himself from operations, he may soon find himself subsisting on a diet of abstractions, leaving the choice of what he eats in the hands of his subordinates. As Kenneth Boulding puts it: "The very purpose of a hierarchy is to prevent information from reaching higher layers. It operates as an information filter, and there are little wastebaskets all along the way."[1]

What kinds of action does a successful executive take to keep his information live and accurate? Here is an example:

One company president that I worked with sensed that his vice presidents were insulating him from some of the vital issues being discussed at lower levels. He accepted a proposal for a formal management development program primarily because it afforded him an opportunity to discuss company problems with middle managers several layers

1. From a speech at a meeting sponsored by the Crowell Collier Institute of Continuing Education in New York, as reported in *Business Week*, February 18, 1967, p. 202.

removed from him in the organization. By meeting with small groups of these men in an academic setting, he learned much about their preoccupations, and also about those of his vice presidents. And he accomplished his purposes without undermining the authority of line managers.

Focusing Time and Energy

The second skill of the good manager is that he knows how to save his energy and hours for those few particular issues, decisions, or problems to which he should give his personal attention. He knows the fine and subtle distinction between keeping fully informed about operating decisions and allowing the organization to force him into participating in these decisions or, even worse, making them. Recognizing that he can bring his special talents to bear on only a limited number of matters, he chooses those issues which he believes will have the greatest long-term impact on the company, and on which his special abilities can be most productive. Under ordinary circumstances he will limit himself to three or four major objectives during any single period of sustained activity.

What about the situations he elects *not* to become involved in as a decision maker? He makes sure (using the skill first mentioned) that the organization keeps him informed about them at various stages; he does not want to be accused of indifference to such issues. He trains his subordinates not to bring the matters to him for a decision. The communication to him from below is essentially one of: "Here is our sizeup, and here's what we propose to do." Reserving his hearty encouragement for those projects that hold superior promise of a contribution to total corporate strategy, he simply acknowledges receipt of information on other matters. When he sees a problem where the organization needs his help, he finds a way to transmit his know-how short of giving orders—usually by asking perceptive questions.

Playing the Power Game

To what extent do successful top executives push their ideas and proposals through the organization? The rather common notion that the "prime mover" continually creates and forces through new programs, like a powerful majority leader in a liberal Congress, is in my opinion very misleading.

The successful manager is sensitive to the power structure in the organization. In considering any major current proposal, he can plot the position of the various individuals and units in the organization on a scale ranging from complete, outspoken support down to determined, sometimes bitter, and oftentimes well-cloaked opposition. In the middle of the scale is an area of comparative indifference. Usually, several aspects of a proposal will fall into this area, and *here is where he knows he can operate*. He assesses the depth and nature of the blocs in the organization. His perception permits him to move through what I call *corridors* of comparative indifference. He seldom challenges when a corridor is blocked, preferring to pause until it has opened up.

Related to this particular skill is his ability to recognize the need for a few trial-balloon launchers in the organization. He knows that the organization will tolerate only a certain number of proposals that emanate from the apex of the pyramid. No matter how sorely he may be tempted to stimulate the organization with a flow of his own ideas, he knows he must work through idea men in different parts of the organization. As he studies the reactions of key individuals and groups to the trial balloons these men send up, he is able to make a better assessment of how to limit the emasculation of the various proposals. For seldom does he find a proposal that is supported by all quarters of the organization. The emergence of strong support in certain quarters is almost sure to evoke strong opposition in others.

VALUE OF SENSE OF TIMING

Circumstances like these mean that a good sense of timing is a priceless asset for a top executive. Let me illustrate:

A vice president had for some time been convinced that his company lacked a sense of direction and needed a formal long-range planning activity to fill the void. Up to the time in question, his soft overtures to other top executives had been rebuffed. And then he spotted an opening.

A management development committee proposed a series of weekend meetings for second-level officers in the company. After extensive debate, but for reasons not announced, the president rejected this proposal. The members of the committee openly resented what seemed to them an arbitrary rejection.

The vice president, sensing a tense situation, suggested to the president that the same officers who were to have attended the weekend management development seminars be organized into a long-range planning committee. The timing of his suggestion was perfect. The president, looking for a bone to toss to the committee, acquiesced immediately, and the management development committee in its next meeting enthusiastically endorsed the idea.

This vice president had been conducting a kind of continuing market research to discover how to sell his long-range planning proposal. His previous probes of the "market" had told him that the president's earlier rejections of his proposal were not so final as to preclude an eventual shift in the corridors of attitude I have mentioned.

The vice president caught the committee in a conciliatory mood, and his proposal rode through with colors flying.

As a good manager stands at a point in time, he can identify a set of goals he is interested in, albeit the outline of them may be pretty hazy. His timetable, which is also pretty hazy, suggests that some must be accomplished sooner than others, and that some may be safely postponed for several months or years. He has a still hazier notion of how he can reach these goals. He assesses key individuals and groups. He knows that each has its own set of goals, some of which he understands rather thoroughly and others about which he can only speculate. He knows also that these individuals and groups represent blocks to certain programs or projects, and that these points of opposition must be taken into account. As the day-to-day operating decisions are made, and as proposals are responded to both by individuals and by groups, he perceives more clearly where the corridors of comparative indifference are. He takes action accordingly.

The Art of Imprecision

The fourth skill of the successful manager is knowing how to satisfy the organization that it has a sense of direction *without ever actually getting himself committed publicly to a specific set of objectives.* This is not to say that he does not have objectives—personal and corporate, long-term and short-term. They are significant guides to his thinking, and he modifies them continually as he better understands the resources he is working with, the competition, and the changing market demands. But as the organization clamors for statements of objectives, these are samples of what they get back from him:

"Our company aims to be number one in its industry."
"Our objective is growth with profit."
"We seek the maximum return on investment."
"Management's goal is to meet its responsibilities to stockholders, employees, and the public."

In my opinion, statements such as these provide almost no guidance to the various levels of management. Yet they are quite readily accepted as objectives by large numbers of intelligent people.

MAINTAINING VIABILITY

Why does the good manager shy away from precise statements of his objectives for the organization? The main reason is that he finds it impossible to set down specific objectives that will be relevant for any reasonable period into the future. Conditions in business change continually and rapidly, and corporate strategy must be revised to take the changes into account. The more explicit the statement of strategy, the more difficult it becomes to persuade the organization to turn to different goals when needs and conditions shift.

The public and the stockholders, to be sure, must perceive the organization as having a well-defined set of objectives and a clear sense of direction. But in reality the good top manager is seldom so certain of the direction which should be taken. Better than anyone else, he senses the many, many threats to his company—threats that lie in the economy, in the actions of competitors, and, not least, within his own organization.

He also knows that it is impossible to state objectives clearly enough so that everyone in the organization understands what they mean. Objectives get communicated only over time by a consistency or pattern in operating decisions. Such decisions are more meaningful than words. In instances where precise objectives are spelled out, the organization tends to interpret them so they fit its own needs.

Subordinates who keep pressing for more precise objectives are in truth working against their own best interests. Each time the objectives are stated more specifically, a subordinate's range of possibilities for operating are reduced. The narrower field means less room to roam and to accommodate the flow of ideas coming up from his part of the organization.

AVOIDING POLICY STRAITJACKETS

The successful manager's reluctance to be precise extends into the area of policy decisions. He seldom makes a forthright statement of policy. He may be aware that in some companies there are executives who spend more time in arbitrating disputes caused by stated policies than in moving the company forward. The management textbooks contend that well-defined policies are the sine qua non of a well-managed company. My research does not bear out this contention. For example:

The president of one company with which I am familiar deliberately leaves the assignments of his top officers vague and refuses to define policies for them. He passes out new assignments with seemingly no pattern in mind and consciously sets up competitive ventures among his subordinates. His methods, though they would never be sanctioned by a classical organization planner, are deliberate—and, incidentally, quite effective.

Since able managers do not make policy decisions, does this mean that well-managed companies operate without policies? Certainly not. But the policies are those that evolve over time from an indescribable mix of operating decisions. From any single operating decision might have come a very minor dimension of the policy as the organization understands it; from a series of decisions comes a pattern of guidelines for various levels of the organization.

The skillful manager resists the urge to write a company creed or to compile a policy manual. Preoccupation with detailed statements of corporate objectives and departmental goals and with comprehensive organization charts and job descriptions—this is often the first symptom of an organization that is in the early stages of atrophy.

The "management by objectives" school, so widely heralded in recent years, suggests that detailed objectives be spelled out at all levels in the corporation. This method is feasible at lower levels of management, but it becomes unworkable at the upper levels. The top manager must think out objectives in detail, but ordinarily some of the objectives must be withheld, or at least communicated to the organization in modest doses. A conditioning process that may stretch over months or years is necessary in order to prepare the organization for radical departures from what it is currently striving to attain.

Suppose, for example, that a president is convinced his company must phase out of the principal business it has been in for 35 years. Although making this change of course is one of his objectives, he may well feel that he cannot disclose the idea even to his vice presidents, whose total know-how is in the present business. A blunt announcement that the company is changing horses would be too great a shock for most of them to bear. And so he begins moving toward this goal but without a full disclosure to his management group.

A detailed spelling out of objectives may only complicate the task of reaching them. Specific, detailed statements give the opposition an opportunity to organize its defenses.

Muddling with a Purpose

The fifth, and most important, skill I shall describe bears little relation to the doctrine that management is (or should be) a comprehensive, systematic, logical, well-programmed science. Of all the heresies set forth here, this should strike doctrinaires as the rankest of all!

The successful manager, in my observation, recognizes the futility of trying to push total packages or programs through the organization. He is willing to take less than total acceptance in order to achieve modest progress toward his goals. Avoiding debates on principles, he tries to piece together particles that may appear to be incidentals into a program that moves at least part of the way toward his objectives. His attitude is based on optimism and persistence. Over and over he says to himself, "There must be some parts of this proposal on which we can capitalize."

Whenever he identifies relationships among the different proposals before him, he knows that they present opportunities for combination and restructuring. It follows that he is a man of wide-ranging interests and curiosity. The more things he knows about, the more opportunities he will have to discover parts which are related. This process does not require great intellectual brilliance or unusual creativity. The wider-ranging his interests, the more likely that he will be able to tie together several unrelated proposals. He is skilled as an analyst, but even more talented as a conceptualizer.

If the manager has built or inherited a solid organization, it will be difficult for him to come up with an idea that no one in the company has ever thought of before. His most significant contribution may be that he can see relationships that no one else has seen. Take this example:

A division manager had set as one of his objectives, at the start of a year, an improvement in product quality. At the end of the year, in reviewing his progress toward this objective, he could identify three significant events that had brought about a perceptible improvement.

First, the head of the quality control group, a veteran manager who was doing only an adequate job, asked early in the year for assignment to a new research group. This opportunity permitted the division manager to install a promising young engineer in this key spot.

A few months later, opportunity number two came along. The personnel department proposed a continuous program of checking the effectiveness of training methods for new employees. The proposal was acceptable to the manufacturing group. The division manager's only contribution was to suggest that the program should include a heavy emphasis on employees' attitudes toward quality.

Then a third opportunity arose when one of the division's best customers discovered that the wrong material had been used for a large lot of parts. The heat generated by this complaint made it possible to institute a completely new system of procedures for inspecting and testing raw materials.

As the division manager reviewed the year's progress on product quality, these were the three most important developments. None of them could have been predicted at the start of the year, but he was quick to see the potential in each as it popped up in the day-to-day operating routines.

EXPLOITATION OF CHANGE

The good manager can function effectively only in an environment of continual change. A *Saturday Review* cartoonist has caught the idea as he pictures an executive seated at a massive desk instructing his secretary to "send in a deal; I feel like wheelin'." Only with many changes in the works can the manager discover new combinations of opportunities and open up new corridors of comparative indifference. His stimulation to creativity comes from trying to make something useful of the proposal or idea in front of him. He will try to make strategic change a way of life in the organization and continually review the strategy even though current results are good.

Charles Lindblom has written an article with an engaging title, "The Science of Muddling Through."[2] In this paper he describes what he calls "the rational comprehensive method" of decision making. The essence of this method is that the decision maker, for each of his problems, proceeds deliberately, one step at a time, to collect complete data; to analyze the data thoroughly; to study a wide range of alternatives, each with its own risks and consequences; and, finally, to formulate a detailed course of action. Lindblom immediately dismisses "the rational comprehensive method" in favor of what he calls "successive limited comparisons." He sees the decision maker as comparing the alternatives that are open to him in order to learn which most closely meets the objectives he has in mind. Since this is not so much a rational process as an opportunistic one, he sees the manager as a muddler, but a muddler with a purpose.

H. Igor Ansoff, in his book, *Corporate Strategy*,[3] espouses a similar notion as he describes what he calls the "cascade approach." In his view, possible decision rules are formulated in gross terms and are successively refined through several stages as the emergence of a solution proceeds. This process gives the appearance of solving the problem several times over, but with successively more precise results.

Both Lindblom and Ansoff are moving us closer to an understanding of how managers really think. The process is not highly abstract; rather, the manager searches for a means of drawing into a pattern the thousands of incidents that make up the day-to-day life of a growing company.

CONTRASTING PICTURES

It is interesting to note, in the writings of several students of management, the emergence of the concept that, rather than making decisions, the leader's principal task is maintaining operating conditions which permit the various decision-making systems to function effectively. The supporters of this theory, it

2. *Readings in Managerial Psychology,* edited by Harold J. Leavitt and Louis R. Pondy (Chicago, University of Chicago Press, 1964), p. 61.
3. New York, McGraw-Hill Book Company, Inc., 1965.

seems to me, overlook the subtle turns of direction that the leader can provide. He cannot add purpose and structure to the balanced judgments of subordinates if he simply rubber-stamps their decisions. He must weigh the issues and reach his own decision.

Richard M. Cyert and James G. March contend that in real life managers do not consider all the possible courses of action, that their search ends once they have found a satisfactory alternative. In my sample, good managers are not guilty of such myopic thinking. Unless they mull over a wide range of possibilities, they cannot come up with the imaginative combinations of ideas that characterize their work.

Many of the articles about successful executives picture them as great thinkers who sit at their desks drafting master blueprints for their companies. The successful top executives I have seen at work do not operate this way. Rather than produce a full-grown decision tree, they start with a twig, help it grow, and ease themselves out on the limbs only after they have tested to see how much weight the limbs can stand.

In my picture, the general manager sits in the midst of a continuous stream of operating problems. His organization presents him with a flow of proposals to deal with the problems. Some of these proposals are contained in voluminous, well-documented, formal reports; some are as fleeting as the walk-in visit from a subordinate whose latest inspiration came during the morning's coffee break. Knowing how meaningless it is to say, "This is a finance problem," or, "That is a communications problem," the manager feels no compulsion to classify his problems. He is, in fact, undismayed by a problem that defies classification. As the late Gary Steiner, in one of his speeches, put it, "He has a high tolerance for ambiguity."

In considering each proposal, the general manager tests it against at least three criteria:

1. Will the total proposal—or, more often, will some part of the proposal— move the organization toward the objectives he has in mind?

2. How will the whole or parts of the proposal be received by the various groups and subgroups in the organization? Where will the strongest opposition come from, which group will furnish the strongest support, and which group will be neutral or indifferent?

3. How does the proposal relate to programs already in process or currently proposed? Can some parts of the proposal under consideration be added on to a program already under way, or can they be combined with all or parts of other proposals in a package that can be steered through the organization?

As another example of a general manager at work, let me describe the train of events that led to a parent company president's decision to attempt to consolidate two of his divisions:

> Let us call the executive Mr. Brown. One day the manager of Division A came to him with a proposal that his division acquire a certain company. That company's founder and president—let us call him Mr. Johansson—had a phenomenal record of inventing new products, but earnings in his company had been less than phenomenal. Johansson's asking price for his company was high when evaluated against the earnings record.
>
> Not until Brown began to speculate on how Johansson might supply fresh vigor for new products in Division A did it appear that perhaps a premium price could be justified. For several years Brown had been unsuccessful in stimulating the manager of that division to see that he must bring in new products to replace those that were losing their place in the market.
>
> The next idea that came to Brown was that Johansson might invent not only for Division A but also for Division B. As Brown analyzed how this might be worked out organizationally, he began to think about the markets being served by divisions A and B. Over the years, several basic but gradual changes in marketing patterns had occurred, with the result that the marketing considerations that had dictated the establishment of separate divisions no longer prevailed. Why should the company continue to support the duplicated overhead expenses in the two divisions?
>
> As Brown weighed the issues, he concluded that by consolidating the two divisions, he could also shift responsibilities in the management groups in ways that would strengthen them overall.

If we were asked to evaluate Brown's capabilities, how would we respond? Putting aside the objection that the information is too sketchy, our tendency might be to criticize Brown. Why did he not identify the changing market patterns in his continuing review of company position? Why did he not force the issue when the division manager failed to do something about new product development? Such criticism would reflect "the rational comprehensive method" of decision making.

But, as I analyze the gyrations in Brown's thinking, one characteristic stands out. He kept searching for the follow-on opportunities that he could fashion out of the original proposal, opportunities that would stand up against the three criteria earlier mentioned. In my book, Brown would rate as an extremely skillful general manager.

Conclusion

To recapitulate, the general manager possesses five important skills. He knows how to:

1. *Keep open many pipelines of information.* No one will quarrel with the desirability of an early warning system that provides varied viewpoints on an issue. However, very few managers know how to practice this skill, and the books on management add precious little to our understanding of the techniques that make it practicable.

2. *Concentrate on a limited number of significant issues.* No matter how skillful the manager is in focusing his energies and talents, he is inevitably caught up in a number of inconsequential duties. Active leadership of an organization demands a high level of personal involvement, and personal involvement brings with it many time-consuming activities that have an infinitesimal impact on corporate strategy. Hence this second skill, while perhaps the most logical of the five, is by no means the easiest to apply.

3. *Identify the corridors of comparative indifference.* Are there inferences here that the good manager has no ideas of his own, that he stands by until his organization proposes solutions, that he never uses his authority to force a proposal through the organization? Such inferences are not intended. The message is that a good organization will tolerate only so much direction from the top; the good manager therefore is adept at sensing how hard he can push.

4. *Give the organization a sense of direction with open-ended objectives.* In assessing this skill, keep in mind that I am talking about top levels of management. At lower levels, the manager should be encouraged to write down his objectives, if for no other reason than to ascertain if they are consistent with corporate strategy.

5. *Spot opportunities and relationships in the stream of operating problems and decisions.* Lest it be concluded from the description of this skill that the good manager is more an improviser than a planner, let me emphasize that he is a planner and encourages planning by his subordinates. Interestingly, though, professional planners may be irritated by a good general manager. Most of them complain about his lack of vision. They devise a master plan, but the president (or other operating executive) seems to ignore it, or to give it minimum acknowledgment by borrowing bits and pieces for implementation. They seem to feel that the power of a good master plan will be obvious to everyone, and its implementation automatic. But the general manager knows that even if the plan is sound and imaginative, the job has only begun. The long, painful task of implementation will depend on his skill, not that of the planner.

PRACTICAL IMPLICATIONS

If this analysis of how skillful general managers think and operate has validity, then it should help us see several problems in a better light.

Investment Analysis:

The investment community is giving increasing attention to sizing up the management of a company being appraised. Thus far, the analysts rely mainly on results or performance rather than on a probe of management skills. But current performance can be affected by many variables, both favorably and unfavorably, and is a dangerous base for predicting what the management of a company will produce in the future. Testing the key managers of a company against the five skills described holds promise for evaluating the caliber of a management group.

Incidentally, I believe that the manager who is building his own company and the man who is moving up through the hierarchy of a larger organization require essentially the same capabilities for success.

The Urge To Merge:

In today's frenzy of acquisitions and mergers, why does a management usually prefer to acquire a company rather than to develop a new product and build an organization to make and sell it? One of the reasons can be found in the way a general manager thinks and operates. He finds it difficult to sit and speculate theoretically about the future as he and his subordinates fashion a plan to exploit a new product. He is much more at home when taking over a going concern, even though he anticipates he will inherit many things he does not want. In the day-to-day operation of a going concern, he finds the milieu to maneuver and conceptualize.

Promotion Practices:

Scarcely any manager in any business can escape the acutely painful responsibility to identify men with potential for growth in management and to devise methods for developing them for broader responsibilities. Few line managers or staff professionals have genuine confidence in the yardsticks and devices they use now. The five skills offer possibilities for raising an additional set of questions about management appraisal methods, job rotation practices, on-the-job development assignments, and the curricula of formal in-house management development programs.

One group of distinguished executives ignores with alarming regularity the implications of the five skills. These are the presidents of multidivision companies who "promote" successful division managers to the parent company level as staff officers. Does this recurring phenomenon cast doubt on the validity of my theory? I think not. To the contrary, strong supporting evidence for my thesis can be found in the results of such action. What happens is that line managers thus "promoted" often end up on the sidelines, out of the game for the rest of their careers. Removed from the tumult of operations, the environment that I contend is critical for their success, many of them just wither away in their high-status posts as senior counselors and never become effective.

Appendix to Chapter 6

Basis of Conclusions in This Article

I have reached the conclusions outlined here after working closely with many managers in many different companies. In truth, the managers were not preselected with research in mind. Never did I tell the man that he was being studied, nor was I in fact studying his behavior. Research was not the purpose of our relationship. We were collaborating to solve some real problem.

Researching the management process when the manager is aware that he is being studied sometimes produces strange results. Rarely is a good executive able to think objectively about the management process as it is exemplified in his own methods. When he tries to explain to a researcher or writer, he tends to feel compelled to develop rational, systematic explanations of how he does his job—explanations that in my opinion are largely fictional.

A manager cannot be expected to describe his methods even if he understands them. They border on manipulation, and the stigma associated with manipulation can be fatal. If the organization ever identifies him as a manipulator, his job becomes more difficult. No one willingly submits to manipulation, and those around him organize to protect themselves. And yet every good manager does have to manipulate.

My definition of a good manager is a simple one: under competitive industry conditions, he is able to move his organization significantly toward the goals he has set, whether measured by higher return on investment, product improvement, development of management talent, faster growth in sales and earnings, or some other standard. Bear in mind that this definition does not refer to the administrator whose principal role is to maintain the status quo in a company or in a department. Keeping the wheels turning in a direction already set is a relatively simple task, compared to that of directing the introduction of a continuing flow of changes and innovations, and preventing the organization from flying apart under the pressure.   —*The Author*

7. Putting Judgment Back into Decisions

Larry E. Greiner, D. Paul Leitch, and Louis B. Barnes

Do modern information systems, which provide management with computer-generated indexes of performance, help managers to make sound judgments about an organization's effectiveness? An extensive study made by the authors in a large organization raises serious doubts. The evidence from the study indicates that informed managers still rely much more on qualitative than quantitative criteria in appraising performance, even when the quantitative measures are available and in use. Furthermore, those managers who use more subjective data tend to agree more with one another than those who depend on highly quantified information. The findings have significant implications for management training and for the planning of information systems.

Top managers are currently inundated with reams of information concerning the performance of organizational units under their supervision. Behind this information explosion lies a seemingly logical assumption made by information specialists and frequently accepted by line managers: if top management can be supplied with more "objective" and "accurate" *quantified* information, they will make "better" judgments about the performance of their operating units.

But how valid is this assumption? A research study we have recently completed indicates that quantified performance information may have a more limited role than is currently assumed or envisioned; in fact, managers rely more on subjective information than they do on so-called "objective" statistics in assessing the overall performance of lower-level units.

The Human Factor

Despite the increasing desire for and trend toward the quantification of performance results, most managers are the first to admit that their performance

AUTHORS' NOTE: We are grateful to the Internal Revenue Service and the Division of Research, Harvard Business School, for supporting this study.

assessments begin and end with human judgment. Managers determine what kinds of performance information to collect; and later, when this information is in front of them, they study the data, make up their minds, and decide what to do. For example, here is how a vice president of finance in a large steel company describes the importance of human judgment in assessing organization performance: "We have capital budgets, we have fixed budgets, we have variable budgets, we have standard costs. We have the full assortment. None of our controls is 100% effective. None replaces subjective judgment."[1]

There are several reasons why managerial judgment is critical in evaluating the performance of lower-level units in today's organizations:

□ Organizations are becoming so large and complex that, as yet, no universal mathematical formulas exist for encompassing all the variables that reflect the total performance of a particular subunit.

□ Events within and around an organization change so rapidly that indicators of "good" performance last year may not be appropriate this year.

□ Managers are frequently aware of nonquantifiable factors that information specialists don't usually hear about or record on their standard forms.

□ Ultimately, it is managers, not computers, that must make decisions based on their assessments of performance. If a manager makes a "biased" judgment of performance, then his actions are also likely to be "biased."

In this article, we shall describe the purpose and methods of our study. Then we will present the major findings, which at times are coupled with some broad implications for management. Finally, we shall conclude with more specific suggestions for improving the quality of performance judgments in organizations.

In particular, we shall consider these important questions that bear on the judgmental process:

□ How important relatively are quantitative and qualitative criteria to managers in making judgments of performance? (If quantitative criteria are less important than assumed, then the organization may be able to redirect the activities of computers and staff analysts to use them more efficiently.)

□ Are managers consistent from one day to the next in their judgments?

□ Do managers agree more on current effectiveness than they do on changes in effectiveness over time?

□ Can managers actually agree with each other in assessing the performance of organizational units beneath them? (If they can't, then they are likely to give off conflicting signals to lower levels.)

1. Letter from Robert Jacobs, "From the Thoughtful Businessman," HBR January - February 1967, p. 48.

☐ Must managers agree on specific criteria if they are to agree in their overall judgments about performance?

☐ Does a manager's position in the organization affect his judgments of performance? (If it does, misunderstandings among managerial levels are likely to ensue.)

How the Study Was Made

We conducted our investigation in a large government agency, the Internal Revenue Service. Although the IRS is not a business organization, it does contain many elements common to most large, complex organizations. More than 60,000 people are employed by the IRS in either the national office headquarters or the 7 regional and 58 district offices, or the 7 computer service centers. The IRS organization is also divided functionally into several major divisions, with each division having a representative group at all regional and most district offices. The measurement of performance is a key concern of IRS managers; many statistical indicators of performance are regularly collected, including indexes of costs, output, and morale.

Top management in the IRS became interested in having a study made partly out of curiosity about the reliability of their performance assessments of district operations. Despite their access to many quantitative performance measures, they readily acknowledged that their overall assessments of district performance depended, in the final analysis, on subjective judgment. At the national office level, managers were interested in knowing if they agreed with their counterparts at the regional level, and vice versa. In addition, managers at all levels were curious about the degree to which they relied on quantitative versus qualitative information in forming their judgments.

The study focused on three types of performance evaluation mentioned most frequently in initial interviews with IRS managers at the national and regional levels:

1. The current effectiveness of divisional subunits within a district. (This is important because it provides early signs of problems in the making.)

2. The performance improvement of these units over the preceding 18 months. (This adds perspective to the judgments of current effectiveness, especially when a currently high-performing unit is slipping or a low-performing unit is improving.)

3. Specific reasons for a unit's performance improvement, or lack of it. (This provides more precise clues for taking corrective action. For example, corrective action might be quite different if the reason were judged to be an uncontrollable "natural disaster" rather than a "lack of leadership.")

THE JUDGING PROCEDURE

To investigate how the IRS top managers evaluated these three performance dimensions, we formed 15 panels, representing 5 headquarters divisions and 10 regional divisions; see *Exhibit 1*. Each panel consisted of 2 to 5 managers acting as judges. Insofar as possible, judges were selected for their familiarity with the performance of their particular divisions at the district level and for their "objectivity" in assessing subunit performance.

The procedure we used to study the performance judgments of these 15 panels is described in *Exhibit II*. We have covered this method in some detail because, as we shall suggest later, other organizations may be interested in

Exhibit I. Location of judges' panels

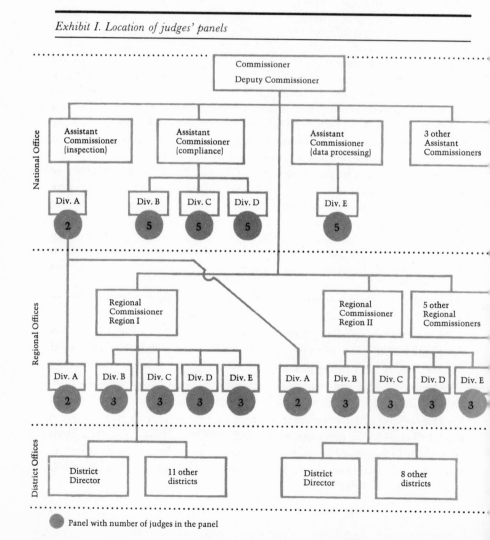

Panel with number of judges in the panel

Exhibit II. Steps in the judging procedure

Step 1: Each judge received a folder containing a range of performance information on each unit to be evaluated. This was done to provide a common starting point. The information covered an 18-month time period. Some of it was statistical (for example, productivity indexes), and some was more subjective (such as "personnel management" conditions). Each judge was asked to study this information thoroughly for two days, then put it away and not look at it again.

Step 2: Each judge received two identical decks of cards. One deck was to be used for judging overall current effectiveness, while the other was for judging overall performance improvement over 18 months. Each card within a deck listed a pair of comparable divisional units from two different district offices (for example, Division A from District 1 as compared with Division A, District 2). All possible combinations of district pairs were covered in each deck. Numerous precautions were taken in the construction of each deck to prevent bias. For example, the order in which pairs were presented was determined by a random number table so as to delete any effects due to order of presentation. Also, each unit appeared the same number of times on the left side as it did on the right side of each card so as to cancel effects of placement.

Steps 3 & 4: Each judge was instructed to circle the unit on each card that had the higher performance, using one deck for judging current effectiveness and the second deck for evaluating improvement. Half the judges were asked to make their effectiveness judgments first, while the other half made their improvement judgments first. This was done to counter any biasing effects arising from making one type of judgment before the other. In addition, judges were asked not to confer with other judges, so as to ensure that each judge was making an independent assessment.

Steps 5 & 6: Three days after Steps 3 & 4 were completed, each judge was given two more decks of cards, both identical in format to the first two decks. His instructions were to repeat exactly the procedure followed in making the first judgments. Our intent here was to find out if judgments were stable from one time period to the next.

Step 7: As a final step, each judge was asked to write three reasons on the back of each card in the improvement deck to explain why he had picked one unit over another. From this information, we hoped to learn more about the specific criteria that each judge was using.

undertaking similar studies. (This is the first study, as far as we know, that has designed and utilized a methodology for systematically examining managerial judgments of subunit performance.)

When each judge had completed the procedure described in *Exhibit II,* he sent his data cards directly to us for analysis. Our analytical procedure was based largely on a mathematical technique called correlation analysis. First, we totaled the number of times that each judge chose one unit over another. From these totals we computed for each judge a rank order of those units evaluated by him; the unit chosen most over other units received a rank of "1," and so forth

Exhibit III. Level of overall agreement

	Current effectiveness	Performance improvement over 18 months
Average correlation of agreement within 15 panels	+.76	+.71
Average correlation of agreement between Day 1 and Day 3 judgments for 50 judges	+.90	+.83

down the list. Then this rank order was correlated against the rank orders for the other judges in each panel. This produced a "level of agreement" *within* each of the 15 panels.

Additional correlations were also computed *between* panels by comparing an overall rank order for each panel (based on an average of individual rank orders) with the overall rank order for other panels. Perfect agreement between rank orders, as measured by a statistical correlation, was +1.00, while perfect disagreement was −1.00. There is no fixed rule for determining an "acceptable" correlation of agreement, although the following guideline tends to be commonly used in research:

+.9 or −.9 = high correlation
+.7 or −.7 = substantial correlation
+.5 or −.5 = moderate correlation
+.3 or −.3 = low correlation

Agreement Among Managers

A basic and critical question for any management is: Can our managers agree with one another about the performance of units under their supervision? Pessimists contend that managers cannot mentally assimilate and agree on all the complex performance data available, or that managers are such an idiosyncratic lot psychologically that it is impossible for them to agree with one another. On the other hand, optimists argue that managers are quite adept at simplifying complex information, being far more logical and objective than the pessimists might believe.

Our findings strongly support the optimists. While we cannot answer the agreement question for *all* organizations, *Exhibit III* does reveal that the particular managers we studied were, in general, able to reach a substantial level of agreement in their overall judgments of *both* current effectiveness and performance improvement. There was also a high correlation between their first-day and third-day judgments on both performance measurements.

The critical reader should ask, of course, if high agreement was merely a product of common "bias" among the judges within each panel. If such a bias did exist, this would be disturbing because IRS managers, while in overall agreement, could be making inaccurate assessments. One check on the amount of bias was to examine the extent of agreement between each divisional panel at the regional level and its counterpart panel at the national office. These panels all reported to different bosses and were separated by large physical distances. Under these conditions of limited authority and interaction we felt that high agreement between national and regional office panels could not be explained in terms of a commonly shared bias.

The findings indeed revealed considerable agreement between regional and national office panels from each of the five divisions: an average of +.75 for their current effectiveness judgments and +.65 for their performance improvement judgments. Therefore, we think it reasonable to infer that common bias was not a strong contributing factor toward high agreement.

The improvement evaluation is obviously a complex assessment, which includes many subjective considerations and also requires a longer time perspective. Yet IRS managers seemed to find themselves on relatively the same historical wave length. This finding is important because a manager's awareness of performance trends is often what tempers his action-taking plans. Lack of agreement about trends could produce not only inappropriate actions but also conflicting decisions from different managers.

At the same time, we should point out that a considerable range existed between panels with the lowest and highest levels of internal agreement. For current-effectiveness judgments, the lowest agreement panel had an internal correlation of +.16, while the highest agreement panel had +.99. For performance-improvement judgments, the internal correlation was +.10 for the lowest agreement panel and +1.00 for the highest panel. Thus, a large majority of panels revealed substantial internal agreement, while a few panels revealed much disagreement. This suggests the importance of discovering the factors that block agreement on some panels and the factors that cause high agreement on others.

EFFECT OF DISTANCE

We found two important organizational variables that seemed to distinguish between high- and low-agreement panels. The most potent variable appeared to be "organizational distance." *Exhibit IV* shows not only that members of national office panels (two levels removed from districts) agreed less with one another in comparison with judges on regional office panels (one level removed), but also that their judgments were less stable from Day 1 to Day 3.

We prefer the term *organizational distance* to *physical distance* because the Region I office and its 12 districts were located within 600 miles of Washington, while the Region II office and its 9 districts were situated more than 1,300 miles away. Yet national office panels did not reach any more agreement about the closer Region I districts than they did about the more remote Region II districts. It appears that sitting close to the top of the organizational pyramid is not necessarily the easiest or best vantage point for assessing field unit performance. Undoubtedly, certain information disappears in the gap between levels, never reaching the top.

For us, these findings raise doubts about concentrating too much decision-making power at the top of large organizations when the decision to be made is based on the evaluation of performance. They also cause one to question an overreliance on centralized information systems. Centralized systems, because of their remoteness and need for uniformity, may be particularly insensitive to what is happening in each field unit.

Exhibit IV. Relationship between organizational distance and level of overall agreement

	Current effectiveness	Performance improvement over 18 months
Average correlation of agreement within:		
5 national office panels	+.53	+.41
10 regional office panels	+.84	+.81
Average correlation of agreement between Day 1 and Day 3 judgements for:		
22 national judges	+.80	+.71
28 regional office judges	+.93	+.87

THE EFFECT OF SIZE

A second important, but less pronounced, organizational variable was the size of functional divisions. *Exhibit V* reveals that panels from the two largest agency divisions (A and B), each of which employed more than twice as many people as any other division, reached lower levels of agreement. These large division panels, regardless of their level in the organization, seemed to have particular difficulty in assessing performance improvement over time.

Managers in large divisions are often physically and organizationally sepa-

Exhibit V. *Relationship between organization size and level of overall agreement*

	Current effectiveness	Performance improvement over 18 months
Average correlation of agreement within:		
6 large division panels	+.73	+.48
9 small division panels	+.82	+.86
Average correlation of agreement between Day 1 and Day 3 judgments for:		
22 large division judges	+.83	+.73
28 small division judges	+.92	+.89

rated; they also become more specialized in their job functions. As a result, their communications are likely to be less frequent and conducted from narrower frames of reference. Further evidence of this communications breakdown was found in the fact that large division panels from the national office agreed with their counterpart panels at the regional offices only at the level of +.46 when judging performance improvement, while national and regional panels from small divisions agreed with each other at a much higher level, +.83, in judging improvement. Apparently, the communications pipeline between national and regional levels was more open in small divisions.

Both *Exhibit IV* and *Exhibit V* make clear that the performance judgments of IRS managers are affected by their positions in the organizations. We suspect that the same findings apply to other large organizations as well. If a manager is located at headquarters, he is less likely to agree with his colleagues. In addition, if he is in a large division, he is less likely to agree not only with his peers at headquarters but also with managers at the next lower level in his division. Judgments of current effectiveness probably will not be as strongly affected by these organizational forces as are judgments of performance improvement.

Lower level managers, because they can agree more with each other, may be able to teach higher level managers a few of their trade secrets. Some clues to these trade secrets became more obvious when we focused on the specific criteria used by high-agreement panels.

Criteria for Judgment

While broader organizational forces (distance and size) produced variations in judgment, the specific criteria used by judges also contributed to differences in

Exhibit VI. Most frequently mentioned criteria

Rank	Rating on 5-point scale*
1. Quality and effectiveness of management	4
2. Productivity measurements	1
3. Manpower utilization	4
4. Overall improvement, status quo, or decline	3
5. Inventory level of uncollected TDAs (taxpayer delinquent accounts)	1
6. Progress and achievement of established objectives and planned programs	4
7. Morale	4
8. Management participation and concern in local problem solving	5
9. Potential available and use to which potential is put	4
10. Improved quality and composition and balance of fieldwork	5

*1=highly quantitative; 2=more quantitative than qualitative; 3=mixed quantitative and qualitative; 4=more qualitative than quantitative; and 5=highly qualitative.

agreement. An analysis was made of the criteria filled out by judges on the reverse sides of their "performance improvement" cards.

As a first step, we arranged for an independent group of IRS analysts in Washington to categorize the criteria reported by the 50 judges. This group of analysts individually rated each of the reasons given by the judges on a 5-point scale: a rating of 4 or 5 was given to highly qualitative criteria, a 3 to mixed qualitative and quantitative criteria, and a 1 or 2 to highly quantitative criteria. One example of a qualitative criterion was "management is setting challenging goals," while a quantitative one was "time spent per average case."

Exhibit VI shows the ranking of the 10 most frequently mentioned criteria. The phrasing of these criteria was done by the IRS national office analysts, who inferred the categories from a variety of specific phrases found on the judges' cards. Some categories are unique to IRS operations, but they indicate general types of criteria that could apply to other organizations as well. Important here is the fact that a large majority of items (7 out of 10) are qualitative (rated 4 or 5 on the rating scale), although two strongly quantitative criteria (rated 1) were also mentioned by the judges. The most important criterion was "quality and

Exhibit VII. Consensus about criteria

	Used by all members	Used by some but not all members	Used by only one member
Four high-agreement panels	44%	15%	41%
Four low-agreement panels	12	17	71

effectiveness of management"; it was used by judges in 13 of the 15 panels.

From this initial categorizing process, we found that 92 different criteria were used by the entire group of judges. These criteria divided themselves into 39% qualitative, 22% mixed, and 39% quantitative, based on the ratings assigned by the IRS analysts. Of significant interest here is the fact that such a high percentage of qualitative criteria were used. The IRS devotes considerable manpower and money to quantifying performance results; yet these numerical results played a more limited role than we suspected.

NUMBER OF FACTORS

Next we compared the criteria used by four high-agreement panels (those panels with an internal correlation of +.84 or better) with the criteria used by four low-agreement panels (those with an internal correlation of +.30 or lower). Here we did not find any significant difference in the total number of criteria used; that is, low-agreement panels did not appear to be confusing themselves with too many criteria. High-agreement panels averaged 11.8 different criteria per panel, and low-agreement panels, 12.8. One high-agreement panel used as few as 7 criteria, while another used 20. Approximately the same range of total criteria (6 to 20) was found among low-agreement panels.

POINTS OF AGREEMENT

An important distinction was discovered in the extent of *common* criteria used by high-agreement panels. *Exhibit VII* reveals that 44% of the criteria used in each high-agreement panel were commonly used by *every* judge within that panel. Only 12% of the criteria used in low-agreement panels were common to every judge.

We conclude from *Exhibit VII* that lack of agreement about specific criteria probably results in lack of agreement about the overall performance of a unit. At the same time, we should point out that "perfect" agreement on specific criteria is not essential; a high percentage of criteria (41%) were unique to individual judges in high-agreement panels. Apparently, many judges took somewhat different reasoning paths to arrive at essentially the same end result.

A broad implication here is that, while managements should work toward agreement on criteria for evaluating overall performance, they should also leave some latitude for each manager to select his own reasons. All too many managements spend endless meeting hours trying to agree on a limited number of criteria. According to our findings, this costly and often frustrating task may not be necessary.

Exhibit VIII. Type of criteria and level of overall agreement

| | Types of criteria used | | |
	Quantitative	Mixed	Qualitative
Four high-agreement panels	17%	14%	69%
Four low-agreement panels	68	12	20

QUALITATIVE CRITERIA

One very significant finding was that high-agreement panels used considerably more qualitative than quantitative criteria in making their decisions. *Exhibit VIII* shows that 69% of the criteria used by high-agreement panels were qualitative, compared to only 20% for low-agreement panels. Low-agreement panels used 68% quantitative criteria yet could reach only an overall agreement level of no better than +.31. Furthermore, we found that the only criteria that low-agreement panels could completely agree on were *quantitative* criteria; there was far less agreement on qualitative criteria. This suggests that if managers want to be more in line with their colleagues in assessing total performance, they need not only to use *a greater proportion of qualitative criteria, but also to develop more consensus on the specific qualitative criteria to be used.*

Why would qualitative evidence be relied on so heavily by high-agreement panels, and why might these criteria lead them to greater overall agreement? As we interpret our findings, there are at least three reasons:

1. Qualitative factors probably give *more concrete, more sensitive,* and *more current* clues to the underlying strengths of a unit; whereas statistics, despite their apparent preciseness, are usually averages or aggregates that fail to portray the complex events behind them.

2. Qualitative criteria present clearer leads for required corrective action; whereas statistical results may give little indication of *why* events happened as they did.

3. Qualitative criteria tend to be broader because they are not tied to particular measurable points; whereas quantitative criteria, just because they have to be particularized to certain narrow segments of field operations in order to be measured, may result in very diverse inferences being drawn from them in judging overall performance.

Applying the Results

Up to this point, we have mentioned some general implications of our findings; now we would like to draw them together and offer some specific suggestions for action:

☐ Most important is the need to recognize that managers—not computers, numbers, or information systems—are the critical element in the assessment of subunit performance.

Statistical reports have increasingly taken on the revered status of "objectivity," while managerial judgments have too often been sidetracked as overly "subjective" or "opinionated." Thus we find organizations building larger headquarters staffs to process ever larger amounts of statistical performance information, much of which is never used.

☐ All organizations ought to be vitally concerned with studying how their managers actually assess subunit performance. While organizations frequently spend large sums of money generating more and more information about subunit performance, they seldom consider what information is actually used or needed by their managers. Nor do they always recognize the importance of achieving a high level of agreement among top managers about subunit performance. If managers cannot agree, there is something amiss, either with the company's information system or with the managers and their organizational environment.

We therefore suggest that organizations take periodic "X rays" of their judgmental process. The study methodology used in the IRS is one useful approach. The findings can be used both for training managers to reach more informed judgments about subunit performance, and for designing information systems that will provide more help to managers in making their judgments.

☐ Management training should use research findings derived from the actual company environment to design programs that fit the needs of its particular management group. To do this, the key management group participating in the study could be brought together to hear and discuss the significant findings.

The critical questions before these managers should be: (a) Why do we have these results? (b) What do we do about them? The answers, of course, will vary with each organization and its unique findings. But the general thrust of actions afterward should be more informed and constructive.

For example, a top management group may decide to pay greater attention to the judgments of its field managers. Or agreement may be reached to place greater and more explicit emphasis on qualitative criteria. Or the present information system may be altered to provide data on those criteria that are most frequently used, while eliminating data on those that are not heavily used.

The next step would be to discuss the findings within smaller functional groupings. It would be useful for those groups in lowest agreement to sit down and discuss why they see subunits from such different perspectives. They may discover, in the process of this examination, that they fail to discuss their observations sufficiently with each other. Or they may find that each is using too diverse a set of criteria, and that more consensus needs to be reached on particular criteria.

☐ The formal information system must be designed to complement these changes if they are to be put into practice. For instance, it makes little sense for a company computer to continue providing data on 50 variables when its managers are in substantial agreement after using data on only 15 variables.

A real challenge for some organizations is to build more qualitative information into their formal systems. One method used in some companies is to request a written narrative with each submission of statistics from the field. Another method is to hold periodic, in-depth discussions involving several managers from different levels so that each can contribute whatever qualitative data are available to him.

Organizations might also consider the possibility of incorporating a judgmental procedure, such as the one used in this study, into an organization's ongoing process of performance assessment. Managements need to consider the challenge of systematically recording managerial judgments as much as they systematize statistical results. Lower-level managers can attest to their feelings of frustration when one upper-level manager tells one of them that he is doing a "good" job while another upper-level manager downgrades him. On the other hand, if this same manager knows that five upper-level managers systematically agree in ranking his unit at the "tail end" of the pack, he cannot as easily rationalize his position.

Our suggestion at this early stage, however, is to experiment with, but not institutionalize, a more systematic judging procedure, perhaps in only one division of a large company. Every formal system, if taken too seriously and rigidly, can become more of a hindrance than a help. There are always bugs to be worked out of these systems before giving them wider application.

Conclusion

A major task of any management is to know what is *actually* taking place within its organization. One critical, but seldom examined, function is the manner in which key managers assess the performance of units under their supervision. In the absence of knowledge, numerous myths and assumptions have abounded. Particularly noticeable is a growing mistrust of the reliability of managerial judgments. Signs of this mistrust are reflected in current trends toward more statistics, more computers, more information specialists, and more centralized information systems—the IRS, where this study was conducted, being no exception.

Yet the findings of this study seriously dispute many of these newer trends and assumptions. Notably:

1. Managers can generally agree with each other about the current effectiveness and performance trends of subunits under them.

2. Their judgments seem to be quite stable from one day to the next.

3. Managers who agree most with their colleagues tend to come from levels closest to the field; work in smaller divisions; use more commonly shared criteria; and rely more on qualitative than on quantitative criteria.

These conclusions must be qualified to the extent that they are based on *one study in a single nonbusiness organization.* Therefore, we should treat them more as propositions to be tested further than as final answers.

However, we believe these findings place a new challenge before every management: to seek new ways of studying, assisting, and restoring confidence in the performance judgments of their managers. This will not occur magically. First, a concerned management will have to investigate and identify its current practices for judging performance. Then, it will have to use the study findings to train its managers in improving their judgmental practices. Finally, it will have to strive to make its information system a more helpful servant rather than an irrelevant master.

8. The Manager's Job: Folklore and Fact

Henry Mintzberg

Just what does the manager do? For years the manager, the heart of the organization, has been assumed to be like an orchestra leader, controlling the various parts of his organization with the ease and precision of a Seiji Ozawa. However, when one looks at the few studies that have been done—covering managerial positions from the president of the United States to street gang leaders—the facts show that managers are not reflective, regulated workers, informed by their massive MIS systems, scientific, and professional. The evidence suggests that they play a complex, intertwined combination of interpersonal, informational, and decisional roles. The author's message is that if managers want to be more effective, they must recognize what their job really is and then use the resources at hand to support rather than hamper their own nature. Understanding their jobs as well as understanding themselves takes both introspection and objectivity on the managers' part. At the end of the article the author includes a set of self-study questions to help provide that insight.

If you ask a manager what he does, he will most probably tell you that he plans, organizes, coordinates, and controls. Then watch what he does. Don't be surprised if you can't relate what you see to these four words.

When he is called and told that one of his factories has just burned down, and he advises the caller to see whether temporary arrangements can be made to supply customers through a foreign subsidiary, is he planning, organizing, coordinating, or controlling? How about when he presents a gold watch to a retiring employee? Or when he attends a conference to meet people in the trade? Or on returning from that conference, when he tells one of his employees about an interesting product idea he picked up there?

The fact is that these four words, which have dominated management vocabulary since the French industrialist Henri Fayol first introduced them in 1916, tell us little about what managers actually do. At best, they indicate some vague objectives managers have when they work.

The field of management, so devoted to progress and change, has for more than half a century not seriously addressed *the* basic question: What do managers do? Without a proper answer, how can we teach management? How can we design planning or information systems for managers? How can we improve the practice of management at all?

Our ignorance of the nature of managerial work shows up in various ways in the modern organization—in the boast by the successful manager that he never spent a single day in a management training program; in the turnover of corporate planners who never quite understood what it was the manager wanted; in the computer consoles gathering dust in the back room because the managers never used the fancy on-line MIS some analyst thought they needed. Perhaps most important, our ignorance shows up in the inability of our large public organizations to come to grips with some of their most serious policy problems.

Somehow, in the rush to automate production, to use management science in the functional areas of marketing and finance, and to apply the skills of the behavioral scientist to the problem of worker motivation, the manager—that person in charge of the organization or one of its subunits—has been forgotten.

My intention in this article is simple: to break the reader away from Fayol's words and introduce him to a more supportable, and what I believe to be a more useful, description of managerial work. This description derives from my review and synthesis of the available research on how various managers have spent their time.

In some studies, managers were observed intensively ("shadowed" is the term some of them used); in a number of others, they kept detailed diaries of their activities; in a few studies, their records were analyzed. All kinds of managers were studied—foremen, factory supervisors, staff managers, field sales managers, hospital administrators, presidents of companies and nations, and even street gang leaders. These "managers" worked in the United States, Canada, Sweden, and Great Britain.

A synthesis of these findings paints an interesting picture, one as different from Fayol's classical view as a cubist abstract is from a Renaissance painting. In a sense, this picture will be obvious to anyone who has ever spent a day in a manager's office, either in front of the desk or behind it. Yet, at the same time, this picture may turn out to be revolutionary, in that it throws into doubt so much of the folklore that we have accepted about the manager's work.

I first discuss some of this folklore and contrast it with some of the discoveries of systematic research—the hard facts about how managers spend their time. Then I synthesize these research findings in a description of ten roles that seem to describe the essential content of all managers' jobs. In a concluding section, I discuss a number of implications of this synthesis for those trying to achieve more effective management, both in classrooms and in the business world.

Some Folklore and Facts About Managerial Work

There are four myths about the manager's job that do not bear up under careful scrutiny of the facts.

1. *Folklore: The manager is a reflective, systematic planner.* The evidence on this issue is overwhelming, but not a shred of it supports this statement.

Fact: Study after study has shown that managers work at an unrelenting pace, that their activities are characterized by brevity, variety, and discontinuity, and that they are strongly oriented to action and dislike reflective activities. Consider this evidence:

☐ Half the activities engaged in by the five chief executives of my study lasted less than nine minutes, and only 10% exceeded one hour.[1] A study of 56 U.S. foremen found that they averaged 583 activities per eight-hour shift, an average of 1 every 48 seconds.[2] The work pace for both chief executives and foremen was unrelenting. The chief executives met a steady stream of callers and mail from the moment they arrived in the morning until they left in the evening. Coffee breaks and lunches were inevitably work related, and ever-present subordinates seemed to usurp any free moment.

☐ A diary study of 160 British middle and top managers found that they worked for a half hour or more without interruption only about once every two days.[3]

☐ Of the verbal contacts of the chief executives in my study, 93% were arranged on an ad hoc basis. Only 1% of the executives' time was spent in open-ended observational tours. Only 1 out of 368 verbal contacts was unrelated to a specific issue and could be called general planning. Another researcher finds that "in *not one single case* did a manager report the obtaining of important external information from a general conversation or other undirected personal communication."[4]

☐ No study has found important patterns in the way managers schedule

1. All the data from my study can be found in Henry Mintzberg, *The Nature of Managerial Work* (New York: Harper & Row, 1973).

2. Robert H. Guest, "Of Time and the Foreman," *Personnel*, May 1956, p. 478.

3. Rosemary Stewart, *Managers and Their Jobs* (London: Macmillan, 1967); see also Sune Carlson, *Executive Behaviour* (Stockholm: Strömbergs, 1951), the first of the diary studies.

4. Francis J. Aguilar, *Scanning the Business Environment* (New York: Macmillan, 1967), p. 102.

their time. They seem to jump from issue to issue, continually responding to the needs of the moment.

Is this the planner that the classical view describes? Hardly. How, then, can we explain this behavior? The manager is simply responding to the pressures of his job. I found that my chief executives terminated many of their own activities, often leaving meetings before the end, and interrupted their desk work to call in subordinates. One president not only placed his desk so that he could look down a long hallway but also left his door open when he was alone—an invitation for subordinates to come in and interrupt him.

Clearly, these managers wanted to encourage the flow of current information. But more significantly, they seemed to be conditioned by their own work loads. They appreciated the opportunity cost of their own time, and they were continually aware of their ever-present obligations—mail to be answered, callers to attend to, and so on. It seems that no matter what he is doing, the manager is plagued by the possibilities of what he might do and what he must do.

When the manager must plan, he seems to do so implicitly in the context of daily actions, not in some abstract process reserved for two weeks in the organization's mountain retreat. The plans of the chief executives I studied seemed to exist only in their heads—as flexible, but often specific, intentions. The traditional literature notwithstanding, the job of managing does not breed reflective planners; the manager is a real-time responder to stimuli, an individual who is conditioned by his job to prefer live to delayed action.

2. *Folklore: The effective manager has no regular duties to perform.* Managers are constantly being told to spend more time planning and delegating, and less time seeing customers and engaging in negotiations. These are not, after all, the true tasks of the manager. To use the popular analogy, the good manager, like the good conductor, carefully orchestrates everything in advance, then sits back to enjoy the fruits of his labor, responding occasionally to an unforeseeable exception.

But here again the pleasant abstraction just does not seem to hold up. We had better take a closer look at those activities managers feel compelled to engage in before we arbitrarily define them away.

Fact: In addition to handling exceptions, managerial work involves performing a number of regular duties, including ritual and ceremony, negotiations, and processing of soft information that links the organization with its environment. Consider some evidence from the research studies:

☐ A study of the work of the presidents of small companies found that they engaged in routine activities because their companies could not afford staff specialists and were so thin on operating personnel that a single absence often required the president to substitute.[5]

☐ One study of field sales managers and another of chief executives suggest that it is a natural part of both jobs to see important customers, assuming the managers wish to keep those customers.[6]

☐ Someone, only half in jest, once described the manager as that person who sees visitors so that everyone else can get his work done. In my study, I found that certain ceremonial duties—meeting visiting dignitaries, giving out gold watches, presiding at Christmas dinners—were an intrinsic part of the chief executive's job.

☐ Studies of managers' information flow suggest that managers play a key role in securing "soft" external information (much of it available only to them because of their status) and in passing it along to their subordinates.

3. *Folklore: The senior manager needs aggregated information, which a formal management information system best provides.* Not too long ago, the words *total information system* were everywhere in the management literature. In keeping with the classical view of the manager as that individual perched on the apex of a regulated, hierarchical system, the literature's manager was to receive all his important information from a giant, comprehensive MIS.

But lately, as it has become increasingly evident that these giant MIS systems are not working—that managers are simply not using them—the enthusiasm has waned. A look at how managers actually process information makes the reason quite clear. Managers have five media at their command—documents, telephone calls, scheduled and unscheduled meetings, and observational tours.

Fact: Managers strongly favor the verbal media—namely, telephone calls and meetings. The evidence comes from every single study of managerial work. Consider the following:

☐ In two British studies, managers spent an average of 66% and 80% of their time in verbal (oral) communication.[7] In my study of five American chief executives, the figure was 78%.

☐ These five chief executives treated mail processing as a burden to be dispensed with. One came in Saturday morning to process 142 pieces of mail in just over three hours, to "get rid of all the stuff." This same manager looked at

    5. Unpublished study by Irving Choran, reported in Mintzberg, *The Nature of Managerial Work.*
    6. Robert T. Davis, *Performance and Development of Field Sales Managers* (Boston: Division of Research, Harvard Business School, 1957); George H. Copeman, *The Role of the Managing Director* (London: Business Publications, 1963).
    7. Stewart, *Managers and Their Jobs;* Tom Burns, "The Directions of Activity and Communication in a Departmental Executive Group," *Human Relations* 7, no. 1 (1954): 73.

the first piece of "hard" mail he had received all week, a standard cost report, and put it aside with the comment, "I never look at this."

□ These same five chief executives responded immediately to 2 of the 40 routine reports they received during the five weeks of my study and to four items in the 104 periodicals. They skimmed most of these periodicals in seconds, almost ritualistically. In all, these chief executives of good-sized organizations initiated on their own—that is, not in response to something else—a grand total of 25 pieces of mail during the 25 days I observed them.

An analysis of the mail the executives received reveals an interesting picture— only 13% was of specific and immediate use. So now we have another piece in the puzzle: not much of the mail provides live, current information—the action of a competitor, the mood of a government legislator, or the rating of last night's television show. Yet this is the information that drove the managers, interrupting their meetings and rescheduling their workdays.

Consider another interesting finding. Managers seem to cherish "soft" information, especially gossip, hearsay, and speculation. Why? The reason is its timeliness; today's gossip may be tomorrow's fact. The manager who is not accessible for the telephone call informing him that his biggest customer was seen golfing with his main competitor may read about a dramatic drop in sales in the next quarterly report. But then it's too late.

To assess the value of historical, aggregated, "hard" MIS information, consider two of the manager's prime uses for his information—to identify problems and opportunities[8] and to build his own mental models of the things around him (e.g., how his organization's budget system works, how his customers buy his product, how changes in the economy affect his organization, and so on). Every bit of evidence suggests that the manager identifies decision situations and builds models not with the aggregated abstractions an MIS provides, but with specific tidbits of data.

Consider the words of Richard Neustadt, who studied the information-collecting habits of Presidents Roosevelt, Truman, and Eisenhower:

It is not information of a general sort that helps a President see personal stakes; not summaries, not surveys, not the *bland amalgams*. Rather . . . it is the odds and ends of *tangible detail* that pieced together in his mind illuminate the underside of issues put before him. To help himself he must reach out as widely as he can for every scrap of fact, opinion, gossip, bearing on his interests and relationships as President. He must become his own director of his own central intelligence.[9]

8. H. Edward Wrapp, "Good Managers Don't Make Policy Decisions," HBR September-October 1967, p. 91.
9. Richard E. Neustadt, *Presidential Power* (New York: John Wiley, 1960), pp. 153-154; italics added.

The manager's emphasis on the verbal media raises two important points:

First, verbal information is stored in the brains of people. Only when people write this information down can it be stored in the files of the organization—whether in metal cabinets or on magnetic tape—and managers apparently do not write down much of what they hear. Thus the strategic data bank of the organization is not in the memory of its computers but in the minds of its managers.

Second, the manager's extensive use of verbal media helps to explain why he is reluctant to delegate tasks. When we note that most of the manager's important information comes in verbal form and is stored in his head, we can well appreciate his reluctance. It is not as if he can hand a dossier over to someone; he must take the time to "dump memory"—to tell that someone all he knows about the subject. But this could take so long that the manager may find it easier to do the task himself. Thus the manager is damned by his own information system to a "dilemma of delegation"—to do too much himself or to delegate to his subordinates with inadequate briefing.

4. *Folklore: Management is, or at least is quickly becoming, a science and a profession.* By almost any definitions of *science* and *profession,* this statement is false. Brief observation of any manager will quickly lay to rest the notion that managers practice a science. A science involves the enaction of systematic, analytically determined procedures or programs. If we do not even know what procedures managers use, how can we prescribe them by scientific analysis? And how can we call management a profession if we cannot specify what managers are to learn? For after all, a profession involves "knowledge of some department of learning or science" *(Random House Dictionary).*[10]

Fact: The managers' programs—to schedule time, process information, make decisions, and so on—remain locked deep inside their brains. Thus, to describe these programs, we rely on words like *judgment* and *intuition,* seldom stopping to realize that they are merely labels for our ignorance.

I was struck during my study by the fact that the executives I was observing—all very competent by any standard—are fundamentally indistinguishable from their counterparts of a hundred years ago (or a thousand years ago, for that matter). The information they need differs, but they seek it in the same way—by word of mouth. Their decisions concern modern technology, but the procedures they use to make them are the same as the procedures of the

10. For a more thorough, though rather different, discussion of this issue, see Kenneth R. Andrews, "Toward Professionalism in Business Management," HBR March-April 1969, p. 49.

nineteenth-century manager. Even the computer, so important for the special-ized work of the organization, has apparently had no influence on the work procedures of general managers. In fact, the manager is in a kind of loop, with increasingly heavy work pressures but no aid forthcoming from management science.

Considering the facts about managerial work, we can see that the manager's job is enormously complicated and difficult. The manager is overburdened with obligations; yet he cannot easily delegate his tasks. As a result, he is driven to overwork and is forced to do many tasks superficially. Brevity, fragmentation, and verbal communication characterize his work. Yet these are the very characteristics of managerial work that have impeded scientific attempts to improve it. As a result, the management scientist has concentrated his efforts on the specialized functions of the organization, where he could more easily analyze the procedures and quantify the relevant information.[11]

But the pressures of the manager's job are becoming worse. Where before he needed only to respond to owners and directors, now he finds that subordinates with democratic norms continually reduce his freedom to issue unexplained orders, and a growing number of outside influences (consumer groups, govern-ment agencies, and so on) expect his attention. And the manager has had nowhere to turn for help. The first step in providing the manager with some help is to find out what his job really is.

Back to a Basic Description of Managerial Work

Now let us try to put some of the pieces of this puzzle together. Earlier, I defined the manager as that person in charge of an organization or one of its subunits. Besides chief executive officers, this definition would include vice presidents, bishops, foremen, hockey coaches, and prime ministers. Can all of these people have anything in common? Indeed they can. For an important starting point, all are vested with formal authority over an organizational unit. From formal authority comes status, which leads to various interpersonal relations, and from these comes access to information. Information, in turn, enables the manager to make decisions and strategies for his unit.

The manager's job can be described in terms of various "roles," or organized sets of behaviors identified with a position. My description, shown in *Exhibit I*,

11. C. Jackson Grayson, Jr., in "Management Science and Business Practice," HBR July-August 1973, p. 41, explains in similar terms why, as chairman of the Price Commission, he did not use those very techniques that he himself promoted in his earlier career as a management scientist.

Exhibit I The manager's roles

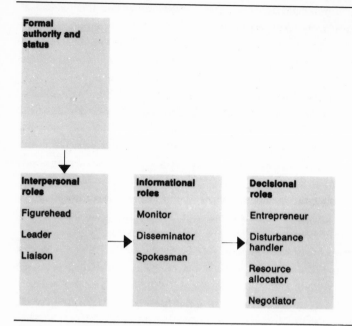

comprises ten roles. As we shall see, formal authority gives rise to the three interpersonal roles, which in turn give rise to the three informational roles; these two sets of roles enable the manager to play the four decisional roles.

INTERPERSONAL ROLES

Three of the manager's roles arise directly from his formal authority and involve basic interpersonal relationships.

1. First is the *figurehead* role. By virtue of his position as head of an organizational unit, every manager must perform some duties of a ceremonial nature. The president greets the touring dignitaries, the foreman attends the wedding of a lathe operator, and the sales manager takes an important customer to lunch.

The chief executives of my study spent 12% of their contact time on ceremonial duties; 17% of their incoming mail dealt with acknowledgments and requests related to their status. For example, a letter to a company president requested free merchandise for a crippled schoolchild; diplomas were put on the desk of the school superintendent for his signature.

Duties that involve interpersonal roles may sometimes be routine, involving little serious communication and no important decision making. Nevertheless, they are important to the smooth functioning of an organization and cannot be ignored by the manager.

2. Because he is in charge of an organizational unit, the manager is responsible for the work of the people of that unit. His actions in this regard constitute the *leader* role. Some of these actions involve leadership directly—for example, in most organizations the manager is normally responsible for hiring and training his own staff.

In addition, there is the indirect exercise of the leader role. Every manager must motivate and encourage his employees, somehow reconciling their individual needs with the goals of the organization. In virtually every contact the manager has with his employees, subordinates seeking leadership clues probe his actions: "Does he approve?" "How would he like the report to turn out?" "Is he more interested in market share than high profits?"

The influence of the manager is most clearly seen in the leader role. Formal authority vests him with great potential power; leadership determines in large part how much of it he will realize.

3. The literature of management has always recognized the leader role, particularly those aspects of it related to motivation. In comparison, until recently it has hardly mentioned the *liaison* role, in which the manager makes contacts outside his vertical chain of command. This is remarkable in light of the finding of virtually every study of managerial work that managers spend as much time with peers and other people outside their units as they do with their own subordinates—and, surprisingly, very little time with their own superiors.

In Rosemary Stewart's diary study, the 160 British middle and top managers spent 47% of their time with peers, 41% of their time with people outside their unit, and only 12% of their time with their superiors. For Robert H. Guest's study of U.S. foremen, the figures were 44%, 46%, and 10%. The chief executives of my study averaged 44% of their contact time with people outside their organizations, 48% with subordinates, and 7% with directors and trustees.

The contacts the five CEOs made were with an incredibly wide range of people: subordinates; clients, business associates, and suppliers; and peers—managers of similar organizations, government and trade organization officials, fellow directors on outside boards, and independents with no relevant organizational affiliations. The chief executives' time with and mail from these groups is shown in *Exhibit II* on page 114. Guest's study of foremen shows, likewise, that their contacts were numerous and wide-ranging, seldom involving fewer than 25 individuals, and often more than 50.

As we shall see shortly, the manager cultivates such contacts largely to find

Exhibit II The chief executives' contacts

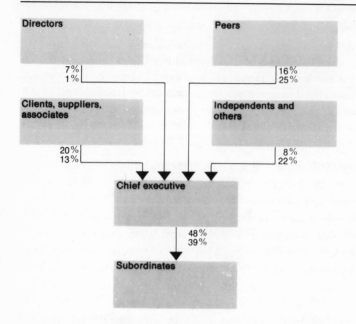

Note:The top figure indicates the proportion of total contact time spent with each group and the bottom figure, the proportion of mail from each group.

information. In effect, the liaison role is devoted to building up the manager's own external information system—informal, private, verbal, but, nevertheless, effective.

INFORMATIONAL ROLES

By virtue of his interpersonal contacts, both with his subordinates and with his network of contacts, the manager emerges as the nerve center of his organizational unit. He may not know everything, but he typically knows more than any member of his staff.

Studies have shown this relationship to hold for all managers, from street gang leaders to U.S. presidents. In *The Human Group,* George C. Homans explains how, because they were at the center of the information flow in their own gangs and were also in close touch with other gang leaders, street gang leaders were better informed than any of their followers.[12] And Richard

12. George C. Homans, *The Human Group* (New York: Harcourt, Brace & World, 1950), based on the study by William F. Whyte entitled *Street Corner Society,* rev. ed. (Chicago: University of Chicago Press, 1955).

Neustadt describes the following account from his study of Franklin D. Roosevelt:

The essence of Roosevelt's technique for information-gathering was competition. "He would call you in," one of his aides once told me, "and he'd ask you to get the story on some complicated business, and you'd come back after a couple of days of hard labor and present the juicy morsel you'd uncovered under a stone somewhere, and *then* you'd find out he knew all about it, along with something else you *didn't* know. Where he got this information from he wouldn't mention, usually, but after he had done this to you once or twice you got damn careful about *your* information."[13]

We can see where Roosevelt "got this information" when we consider the relationship between the interpersonal and informational roles. As leader, the manager has formal and easy access to every member of his staff. Hence, as noted earlier, he tends to know more about his own unit than anyone else does. In addition, his liaison contacts expose the manager to external information to which his subordinates often lack access. Many of these contacts are with other managers of equal status, who are themselves nerve centers in their own organization. In this way, the manager develops a powerful data base of information.

The processing of information is a key part of the manager's job. In my study, the chief executives spent 40% of their contact time on activities devoted exclusively to the transmission of information; 70% of their incoming mail was purely informational (as opposed to requests for action). The manager does not leave meetings or hang up the telephone in order to get back to work. In large part, communication *is* his work. Three roles describe these informational aspects of managerial work.

1. As *monitor,* the manager perpetually scans his environment for information, interrogates his liaison contacts and his subordinates, and receives unsolicited information, much of it as a result of the network of personal contacts he has developed. Remember that a good part of the information the manager collects in his monitor role arrives in verbal form, often as gossip, hearsay, and speculation. By virtue of his contacts, the manager has a natural advantage in collecting this soft information for his organization.

2. He must share and distribute much of this information. Information he gleans from outside personal contacts may be needed within his organization. In his *disseminator* role, the manager passes some of his privileged information directly to his subordinates, who would otherwise have no access to it. When his subordinates lack easy contact with one another, the manager will sometimes pass information from one to another.

13. Neustadt, *Presidential Power,* p. 157.

3. In his *spokesman* role, the manager sends some of his information to people outside his unit—a president makes a speech to lobby for an organization cause, or a foreman suggests a product modification to a supplier. In addition, as part of his role as spokesman, every manager must inform and satisfy the influential people who control his organizational unit. For the foreman, this may simply involve keeping the plant manager informed about the flow of work through the shop.

The president of a large corporation, however, may spend a great amount of his time dealing with a host of influences. Directors and shareholders must be advised about financial performance; consumer groups must be assured that the organization is fulfilling its social responsibilities; and government officials must be satisfied that the organization is abiding by the law.

DECISIONAL ROLES

Information is not, of course, an end in itself; it is the basic input to decision making. One thing is clear in the study of managerial work: the manager plays the major role in his unit's decision-making system. As its formal authority, only he can commit the unit to important new courses of action; and as its nerve center, only he has full and current information to make the set of decisions that determines the unit's strategy. Four roles describe the manager as decision maker:

1. As *entrepreneur,* the manager seeks to improve his unit, to adapt it to changing conditions in the environment. In his monitor role, the president is constantly on the lookout for new ideas. When a good one appears, he initiates a development project that he may supervise himself or delegate to an employee (perhaps with the stipulation that he must approve the final proposal).

There are two interesting features about these development projects at the chief executive level. First, these projects do not involve single decisions or even unified clusters of decisions. Rather, they emerge as a series of small decisions and actions sequenced over time. Apparently, the chief executive prolongs each project so that he can fit it bit by bit into his busy, disjointed schedule and so that he can gradually come to comprehend the issue, if it is a complex one.

Second, the chief executives I studied supervised as many as 50 of these projects at the same time. Some projects entailed new products or processes; others involved public relations campaigns, improvement of the cash position, reorganization of a weak department, resolution of a morale problem in a foreign division, integration of computer operations, various acquisitions at different stages of development, and so on.

The chief executive appears to maintain a kind of inventory of the development projects that he himself supervises—projects that are at various stages of development, some active and some in limbo. Like a juggler, he keeps a number of projects in the air; periodically, one comes down, is given a new burst of energy, and is sent back into orbit. At various intervals, he put new projects on-stream and discards old ones.

2. While the entrepreneur role describes the manager as the voluntary initiator of change, the *disturbance handler* role depicts the manager involuntarily responding to pressures. Here change is beyond the manager's control. He must act because the pressures of the situation are too severe to be ignored: a strike looms, a major customer has gone bankrupt, or a supplier reneges on his contract.

It has been fashionable, I noted earlier, to compare the manager to an orchestra conductor, just as Peter F. Drucker wrote in *The Practice of Management:*

> The manager has the task of creating a true whole that is larger than the sum of its parts, a productive entity that turns out more than the sum of the resources put into it. One analogy is the conductor of a symphony orchestra, through whose effort, vision and leadership individual instrumental parts that are so much noise by themselves become the living whole of music. But the conductor has the composer's score; he is only interpreter. The manager is both composer and conductor.[14]

Now consider the words of Leonard R. Sayles, who has carried out systematic research on the manager's job:

> [The manager] is like a symphony orchestra conductor, endeavouring to maintain a melodious performance in which the contributions of the various instruments are coordinated and sequenced, patterned and paced, while the orchestra members are having various personal difficulties, stage hands are moving music stands, alternating excessive heat and cold are creating audience and instrument problems, and the sponsor of the concert is insisting on irrational changes in the program.[15]

In effect, every manager must spend a good part of his time responding to high-pressure disturbances. No organization can be so well run, so standardized, that it has considered every contingency in the uncertain environment in advance. Disturbances arise not only because poor managers ignore situations until they reach crisis proportions, but also because good managers cannot possibly anticipate all the consequences of the actions they take.

3. The third decisional role is that of *resource allocator*. To the manager falls

14. Peter F. Drucker, *The Practice of Management* (New York: Harper & Row, 1954), pp. 341-342.
15. Leonard R. Sayles, *Managerial Behavior* (New York: McGraw-Hill, 1964), p. 162.

the responsibility of deciding who will get what in his organizational unit. Perhaps the most important resource the manager allocates is his own time. Access to the manager constitutes exposure to the unit's nerve center and decision maker. The manager is also charged with designing his unit's structure, that pattern of formal relationships that determines how work is to be divided and coordinated.

Also, in his role as resource allocator, the manager authorizes the important decisions of his unit before they are implemented. By retaining this power, the manager can ensure that decisions are interrelated; all must pass through a single brain. To fragment this power is to encourage discontinuous decision making and a disjointed strategy.

There are a number of interesting features about the manager's authorizing others' decisions. First, despite the widespread use of capital budgeting procedures—a means of authorizing various capital expenditures at one time—executives in my study made a great many authorization decisions on an ad hoc basis. Apparently, many projects cannot wait or simply do not have the quantifiable costs and benefits that capital budgeting requires.

Second, I found that the chief executives faced incredibly complex choices. They had to consider the impact of each decision on other decisions and on the organization's strategy. They had to ensure that the decision would be acceptable to those who influence the organization, as well as ensure that resources would not be overextended. They had to understand the various costs and benefits as well as the feasibility of the proposal. They also had to consider questions of timing. All this was necessary for the simple approval of someone else's proposal. At the same time, however, delay could lose time, while quick approval could be ill considered and quick rejection might discourage the subordinate who had spent months developing a pet project.

One common solution to approving projects is to pick the man instead of the proposal. That is, the manager authorizes those projects presented to him by people whose judgment he trusts. But he cannot always use this simple dodge.

4. The final decisional role is that of *negotiator*. Studies of managerial work at all levels indicate that managers spend considerable time in negotiations: the president of the football team is called in to work out a contract with the holdout superstar; the corporation president leads his company's contingent to negotiate a new strike issue; the foreman argues a grievance problem to its conclusion with the shop steward. As Leonard Sayles puts it, negotiations are a "way of life" for the sophisticated manager.

These negotiations are duties of the manager's job; perhaps routine, they are not to be shirked. They are an integral part of his job, for only he has the authority to commit organizational resources in "real time," and only he has the nerve center information that important negotiations require.

THE INTEGRATED JOB

It should be clear by now that the ten roles I have been describing are not easily separable. In the terminology of the psychologist, they form a gestalt, an integrated whole. No role can be pulled out of the framework and the job be left intact. For example, a manager without liaison contacts lacks external information. As a result, he can neither disseminate the information his employees need nor make decisions that adequately reflect external conditions. (In fact, this is a problem for the new person in a managerial position, since he cannot make effective decisions until he has built up his network of contacts.)

Here lies a clue to the problems of team management.[16] Two or three people cannot share a single managerial position unless they can act as one entity. This means that they cannot divide up the ten roles unless they can very carefully reintegrate them. The real difficulty lies with the informational roles. Unless there can be full sharing of managerial information—and, as I pointed out earlier, it is primarily verbal—team management breaks down. A single managerial job cannot be arbitrarily split, for example, into internal and external roles, for information from both sources must be brought to bear on the same decisions.

To say that the ten roles form a gestalt is not to say that all managers give equal attention to each role. In fact, I found in my review of the various research studies that

□ sales managers seem to spend relatively more of their time in the interpersonal roles, presumably a reflection of the extrovert nature of the marketing activity;

□ production managers give relatively more attention to the decisional roles, presumably a reflection of their concern with efficient work flow;

□ staff managers spend the most time in the informational roles, since they are experts who manage departments that advise other parts of the organization.

Nevertheless, in all cases the interpersonal, informational, and decisional roles remain inseparable.

Toward More Effective Management

What are the messages for management in this description? I believe, first and foremost, that this description of managerial work should prove more important to managers than any prescription they might derive from it. That is to say, *the*

16. See Richard C. Hodgson, Daniel J. Levinson, and Abraham Zaleznik, *The Executive Role Constellation* (Boston: Division of Research, Harvard Business School, 1965), for a discussion of the sharing of roles.

manager's effectiveness is significantly influenced by his insight into his own work. His performance depends on how well he understands and responds to the pressures and dilemmas of the job. Thus managers who can be introspective about their work are likely to be effective at their jobs. The Appendix on page 123 offers 14 groups of self-study questions for managers. Some may sound rhetorical; none is meant to be. Even though the questions cannot be answered simply, the manager should address them.

Let us take a look at three specific areas of concern. For the most part, the managerial logjams—the dilemma of delegation, the data base centralized in one brain, the problems of working with the management scientist—revolve around the verbal nature of the manager's information. There are great dangers in centralizing the organization's data bank in the minds of its managers. When they leave, they take their memory with them. And when subordinates are out of convenient verbal reach of the manager, they are at an informational disadvantage.

1. *The manager is challenged to find systematic ways to share his privileged information.* A regular debriefing session with key subordinates, a weekly memory dump on the dictating machine, the maintaining of a diary of important information for limited circulation, or other similar methods may ease the logjam of work considerably. Time spent disseminating this information will be more than regained when decisions must be made. Of course, some will raise the question of confidentiality. But managers would do well to weigh the risks of exposing privileged information against having subordinates who can make effective decisions.

If there is a single theme that runs through this article, it is that the pressures of his job drive the manager to be superficial in his actions—to overload himself with work, encourage interruption, respond quickly to every stimulus, seek the tangible and avoid the abstract, make decisions in small increments, and do everything abruptly.

2. *Here again, the manager is challenged to deal consciously with the pressures of superficiality by giving serious attention to the issues that require it, by stepping back from his tangible bits of information in order to see a broad picture, and by making use of analytical inputs.* Although effective managers have to be adept at responding quickly to numerous and varying problems, the danger in managerial work is that they will respond to every issue equally (and that means abruptly) and that they will never work the tangible bits and pieces of informational input into a comprehensive picture of their world.

As I noted earlier, the manager uses these bits of information to build models of his world. But the manager can also avail himself of the models of the specialists. Economists describe the functioning of markets, operations researchers simulate financial flow processes, and behavioral scientists explain the needs and goals of people. The best of these models can be searched out and learned.

In dealing with complex issues, the senior manager has much to gain from a close relationship with the management scientists of his own organization. They have something important that he lacks—time to probe complex issues. An effective working relationship hinges on the resolution of what a colleague and I have called "the planning dilemma."[17] Managers have the information and the authority; analysts have the time and the technology. A successful working relationship between the two will be effected when the manager learns to share his information and the analyst learns to adapt to the manager's needs. For the analyst, adaptation means worrying less about the elegance of the method and more about its speed and flexibility.

It seems to me that analysts can help the top manager especially to schedule his time, feed in analytical information, monitor projects under his supervision, develop models to aid in making choices, design contingency plans for disturbances that can be anticipated, and conduct "quick-and-dirty" analysis for those that cannot. But there can be no cooperation if the analysts are out of the mainstream of the manager's information flow.

3. *The manager is challenged to gain control of his own time by turning obligations to his advantage and by turning those things he wishes to do into obligations.* The chief executives of my study initiated only 32% of their own contacts (and another 5% by mutual agreement). And yet to a considerable extent they seemed to control their time. There were two key factors that enabled them to do so.

First, the manager has to spend so much time discharging obligations that if he were to view them as just that, he would leave no mark on his organization. The unsuccessful manager blames failure on the obligations; the effective manager turns his obligations to his own advantage. A speech is a chance to lobby for a cause; a meeting is a change to reorganize a weak department; a visit to an important customer is a chance to extract trade information.

Second, the manager frees some of his time to do those things that he—perhaps no one else—thinks important by turning them into obligations. Free time is made, not found, in the manager's job; it is forced into the schedule. Hoping to leave some time open for contemplation or general planning is tantamount to hoping that the pressures of the job will go away. The manager who wants to innovate initiates a project and obligates others to report back to him; the manager who needs certain environmental information establishes

17. James S. Hekimian and Henry Mintzberg, "The Planning Dilemma," *The Management Review*, May 1968, p. 4.

channels that will automatically keep him informed; the manager who has to tour facilities commits himself publicly.

THE EDUCATOR'S JOB

Finally, a word about the training of managers. Our management schools have done an admirable job of training the organization's specialists—management scientists, marketing researchers, accountants, and organizational development specialists. But for the most part they have not trained managers.[18]

Management schools will begin the serious training of managers when skill training takes a serious place next to cognitive learning. Cognitive learning is detached and informational, like reading a book or listening to a lecture. No doubt much important cognitive material must be assimilated by the manager-to-be. But cognitive learning no more makes a manager than it does a swimmer. The latter will drown the first time he jumps into the water if his coach never takes him out of the lecture hall, gets him wet, and gives him feedback on his performance.

In other words, we are taught a skill through practice plus feedback, whether in a real or simulated situation. Our management schools need to identify the skills managers use, select students who show potential in these skills, put the students into situations where these skills can be practiced, and then give them systematic feedback on their performance.

My description of managerial work suggests a number of important managerial skills—developing peer relationships, carrying out negotiations, motivating subordinates, resolving conflicts, establishing information networks and subsequently disseminating information, making decisions in conditions of extreme ambiguity, and allocating resources. Above all, the manager needs to be introspective about his work so that he may continue to learn on the job.

Many of the manager's skills can, in fact, be practiced, using techniques that range from role playing to videotaping real meetings. And our management schools can enhance the entrepreneurial skills by designing programs that encourage sensible risk taking and innovation.

No job is more vital to our society than that of the manager. It is the manager who determines whether our social institutions serve us well or whether they squander our talents and resources. It is time to strip away the folklore about managerial work, and time to study it realistically so that we can begin the difficult task of making significant improvements in its performance.

---

18. See J. Sterling Livingston, "Myth of the Well-Educated Manager," HBR January-February 1971, p. 79.

1. Where do I get my information, and how? Can I make greater use of my contacts to get information? Can other people do some of my scanning for me? In what areas is my knowledge weakest, and how can I get others to provide me with the information I need? Do I have powerful enough mental models of those things I must understand within the organization and in its environment?

2. What information do I disseminate in my organization? How important is it that my subordinates get my information? Do I keep too much information to myself because dissemination of it is time-consuming or inconvenient? How can I get more information to others so they can make better decisions?

3. Do I balance information collecting with action taking? Do I tend to act before information is in? Or do I wait so long for all the information that opportunities pass me by and I become a bottleneck in my organization?

4. What pace of change am I asking my organization to tolerate? Is this change balanced so that our operations are neither excessively static nor overly disrupted? Have we sufficiently analyzed the impact of this change on the future of our organization?

5. Am I sufficiently well informed to pass judgment on the proposals that my subordinates make? Is it possible to leave final authorization for more of the proposals with subordinates? Do we have problems of coordination because subordinates in fact now make too many of these decisions independently?

6. What is my vision of direction for this organization? Are these plans primarily in my own mind in loose form? Should I make them explicit in order to guide the decisions of others in the organization better? Or do I need flexibility to change them at will?

7. How do my subordinates react to my managerial style? Am I sufficiently sensitive to the powerful influence my actions have on them? Do I fully understand their reactions to my actions? Do I find an appropriate balance between encouragement and pressure? Do I stifle their initiative?

8. What kind of external relationships do I maintain, and how? Do I spend

too much of my time maintaining these relationships? Are there certain types of people whom I should get to know better?

9. Is there any system to my time scheduling, or am I just reacting to the pressures of the moment? Do I find the appropriate mix of activities, or do I tend to concentrate on one particular function or one type of problem just because I find it interesting? Am I more efficient with particular kinds of work at special times of the day or week? Does my schedule reflect this? Can someone else (in addition to my secretary) take responsibility for much of my scheduling and do it more systematically?

10. Do I overwork? What effect does my work load have on my efficiency? Should I force myself to take breaks or to reduce the pace of my activity?

11. Am I too superficial in what I do? Can I really shift moods as quickly and frequently as my work patterns require? Should I attempt to decrease the amount of fragmentation and interruption in my work?

12. Do I orient myself too much toward current, tangible activities? Am I a slave to the action and excitement of my work, so that I am no longer able to concentrate on issues. Do key problems receive the attention they deserve? Should I spend more time reading and probing deeply into certain issues? Could I be more reflective? Should I be?

13. Do I use the different media appropriately? Do I know how to make the most of written communication? Do I rely excessively on face-to-face communication, thereby putting all but a few of my subordinates at an informational disadvantage? Do I schedule enough of my meetings on a regular basis? Do I spend enough time touring my organization to observe activity at first hand? Am I too detached from the heart of my organization's activities, seeing things only in an abstract way?

14. How do I blend my personal rights and duties? Do my obligations consume all my time? How can I free myself sufficiently from obligations to ensure that I am taking this organization where I want it to go? How can I turn my obligations to my advantage?

9. Zen and the Art of Management

Richard Tanner Pascale

For many in the West, the term Zen connotes puzzling aspects of Eastern culture. This article attempts to unlock these puzzles as they apply to management of organizations. In the most exhaustive study to date of Japanese-managed companies in the United States and Japan, the author finds that when technology and government factors are equal, the Japanese companies' U.S. subsidiaries do not outperform their American counterparts (despite what has been reported in the U.S. press). Furthermore, and contrary to the conventional wisdom, American managers use a participative decision-making style as often as Japanese managers do. The author explores nuances of the administrative process that appear to account for more effective organizational functioning. He concludes that the arts employed by successful Japanese and American managers include subtle ways of dealing with others in the organization, such as permitting a certain situation to remain ambiguous instead of striving for a premature conclusion. While American managers are often as skillful in these areas as the Japanese, an Eastern perspective makes many of these tools more tangible and their potential more evident.

For 20 years or more students of management have labored to minimize its mystique, reduce our dependence on "gut feel," and establish a more scientific basis for managerial behavior. All the while, practitioners have been cautious in embracing these pursuits; casting a wary eye on "textbook" solutions, they assert that management is an art as much as a science.

Yet even the most skeptical admit that some benefit has accrued from these efforts. All realms of management, from finance to human relations, have felt the impact of analytical inquiry.

One common theme in this evolution of a "management science" has been the desire to make explicit the tools and processes that managers have historically

AUTHOR'S NOTE: I·wish to thank the National Commission on Productivity and the Weyerhaeuser Foundation for support of the research that formed the basis for this article, and Anthony G. Athos for his helpful comments on the manuscript.

employed intuitively. With just such a goal in mind, I embarked in 1974 on a study of Japanese-managed companies in the United States and Japan. The purpose was to ascertain what elements of the communications and decision-making processes contributed to the reported high performance of Japanese companies.

A number of respected observers of Japanese ways had attributed their success in part to such practices as "bottom-up" communication, extensive lateral communication across functional areas, and a pronounced use of participative- (or consensus-) style decision making that supposedly leads to higher-quality decisions and implementation. The research consisted of interviews of and questionnaires administered to more than 215 managers and 1,400 workers in 26 companies and 10 industries.

I made communication audits of the number of telephone calls and face-to-face contacts initiated and received by managers of Japanese companies in Japan, of their subsidiaries in the United States, and of near-identical American companies matched on an industry-by-industry basis. I took pains to document the size and length of meetings and the volume of formal correspondence and informal notes, to observe the frequency of interaction in managerial office areas, and to obtain managers' perceptions of the nature and quality of the decision making and implementation process.

What did I find? First, Japanese-managed businesses in both countries are not much different from American-owned companies: they use the telephone to about the same degree and write about the same number of letters. In their decision-making processes, both in the U.S. subsidiaries and in Japan, the Japanese do not use a participative style any more than Americans do. Actually, I discovered only two significant differences between Japanese and American companies:[1]

1. Three times as much communication was initiated at lower levels of management in the Japanese companies, then percolated upward.

2. While managers of Japanese companies rated the quality of their decision making the same as did their American counterparts, they perceived the quality of *implementation* of those decisions to be better.

These findings puzzled me. How could the style of decision making (in particular, the degree of participation) and quality of decisions be the same in the two groups, yet the quality of implementation be different? Evidently, the greater reliance by the Japanese on bottom-up communication played a role, but the causal relationship remained unclear.

A senior executive at Sony provided a clue. "To be truthful," the Japanese

1. For a detailed report of these findings see my article, "Communications and Decision Making Across Cultures: Japanese and American Comparisons," *Administrative Science Quarterly*, March, 1978.

manager said, "probably 60% of the decisions I make are my decisions. But I keep my intentions secret. In discussions with subordinates, I ask questions, pursue facts, and try to nudge them in my direction without disclosing my position. Sometimes I end up changing my position as the result of the dialogue. But whatever the outcome, they feel a part of the decision. Their involvement in the decision also increases their experience as managers."

Many others, American as well as Japanese, alluded in interviews to the same technique. "It does not make so much difference," reflected an American who ran a ball-bearing plant in New Hampshire, "if decisions are top down as it does how the top-down decision maker goes about touching bases. If he begins with an open question, he can often guide his subordinates to a good solution."

In these statements, and in others like them, is the genesis of this paper. The important discovery of this research was not, as expected, that Japanese do some things differently and better. While that is true to a limited extent, the more significant finding is that successful managers, *regardless of nationality,* share certain common characteristics that are related to subtleties of the communications process.

The term *Zen* in the title of this article is used figuratively to denote these important nuances in interpersonal communication often enshrouded in a veil of mystique. The phenomenon does not correspond to the analytical dimension of consecutive deductive responses. Nor is it directly akin to the human relations dimension that highlights the virtues of problem confrontation, participation, and openness. I refer to this Zen-like quality as the *implicit* dimension. It is as distinct from the other, better-known dimensions of management as time is from the other three dimensions of physical space.

In trying to explain the implicit dimension, I find that the traditional language of management gets in the way. To work around the difficulty, it is helpful to explore this dimension through the lens of the Eastern metaphor. After many interviews with American and Japanese managers, I have come to believe that the perspective imbedded in Eastern philosophy, culture, and values helps make the implicit dimension more visible. Whereas Japanese managers find certain insights within easy reach of their Eastern way of thinking, American managers, while often just as skillful, must swim upstream culturally, so to speak.

Ambiguity as a Managerial Tool

Much of the lore of management in the West regards ambiguity as a symptom of a variety of organizational ills whose cure is larger doses of rationality, specificity, and decisiveness. But is ambiguity sometimes desirable?

Ambiguity may be thought of as a shroud of the unknown surrounding certain events. The Japanese have a word for it, *ma,* for which there is no English translation. The word is valuable because it gives an explicit place to the unknowable aspect of things. In English we may refer to an empty space between the chair and the table; the Japanese don't say the space is empty but "full of nothing." However amusing the illustration, it goes to the core of the issue. Westerners speak of what is unknown primarily in reference to what is known (like the space between the chair and the table), while most Eastern languages give honor to the unknown in its own right. Consider this Tao verse:

> Thirty spokes are made one by holes in a hub
> Together with the vacancies between them, they comprise a wheel.
> The use of clay in moulding pitchers
> Comes from the hollow of its absence;
> Doors, windows, in a house
> Are used for their emptiness:
> Thus we are helped by what is not
> To use what is.[2]

Of course, there are many situations that a manager finds himself in where being explicit and decisive is not only helpful but necessary. There is considerable advantage, however, in having a dual frame of reference—recognizing the value of both the clear and the ambiguous. The point to bear in mind is that in certain situations ambiguity may serve better than absolute clarity.

When an executive has access to too much data for human processing, he needs to simplify. If he has examined, say, different pricing schemes for 12 months and has identified all the choices available to him, the time has probably come to decide on one of them. "Deciding" in these circumstances has the benefit of curtailing the wheel spinning, simplifying things, and resolving anxiety for oneself and others.

But there is another kind of problem—for example, merging the production and engineering departments—where experience may suggest that the issue is more complicated than the bare facts indicate. Frequently the issue crops up around changes that arouse human feelings. Under these circumstances the notion of ambiguity is useful. Rather than grasping for a solution, the administrator may take the interim step of "deciding" how to proceed. The process of "proceeding" in turn generates further information; you move toward your goal through a sequence of tentative steps rather than bold-stroke actions. The distinction is between having enough data to *decide* and having enough data to *proceed.*

2. Witter Bynner, *The Way of Life According to Lao Tzu* (New York: Capricorn Books, 1944), p. 30.

If an executive's perception of the problem and the means of implementation involve groups of persons at different levels of the organization with different mandates (like unions and professional groups) and the distribution of power is such that he lacks full control, successful implementation usually requires tentativeness. The notion of ambiguity helps make tentativeness legitimate.

Ambiguity has two important connotations for management. First, it is a useful concept in thinking about how we deal with others, orally and in writing. Second, it provides a way of legitimizing the loose rein that a manager permits in certain organizational situations where agreement needs time to evolve or where further insight is needed before conclusive action can be taken.

CARDS OFF THE TABLE

To watch a skilled manager use ambiguity is to see an art form in action. Carefully selecting his words, constructing a precise tension between the oblique and the specific, he picks his way across difficult terrain. In critiquing a subordinate's work, for example, the executive occasionally finds it desirable to come close enough to the point to ensure that the subordinate gets the message but not so close as to "crowd" him and cause defensiveness.

A Japanese manager conducts the dialogue in circles, widening and narrowing them to correspond to the subordinate's sensitivity to the feedback. He may say, "I'd like you to reflect a bit further on your proposal." Translated into Western thought patterns, this sentence would read, "You're dead wrong and you'd better come up with a better idea."[3] The first approach allows the subordinate to exist with his pride intact.

Part of our drive for the explicit stems from the Western notion that it's a matter of honor to "get the cards on the table." This attitude rests on the assumption that, no matter how much it hurts, it's good for you; and the sign of a good manager is his ability to give and take negative feedback.

No doubt there is a good deal of merit in this conventional wisdom. But between the mythology of our management lore and our foibles as human beings often lies the true state of things. It is desirable to get the facts and know where one stands. But it is also human to feel threatened, particularly when personal vulnerability is an issue.

There is no reason to believe that Westerners have less pride than the Japanese have or feel humiliation less poignantly than the Japanese do. An American Management Association survey indicates that issues involving self-respect mattered greatly to more than two-thirds of the persons sampled.[4]

3. Frank Gibney, "The Japanese and Their Language," *Encounter,* March 1975, p. 33.
4. G. McLean Preston and Katherine Jillson, "The Manager and Self-Respect," *AMA Survey Report* (New York: AMACOM, 1975).

Eastern cultures are sensitive to the concept of "face"; Westerners, however, regard it as a sign of weakness. Yet look back on instances in organizations where an individual, publicly embarrassed by another, hurt himself and the organization just to even the score. The evidence suggests that explicitly crowding a person into a corner may in many instances be not only unwarranted but also counterproductive.

Delivering oneself of the need to "speak the truth" often masks a self-serving sense of brute integrity. "Clearing the air" can be more helpful to the "clearer" than to others who are starkly revealed. The issue of brute integrity is not just an outcome of a certain cultural tendency to speak plainly and bluntly, nor is it wholly explainable in terms of our assumptions about authority and hierarchy and the relationships between bosses and subordinates. At a deeper level, it has a sexist component. In our culture, simple, straightforward, simplistic confrontation—a kind of high noon shoot-'em-out—is mixed with notions of what masculinity is. Unfortunately, shoot-'em-outs work best when the other guy dies. If you have to work with that person on a continuing basis, macho confrontations complicate life immensely.

In contrast, ambiguity, in reference to sensitivity and feelings, is alleged in the Western world to be female. But if we set aside the stereotypes and contemplate the consequences of these two modes of behavior on organizational life, we may discover that primitive notions of masculinity work no better in the office over the long term than they do in bed.

Are brute integrity and explicit communication worth the price of the listener's goodwill, open-mindedness, and receptivity to change? Explicit communication is a cultural assumption, not a linguistic imperative. Many executives develop the skills necessary to vary their position along the spectrum from explicitness to ambiguity.

MORE "URA" THAN "OMOTE"

Earlier I noted the value of ambiguity in permitting time and space for certain situations to take clearer shape or reach an accommodation of their own. A certain looseness in the definition of the relationship between things can permit a workable arrangement to evolve, whereas premature action may freeze things into rigidity. For example, one of the most persistent afflictions in American organizations is the penchant to make formal announcements. Most things one does announce themselves.

The Japanese manager comes culturally equipped with a pair of concepts, *omote* (in front) and *ura* (behind the scenes). These ideas correspond to the Latin notions of de jure and de facto, with one important distinction: the Japanese think of *ura* as constituting *real life; omote* is the ceremonial function for the benefit of others. The Japanese relegate the making of announcements to a secondary place that follows after all the action has taken place behind the scenes.

"You Americans are fond of announcing things," said one Japanese manager in the study. "It sets everything astir. The other day we decided to try out having our personnel department handle certain requests that traditionally had been handled by the production people. Our American vice president insisted on announcing it. Well, the production department had always handled its own personnel affairs and got its back up. Rumors commenced about whether the personnel people were in ascendence, building an empire, and so forth. Given the tentativeness of the system we were trying out, why not just begin by quietly asking that certain matters be referred to personnel? Before long, the informal organization will accustom itself to the new flow. Clearly you can't do this all the time, but some of the time it certainly works."

To announce what you want to happen, you have to make statements concerning a lot of things that you don't know about yet. If certain processes and relationships are allowed to take their own shape first, however, your announcement will probably have to be made just once because you will only be confirming what has already happened. Consider how differently attempts at organizational change might proceed if they embraced the Eastern orientation. Instead of turning the spotlight on the intended move, parading the revised organization charts and job descriptions, management would reassign tasks incrementally, gradually shift boundaries between functions, and issue the announcement only when the desired change had become a de facto reality. In some situations this is the better way.

"Impossible!" some will argue. "People resist change. Only by announcing your intentions can you bring the organization into line." But is it really "into line"? Unquestionably, decrees have their part to play in some organizational actions. But more often than not, the sudden lurch to a new order belies an informal process of resistance that works with enduring effectiveness. One has only to look at the Department of Health, Education, and Welfare for an illustration of this phenomenon. A congressional mandate and 20 years' worth of frustrated presidents have not greatly altered the character of the three distinct bureaus constituting that agency.

The notion of achieving gradual change, rather than launching a head-on assault, runs deep in Eastern culture. It provides a manager with a context for thinking about outflanking organizational obstacles and in time letting them wither away. "It is well to persist like water," counsels the Tao saying. "For back it comes, again and again, wearing down the rigid strength which cannot yield to withstand it."[5]

5. Bynner, *The Way of Life According to Lao Tzu*, p. 74.

With such an orientation one can accept the inevitability of obstacles rather than view them with righteous indignation—as some Western managers are inclined to do. And as the Tao saying suggests, acceptance does not convey fatalistic resignation. Rather, it points toward the value of patiently flowing with a solution while in due time it overcomes the obstacles in its path.

To Get Recognition, Give It Away

One way of thinking about the rewards employees receive is in terms of a triad: promotion, remuneration, and recognition. Of the three forms of reward, the first two are relatively unresponsive in the day-to-day operation of an organization. Promotions and wage hikes seldom come oftener than six months apart. On a daily basis, recognition is the reward most noticed and sought after. In the American Management Association survey to which I allude earlier, 49% of the respondents indicated that recognition for what they did was their most important reward.

Recognition may become an increasingly important "fringe benefit," since a central problem facing American society is how to reward people in a period of slowed growth when employees win promotions and raises less often. Enriching our understanding of recognition and the role it plays may provide some helpful guidance.

Recognition is a powerful operating incentive. People who live in organizations develop uncanny sensitivity to where it is flowing. If you ask a person to change, one of the most relevant rewards you can provide in return is recognition. If, on the contrary, you try to induce change but you are seen as unwilling to share the recognition, you are not apt to get very far. It is an ironic axiom of organization that if you are willing to give up recognition, in return you gain increased power to bring about effective change.

The Eastern frame of thinking embodies the dual nature of recognition, as this Tao proverb shows:

> A wise man has a simple wisdom
> Which other men seek.
> Without taking credit
> Is accredited.
> Laying no claim
> Is acclaimed.[6]

We are all acquainted with "expressed" recognition, the big prize that modern organizational knights vie for. "B.L.T." is the recognition sandwich

6. Bynner, *The Way of Life According to Lao Tzu*, pp. 28 and 38.

... "bright lights and trumpets," that is. When you receive a B.L.T., everybody knows about it. But Eastern thinking reminds us of a second variety, which might be called implied recognition. It is subtle but no less tangible, and it is acquired over time.

In its positive form it is the reputation of being trustworthy, skilled in making things happen in the organization, and accomplished in getting things done through people. In its negative manifestation one is regarded as using people, prone to cutting corners, and out for oneself. Implied recognition can be given in a variety of ways that may seem insignificant, except to the recipient. An effort to seek another's opinion, for example, communicates respect for his insight. So does an invitation to participate in a significant meeting from which the person might otherwise have been excluded.

The phenomenon of implied recognition generally plays an important role in organizations that run smoothly. Problems arise when organizations overemphasize incentives that rivet attention on expressed recognition and undermine regard for implied recognition. As a result, all the members of the "team" try to grab the ball and nobody blocks. They seldom win consistently. But why grab from others what they will give you voluntarily? When you make sure you get the credit you deserve, in the long run you get less of it than you would otherwise.

Eastern perspective provides a further insight. It reminds us that the real organization you are working for is the organization called yourself. The problems and challenges of the organization that you are working for "out there" and the one "in here" are not two separate things. They grow toward excellence together. The sense of the "implied" for accommodation and timing and the sense of the "expressed" for the jugular must be woven together like strands in a braided rope, alternatively appearing and disappearing from sight but part of the whole. Good executives master the art *and* the science of management—not just one or the other.

Leaders Go Straight—Around the Circle

Western concepts of leadership embrace a number of images—strength, firmness, determination, and clarity of vision. In American management lore, leaders are seen as lonely figures capable of decisive action in the face of adversity.[7] Eastern thinking views leadership in significantly different ways. Whereas Western leaders are supposedly selected from among those who are

7. For a discussion of the myths versus the realities of management behavior and leadership, see Leonard Sayles, *Managerial Behavior* (New York: McGraw-Hill, 1964), especially pp. 41–45; also see Henry Mintzberg, "The Manager's Job: Folklore and Fact," HBR July-August 1975, p. 49.

outstanding, Eastern culture values leaders who stand "in" rather than stand "out."

In Judeo-Christian cultures, words very nearly possess sacredness. Men are willing to sacrifice for, live by, and die for words. We cling to them and make them swell with meaning; they are shafts of light that give form to our experiential darkness. Anthony G. Athos of the Harvard Business School notes the distinction between two everyday words, *choice* and *decision*. Managers, we are taught, "make decisions"; lovers "choose." The former term implies mastery; the latter conveys a difficult selection among choices, in which we can gain some things only by giving up others.[8]

Athos's insight is particularly important for managers because the word *decision* and the phrase *decision making* conjure up an extensive mythology of meaning. Good decision makers, our mythology tells us, have command of the facts, are aware of the options, and select from among them the best one.

The Japanese, however, do not even have a term for decision making in the Western sense. This linguistic curiosity reflects something deeper, a tendency of the culture to acknowledge the ambivalence experienced when our mastery of situations is imperfect. Faced with difficult trade-offs, Japanese "choose" one over the other; Westerners like to think they "decide."

The lore of Eastern management more fully acknowledges the inevitable sense of incompleteness that stems from having to choose. It sensitizes its managers to the illusions of mastery and trains them to suspect the accompanying belief that anything is ever truly decided. Whereas the mythology of Western management tends to cast solutions as fixed and final, Eastern philosophical tradition emphasizes individual accommodation to a continuously unfolding set of events.

Think of the consequences of these outlooks as managers of these two cultures go about living up to their cultural imperatives. Eastern managers accept ambivalence. When faced with the necessity to "juggle," they do so with reassurance that the experience is congruent with what management is all about. Faced with the same set of events, some American managers may feel uneasy. This problem is exacerbated by the absence of cultural underpinnings for thinking about certain activities in which mastery of the situation is either impossible or downright undesirable. (Also, their language is not attuned to expression of this mode of thinking.)

The Western notion of mastery is closely linked with deep-seated assumptions about the self. The professional life of some Westerners, and certainly many who move into management positions, is dedicated to strengthening the ego in an effort to assert and maintain control over their environment and

8. Anthony G. Athos, "Choice and Decision," unpublished working paper, 1973.

their destiny. In contrast, the Eastern frame of reference views pragmatically appropriate limitations of the ego as a virtue.

To the Easterner, overt strength is not unequivocally a desired attribute. This notion of strength may be likened to the endurance of coral reefs that survive the massive forces of sea and wind during typhoons. Reefs do not attempt to resist the sea like defiant walls of man-made steel and concrete. Instead, the reef extends wedges out in a seaward direction. The waves deflect off these wedges, one against the other. Consequently their power, rather than directed at the reef, is turned against itself. The reef does not insist on standing higher than the sea. In times of typhoon, the waves wash over the reef. And it survives.

Let things flow. "Success is going straight—around the circle," says the Chinese adage. How often in organizations does the forcing of events precipitate needless resistance and even crisis? Yet the Western notion of leadership, fueled by the high value placed on logical, purposive, goal-blinded action, impels many to leap before they look.[9]

Dam up a river. In time the water rises until a trickle finds its way around the obstruction, gradually increasing in flow and force until its original course is resumed. Managers, of course, do not have to watch torrents of frustration and energy needlessly build up behind an organizational obstruction. But perhaps the solution is not always to dynamite away the obstruction; sometimes it is to trace a way around it with a light touch, enough to get a trickle flowing. Let the flow of events do the rest of the work. By embracing an alternative concept of leadership, managers can choose, where appropriate, to seek a contributing place in the flow of things rather than impose a false sense of mastery over events.

For Employees, Idiosyncrasies vs. Systems

The typical Western organization prides itself on having made a science of the secular virtues of efficiency and impartiality. In trying to cope with the slowed growth and economic uncertainty of recent years, organizations have intensified the emphasis on efficiency. A different set of forces has put emphasis on impartiality—among them the regulations aimed at eliminating discrimination of all kinds. The dilemma is how to treat people as equal without treating them as the same. Many organizations appear to be insensitive to this distinction. As a result they, like white bread or pure sugar, become bland and somewhat unhealthful; all the vital human elements seem to get refined away.

I should acknowledge that many Western executives show deep concern for

9. For a discussion of this "flowing" phenomenon in a Western context, see James D. Thompson, *Organizations in Action* (New York: McGraw-Hill, 1967), p. 149.

the people working for them. In a survey of American managers, psychologist Jay Hall found that those most highly rated in interpersonal skills were generally regarded as the most competent by their bosses. "Good managers," Hall wrote, "use an integrative style of management in which production goals and people's needs are equally important."[10]

Obviously, organizations need efficient systems to accomplish their tasks. But enough is enough, and more may be too much. The human touch is often lacking, and its absence breeds isolation and detachment. Lonely people perform instrumental functions as if they truly were interchangeable parts in a great machine. The explanation, I suppose, is that the increasing physical density of workers in our landscaped offices and automated factories has nothing to do with the psychic distances. Hard-edged procedures enhance this sense of aloneness.

Japanese companies, despite their evident prowess at adopting Western technology, have not followed the Western pattern where trade-offs between human relationships and secular efficiencies are concerned. Of more than 600 American employees of Japanese corporations interviewed in my study (including 100 managers and 500 workers) almost all expressed an awareness of the more personalized approach of their employers. The Japanese have a word describing a special quality of master potters who make the "perfect" bowl. The bowl is endowed with an ever-so-slight imperfection—a constant reminder of the object's relation to the humanity of the maker. The master knows that the perfection of mass-produced bowls is less satisfying than ones that lean a little. In this context, it might be said that Japanese companies lean a little.

The Japanese distinguish between our notion of "organization" and their notion of "the company." In their minds, the term organization refers only to the system; their concept of the company includes its underlying character as well. A company's character describes a shared sense of values long held by members and enforced by group norms. The result is an institutional way of doing things that is different from what efficiency alone would require. The "company" may accomplish the same tasks as an "organization" does, but it occupies more space, moves with more weight, and reflects a commitment to larger ends than just the accomplishment of a mission.

In Japan, companies are thought of as taking all of an employee. (In the United States the prevailing notion is that they take a piece of an employee.) The relationship is akin to the binding force of the family. Lacking such a philosophy, Western organizations tend to rely on what bureaucracies do best—championing "systems solutions"—rather than deal with the idiosyncratic

10. Jay Hall, "What Makes a Manager Good, Bad, or Average?" *Psychology Today*, August 1976, p. 52.

requirements of human nature. The result can isolate people into the lonely illusion of objectivity.

IS THE BOTTOM LINE THE MEASURE?

From the Japanese vantage point, the sense of incompleteness in our working lives stems from a divergence between what many people seek and what most Western organizations provide. Most people bring three kinds of needs to their organizational existence: a need to be rewarded for what they achieve, a need to be accepted as a unique person, and a need to be appreciated not only for the function performed but also as a human being. The term "reward," as used here, refers to the tangible payments one receives from an organization (such as salary and promotions) in exchange for services provided.

I use this narrow, rather instrumental definition of rewards to distinguish it from "acceptance" and "appreciation," which represent other kinds of benefits sought. In this context, acceptance refers to the quality of being known in a human sense rather than simply valued for the function one performs. The worker feels acceptance when people and organizations know him for who he is and make allowance for that uniqueness in their relationship with him. Appreciation goes a step further, conveying not only an acknowledgment by others of a person's distinctness but also a valuation of it in a positive and supportive way.

In an effort to express their commitment to people, the Japanese companies in the United States that I studied spent on average more than three times as much per employee on social and recreational facilities and activities than their American counterparts ($48.85 per employee per year versus $14.85). Some of these programs were probably largely symbolic, but many also fostered increased off-the-job contact among employees. The benefit was to "personalize" the particular company.

Perhaps a more direct vehicle for providing acceptance and appreciation is the Japanese policy of supporting spans of control at the supervisory level. This practice resulted in twice as much contact between workers and their foremen as in American companies, measured by employees per first-line supervisor (30.1 versus 13.5). The supervisors in Japanese-managed companies more often worked alongside the subordinates, engaged in personal counseling more extensively, and permitted more interaction among workers than the American companies did.[11]

What was the outcome? The evidence is sufficiently mixed to gratify both

11. Richard Tanner Pascale and Mary Ann Maguire, "The Company and the Worker: Japanese and American Comparisons," Graduate School of Business, Stanford University, 1977.

skeptics and advocates. There was no difference in production; the average output per unit of labor was about the same. Moreover, the Japanese companies experienced somewhat higher levels of tardiness and absenteeism. In respect to job satisfaction, the results were more favorable for Japanese-managed businesses in the United States. Their managers and workers expressed much more satisfaction with their jobs than did their counterparts in American companies.

Why bother, it might be asked, if the result has no impact on the bottom line? By Eastern standards the bottom line misses the point. It was Socrates (not an Eastern philosopher) who observed that "man is the measure of all things." Eastern perspective brings his meaning into fuller view. To the Eastern mind, it is "man," not the "bottom line," that is the ultimate measure of all things. He is not the source of all things, as some who view man in total command of his destiny might proclaim. Nor is he the objectified contributor to all things, as some organizations appear to presume in weighing his contributions against their costs.

A Japanese, while concerned with the bottom line, is not single-minded about it as many Westerners are. Rather, he proceeds with a dual awareness—that there is a second ledger in which "success" is debited or credited in terms of his contribution to the quality of relationships that ensue. So the professional manager defines his role not only as one who accomplishes certain organizational tasks but also as an essential intermediary in the social fabric.

Are Feathers More Effective than Sledgehammers?

This discussion has utilized Eastern ideas as a metaphor for exploring the process of management. One central theme is that it is not just particular notions—such as ambiguity or implied recognition—that can be helpful but the cultural context underlying these notions as well. I have tried to suggest that a combination of culture, words, philosophy, and values provides each of us with a particular outlook. The Eastern outlook is adopted not because it is "best" but because it sheds a different light on certain aspects of management. The Eastern perspective provides not so much a new set of tools (for, as I have noted repeatedly, many skilled American managers use these tools) but rather legitimacy for using these tools in some situations where they are appropriate.

From the Eastern vantage point, process is where managers live. This vantage point dwells on the chemistry of human relationships, as well as on the mechanics of human accomplishment, and it provides a way of thinking that assigns a particular value to human needs as well as to systems and economic requirements. Appreciation of the underpinnings of this outlook is fundamental to the thrust of this article. For if they are bounded by our traditional set of Western assumptions, many of the ideas here become empty techniques.

Management assumptions act as fences—keeping some things in and other things out of our awareness. As we have seen, there are many fences, not of wood but shaped by our words, values, and management ideology. I submit that a nontrivial set of management problems might be better understood if viewed from the other side of our Western fence. Undoubtedly, a very high degree of personal development is necessary to embrace both of these outlooks, to know when each is appropriate and to acquire the skills that each requires.

This suggests a cautionary note for the Western manager: in addition to approaching things purposively, defining problems crisply, and identifying his objectives explicitly (which are desirable but not necessarily sufficient traits to manage all problems skillfully), he may also wish to bear in mind that our Western world view diminishes our sensitivity and skill in managing certain kinds of problems. Such insight may enable us to avoid using sledgehammers when feathers will do. Eastern ideas provide a metaphor for the acquisition of such skill. "Truth lurks in metaphors."[12]

12. Anthony G. Athos, "Satan Is Left-Handed," *Association of Humanistic Psychology Newsletter*, December 1975.

10. Your Innate Asset for Combating Stress

Herbert Benson

As much as any group in history, modern administrators are overworked, pressured, and squeezed, often to the point of physical illness or emotional misery. Their characteristic ambitions constantly lead them into struggles that stretch their capacities. Many cannot stand up to it; their reactions range from subtle malaise to heart attacks. Fortunately, there is an extremely simple technique by which the executive can alter his physiology from the stressful mode toward calm—even decreasing his blood pressure. It can be practiced easily and with immense rewards in physical and emotional well-being. This article has been written expressly to provide the harried manager with the medical rationales for using the technique and to persuade him to practice it for the sake of his own health. In his conclusion the author even suggests that every company do ALL its employees a good turn by offering an alternative to the coffee break—the relaxation response break. Once an executive has tried it out, he may agree with this suggestion.

Emotional stress is a well-known aspect of the modern Western world and is especially prevalent in the business community. Our society has experienced rapid technological progress; the business community has been an integral part of this progress and, like the rest of the society, has experienced both beneficial and deleterious effects. Members of the business community have been forced to make certain behavioral adjustments—notably, a faster pace and a more pressured life—and behavioral adjustments of this sort induce stress. Although some individuals are aware of the physiologically harmful effects of stress, few know how to prevent or alleviate them. Victimized by the stressful world they have helped to create, many executives have accepted stress as a necessary component of their existence.

AUTHOR'S NOTE: The work on which this article is based has been supported by funds from the U.S. Public Health Service and the General Service Foundation. The editorial assistance of Helen P. Klemchuk and Martha M. Greenwood and the secretarial help of Nancy E. MacKinnon in the preparation of this article are gratefully acknowledged.

However, there is a simple way for the individual to alleviate stress and thus moderate or control many of its undesirable effects—effects that may range from simple anxiety to heart disease. The "relaxation response," an integrated physiologic response, appears to counteract the harmful physiologic effects of stress. It can be elicited by a simple mental technique.

The essential elements of the technique have long been familiar to man, and although they have usually been framed in the vocabularies of religions and cults where the elicitation of the relaxation response has played an important role, the response and the technique can be described in ordinary language. Moreover, the technique and the response can be beneficially applied by all the individuals of the community, including the executive.

The Concept of Stress

The concept of stress has been difficult to define and difficult to quantify.[1] Stress can be usefully defined through its physiologic correlates, particularly elevations in blood pressure. Elevated blood pressure is consistently related to environmental situations that require behavioral adjustment by the individual and thus may be described as stressful. The behavioral adjustments associated with socioeconomic mobility, cultural change, urbanization, and migration are examples of such environmental situations.

Relevant findings were obtained in a comparison of high school and college graduates in managerial positions within the same corporation. The high school graduates experienced more general illness during the one-year period of observation and displayed more signs of cardiovascular disease and high blood pressure (hypertension). The investigators in this study postulated that the high school graduates perceived more threats and challenges in their life situations than the college graduates because of the greater discrepancy between their lives and their childhood experiences: the relative ill health of the high school graduates is regarded as part of the price they pay for "getting ahead in the world."

In other investigations, undertaken in several Pacific islands, higher blood pressure was found to be associated with the degree of Westernization. Migration from rural to urban areas in these same islands was also correlated with a rise in the prevalence of elevated blood pressure. Adrian M. Ostfeld and Richard B. Shekelle of the University of Illinois clearly summarized why these situations apparently require behavioral adjustment:

1. Mary C. Gutmann and Herbert Benson, "Interaction of Environmental Factors and Systemic Arterial Blood Pressure: A Review," *Medicine,* November 1971, p. 543.

There has been an appreciable increase in uncertainty of human relations as man has gone from the relatively primitive and more rural to the urban and industrial. Contemporary man in much of the world is faced every day with people and with situations about which there is uncertainty of outcome, wherein appropriate behavior is not prescribed and validated by tradition, where the possibility of bodily or psychological harm exists, where running or fighting is inappropriate, and where mental vigilance is called for.[2]

THE FIGHT-OR-FLIGHT RESPONSE

Stressful situations that require behavioral adjustment appear to elevate blood pressure by means of a physiologic response popularly referred to as the "fight-or-flight response," first described by Dr. Walter B. Cannon of the Harvard Medical School. When an animal perceives a threatening situation, its reflexive response is an integrated physiologic response that prepares it for running or fighting. This response is characterized by coordinated increases in metabolism (oxygen consumption), blood pressure, heart rate, rate of breathing, amount of blood pumped by the heart, and amount of blood pumped to the skeletal muscles.

The existence of this integrated response in lower animals was substantiated by the Swiss Nobel laureate Dr. Walter R. Hess. By stimulating the brain of the cat, he demonstrated that the controlling center for the fight-or-flight response is located within a specific area of the brain called the hypothalamus. When this area is electrically stimulated, the brain and other portions of the nervous system respond by controlled outpouring of epinephrine and norepinephrine (also called adrenalin and noradrenalin), which leads to the physiologic changes noted in the fight-or-flight response. These two compounds are the major chemical mediating substances of the sympathetic nervous system. Significantly, the overactivity of this functional division of the nervous system has been implicated in the development of many serious diseases. Thus the fight-or-flight response is an integrated physiologic mechanism leading to coordinated activation of the sympathetic nervous system.

A Czech scientist, Dr. Jan Brod, and his associates have demonstrated the physiologic characteristics of the fight-or-flight response in man in the laboratory setting. First, control measurements were made in a group of healthy young adults in a resting position. These subjects were then given a mental-arithmetic problem to solve: from a four-digit number like 1,194, subtract consecutive serial 17s. A metronome was set clicking in the background, and others around

2. "Psychological Variables and Blood Pressure," in *The Epidemiology of Hypertension,* edited by J. Stamler, R. Stamler, and T. N. Pullman (New York, Grune and Stratton, 1967), p. 321.

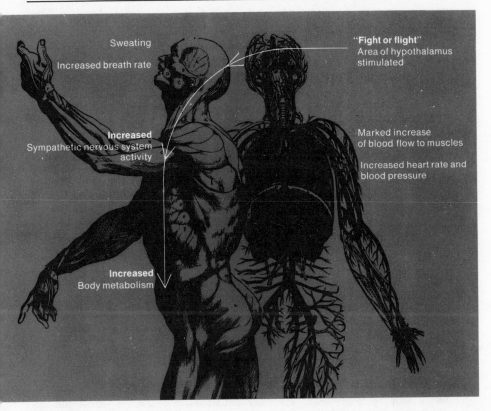

the subjects made statements such as: "I did better than that. You're not doing very well." Then new measurements were taken of blood pressure, blood pumped by the heart, and blood pumped to the skeletal muscles. All had increased. *Exhibit I* is an illustration of the physiologic characteristics associated with the fight-or-flight response.

Other situations requiring behavioral adjustment also lead to the fight-or-flight response. All human beings use the same basic physiologic mechanisms to respond to individually meaningful, stressful events.

Although the fight-or-flight response is still a necessary and useful physiologic feature for survival, the stresses of today's society have led to its excessive elicitation; at the same time, its behavioral features, such as running or fighting, are usually socially inappropriate or unacceptable. These circumstances may lead to persistent hypertension. Those who experience greater environmental stress and, therefore, more frequent elicitation of the fight-or-flight response have a greater chance of developing chronic hypertension (that is, chronic high blood pressure).

The importance of hypertension

High blood pressure, or hypertension, is of far greater significance to man than as just an index of stressful circumstances. It is one of the important factors—if not the most important—predisposing man to heart attack and stroke. These diseases of the heart and brain account for more than 50% of the deaths each year within the United States. Therefore, it is not surprising that various degrees of hypertension are present in 15% to 33% of the adult population of the United States, affecting between 23 million and 44 million individuals.

Heart attacks and strokes have always been diseases leading to death, predominantly in the elderly. However, it is highly disturbing that these diseases are now affecting a younger population. The late American cardiologist Dr. Samuel Levine pointed out that in families he followed for decades in which both fathers and sons experienced heart attacks, the average age at the time of the first attack was 13 years earlier for the sons than for their fathers. Many cardiologists feel that we are in the midst of an epidemic of these diseases. If hypertension could be prevented, this epidemic might be alleviated. Consequently, situations requiring behavioral adjustment, which may lead to hypertension, are of considerable concern.

THE RELAXATION RESPONSE

What can be done about everyday situations that lead to stress and its consequences? It is unlikely that the rapid pace of Western life will slow down significantly; and as far as our present standard of living depends on that pace, it is unlikely that most executives would want it to slow down. The need for behavioral adjustment will probably continue, and therefore individuals should learn to counteract the harmful effects of the physiologic response to stress. One possibility is the regular elicitation of the relaxation response.[3]

The relaxation response is an innate, integrated set of physiologic changes opposite to those of the fight-or-flight response. It can be elicited by psychologic means. Hess first described this response in the cat. He electrically stimulated another specific area of the hypothalamus and elicited what he called "a protective mechanism against overstress [which promotes] restorative processes."[4]

3. See Herbert Benson, John F. Beary, and Mark P. Carol, "The Relaxation Response," *Psychiatry*, February 1974, p. 37.
4. Walter R. Hess, *Functional Organization of the Diencephalon* (New York, Grune and Stratton, 1957), p. 40.

Like the fight-or-flight response, the relaxation response is also present in man. Until recently, the relaxation response has been elicited primarily by meditational techniques—the reader will find information about the effects of some of these techniques in *Exhibit II*. The practice of one well-investigated technique, transcendental meditation (TM), results in physiologic changes that are consistent with generalized decreased sympathetic nervous system activity[5] and are thus opposite to the fight-or-flight response. There is a simultaneous decrease in the body's metabolism, in heart rate, and in rate of breathing. These changes are distinctly different from the physiologic changes noted during quiet sitting or sleep. Blood pressure remains unchanged during the practice of transcendental meditation; however, pressures appear lower in general among meditators than among individuals who do not practice meditation. *Exhibit III* is an illustration of the physiologic characteristics associated with the relaxation response.

A Very Simple Technique

The basic technique for the elicitation of the relaxation response is extremely simple. Its elements have been known and used for centuries in many cultures throughout the world. Historically, the relaxation response has usually been elicited in a religious context. The reader who is interested in the historical background of the response and its universality may enjoy the appendix to this article.

Four basic elements are common to all these practices: a quiet environment, a mental device, a passive attitude, and a comfortable position. A simple, mental, noncultic technique based on these four elements has recently been used in my laboratory. Subjects are given the following description of the four elements in the technique:

1. A quiet environment. One should choose a quiet, calm environment with as few distractions as possible. Sound, even background noise, may prevent the elicitation of the response. Choose a convenient, suitable place—for example, at an office desk in a quiet room.

2. A mental device. The meditator employs the constant stimulus of a single-syllable sound or word. The syllable is repeated silently or in a low, gentle tone. The purpose of the repetition is to free oneself from logical, externally oriented

5. See R. Keith Wallace, Herbert Benson, and Archie F. Wilson, "A Wakeful Hypometabolic Physiologic State," *American Journal of Physiology,* September 1971, p. 795; see also R. Keith Wallace and Herbert Benson, "The Physiology of Meditation," *Scientific American,* February 1972, p. 84.

Exhibit II. Comparison of methods for inducing the relaxation response

Technique	Physiologic measurement					
	Oxygen consumption	Respiratory rate	Heart rate	Alpha waves	Blood pressure	Muscle tension
Transcendental meditation	Decreases	Decreases	Decreases	Increases	Decreases	Not measured
Zen and yoga	Decreases	Decreases	Decreases	Increases	No change	Not measured
Autogenic training	Not measured	Decreases	Decreases	Increases	Inconclusive results	Decreases
Progressive relaxation	Not measured	Not measured	Not measured	Not measured	Inconclusive results	Decreases
Hypnosis with suggested deep relaxation	Decreases	Decreases	Decreases	Not measured	Inconclusive results	Decreases
Sentic cycles	Decreases	Decreases	Decreases	Not measured	Not measured	Not measured

Exhibit III Physiologic changes associated with the relaxation response

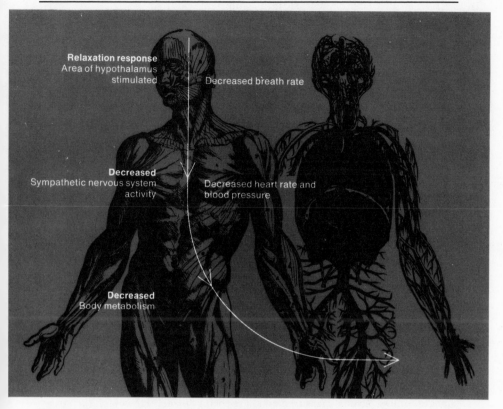

Relaxation response
Area of hypothalamus stimulated

Decreased breath rate

Decreased
Sympathetic nervous system activity

Decreased heart rate and blood pressure

Decreased
Body metabolism

thought by focusing solely on the stimulus. Many different words and sounds have been used in traditional practices. Because of its simplicity and neutrality, the use of the syllable *one* is suggested.

3. A passive attitude. The purpose of the response is to help one rest and relax, and this requires a completely passive attitude. One should not scrutinize his performance or try to force the response, because this may well prevent the response from occurring. When distracting thoughts enter the mind, they should simply be disregarded.

4. A comfortable position. The meditator should sit in a comfortable chair in as restful a position as possible. The purpose is to reduce muscular effort to a minimum. The head may be supported; the arms should be balanced or supported as well. The shoes may be removed and the feet propped up several inches, if desired. Loosen all tight-fitting clothing.

ELICITING THE RELAXATION RESPONSE

Using these four basic elements, one can evoke the response by following the simple, mental, noncultic procedure that subjects have used in my laboratory:

☐ In a quiet environment, sit in a comfortable position.

☐ Close your eyes.

☐ Deeply relax all your muscles, beginning at your feet and progressing up to your face—feet, calves, thighs, lower torso, chest, shoulders, neck, head. Allow them to remain deeply relaxed.

☐ Breathe through your nose. Become aware of your breathing. As you breathe out, say the word *one* silently to yourself. Thus: breathe in . . . breathe out, with *one*. In . . . out, with *one*. . . .

☐ Continue this practice for 20 minutes. You may open your eyes to check the time, but do not use an alarm. When you finish, sit quietly for several minutes, at first with your eyes closed and later with your eyes open.

Remember not to worry about whether you are successful in achieving a deep level of relaxation—maintain a passive attitude and permit relaxation to occur at its own pace. When distracting thoughts occur, ignore them and continue to repeat *one* as you breathe. The technique should be practiced once or twice daily, and not within two hours after any meal, since the digestive processes seem to interfere with the elicitation of the expected changes.

With practice, the response should come with little effort. Investigations have shown that only a small percentage of people do not experience the expected physiologic changes.[6] (However, it has been noted that people who are undergoing psychoanalysis for at least two sessions a week experience difficulty in eliciting the response.)

A person cannot be certain that the technique is eliciting these physiologic changes unless actual measurements are being made. However, the great majority of people report feelings of relaxation and freedom from anxiety during the elicitation of the relaxation response and during the rest of the day as well. These feelings of well-being are akin to those often noted after physical exercise, but without the attendant physical fatigue.

The practice of this technique evokes some of the same physiologic changes noted during the practice of other techniques, such as those listed in *Exhibit II*. These physiologic changes are significant decreases in body metabolism—oxygen consumption and carbon dioxide elimination—and rate of breathing. Decreased oxygen consumption is the most sensitive index of the elicitation of the relaxation response.

Techniques that elicit the relaxation response should not be confused with biofeedback. Through biofeedback training, a subject can be made aware of an otherwise unconscious physiologic function, such as his heart rate, and learn to

6. See Wallace, Benson, and Wilson, op. cit.; see also John F. Beary and Herbert Benson, "A Simple Psychophysiologic Technique Which Elicits the Hypometabolic Changes of the Relaxation Response," *Psychosomatic Medicine,* March-April 1974, p. 115.

alter it voluntarily. He uses a device that measures the function—heart rate, for example—and "feeds back" to him information corresponding to each beat of his heart. He can then be rewarded (or reward himself) for increases or decreases in his heart rate and thus learn partial heart rate control. Other physiologic functions that have been shown partially controllable through biofeedback are blood pressure, skin temperature, muscle tension, and certain patterns of brain waves, such as alpha waves.

But whereas biofeedback requires physiologic monitoring equipment and can usually be focused on only one physiologic function at a time, elicitation of the relaxation response requires no equipment and affects several physiologic functions simultaneously.

THERAPEUTIC POSSIBILITIES FOR HYPERTENSION

I suggest that voluntary, regular elicitation of the relaxation response can counterbalance and alleviate the effects of the environmentally induced, but often inappropriate, fight-or-flight response.

For example, the regular elicitation of the relaxation response is useful in lowering the blood pressure of hypertensive subjects.[7] Individuals atending an introductory transcendental meditation lecture were asked whether they had high blood pressure and, if so, whether they would be willing to participate in a study of the effects of meditation on high blood pressure. Over 80 subjects with high blood pressure volunteered for the study. They agreed to postpone learning meditation for six weeks while their blood pressures were periodically measured and recorded to establish their premeditation blood pressures. At the end of the six-week period, the subjects were trained to elicit the relaxation response through transcendental meditation.

After at least two weeks of twice-daily meditation, the subjects' blood pressures were measured approximately every two weeks for at least nine weeks. Measurements were made at random times of the day but never during meditation. Throughout this entire period, the subjects were instructed to remain under the care of their physicians and to make only those changes in their medications that were prescribed by their physicians.

Of the original group, about 50 individuals altered the type or dosage of their

7. See Herbert Benson, Barbara R. Marzetta, and Bernard A. Rosner, "Decreased Blood Pressure Associated with the Regular Elicitation of the Relaxation Response: A Study of Hypertensive Subjects," in *Contemporary Problems in Cardiology*, Vol. I: *Stress and the Heart*, edited by R. S. Eliot (Mt. Kisco, New York, Futura, 1974), p. 293; see also Herbert Benson, Bernard A. Rosner, Barbara R. Marzetta, and Helen Klemchuk, "Decreased Blood-Pressure in Pharmacologically Treated Hypertensive Patients Who Regularly Elicited the Relaxation Response," *The Lancet*, February 23, 1974, p. 289.

antihypertensive medications during the course of the experiment. The data on these individuals were excluded from the study to avoid possible inaccurate interpretations caused by the altered regimens. There remained over 30 subjects who either did not alter their medications or took no antihypertensive medications. Comparisons were then made between these subjects' blood pressures before and after learning meditation.

During the premeditation (control) period, the subjects' systolic blood pressures averaged 140 to 150 millimeters of mercury. (Systolic pressure is the measure of the highest component of blood pressure.) After nine weeks of regular elicitation of the relaxation response, this average dropped into the range of 130 to 140 millimeters. Their diastolic pressures (the lowest component of blood pressure) averaged 90 to 95 millimeters during the control period and dropped into the range of 85 to 90 millimeters by the ninth week of meditation. These decreases reflect a statistically significant change in blood pressure, from what is considered the borderline hypertensive range to the normal range of blood pressure.[8]

An equally important result of the experiment was the change in blood pressure in the subjects who chose to stop meditation. Within four weeks both their systolic and their diastolic pressures had returned to their initial hypertensive levels.

Work remains to be done in this area, but these studies suggest that the regular elicitation of the relaxation response may be another means of lowering blood pressure. At the present time, standard medical therapy for hypertension involves the use of antihypertensive drugs. This pharmacologic method of lowering blood pressure is very effective, but it is sometimes accompanied by unpleasant side effects, and it is expensive. Indications are that the relaxation response affects the same mechanisms and lowers blood pressure by the same means as some antihypertensive drugs. Both act on the sympathetic nervous system.

Although it is unlikely that the regular elicitation of the relaxation response will be adequate therapy by itself for severe or moderate hypertension, it might act synergistically, along with antihypertensive drugs, to lower blood pressure, and may lead to the use of fewer drugs or decreased dosages. In borderline hypertension, the regular elicitation of the relaxation response may be of great value, since it has no pharmacologic side effects and might possibly supplant the use of drugs.

However, no matter how encouraging these initial results appear to be, no person should treat himself for high blood pressure by regularly eliciting the

8. Ibid.

relaxation response. He should use the technique only under the supervision of his physician, who will routinely monitor his blood pressure to make sure it is adequately controlled.

OTHER THERAPEUTIC POSSIBILITIES

Individuals choose various means to alleviate their subjective feelings of stress, and heavy alcohol intake, drug abuse, and cigarette smoking are serious problems in our society. In a recent investigation, 1,862 individuals completed a questionnaire in which they reported a marked decrease in hard-liquor intake, drug abuse, and cigarette smoking after they had begun the elicitation of the relaxation response through the practice of transcendental meditation.[9]

Details on decreased alcohol intake are as follows. Hard liquor was defined as any beverage of alcoholic content other than wine or beer, and its usage was divided into four categories:

1. Total nonusage of alcohol.
2. Light usage—up to three times per month.
3. Medium usage—one to six times per week.
4. Heavy usage—at least once per day.

Prior to the regular practice of meditation, 2.7% were heavy users of hard liquor. This percentage decreased to 0.4% after 21 months of the twice-daily practice of meditation. Medium users comprised 15.8% prior to meditation; after 21 months they were only 2.6%. Light usage of hard liquor decreased from 41.4% to 21.9%. Further, heavy and medium users tended to become light users or nonusers as they continued to meditate; and, whereas 40.1% were nonusers of alcohol prior to learning meditation, this percentage had increased to 75.1% after 21 or more months of meditation.

This questionnaire also surveyed the drug-abuse patterns of the group—that is, the usage of marijuana, amphetamines, barbiturates, narcotics, LSD and other hallucinogens. Following the start of the regular practice of meditation, there was a marked decrease in the number of drug abusers in all categories; and, as the practice was continued, there was a progressive decrease in drug abuse. After 21 months, most subjects were using no drugs at all.

For example, in the 6-month period before starting the practice of meditation, about 80% of this sample used marijuana, and of those about 28% were heavy users. After regularly eliciting the relaxation response for approximately 6 months, 37% used marijuana, and of those only 6% were heavy users. After 21

9. Herbert Benson and R. Keith Wallace, "Decreased Drug Abuse With Transcendental Meditation—A Study of 1,862 Subjects," in *Drug Abuse—Proceedings of the International Conference,* edited by C. J. D. Zarafonetis (Philadelphia, Lea and Febiger, 1972), p. 369.

months of the practice, 12% continued to use marijuana, and of those almost all were light users; only one individual was a heavy user.

There was an even greater decrease in the abuse of LSD. Before starting the practice of meditation, 48% of the subjects had used LSD, and of these about 14% were heavy users (at least once per week). After 3 months of meditation, 12% of the subjects still took LSD, but after 21 months only 3% still took it.

For other drugs there were similar increases in numbers of nonusers after starting the practice of meditation. After 21 months, nonusers of the other hallucinogens rose from 61% to 96%; for the narcotics, from 83% to 99%; for the amphetamines, from 68% to 99%; and for the barbiturates, from 83% to 99%.

The smoking habits of the subjects also changed. Approximately 48% smoked cigarettes before starting meditation, and 27% of the sample were heavy users (at least one pack per day). After 21 months of meditation, only 16% still smoked cigarettes, and only 5.8% were heavy smokers.

This particular investigation was biased in several ways. The data were retrospective and subject to the limitation of personal recall. The group was not a random sample, nor was it chosen to be representative of the general population. Further, there was no control population; there are no data concerning the patterns of alcohol intake, drug abuse, and cigarette smoking of a matched sample of nonmeditators. Only a prospective investigation can eliminate these biases. However, these data, as well as data from the other studies cited, suggest strongly that a beneficial effect may be derived from elicitation of the relaxation response.

I must emphasize again, however, that the relaxation response should not be viewed as a potential panacea for medical problems. An investigation of the response in the therapy of severe migraine and certain other kinds of headache, for example, has demonstrated the response to be of limited usefulness in these illnesses; it is recommended that this particular therapy be tried when other therapies of headache have proved unsuccessful.[10] *Thus, the relaxation response should not be practiced for preventive or therapeutic medical benefits unless done so with the approval of a physician.*

A note on side effects

The side effects of the extensive practice of the relaxation response are worth brief discussion, although they have not been well documented.

When the response is elicited for two limited daily periods of 20 to 30 minutes, no adverse side effects have been observed. When the response is elicited more frequently—for example, for many hours daily over a period of

10. Herbert Benson, Helen Klemchuk, and John R. Graham, "The Usefulness of the Relaxation Response in the Therapy of Headache," *Headache*, Vol. 14, pp. 49–52, 1974.

several days—some individuals have experienced a withdrawal from life and have developed symptoms that range from insomnia to hallucinatory behavior. These side effects of the excessive elicitation of the relaxation response are difficult to evaluate on a retrospective basis, since many people with preexisting psychiatric problems might be drawn to any technique that evangelistically promises relief from tension and stress.

However, it is unlikely that the twice daily elicitation of the response would do any more harm than would regular prayer.

Benefits for the Business Community

As noted above, well over 50% of our present U.S. population will die of heart disease and related conditions, and these diseases appear to be attacking Americans at younger and younger ages. The frequent elicitation of the fight-or-flight response has been strongly implicated in the development of these diseases. The regular use of the relaxation response in our daily lives may counteract the harmful effects of the fight-or-flight response and thereby mitigate these extremely prevalent and dire diseases.

However, modern Western society has turned away from many of the traditional techniques that elicit the relaxation response, such as prayer. Our society has thus lost an important means of alleviating stress and maintaining equilibrium in a changing world. We can probably greatly benefit by the reintroduction of the relaxation response into our society.

Because of its far-reaching influence in our society, the business sector could take the lead in this reintroduction. For example, programs could be established in which time is made available for employees to practice the relaxation response. Voluntary participants could choose whatever mode they wish: a familiar mode, like certain types of prayer, or the simple, noncultic, mental technique previously described. A quiet environment is desirable, but a person can elicit the response at his or her desk or at any comfortable seat. A "relaxation response break" might be substituted for the coffee break. This may improve employees' ability to deal with stress and increase their sense of well-being. Not only may such an application prove beneficial to the individual—it may have further, broader benefits and ramifications for industry as a whole.

For centuries, people have used various techniques to elicit the relaxation response, but it is only now that we are recognizing its potential physiologic benefits. The relaxation response is innate. Members of industry need only take the time to bring it forth. Finally, in our society, the executive certainly has the power to effectively champion the use of this simple but remarkably salutary response, by making time available to bring it forth.

Appendix: A Historical Note

The elicitation of the relaxation response has been a part of many secular and religious practices for centuries.

In the West, a fourteenth-century Christian treatise entitled *The Cloud of Unknowing* discusses how to attain an alleged union with God. The anonymous author states that this goal cannot be reached in the ordinary levels of human consciousness but requires the use of "lower" levels. These levels are reached by eliminating all distractions and physical activity, all worldly things, including all thoughts. As a means of "beating down thought," the use of a single-syllable word, such as "God" or "love," should be repeated:

> Choose whichever one you prefer, or, if you like, choose another that suits your taste, provided that it is of one syllable. And clasp this word tightly in your heart so that it never leaves it no matter what may happen. This word shall be your shield and your spear.... With this word you shall strike down thoughts of every kind and drive them beneath the cloud of forgetting. After that, if any thoughts should press upon you ... answer him with this word only and with no other words.

According to the writer, there will be moments when "every created thing may suddenly and completely be forgotten. But immediately after each stirring, because of the corruption of the flesh, [the soul] drops down again to some thought or some deed." An important instruction for success is "do not by another means work in it with your mind or with your imagination."

Another Christian work, *The Third Spiritual Alphabet,* written in the tenth century by Fray Francisco de Osuna, describes an altered state of consciousness. He wrote that "contemplation requires us to blind ourselves to all that is not God," and that one should be deaf and dumb to all else and must "quit all obstacles, keeping your eyes bent on the ground." The method can be either a short, self-composed prayer, repeated over and over, or simply saying *no* to thoughts when they occur. This exercise was to be performed for one hour in the morning and evening and taught by a qualified teacher.

NOTE: This historical discussion appears in part in Benson, Beary, and Carol, "The Relaxation Response."

Fray Francisco wrote that such an exercise would help in all endeavors, making individuals more efficient in their tasks and the tasks more enjoyable; that all men, especially the busy, secular as well as religious, should be taught this meditation because it is a refuge to which one can retreat when faced with stressful situations.

Christian meditation and mysticism were well developed within the Byzantine church and known as Hesychasm. Hesychasm involved a method of repetitive prayer that was described in the fourteenth century at Mount Athos in Greece by Gregory of Sinai and was called "The Prayer of the Heart" or "The Prayer of Jesus." It dates back to the beginnings of Christianity. The prayer itself was called secret meditation and was transmitted from older to younger monks through an initiation rite. Emphasis was placed on having a skilled instructor. The method of prayer recommended by these monks was as follows:

Sit down alone and in silence. Lower your head, shut your eyes, breathe out gently, and imagine yourself looking into your own heart. Carry your mind, i.e., your thoughts, from your head to your heart. As you breathe out, say 'Lord Jesus Christ, have mercy on me.' Say it moving your lips gently, or simply say it in your mind. Try to put all other thoughts aside. Be calm, be patient, and repeat the process very frequently.

In Judaism, similar practices date back to the time of the second temple in the second century B.C. and are found in one of the earliest forms of Jewish mysticism, Merkabalism. In this practice of meditation, the subject sat with his head between his knees and whispered hymns, songs, and repeated a name of a magic seal.

In the thirteenth century A.D., the works of Rabbi Abulafia were published, and his ideas became a major part of Jewish cabalistic tradition. Rabbi Abulafia felt that the normal life of the soul is kept within limits by our sensory perceptions and emotions, and since these perceptions and emotions are concerned with the finite, the soul's life is finite. Man, therefore, needs a higher form of perception that, instead of blocking the soul's deeper regions, opens them up. An "absolute" object on which to meditate is required. Rabbi Abulafia found this object in the Hebrew alphabet. He developed a mystical system of contemplating the letters of God's name. Rabbi Ben Zion Bokser describes Rabbi Abulafia's prayer:

Immersed in prayer and meditation, uttering the divine name with special modulations of the voice and with special gestures, he induced in himself a state of ecstasy in which he believed the soul had shed its material bonds and, unimpeded, returned to its divine source.[1]

---

1. *From the World of the Cabbalah* (New York, Philosophical Library, 1954), p. 9.

The purpose of this prayer and methodical meditation is to experience a new state of consciousness in which all relation to the senses is severed. Gershom Gerhard Scholem compares this state to music and yoga. He feels that Abulafia's teachings "represent but a Judaized version of that ancient spiritual technique which has found its classical expression in the practices of the Indian mystics who follow the system known as *Yoga*." Scholem continues:

> To cite only one instance out of many, an important part in Abulafia's system is played by the technique of breathing; now this technique has found its highest development in the Indian *Yoga,* where it is commonly regarded as the most important instrument of mental discipline. Again, Abulafia lays down certain rules of body posture, certain corresponding combinations of consonants and vowels, and certain forms of recitation, and in particular some passages of his book *The Light of the Intellect* give the impression of a Judaized treatise on *Yoga.* The similarity even extends to some aspects of the doctrine of ecstatic vision, as preceded and brought about by these practices.[2]

The basic elements that elicit the relaxation response in certain practices of Christianity and Judaism are also found in Islamic mysticism or Sufism. Sufism developed in reaction to the external rationalization of Islam and made use of intuitive and emotional faculties that are claimed to be dormant until utilized through training under the guidance of a teacher. The method of employing these faculties is known as dhikr. It is a means of excluding distractions and of drawing nearer to God by the constant repetition of His name, either silently or aloud, and by rhythmic breathing. Music, musical poems, and dance are also employed in their ritual of dhikr, for it was noticed that they could help induce states of ecstasy.

Originally, dhikr was only practiced by the members of the society who made a deliberate choice to redirect their lives to God as the preliminary step in the surrender of the will. Upon initiation into his order, the initiate received the *wird,* a secret, holy sound. The old Masters felt that the true encounter with God could not be attained by all, for most men are born deaf to mystical sensitivity. However, by the twelfth century, this attitude had changed. It was realized that this ecstasy could be induced in the ordinary man in a relatively short time by rhythmic exercises involving posture, control of breath, coordinated movements, and oral repetitions.

In the Western world, the relaxation response elicited by religious practices was not part of the routine practice of religions, but rather was associated with the mystical tradition. In the East, however, meditation that elicited the relaxation response was developed much earlier and became a major element in religion as well as in everyday life. Writings from Indian scriptures, the

2. *Major Trends in Jewish Mysticism* (New York, Schocken Books, 1967), p. 139.

Upanishads, dated sixth century B.C., note that individuals might attain "a unified state with the Brahman [the Deity] by means of restraint of breath, withdrawal of senses, meditation, concentration, contemplation, and absorption."

There are a multitude of Eastern religions and ways of life, including Zen and yoga, with their many variants, which can elicit the relaxation response. They employ mental and physical methods, including the repetition of a word or sound, the exclusion of meaningful thoughts, a quiet environment, and a comfortable position, and they stress the importance of a trained teacher. One of the meditative practices of Zen Buddhism, za-zen, employs a yogalike technique of the coupling of respiration and counting to ten, e.g., one on inhaling, two on exhaling, and so on, to ten. With time, one stops counting and simply "follows the breath" in order to achieve a state of no thought, no feeling, to be completely in nothing.

Shintoism and Taoism are important religions of Japan and China. A method of prayer in Shintoism consists of sitting quietly, inspiring through the nose, holding inspiration for a short time, and expiring through the mouth, with eyes directed toward a mirror at their level. Throughout the exercise, the priest repeats ten numbers, or sacred words, pronounced according to the traditional religious teachings. Fujisawa noted, "It is interesting that this grand ritual characteristic of Shintoism in doubtlessly the same process as *Yoga*." Taoism, one of the traditional religions of China, employs, in addition to methods similar to Shinto, concentration on nothingness to achieve absolute tranquility.

Similar meditational practices are found in practically every culture of man. Shamanism is a form of mysticism associated with feelings of ecstasy and is practiced in conjunction with tribal religions in North and South America, Indonesia, Oceania, Africa, Siberia, and Japan. Each shaman has a song or chant to bring on trances, usually entering into solitude to do so. Music, especially the drum, plays an important part in Shamanistic trances.

Many less traditional religious practices are flourishing in the United States. One aim of the practices is achievement of an altered state of consciousness, which is induced by techniques similar to those that elicit the relaxation response. Subub, Nichiren Sho Shu, Hare Krishna, Scientology, Black Muslimism, the Meher Baba group, and the Association for Research and Enlightenment are but a few of these.

In addition to techniques that elicit the relaxation response within a religious context, secular techniques also exist. The so-called nature mystics have been able to elicit the relaxation response by immersing themselves in quiet, often in the quiet of nature. Wordsworth believed that when his mind was freed from preoccupation with disturbing objects, petty cares, "little enmities and low desires," he could reach a condition of equilibrium, which he describes as a "wise passiveness" or "a happy stillness of the mind." Wordsworth believed that anyone could deliberately induce this condition in himself by a kind of relaxation of the will. Thoreau made many references to such feelings attained by sitting for hours alone with nature. Indeed, Thoreau compares himself to a yogi. William James describes similar experiences. For the reader who wishes to pursue the topic further, a treatise on other such experiences may be found in Raynor C. Johnson's *Watcher on the Hills* (Mystic, Connecticut, Lawrence Verry Inc., 1951).

Part III
Developing People's Talents

Preface

In general, we know how to teach others how to read, write, program computers, and make statistical analyses. All these things may not be easy to do, but we know how to teach them and we know how to tell if someone has learned them or not. It is not as easy, however, to develop the intuitive, nonrational sides of people. A person can be taught to put symbols on a piece of paper, but can he or she be "taught" how to create a poem, or make a wise decision.

In business the same problem exists. There is no lack of successful managerial development programs that teach technical skills. But how about courses that teach qualities that leaders require: interpersonal skills, judgment, or creativity? There have been attempts, such as sensitivity training courses, to teach these things, but in general most attempts to develop the intuitive side of a manager have been minimal, as well as haphazard.

Even more problematic, as Abraham Zaleznik points out in "Managers and Leaders: Are They Different?," most bureaucratic, rational, and orderly structures are actually inimical to the development of leaders. Large bureaucratic organizations limit personal relationships, which are essential to developing interpersonal skills.

The articles in this section show how through personal relationships and empathetic modeling people can learn and develop new skills as well as acquire leadership qualities in an organizational setting. In all cases, a manager's treatment of a subordiante is the crucial factor in that subordinate's development. According to J. Sterling Livingston, a manager's expectations are the key to a subordinate's performance. He writes in "Pygmalion in Management" that managers effective in developing people pick those people they know will succeed and then treat them that way. The success lies in the employee's perceiving that confidence.

11. Managers and Leaders: Are They Different?

Abraham Zaleznik

Most societies, and that includes business organizations, are caught between two conflicting needs: one for managers to maintain the balance of operations, and one for leaders to create new approaches and imagine new areas to explore. One might well ask why there is a conflict. Cannot both managers and leaders exist in the same society, or even better, cannot one person be both a manager and a leader? The author of this article does not say that is impossible but suggests that because leaders and managers are basically different types of people, the conditions favorable to the growth of one may be inimical to the other. Exploring the world views of managers and leaders, the author illustrates, using Alfred P. Sloan and Edwin Land among others as examples, that managers and leaders have different attitudes toward their goals, careers, relations with others, and themselves. And tracing their different lines of development, the author shows how leaders are of a psychologically different type than managers; their development depends on their forming a one-to-one relationship with a mentor.

What is the ideal way to develop leadership? Every society provides its own answer to this question, and each, in groping for answers, defines its deepest concerns about the purposes, distributions, and uses of power. Business has contributed its answer to the leadership question by evolving a new breed called the manager. Simultaneously, business has established a new power ethic that favors collective over individual leadership, the cult of the group over that of personality. While ensuring the competence, the control, and the balance of power relations among groups with the potential for rivalry, managerial leadership unfortunately does not necessarily ensure imagination, creativity, or ethical behavior in guiding the destinies of corporate enterprises.

Leadership inevitably requires using power to influence the thoughts and actions of other people. Power in the hands of an individual entails human risks: first, the risk of equating power with the ability to get immediate results; second, the risk of ignoring the many different ways people can legitimately accumulate power; and third, the risk of losing self-control in the desire for power. The need to hedge these risks accounts in part for the development of collective leadership and the managerial ethic. Consequently, an inherent conservatism dominates the culture of large organizations. In *The Second American Revolution,* John D. Rockefeller, 3rd, describes the conservatism of organizations:

An organization is a system, with a logic of its own, and all the weight of tradition and inertia. The deck is stacked in favor of the tried and proven way of doing things and against the taking of risks and striking out in new directions.[1]

Out of this conservatism and inertia organizations provide succession to power through the development of managers rather than individual leaders. And the irony of the managerial ethic is that it fosters a bureaucratic culture in business, supposedly the last bastion protecting us from the encroachments and controls of bureaucracy in government and education. Perhaps the risks associated with power in the hands of an individual may be necessary ones for business to take if organizations are to break free of their inertia and bureaucratic conservatism.

Manager vs. Leader Personality

Theodore Levitt has described the essential features of a managerial culture with its emphasis on rationality and control:

Management consists of the rational assessment of a situation and the systematic selection of goals and purposes (what is to be done?); the systematic development of strategies to achieve these goals; the marshalling of the required resources; the rational design, organization, direction, and control of the activities required to attain the selected purposes; and, finally, the motivating and rewarding of people to do the work.[2]

In other words, whether his or her energies are directed toward goals, resources, organization structures, or people, a manager is a problem solver. The manager asks himself, "What problems have to be solved, and what are the best ways to achieve results so that people will continue to contribute to this organization?" In this conception, leadership is a practical effort to direct affairs; and to fulfill his task, a manager requires that many people operate at different levels of status and responsibility. Our democratic society is, in fact,

1. John D. Rockefeller, 3rd., *The Second American Revolution* (New York: Harper & Row, 1973), p. 72.
2. Theodore Levitt, "Management and the Post Industrial Society," *The Public Interest,* Summer 1976, p. 73.

unique in having solved the problem of providing well-trained managers for business. The same solution stands ready to be applied to government, education, health care, and other institutions. It takes neither genius nor heroism to be a manager, but rather persistence, tough-mindedness, hard work, intelligence, analytical ability and, perhaps most important, tolerance and goodwill.

Another conception, however, attaches almost mystical beliefs to what leadership is and assumes that only great people are worthy of the drama of power and politics. Here, leadership is a psychodrama in which, as a precondition for control of a political structure, a lonely person must gain control of him- or herself. Such an expectation of leadership contrasts sharply with the mundane, practical, and yet important conception that leadership is really managing work that other people do.

Two questions come to mind. Is this mystique of leadership merely a holdover from our collective childhood of dependency and our longing for good and heroic parents? Or is there a basic truth lurking behind the need for leaders that no matter how competent managers are, their leadership stagnates because of their limitations in visualizing purposes and generating value in work? Without this imaginative capacity and the ability to communicate, managers, driven by their narrow purposes, perpetuate group conflicts instead of reforming them into broader desires and goals.

If indeed problems demand greatness, then, judging by past performance, the selection and development of leaders leave a great deal to chance. There are no known ways to train "great" leaders. Furthermore, beyond what we leave to chance, there is a deeper issue in the relationship between the need for competent managers and the longing for great leaders.

What it takes to ensure the supply of people who will assume practical responsibility may inhibit the development of great leaders. Conversely, the presence of great leaders may undermine the development of managers who become very anxious in the relative disorder that leaders seem to generate. The antagonism in aim (to have many competent managers as well as great leaders) often remains obscure in stable and well-developed societies. But the antagonism surfaces during periods of stress and change, as it did in the Western countries during both the Great Depression and World War II. The tension also appears in the struggle for power between theorists and professional managers in revolutionary societies.

It is easy enough to dismiss the dilemma I pose (of training managers while we may need new leaders, or leaders at the expense of managers) by saying that the need is for people who can be *both* managers and leaders. The truth of the matter as I see it, however, is that just as a managerial culture is different from the entrepreneurial culture that develops when leaders appear in organizations, managers and leaders are very different kinds of people. They differ in motivation, personal history, and in how they think and act.

A technologically oriented and economically successful society tends to depreciate the need for great leaders. Such societies hold a deep and abiding faith in rational methods of solving problems, including problems of value, economics, and justice. Once rational methods of solving problems are broken down into elements, organized, and taught as skills, then society's faith in technique over personal qualities in leadership remains the guiding conception for a democratic society contemplating its leadership requirements. But there are times when tinkering and trial and error prove inadequate to the emerging problems of selecting goals, allocating resources, and distributing wealth and opportunity. During such times, the democratic society needs to find leaders who use themselves as the instruments of learning and acting, instead of managers who use their accumulation of collective experience to get where they are going.

The most impressive spokesman, as well as exemplar of the managerial viewpoint, was Alfred P. Sloan, Jr., who, along with Pierre du Pont, designed the modern corporate structure. Reflecting on what makes one management successful while another fails, Sloan suggested that "good management rests on a reconciliation of centralization and decentralization, or 'decentralization with coordinated control.' "[3]

Sloan's conception of management, as well as his practice, developed by trial and error, and by the accumulation of experience. Sloan wrote:

There is no hard and fast rule for sorting out the various responsibilities and the best way to assign them. The balance which is struck . . . varies according to what is being decided, the circumstances of the time, past experience, and the temperaments and skills of the executive involved.[4]

In other words, in much the same way that the inventors of the late nineteenth century tried, failed, and fitted until they hit on a product or method, managers who innovate in developing organizations are "tinkerers." They do not have a grand design or experience the intuitive flash of insight that, borrowing from modern science, we have come to call the "breakthrough."

Managers and leaders differ fundamentally in their world views. The dimensions for assessing these differences include managers' and leaders' orientations toward their goals, their work, their human relations, and their selves.

3. Alfred P. Sloan, Jr., *My Years with General Motors* (New York: Doubleday & Co., 1964), p. 429.
4. Ibid., p. 429.

ATTITUDES TOWARD GOALS

Managers tend to adopt impersonal, if not passive, attitudes toward goals. Managerial goals arise out of necessities rather than desires, and, therefore, are deeply imbedded in the history and culture of the organization.

Frederic G. Donner, chairman and chief executive officer of General Motors from 1958 to 1967, expressed this impersonal and passive attitude toward goals in defining GM's position on product development:

To meet the challenge of the marketplace, we must recognize changes in customer needs and desires far enough ahead to have the right products in the right places at the right time and in the right quantity.

We must balance trends in preference against the many compromises that are necessary to make a final product that is both reliable and good looking, that performs well and that sells at a competitive price in the necessary volume. We must design, not just the cars we would like to build, but more importantly, the cars that our customers want to buy.[5]

Nowhere in this formulation of how a product comes into being is there a notion that consumer tastes and preferences arise in part as a result of what manufacturers do. In reality, through product design, advertising, and promotion, consumers learn to like what they then say they need. Few would argue that people who enjoy taking snapshots *need* a camera that also develops pictures. But in response to novelty, convenience, a shorter interval between acting (taking the snap) and gaining pleasure (seeing the shot), the Polaroid camera succeeded in the marketplace. But it is inconceivable that Edwin Land responded to impressions of consumer need. Instead, he translated a technology (polarization of light) into a product, which proliferated and stimulated consumers' desires.

The example of Polaroid and Land suggests how leaders think about goals. They are active instead of reactive, shaping ideas instead of responding to them. Leaders adopt a personal and active attitude toward goals. The influence a leader exerts in altering moods, evoking images and expectations, and in establishing specific desires and objectives determines the direction a business takes. The net result of this influence is to change the way people think about what is desirable, possible, and necessary.

CONCEPTIONS OF WORK

What do managers and leaders do? What is the nature of their respective work?

Leaders and managers differ in their conceptions. Managers tend to view

5. Ibid., p. 440.

work as an enabling process involving some combination of people and ideas interacting to establish strategies and make decisions. Managers help the process along by a range of skills, including calculating the interests in opposition, staging and timing the surfacing of controversial issues, and reducing tensions. In this enabling process, managers appear flexible in the use of tactics: they negotiate and bargain, on the one hand, and use rewards and punishments, and other forms of coercion, on the other. Machiavelli wrote for managers and not necessarily for leaders.

Alfred Sloan illustrated how this enabling process works in situations of conflict. The time was the early 1920s when the Ford Motor Co. still dominated the automobile industry using, as did General Motors, the conventional water-cooled engine. With the full backing of Pierre du Pont, Charles Kettering dedicated himself to the design of an air-cooled engine, which, if successful, would have been a great technical and market coup for GM. Kettering believed in his product, but the manufacturing division heads at GM remained skeptical and later opposed the new design on two grounds: first, that it was technically unreliable, and second, that the corporation was putting all its eggs in one basket by investing in a new product instead of attending to the current marketing situation.

In the summer of 1923 after a series of false starts and after its decision to recall the copper-cooled Chevrolets from dealers and customers, GM management reorganized and finally scrapped the project. When it dawned on Kettering that the company had rejected the engine, he was deeply discouraged and wrote to Sloan that without the "organized resistance" against the project it would succeed and that unless the project were saved, he would leave the company.

Alfred Sloan was all too aware of the fact that Kettering was unhappy and indeed intended to leave General Motors. Sloan was also aware of the fact that, while the manufacturing divisions strongly opposed the new engine, Pierre du Pont supported Kettering. Furthermore, Sloan had himself gone on record in a letter to Kettering less than two years earlier expressing full confidence in him. The problem Sloan now had was to make his decision stick, keep Kettering in the organization (he was much too valuable to lose), avoid alienating du Pont, and encourage the division heads to move speedily in developing product lines using conventional water-cooled engines.

The actions that Sloan took in the face of this conflict reveal much about how managers work. First, he tried to reassure Kettering by presenting the problem in a very ambiguous fashion, suggesting that he and the Executive Committee sided with Kettering, but that it would not be practical to force the divisions to do what they were opposed to. He presented the problem as being a question of the people, not the product. Second, he proposed to reorganize around the problem by consolidating all functions in a new division that would be responsible for the design, production, and marketing of the new car. This solution, however, appeared as ambiguous as his efforts to placate and keep Kettering in General Motors. Sloan wrote: "My plan was to create an independent pilot operation under the sole jurisdiction of Mr. Kettering, a kind of copper-cooled-car division. Mr. Kettering would designate his own chief engineer and his production staff to solve the technical problems of manufacture."[6]

While Sloan did not discuss the practical value of this solution, which included saddling an inventor with management responsibility, he in effect used this plan to limit his conflict with Pierre du Pont.

In effect, the managerial solution that Sloan arranged and pressed for adoption limited the options available to others. The structural solution narrowed choices, even limiting emotional reactions to the point where the key people could do nothing but go along, and even allowed Sloan to say in his memorandum to du Pont, "We have discussed the matter with Mr. Kettering at some length this morning and he agrees with us absolutely on every point we made. He appears to receive the suggestion enthusiastically and has every confidence that it can be put across along these lines."[7]

Having placated people who opposed his views by developing a structural solution that appeared to give something but in reality only limited options, Sloan could then authorize the car division's general manager, with whom he basically agreed, to move quickly in designing water-cooled cars for the immediate market demand.

Years later Sloan wrote, evidently with tongue in cheek, "The copper-cooled car never came up again in a big way. It just died out, I don't know why."[8]

In order to get people to accept solutions to problems, managers need to coordinate and balance continually. Interestingly enough, this managerial work has much in common with what diplomats and mediators do, with Henry Kissinger apparently an outstanding practitioner. The manager aims at shifting balances of power toward solutions acceptable as a compromise among conflicting values.

What about leaders, what do they do? Where managers act to limit choices, leaders work in the opposite direction, to develop fresh approaches to longstanding problems and to open issues for new options. Stanley and Inge Hoffmann, the political scientists, liken the leader's work to that of the artist. But unlike most artists, the leader himself is an integral part of the aesthetic product. One

6. Ibid., p. 91.
7. Ibid., p. 91.
8. Ibid., p. 93.

cannot look at a leader's art without looking at the artist. On Charles de Gaulle as a political artist, they wrote: "And each of his major political acts, however tortuous the means or the details, has been whole, indivisible and unmistakably his own, like an artistic act."[9]

The closest one can get to a product apart from the artist is the ideas that occupy, indeed at times obsess, the leader's mental life. To be effective, however, the leader needs to project his ideas into images that excite people, and only then develop choices that give the projected images substance. Consequently, leaders create excitement in work.

John F. Kennedy's brief presidency shows both the strengths and weaknesses connected with the excitement leaders generate in their work. In his inaugural address he said, "Let every nation know, whether it wishes us well or ill, that we shall pay any price, bear any burden, meet any hardship, support any friend, oppose any foe, in order to assure the survival and the success of liberty."

This much-quoted statement forced people to react beyond immediate concerns and to identify with Kennedy and with important shared ideals. But upon closer scrutiny the statement must be seen as absurd because it promises a position which if in fact adopted, as in the Viet Nam War, could produce disastrous results. Yet unless expectations are aroused and mobilized, with all the dangers of frustration inherent in heightened desire, new thinking and new choice can never come to light.

Leaders work from high-risk positions, indeed often are temperamentally disposed to seek out risk and danger, especially where opportunity and reward appear high. From my observations, why one individual seeks risks while another approaches problems conservatively depends more on his or her personality and less on conscious choice. For some, especially those who become managers, the instinct for survival dominates their need for risk, and their ability to tolerate mundane, practical work assists their survival. The same cannot be said for leaders who sometimes react to mundane work as to an affliction.

RELATIONS WITH OTHERS

Managers prefer to work with people; they avoid solitary activity because it makes them anxious. Several years ago, I directed studies on the psychological aspects of career. The need to seek out others with whom to work and collaborate seemed to stand out as important characteristics of managers. When asked, for example, to write imaginative stories in response to a picture showing

9. Stanley and Inge Hoffmann, "The Will for Grandeur: de Gaulle as Political Artist," *Daedalus,* Summer 1968, p. 849.

a single figure (a boy contemplating a violin, or a man silhouetted in a state of reflection), managers populated their stories with people. The following is an example of a manager's imaginative story about the young boy contemplating a violin:

> Mom and Dad insisted that junior take music lessons so that someday he can become a concert musician. His instrument was ordered and had just arrived. Junior is weighing the alternatives of playing football with the other kids or playing with the squeak box. He can't understand how his parents could think a violin is better than a touchdown.
>
> After four months of practicing the violin, junior has had more than enough, Daddy is going out of his mind, and Mommy is willing to give in reluctantly to the men's wishes. Football season is now over, but a good third baseman will take the field next spring.[10]

This story illustrates two themes that clarify managerial attitudes toward human relations. The first, as I have suggested, is to seek out activity with other people (i.e., the football team), and the second is to maintain a low level of emotional involvement in these relationships. The low emotional involvement appears in the writer's use of conventional metaphors, even clichés, and in the depiction of the ready transformation of potential conflict into harmonious decisions. In this case, Junior, Mommy, and Daddy agree to give up the violin for manly sports.

These two themes may seem paradoxical, but their coexistence supports what a manager does, including reconciling differences, seeking compromises, and establishing a balance of power. A further idea demonstrated by how the manager wrote the story is that managers may lack empathy, or the capacity to sense intuitively the thoughts and feelings of others. To illustrate attempts to be empathic, here is another story written to the same stimulus picture by someone considered by his peers to be a leader:

> This little boy has the appearance of being a sincere artist, one who is deeply affected by the violin, and has an intense desire to master the instrument.
>
> He seems to have just completed his normal practice session and appears to be somewhat crestfallen at his inability to produce the sounds which he is sure lie within the violin.
>
> He appears to be in the process of making a vow to himself to expend the necessary time and effort to play this instrument until he satisfies himself that he is able to bring forth the qualities of music which he feels within himself.
>
> With this type of determination and carry through, this boy became one of the great violinists of his day.[11]

Empathy is not simply a matter of paying attention to other people. It is also the capacity to take in emotional signals and to make them mean something in a

10. Abraham Zaleznik, Gene W. Dalton, and Louis B. Barnes, *Orientation and Conflict in Career* (Boston: Division of Research, Harvard Business School, 1970), p. 316.
11. Ibid., p. 294.

relationship with an individual. People who describe another person as "deeply affected" with "intense desire," as capable of feeling "crestfallen" and as one who can "vow to himself," would seem to have an inner perceptiveness that they can use in their relationships with others.

Managers relate to people according to the role they play in a sequence of events or in a decision-making *process,* while leaders, who are concerned with ideas, relate in more intuitive and empathic ways. The manager's orientation to people, as actors in a sequence of events, deflects his or her attention away from the substance of people's concerns and toward their roles in a process. The distinction is simply between a manager's attention to *how* things get done and a leader's to *what* the events and decisions mean to participants.

In recent years, managers have taken over from game theory the notion that decision-making events can be one of two types: the win-lose situation (or zero-sum game) or the win-win situation, in which everybody in the action comes out ahead. As part of the process of reconciling differences among people and maintaining balances of power, managers strive to convert win-lose into win-win situations.

As an illustration, take the decision of how to allocate capital resources among operating divisions in a large, decentralized organization. On the face of it, the dollars available for distribution are limited at any given time. Presumably, therefore, the more one division gets, the less is available for other divisions.

Managers tend to view this situation (as it affects human relations) as a conversion issue: how to make what seems like a win-lose problem into a win-win problem. Several solutions to this situation come to mind. First, the manager focuses others' attention on procedure and not on substance. Here the actors become engrossed in the bigger problem of *how* to make decisions, not *what* decisions to make. Once committed to the bigger problem, the actors have to support the outcome since they were involved in formulating decision rules. Because the actors believe in the rules they formulated, they will accept present losses in the expectation that next time they will win.

Second, the manager communicates to his subordinates indirectly, using "signals" instead of "messages." A signal has a number of possible implicit positions in it, while a message clearly states a position. Signals are inconclusive and subject to reinterpretation should people become upset and angry, while messages involve the direct consequence that some people will indeed not like what they hear. The nature of messages heightens emotional response, and, as I have indicated, emotionally makes managers anxious. With signals, the question of who wins and who loses often becomes obscured.

Third, the manager plays for time. Managers seem to recognize that with the passage of time and the delay of major decisions, compromises emerge that take the sting out of win-lose situations; and the original "game" will be superseded by additional ones. Therefore, compromises may mean that one wins and loses simultaneously, depending on which of the games one evaluates.

There are undoubtedly many other tactical moves managers use to change human situations from win-lose to win-win. But the point to be made is that such tactics focus on the decision-making process itself and interest managers rather than leaders. The interest in tactics involves costs as well as benefits, including making organizations fatter in bureaucratic and political intrigue and leaner in direct, hard activity and warm human relationships. Consequently, one often hears subordinates characterize managers as inscrutable, detached, and manipulative. These adjectives arise from the subordinates' perception that they are linked together in a process whose purpose, beyond simply making decisions, is to maintain a controlled as well as rational and equitable structure. These adjectives suggest that managers need order in the face of the potential chaos that many fear in human relationships.

In contrast, one often hears leaders referred to in adjectives rich in emotional content. Leaders attract strong feelings of identity and difference, or of love and hate. Human relations in leader-dominated structures often appear turbulent, intense, and at times even disorganized. Such an atmosphere intensifies individual motivation and often produces unanticipated outcomes. Does this intense motivation lead to innovation and high performance, or does it represent wasted energy?

SENSES OF SELF

In *The Varieties of Religious Experience,* William James describes two basic personality types, "once-born" and "twice-born."[12] People of the former personality type are those for whom adjustments to life have been straightforward and whose lives have been more or less a peaceful flow from the moment of their births. The twice-borns, on the other hand, have not had an easy time of it. Their lives are marked by a continual struggle to attain some sense of order. Unlike the once-borns they cannot take things for granted. According to James, these personalities have equally different world views. For a once-born personality, the sense of self, as a guide to conduct and attitude, derives from a feeling of being at home and in harmony with one's environment. For a twice-born, the sense of self derives from a feeling of profound separateness.

A sense of belonging or of being separate has a practical significance for the kinds of investments managers and leaders make in their careers. Managers see

12. William James, *The Varieties of Religious Experience* (New York: Mentor Books, 1958).

themselves as conservators and regulators of an existing order of affairs with which they personally identify and from which they gain rewards. Perpetuating and strengthening existing institutions enhances a manager's sense of self-worth: he or she is performing in a role that harmonizes with the ideals of duty and responsibility. William James had this harmony in mind—this sense of self as flowing easily to and from the outer world—in defining a once-born personality. If one feels oneself as a member of institutions, contributing to their well-being, then one fulfills a mission in life and feels rewarded for having measured up to ideals. This reward transcends material gains and answers the more fundamental desire for personal integrity which is achieved by identifying with existing institutions.

Leaders tend to be twice-born personalities, people who feel separate from their environment, including other people. They may work in organizations, but they never belong to them. Their sense of who they are does not depend upon memberships, work roles, or other social indicators of identity. What seems to follow from this idea about separateness is some theoretical basis for explaining why certain individuals search out opportunities for change. The methods to bring about change may be technological, political, or ideological, but the object is the same: to profoundly alter human, economic, and political relationships.

Sociologists refer to the preparation individuals undergo to perform in roles as the socialization process. Where individuals experience themselves as an integral part of the social structure (their self-esteem gains strength through participation and conformity), social standards exert powerful effects in maintaining the individual's personal sense of continuity, even beyond the early years in the family. The line of development from the family to schools, then to career, is cumulative and reinforcing. When the line of development is not reinforcing because of significant disruptions in relationships or other problems experienced in the family or other social institutions, the individual turns inward and struggles to establish self-esteem, identity, and order. Here the psychological dynamics center on the experience with loss and the efforts at recovery.

In considering the development of leadership, we have to examine two different courses of life history: (1) development through socialization, which prepares the individual to guide institutions and to maintain the existing balance of social relations; and (2) development through personal mastery, which impels an individual to struggle for psychological and social change. Society produces its managerial talent through the first line of development, while through the second leaders emerge.

Development of Leadership

The development of every person begins in the family. Each person experiences the traumas associated with separating from his or her parents, as well as the pain that follows such frustration. In the same vein, all individuals face the difficulties of achieving self-regulation and self-control. But for some, perhaps a majority, the fortunes of childhood provide adequate gratifications and sufficient opportunities to find substitutes for rewards no longer available. Such individuals, the "once-borns," make moderate identifications with parents and find a harmony between what they expect and what they are able to realize from life.

But suppose the pains of separation are amplified by a combination of parental demands and the individual's needs to the degree that a sense of isolation, of being special, and of wariness disrupts the bonds that attach children to parents and other authority figures? Under such conditions, and given a special aptitude, the origins of which remain mysterious, the person becomes deeply involved in his or her inner world at the expense of interest in the outer world. For such a person, self-esteem no longer depends solely upon positive attachments and real rewards. A form of self-reliance takes hold along with expectations of performance and achievement, and perhaps even the desire to do great works.

Such self-perceptions can come to nothing if the individual's talents are negligible. Even with strong talents, there are no guarantees that achievement will follow, let alone that the end result will be for good rather than evil. Other factors enter into development. For one thing, leaders are like artists and other gifted people who often struggle with neuroses; their ability to function varies considerably even over the short run, and some potential leaders may lose the struggle altogether. Also, beyond early childhood, the patterns of development that affect managers and leaders involve the selective influence of particular people. Just as they appear flexible and evenly distributed in the types of talents available for development, managers form moderate and widely distributed attachments. Leaders, on the other hand, establish, and also break off, intensive one-to-one relationships.

It is a common observation that people with great talents are often only indifferent students. No one, for example, could have predicted Einstein's great achievements on the basis of his mediocre record in school. The reason for mediocrity is obviously not the absence of ability. It may result, instead, from self-absorption and the inability to pay attention to the ordinary tasks at hand. The only sure way an individual can interrupt reverie-like preoccupation and self-absorption is to form a deep attachment to a great teacher or other benevolent person who understands and has the ability to communicate with the gifted individual.

Whether gifted individuals find what they need in one-to-one relationships depends on the availability of sensitive and intuitive mentors who have a vocation in cultivating talent. Fortunately, when the generations do meet and the self-selections occur, we learn more about how to develop leaders and how talented people of different generations influence each other.

While apparently destined for a mediocre career, people who form important one-to-one relationships are able to accelerate and intensify their development through an apprenticeship. The background for such apprenticeships, or the psychological readiness of an individual to benefit from an intensive relationship, depends upon some experience in life that forces the individual to turn inward. A case example will make this point clearer. This example comes from the life of Dwight David Eisenhower, and illustrates the transformation of a career from competent to outstanding.[13]

Dwight Eisenhower's early career in the Army foreshadowed very little about his future development. During World War I, while some of his West Point classmates were already experiencing the war firsthand in France, Eisenhower felt "embedded in the monotony and unsought safety of the Zone of the Interior . . . that was intolerable punishment."[14]

Shortly after World War I, Eisenhower, then a young officer somewhat pessimistic about his career chances, asked for a transfer to Panama to work under General Fox Connor, a senior officer whom Eisenhower admired. The army turned down Eisenhower's request. This setback was very much on Eisenhower's mind when Ikey, his first-born son, succumbed to influenza. By some sense of responsibility for its own, the army transferred Eisenhower to Panama, where he took up his duties under General Connor with the shadow of his lost son very much upon him.

In a relationship with the kind of father he would have wanted to be, Eisenhower reverted to being the son he lost. In this highly charged situation, Eisenhower began to learn from his mentor. General Connor offered, and Eisenhower gladly took, a magnificent tutorial on the military. The effects of this relationship on Eisenhower cannot be measured quantitatively, but, in Eisenhower's own reflections and the unfolding of his career, one cannot overestimate its significance in the reintegration of a person shattered by grief.

As Eisenhower wrote later about Connor,

13. This example is included in Abraham Zaleznik and Manfred F. R. Kets de Vries, *Power and the Corporate Mind* (Boston: Houghton Mifflin, 1975).

14. Dwight D. Eisenhower, *At Ease: Stories I Tell to Friends* (New York: Doubleday, 1967), p. 136.

Life with General Connor was a sort of graduate school in military affairs and the humanities, leavened by a man who was experienced in his knowledge of men and their conduct. I can never adequately express my gratitude to this one gentleman. . . . In a lifetime of association with great and good men, he is the one more or less invisible figure to whom I owe an incalculable debt.[15]

Some time after his tour of duty with General Connor, Eisenhower's breakthrough occurred. He received orders to attend the Command and General Staff School at Fort Leavenworth, one of the most competitive schools in the army. It was a coveted appointment, and Eisenhower took advantage of the opportunity. Unlike his performance in high school and West Point, his work at the Command School was excellent; he was graduated first in his class.

Psychological biographies of gifted people repeatedly demonstrate the important part a mentor plays in developing an individual. Andrew Carnegie owed much to his senior, Thomas A. Scott. As head of the Western Division of the Pennsylvania Railroad, Scott recognized talent and the desire to learn in the young telegrapher assigned to him. By giving Carnegie increasing responsibility and by providing him with the opportunity to learn through close personal observation, Scott added to Carnegie's self-confidence and sense of achievement. Because of his own personal strength and achievement, Scott did not fear Carnegie's aggressiveness. Rather, he gave it full play in encouraging Carnegie's initiative.

Mentors take risks with people. They bet initially on talent they perceive in younger people. Mentors also risk emotional involvement in working closely with their juniors. The risks do not always pay off, but the willingness to take them appears crucial in developing leaders.

CAN ORGANIZATIONS DEVELOP LEADERS?

The examples I have given of how leaders develop suggest the importance of personal influence and the one-to-one relationship. For organizations to encourage consciously the development of leaders as compared with managers would mean developing one-to-one relationships between junior and senior executives and, more important, fostering a culture of individualism and possible elitism. The elitism arises out of the desire to identify talent and other qualities suggestive of the ability to lead and not simply to manage.

The Jewel Companies Inc. enjoy a reputation for developing talented people. The chairman and chief executive officer, Donald S. Perkins, is perhaps a good example of a person brought along through the mentor approach. Franklin J.

15. Ibid., p. 187.

Lunding, who was Perkins's mentor, expressed the philosophy of taking risks with young people this way: "Young people today want in on the action. They don't want to sit around for six months trimming lettuce."[16] This statement runs counter to the culture that attaches primary importance to slow progression based on experience and proved competence. It is a high-risk philosophy, one that requires time for the attachment between senior and junior people to grow and be meaningful, and one that is bound to produce more failures than successes.

The elitism is an especially sensitive issue. At Jewel the MBA degree symbolized the elite. Lunding attracted Perkins to Jewel at a time when business school graduates had little interest in retailing in general, and food distribution in particular. Yet the elitism seemed to pay off: not only did Perkins become the president at age 37, but also under the leadership of young executives recruited into Jewel with the promise of opportunity for growth and advancement, Jewel managed to diversify into discount and drug chains and still remain strong in food retailing. By assigning each recruit to a vice president who acted as sponsor, Jewel evidently tried to build a structure around the mentor approach to developing leaders. To counteract the elitism implied in such an approach, the company also introduced an "equalizer" in what Perkins described as "the first assistant philosophy." Perkins stated:

> Being a good first assistant means that each management person thinks of himself not as the order-giving, domineering boss, but as the first assistant to those who "report" to him in a more typical organizational sense. Thus we mentally turn our organizational charts upside-down and challenge ourselves to seek ways in which we can lead . . . by helping . . . by teaching . . . by listening . . . and by managing in the true democratic sense . . . that is, with the consent of the managed. Thus the satisfactions of leadership come from helping others to get things done and changed—and not from getting credit for doing and changing things ourselves.[17]

While this statement would seem to be more egalitarian than elitist, it does reinforce a youth-oriented culture, since it defines the senior officer's job as primarily helping the junior person.

A myth about how people learn and develop that seems to have taken hold in the American culture also dominates thinking in business. The myth is that people learn best from their peers. Supposedly, the threat of evaluation and even humiliation recedes in peer relations because of the tendency for mutual identification and the social restraints on authoritarian behavior among equals. Peer training in organizations occurs in various forms. The use, for example, of

16. "Jewel Lets Young Men Make Mistakes," *Business Week,* January 17, 1970, p. 90.
17. "What Makes Jewel Shine So Bright," *Progressive Grocer,* September 1973, p. 76.

task forces made up of peers from several interested occupational groups (sales, production, research, and finance) supposedly removes the restraints of authority on the individual's willingness to assert and exchange ideas. As a result, so the theory goes, people interact more freely, listen more objectively to criticism and other points of view and, finally, learn from this healthy interchange.

Another application of peer training exists in some large corporations, such as Philips, N.V. in Holland, where organization structure is built on the principle of joint responsibility of two peers, one representing the commercial end of the business and the other the technical. Formally, both hold equal responsibility for geographic operations or product groups, as the case may be. As a practical matter, it may turn out that one or the other of the peers dominates the management. Nevertheless, the main interaction is between two or more equals.

The principal question I would raise about such arrangements is whether they perpetuate the managerial orientation and preclude the formation of one-to-one relationships between senior people and potential leaders.

Aware of the possible stifling effects of peer relationships on aggressiveness and individual initiative, another company, much smaller than Philips, utilizes joint responsibility of peers for operating units, with one important difference. The chief executive of this company encourages competition and rivalry among peers, ultimately appointing the one who comes out on top for increased responsibility. These hybrid arrangements produce some unintended consequences that can be disastrous. There is no easy way to limit rivalry. Instead, it permeates all levels of the operation and opens the way for the formation of cliques in an atmosphere of intrigue.

A large, integrated oil company has accepted the importance of developing leaders through the direct influence of senior on junior executives. One chairman and chief executive officer regularly selected one talented university graduate whom he appointed his special assistant, and with whom he would work closely for a year. At the end of the year, the junior executive would become available for assignment to one of the operating divisions, where he would be assigned to a responsible post rather than a training position. The mentor relationship had acquainted the junior executive firsthand with the use of power, and with the important antidotes to the power disease called *hubris*—performance and integrity.

Working in one-to-one relationships, where there is a formal and recognized difference in the power of the actors, takes a great deal of tolerance for emotional interchange. This interchange, inevitable in close working arrangements, probably accounts for the reluctance of many executives to become involved in such relationships. *Fortune* carried an interesting story on the departure of a key executive, John W. Hanley, from the top management of

Procter & Gamble, for the chief executive officer position at Monsanto.[18] According to this account, the chief executive and chairman of P&G passed over Hanley for appointment to the presidency and named another executive vice president to this post instead.

The chairman evidently felt he could not work well with Hanley, who, by his own acknowledgment, was aggressive, eager to experiment and change practices, and constantly challenged his superior. A chief executive officer naturally has the right to select people with whom he feels congenial. But I wonder whether a greater capacity on the part of senior officers to tolerate the competitive impulses and behavior of their subordinates might not be healthy for corporations. At least a greater tolerance for interchange would not favor the managerial team player at the expense of the individual who might become a leader.

I am constantly surprised at the frequency with which chief executives feel threatened by open challenges to their ideas, as though the source of their authority, rather than their specific ideas, were at issue. In one case a chief executive officer, who was troubled by the aggressiveness and sometimes outright rudeness of one of his talented vice presidents, used various indirect methods such as group meetings and hints from outside directors to avoid dealing with his subordinate. I advised the executive to deal head-on with what irritated him. I suggested that by direct, face-to-face confrontation, both he and his subordinate would learn to validate the distinction between the authority to be preserved and the issues to be debated.

To confront is also to tolerate aggressive interchange, and has the net effect of stripping away the veils of ambiguity and signaling so characteristic of managerial cultures, as well as encouraging the emotional relationship leaders need if they are to survive.

18. "Jack Hanley Got There by Selling Harder," *Fortune,* November 1976.

12. Pygmalion in Management

J. Sterling Livingston

Pygmalion was a sculptor in Greek mythology who carved a statue of a beautiful woman that subsequently was brought to life. George Bernard Shaw's play, Pygmalion *(the basis for the musical hit* My Fair Lady*), has a somewhat similar theme; the essence is that one person, by his effort and will, can transform another person. And in the world of management, many executives play Pygmalion-like roles in developing able subordinates and in stimulating their performance. What is the secret of their success? How are they different from managers who fail to develop top-notch subordinates? And what are the implications of all this for the problem of excessive turnover and disillusionment among talented young people in business? Such are the questions discussed here. The title of the article was inspired by* Pygmalion in the Classroom, *a book by Professor Robert Rosenthal and Lenore Jacobson that describes the effect of expectations on the intellectual development of children.*

In George Bernard Shaw's *Pygmalion,* Eliza Doolittle explains:

> You see, really and truly, apart from the things anyone can pick up (the dressing and the proper way of speaking, and so on), the difference between a lady and a flower girl is not how she behaves, but how she's treated. I shall always be a flower girl to Professor Higgins, because he always treats me as a flower girl, and always will; but I know I can be a lady to you, because you always treat me as a lady, and always will.

Some managers always treat their subordinates in a way that leads to superior performance. But most managers, like Professor Higgins, unintentionally treat their subordinates in a way that leads to lower performance than they are capable of achieving. The way managers treat their subordinates is subtly influenced by what they expect of them. If a manager's expectations are high, productivity is likely to be excellent. If his expectations are low, productivity is likely to be poor. It is as though there were a law that caused a subordinate's performance to rise or fall to meet his manager's expectations.

The powerful influence of one person's expectations on another's behavior has long been recognized by physicians and behavioral scientists and, more recently, by teachers. But heretofore the importance of managerial expectations for individual and group performance has not been widely understood. I have documented this phenomenon in a number of case studies prepared during the past decade for major industrial concerns. These cases and other evidence available from scientific research now reveal:

☐ What a manager expects of his subordinates and the way he treats them largely determine their performance and career progress.

☐ A unique characteristic of superior managers is their ability to create high performance expectations that subordinates fulfill.

☐ Less effective managers fail to develop similar expectations, and, as a consequence, the productivity of their subordinates suffers.

☐ Subordinates, more often than not, appear to do what they believe they are expected to do.

Impact on Productivity

One of the most comprehensive illustrations of the effect of managerial expectations on productivity is recorded in studies of the organizational experiment undertaken in 1961 by Alfred Oberlander, manager of the Rockaway District Office of the Metropolitan Life Insurance Company.[1] He had observed that outstanding insurance agencies grew faster than average or poor agencies and that new insurance agents performed better in outstanding agencies than in average or poor agencies, regardless of their sales aptitude. He decided, therefore, to group his superior men in one unit to stimulate their performance and to provide a challenging environment in which to introduce new salesmen.

Accordingly, Oberlander assigned his six best agents to work with his best assistant manager, an equal number of average producers to work with an average assistant manager, and the remaining low producers to work with the least able manager. He then asked the superior group to produce two thirds of the premium volume achieved by the entire agency the previous year. He described the results as follows:

Shortly after this selection had been made, the men in the agency began referring to this select group as a "super-staff" since, due to the fact that we were operating this group as a unit, their esprit de corps was very high. Their production efforts over the first 12 weeks far surpassed our most optimistic expectations . . . proving that groups of men of sound ability can be motivated beyond their apparently normal productive

1. See "Jamesville Branch Office (A)," MET003A, and "Jamesville Branch Office (B)," MET003B (Boston, Sterling Institute, 1969).

capacities when the problems created by the poor producer are eliminated from the operation.

Thanks to this fine result, over-all agency performance improved 40 percent and stayed at this figure.

In the beginning of 1962 when, through expansion, we appointed another assistant manager and assigned him a staff, we again utilized this same concept, arranging the men once more according to their productive capacity.

The assistant managers were assigned . . . according to their ability, with the most capable assistant manager receiving the best group, thus playing strength to strength. Our agency over-all production again improved by about 25–30 percent, and so this staff arrangement was continued until the end of the year.

Now in this year of 1963, we found upon analysis that there were so many men . . . with a potential of half a million dollars or more that only one staff remained of those men in the agency who were not considered to have any chance of reaching the half-million-dollar mark.[2]

Although the productivity of the "super-staff" improved dramatically, it should be pointed out that the productivity of men in the lowest unit, "who were not considered to have any chance of reaching the half-million-dollar mark" actually declined and that attrition among these men increased. The performance of the superior men rose to meet their managers' expectations, while that of the weaker men declined as predicted.

SELF-FULFILLING PROPHECIES

However, the "average" unit proved to be an anomaly. Although the district manager expected only average performance from this group, its productivity increased significantly. This was because the assistant manager in charge of the group refused to believe that he was less capable than the manager of the "super-staff" or that the agents in the top group had any greater ability than the agents in his group. He insisted in discussions with his agents that every man in the middle group had greater potential than the men in the "super-staff," lacking only their years of experience in selling insurance. He stimulated his agents to accept the challenge of outperforming the "super-staff." As a result, in each year the middle group increased its productivity by a higher percentage than the "super-staff" did (although it never attained the dollar volume of the top group).

It is of special interest that the self-image of the manager of the "average" unit did not permit him to accept others' treatment of him as an "average"

2. "Jamesville Branch Office (B)," p. 2.

manager, just as Eliza Doolittle's image of herself as a lady did not permit her to accept others' treatment of her as a flower girl. The assistant manager transmitted his own strong feelings of efficacy to his agents, created mutual expectancy of high performance, and greatly stimulated productivity.

Comparable results occurred when a similar experiment was made at another office of the company. Further confirmation comes from a study of the early managerial success of 49 college graduates who were management-level employees of an operating company of the American Telephone and Telegraph Company. David E. Berlew and Douglas T. Hall of the Massachusetts Institute of Technology examined the career progress of these managers over a period of five years and discovered that their relative success, as measured by salary increases and the company's estimate of each man's performance and potential, depended largely on the company's expectations of them.[3]

The influence of one person's expectations on another's behavior is by no means a business discovery. More than half a century ago, Albert Moll concluded from his clinical experience that subjects behaved as they believed they were expected to.[4] The phenomenon he observed, in which "the prophecy causes its own fulfillment," has recently become a subject of considerable scientific interest. For example:

☐ In a series of scientific experiments, Robert Rosenthal of Harvard University has demonstrated that a "teacher's expectation for her pupils' intellectual competence can come to serve as an educational self-fulfilling prophecy.[5]

☐ An experiment in a summer Headstart program for 60 preschoolers compared the performance of pupils under (a) teachers who had been led to expect relatively slow learning by their children, and (b) teachers who had been led to believe their children had excellent intellectual ability and learning capacity. Pupils of the second group of teachers learned much faster.[6]

Moreover, the healing professions have long recognized that a physician's or psychiatrist's expectations can have a formidable influence on a patient's physical or mental health. What takes place in the minds of the patients and the healers, particularly when they have congruent expectations, may determine the outcome. For instance, the havoc of a doctor's pessimistic prognosis has often

3. "Some Determinants of Early Managerial Success," Alfred P. Sloan School of Management Organization Research Program #81-64 (Cambridge, Massachusetts Institute of Technology, 1964), pp. 13–14.

4. Robert Rosenthal and Lenore Jacobson, *Pygmalion in the Classroom* (New York, Holt, Rinehart and Winston, Inc., 1968), p. 11.

5. Ibid., Preface, p. vii.

6. Ibid., p. 38.

been observed. Again, it is well known that the efficacy of a new drug or a new treatment can be greatly influenced by the physician's expectations—a result referred to by the medical profession as a "placebo effect."

When salesmen are treated by their managers as supersalesmen, as the "super-staff" was at Metropolitan Rockaway District Office, they try to live up to that image and do what they know supersalesmen are expected to do. But when salesmen with poor productivity records are treated by their managers as not having "any chance" of success, as the low producers at Rockaway were, this negative expectation also becomes a managerial self-fulfilling prophecy.

Unsuccessful salesmen have great difficulty maintaining their self-image and self-esteem. In response to low managerial expectations, they typically attempt to prevent additional damage to their egos by avoiding situations that might lead to greater failure. They either reduce the number of sales calls they make or avoid trying to "close" sales when that might result in further painful rejection, or both. Low expectations and damaged egos lead them to behave in a manner that increases the probability of failure, thereby fulfilling their managers' expectations. Let me illustrate:

> Not long ago I studied the effectiveness of branch bank managers at a West Coast bank with over 500 branches. The managers who had had their lending authority reduced because of high rates of loss became progressively less effective. To prevent further loss of authority, they turned to making only "safe" loans. This action resulted in losses of business to competing banks and a relative decline in both deposits and profits at their branches. Then, to reverse that decline in deposits and earnings, they often "reached" for loans and became almost irrational in their acceptance of questionable credit risks. Their actions were not so much a matter of poor judgment as an expression of their willingness to take desperate risks in the hope of being able to avoid further damage to their egos and to their careers.

> Thus, in response to the low expectations of their supervisors, who had reduced their lending authority, they behaved in a manner that led to larger credit losses. They appeared to do what they believed they were expected to do, and their supervisors' expectations became self-fulfilling prophecies.

Power of Expectations

Managers cannot avoid the depressing cycle of events that flow from low expectations merely by hiding their feelings from subordinates. If a manager believes a subordinate will perform poorly, it is virtually impossible for him to mask his expectations, because the message usually is communicated unintentionally, without conscious action on his part.

Indeed, a manager often communicates most when he believes he is communicating least. For instance, when he says nothing, when he becomes "cold" and "uncommunicative," it usually is a sign that he is displeased by a subordinate or believes he is "hopeless." The silent treatment communicates negative feelings even more effectively, at times, than a tongue-lashing does. What seems to be critical in the communication of expectations is not what the boss says, so much as the *way he behaves*. Indifferent and noncommittal treatment, more often than not, is the kind of treatment that communicates low expectations and leads to poor performance.

COMMON ILLUSIONS

Managers are more effective in communicating low expectations to their subordinates than in communicating high expectations to them, even though most managers believe exactly the opposite. It usually is astonishingly difficult for them to recognize the clarity with which they transmit negative feelings to subordinates. To illustrate again:

The Rockaway district manager vigorously denied that he had communicated low expectations to the men in the poorest group who, he believed, did not have "any chance" of becoming high producers. Yet the message was clearly received by those men. A typical case was that of an agent who resigned from the low unit. When the district manager told the agent that he was sorry he was leaving, the agent replied, "No, you're not; you're glad." Although the district manager previously had said nothing to the man, he had unintentionally communicated his low expectations to his agents through his indifferent manner. Subsequently, the men who were assigned to the lowest unit interpreted the assignment as equivalent to a request for their resignation.

One of the company's agency managers established superior, average, and low units, even though he was convinced that he had no superior or outstanding subordinates. "All my assistant managers and agents are either average or incompetent," he explained to the Rockaway district manager. Although he tried to duplicate the Rockaway results, his low opinions of his men were communicated—not so subtly—to them. As a result, the experiment failed.

Positive feelings, on the other hand, often do not come through clearly enough. For example:

Another insurance agency manager copied the organizational changes made at the Rockaway District Office, grouping the salesmen he rated highly with the best manager, the average salesmen with an average manager, and so on. However, improvement did not result from the move. The Rockaway district manager therefore investigated the situation. He discovered that the assistant manager in charge of the high-performance unit was unaware that his manager considered him to be the best. In fact, he and the other agents doubted that the agency manager really believed there was any difference in their abilities. This agency manager was a stolid, phlegmatic, unemotional man who treated his men in a rather pedestrian way. Since high expectations had not been communicated to the men, they did not understand the reason for the new organization and could not see any point in it. Clearly, the way a manager *treats* his subordinates, not the way he organizes them, is the key to high expectations and high productivity.

IMPOSSIBLE DREAMS

Managerial expectations must pass the test of reality before they can be translated into performance. To become self-fulfilling prophecies, expectations must be made of sterner stuff than the power of positive thinking or generalized confidence in one's fellow men—helpful as these concepts may be for some other purposes. Subordinates will not be motivated to reach high levels of productivity unless they consider the boss's high expectations realistic and achievable. If they are encouraged to strive for unattainable goals, they eventually give up trying and settle for results that are lower than they are capable of achieving. The experience of a large electrical manufacturing company demonstrates this; the company discovered that production actually declined if production quotas were set too high, because the workers simply stopped trying to meet them. In other words, the practice of "dangling the carrot just beyond the donkey's reach," endorsed by many managers, is not a good motivational device.

Scientific research by David C. McClelland of Harvard University and John W. Atkinson of the University of Michigan[7] has demonstrated that the relationship of motivation to expectancy varies in the form of a bell-shaped curve, as shown in the chart opposite.

The degree of motivation and effort rises until the expectancy of success reaches 50%, then begins to fall even though the expectancy of success continues to increase. No motivation or response is aroused when the goal is perceived as being either virtually certain or virtually impossible to attain.

Moreover, as Berlew and Hall have pointed out, if a subordinate fails to meet performance expectations that are close to his own level of aspirations, he will "lower his personal performance goals and standards, his . . . performance will tend to drop off, and he will develop negative attitudes toward the task activity

7. See John W. Atkinson, "Motivational Determinants of Risk-Taking Behavior," *Psychological Review,* Vol. 64, No. 6, 1957, p. 365.

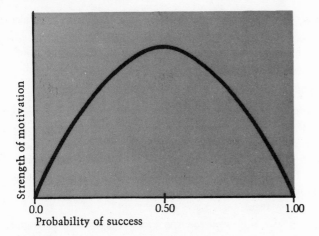

Strength of motivation

0.0   0.50   1.00
Probability of success

or job."[8] It is therefore not surprising that failure of subordinates to meet the unrealistically high expectations of their managers leads to high rates of attrition; such attrition may be voluntary or involuntary.

SECRET OF SUPERIORITY

Something takes place in the minds of superior managers that does not occur in the minds of those who are less effective. While superior managers are consistently able to create high performance expectations that their subordinates fulfill, weaker managers are not successful in obtaining a similar response. What accounts for the difference?

The answer, in part, seems to be that superior managers have greater confidence than other managers in their own ability to develop the talents of their subordinates. Contrary to what might be assumed, the high expectations of superior managers are based primarily on what they think about themselves— about their own ability to select, train, and motivate their subordinates. What the manager believes about himself subtly influences what he believes about his subordinates, what he expects of them, and how he treats them. If he has confidence in his ability to develop and stimulate them to high levels of performance, he will expect much of them and will treat them with confidence that his expectations will be met. But if he has doubts about his ability to stimulate them, he will expect less of them and will treat them with less confidence.

Stated in another way, the superior manager's record of success and his confidence in his ability give his high expectations credibility. As a consequence,

8. David E. Berlew and Douglas T. Hall, "The Socialization of Managers: Effects of Expectations on Performance," *Administrative Science Quarterly,* September 1966, p. 208.

his subordinates accept his expectations as realistic and try hard to achieve them.

The importance of what a manager believes about his training and motivational ability is illustrated by "Sweeney's Miracle,"[9] a managerial and educational self-fulfilling prophecy:

James Sweeney taught industrial management and psychiatry at Tulane University, and he also was responsible for the operation of the Biomedical Computer Center there. Sweeney believed that he could teach even a poorly educated man to be a capable computer operator. George Johnson, a black man who was a former hospital porter, became janitor at the computer center; he was chosen by Sweeney to prove his conviction. In the morning, George Johnson performed his janitorial duties, and in the afternoon Sweeney taught him about computers.

Johnson was learning a great deal about computers when someone at the university concluded that, to be a computer operator, one had to have a certain I.Q. score. Johnson was tested, and his I.Q. indicated that he would not be able to learn to type, much less operate a computer.

But Sweeney was not convinced. He threatened to quit unless Johnson was permitted to learn to program and operate the computer. Sweeney prevailed, and he is still running the computer center. Johnson is now in charge of the main computer room and is responsible for training new employees to program and operate the computer.

Sweeney's expectations were based on what he believed about his own teaching ability, not on Johnson's learning credentials. What a manager believes about his ability to train and motivate subordinates clearly is the foundation on which realistically high managerial expectations are built.

The Critical Early Years

Managerial expectations have their most magical influence on young men. As subordinates mature and gain experience, their self-image gradually hardens, and they begin to see themselves as their career records imply. Their own aspirations, and the expectations of their superiors, become increasingly controlled by the "reality" of their past performance. It becomes more and more difficult for them, and for their managers, to generate mutually high expectations unless they have outstanding records.

Incidentally, the same pattern occurs in school. Rosenthal's experiments with educational self-fulfilling prophecies consistently demonstrate that teachers' expectations are more effective in influencing intellectual growth in younger

9. See Robert Rosenthal and Lenore Jacobson, op. cit., pp. 3–4.

children than in older children. In the lower grade levels, particularly in the first and second grades, the effects of teachers' expectations are dramatic.[10] In the upper grade levels, teachers' prophecies seem to have little effect on a child's intellectual growth, although they do affect his motivation and attitude toward school. While the declining influence of teachers' expectations cannot be completely explained, it is reasonable to conclude that younger children are more malleable, have fewer fixed notions about their abilities, and have less well-established reputations in the schools. As they grow, particularly if they are assigned to "tracks" on the basis of their records, as is now often done in public schools, their beliefs about their intellectual ability and their teachers' expectations of them begin to harden and become more resistant to influence by others.

KEY TO FUTURE PERFORMANCE

The early years in a business organization, when a young man can be strongly influenced by managerial expectations, are critical in determining his future performance and career progress. This is shown by a study at American Telephone and Telegraph Company:

Berlew and Hall found that what the company initially expected of 49 college graduates who were management-level employees was the most critical factor in their subsequent performance and success. The researchers concluded: "The .72 correlation between how much a company expects of a man in his first year and how much he contributes during the next five years is too compelling to be ignored."[11]

Subsequently, the two men studied the career records of 18 college graduates who were hired as management trainees in another of the American Telephone and Telegraph Company's operating companies. Again they found that both expectations and performance in the first year correlated consistently with later performance and success.[12]

Berlew and Hall summarized their research by stating:

"Something important is happening in the first year.... Meeting high company expectations in the critical first year leads to the internalization of positive job attitudes and high standards; these attitudes and standards, in turn, would first lead to and be reinforced by strong performance and success in later years. It should also follow that a new manager who meets the challenge of one highly demanding job will be given subsequently a more demanding job, and his level of contribution will rise as he responds

10. Ibid., pp. 74–81.
11 "Some Determinants of Early Managerial Success," pp. 13–14.
12. "The Socialization of Managers: Effects of Expectations on Performance," p. 219.

to the company's growing expectations of him. The key . . . is the concept of the first year as a *critical period for learning,* a time when the trainee is uniquely ready to develop or change in the direction of the company's expectations." [13]

MOST INFLUENTIAL BOSS

A young man's first manager is likely to be the most influential person in his career. If this manager is unable or unwilling to develop the skills the young man needs to perform effectively, the latter will set lower standards for himself than he is capable of achieving, his self-image will be impaired, and he will develop negative attitudes toward his job, his employer, and—in all probability—his career in business. Since his chances of building a successful career with his employer will decline rapidly, he will leave, if he has high aspirations, in hope of finding a better opportunity. If, on the other hand, his manager helps him achieve his maximum potential, he will build the foundation for a successful career. To illustrate:

With few exceptions, the most effective branch managers at a large West Coast bank were mature men in their forties and fifties. The bank's executives explained that it took considerable time for a man to gain the knowledge, experience, and judgment required to handle properly credit risks, customer relations, and employee relations.

However, one branch manager, ranked in the top 10% of the managers in terms of effectiveness (which included branch profit growth, deposit growth, scores on administrative audits, and subjective rankings by superiors), was only 27 years old. This young man had been made a branch manager at 25, and in two years he not only improved the performance of his branch substantially but also developed his younger assistant manager so that he, in turn, was made a branch manager at 25.

The man had had only average grades in college, but, in his first four years at the bank, he had been assigned to work with two branch managers who were remarkably effective teachers. His first boss, who was recognized throughout the bank for his unusual skill in developing young men, did not believe that it took years to gain the knowledge and skill needed to become an effective banker. After two years, the young man was made assistant manager at a branch headed by another executive, who also was an effective developer of his subordinates. Thus it was that when the young man was promoted to head a branch, he confidently followed the model of his two previous superiors in operating his branch, quickly established a record of outstanding performance, and trained his assistant (as he had been trained) to assume responsibility early.

Contrasting records

For confirming evidence of the crucial role played by a person's first bosses, let us turn to selling, since performance in this area is more easily measured

13. Ibid., pp. 221–222.

than in most managerial areas. Consider the following investigations:

In a study of the careers of 100 insurance salesmen who began work with either highly competent or less-than-competent agency managers, the Life Insurance Agency Management Association found that men with average sales aptitude test scores were nearly five times as likely to succeed under managers with good performance records as under managers with poor records; and men with superior sales aptitude scores were found to be twice as likely to succeed under high-performing managers as under low-performing managers.[14]

The Metropolitan Life Insurance Company determined in 1960 that differences in the productivity of new insurance agents who had equal sales aptitudes could be accounted for only by differences in the ability of managers in the offices to which they were assigned. Men whose productivity was high in relation to their aptitude test scores invariably were employed in offices that had production records among the top third in the company. Conversely, men whose productivity was low in relation to their test scores typically were in the least successful offices. After analyzing all the factors that might have accounted for these variations, the company concluded that differences in the performance of new men were due primarily to differences in the "proficiency in sales training and direction" of the local managers.[15]

A study I conducted of the performance of automobile salesmen in Ford dealerships in New England revealed that superior salesmen were concentrated in a few outstanding dealerships. For instance, 10 of the top 15 salesmen in New England were in 3 (out of approximately 200) of the dealerships in this region; and 5 of the top 15 men were in one highly successful dealership; yet 4 of these men previously had worked for other dealers without achieving outstanding sales records. There seemed to be little doubt that the training and motivational skills of managers in the outstanding dealerships were the critical factor.

ASTUTE SELECTION

While success in business sometimes appears to depend on the "luck of the draw," more than luck is involved when a young man is selected by a superior manager. Successful managers do not pick their subordinates at random or by the toss of a coin. They are careful to select only those who they "know" will succeed. As Metropolitan's Rockaway district manager, Alfred Oberlander, insisted: "Every man who starts with us is going to be a top-notch life insurance man, or he would not have received an invitation to join the team."[16]

When pressed to explain how they "know" whether a man will be successful,

14. Robert T. Davis, "Sales Management in the Field," HBR January-February 1958, p. 91.
15. Alfred A. Oberlander, "The Collective Conscience in Recruiting," address to Life Insurance Agency Management Association Annual Meeting, Chicago, Illinois, 1963, p. 5.
16. Ibid., p. 9.

superior managers usually end up by saying something like, "The qualities are intangible, but I know them when I see them." They have difficulty being explicit because their selection process is intuitive and is based on interpersonal intelligence that is difficult to describe. The key seems to be that they are able to identify subordinates with whom they can probably work effectively—men with whom they are compatible and whose body chemistry agrees with their own. They make mistakes, of course. But they "give up" on a subordinate slowly because that means "giving up" on themselves—on their judgment and ability in selecting, training, and motivating men. Less effective managers select subordinates more quickly and give up on them more easily, believing that the inadequacy is that of the subordinate, not of themselves.

Developing Young Men

Observing that his company's research indicates that "initial corporate expectations for performance (with real responsibility) mold subsequent expectations and behavior," R. W. Walters, Jr., director of college employment at the American Telephone and Telegraph Company, contends that: "Initial bosses of new college hires must be the best in the organization."[17] Unfortunately, however, most companies practice exactly the opposite.

Rarely do new graduates work closely with experienced middle managers or upper-level executives. Normally, they are bossed by first-line managers who tend to be the least experienced and least effective in the organization. While there are exceptions, first-line managers generally are either "old pros" who have been judged as lacking competence for higher levels of responsibility, or they are younger men who are making the transition from "doing" to "managing." Often, these managers lack the knowledge and skill required to develop the productive capabilities of their subordinates. As a consequence, many college graduates begin their careers in business under the worst possible circumstances. Since they know their abilities are not being developed or used, they quite naturally soon become negative toward their jobs, employers, and business careers.

Although most top executives have not yet diagnosed the problem, industry's greatest challenge by far is the underdevelopment, underutilization, and ineffective management and use of its most valuable resource—its young managerial and professional talent.

17. "How to Keep the Go-getters," *Nation's Business,* June 1966, p. 74.

DISILLUSION AND TURNOVER

The problem posed to corporate management is underscored by the sharply rising rates of attrition among young managerial and professional personnel. Turnover among managers one to five years out of college is almost twice as high now as it was a decade ago, and five times as high as two decades ago. Three out of five companies surveyed by *Fortune* magazine in the fall of 1968 reported that turnover rates among young managers and professionals were higher than five years ago.[18] While the high level of economic activity and the shortage of skilled personnel have made job-hopping easier, the underlying causes of high attrition, I am convinced, are underdevelopment and underutilization of a work force that has high career aspirations.

The problem can be seen in its extreme form in the excessive attrition rates of college and university graduates who begin their careers in sales positions. Whereas the average company loses about 50% of its new college and university graduates within three to five years, attrition rates as high as 40% in the *first* year are common among college graduates who accept sales positions in the average company. This attrition stems primarily, in my opinion, from the failure of first-line managers to teach new college recruits what they need to know to be effective sales representatives.

As we have seen, young men who begin their careers working for less-than-competent sales managers are likely to have records of low productivity. When rebuffed by their customers and considered by their managers to have little potential for success, the young men naturally have great difficulty in maintaining their self-esteem. Soon they find little personal satisfaction in their jobs and, to avoid further loss of self-respect, leave their employers for jobs that look more promising. Moreover, as reports about the high turnover and disillusionment of those who embarked on sales careers filter back to college campuses, new graduates become increasingly reluctant to take jobs in sales.

Thus, ineffective first-line sales management sets off a sequence of events that ends with college and university graduates avoiding careers in selling. To a lesser extent, the same pattern is duplicated in other functions of business, as evidenced by the growing trend of college graduates to pursue careers in "more meaningful" occupations, such as teaching and government service.

A serious "generation gap" between bosses and subordinates is another significant cause of breakdown. Many managers resent the abstract academic language and narrow rationalization typically used by recent graduates. As one

18. Robert C. Albrook, "Why It's Harder to Keep Good Executives," *Fortune,* November 1968, p. 137.

manager expressed it to me: "For God's sake, you need a lexicon even to talk with these kids." Noncollege managers often are particularly resentful, perhaps because they feel threatened by the bright young men with book-learned knowledge that they do not understand.

For whatever reason, the "generation gap" in many companies is eroding managerial expectations of new college graduates. For instance, I know of a survey of management attitudes in one of the nation's largest companies that revealed that 54% of its first-line and second-line managers believed that new college recruits were "not as good as they were five years ago." Since what a manager expects of a subordinate influences the way he treats him, it is understandable that new graduates often develop negative attitudes toward their jobs and their employers. Clearly, low managerial expectations and hostile attitudes are not the basis for effective management of new men entering business.

Conclusion

Industry has not developed effective first-line managers fast enough to meet its needs. As a consequence, many companies are underdeveloping their most valuable resource—talented young men and women. They are incurring heavy attrition costs and contributing to the negative attitudes young people often have about careers in business.

For top executives in industry who are concerned with the productivity of their organizations and the careers of young employees, the challenge is clear: it is to speed the development of managers who will treat their subordinates in ways that lead to high performance and career satisfaction. The manager not only shapes the expectations and productivity of his subordinates, but also influences their attitudes toward their jobs and themselves. If he is unskilled, he leaves scars on the careers of the young men, cuts deeply into their self-esteem, and distorts their image of themselves as human beings. But if he is skillful and has high expectations of his subordinates, their self-confidence will grow, their capabilities will develop, and their productivity will be high. More often than he realizes, the manager is Pygmalion.

13. Is Management Really an Art?

Henry M. Boettinger

If, as many have argued, management really is an art, if leadership entails more than analytic and statistical skills, it would make sense for businessmen to look at the creative and performing arts to learn something about their own endeavors. The author investigates what he sees as three indispensable aspects of the artistic process—craft, vision, and communication. Just as artists need to master their crafts, business managers need to perfect their skills in dealing with people and in expressing themselves verbally; just as artists need visions and passion to realize them, managers need imagination and audacity to redesign their organizations; and just as great masters communicate their visions, great leaders inspire those who work for them. To complete this process, managers as well as artists need constructive criticism and models to emulate. Thus one of the obligations of top management is to teach and guide. The author concludes that for its own survival, business should take on the responsibility of nurturing its own leaders.

In sheer banality, few statements exceed the assertion that management is an art. Grizzled managerial veterans sometimes shout it to silence insolent or overeager newcomers who brandish shiny scientific methods during decision-making sessions. On happier occasions, appreciative observers use it to explain unexpected success, when chance and the probability of failure surrender to competence and nerve. And who could deny that such a platitude is in some way descriptive of experience? Surely no sensible person would say that management is not an art. Perhaps if one takes the comparison of management to art seriously, he will find that it has some important implications for modern managerial practice.

Over the past few years, I have sought out successful practitioners and teachers in some endeavors recognized as arts—musical performance, ballet, painting, sculpture, architecture, writing, surgery, cooking, and certain sports of

AUTHOR'S NOTE: The author wishes to acknowledge the support given this article by the Oxford Centre for Management Studies, Oxford University.

the individual type, like fencing and horsemanship. My purpose was to see if they have some attributes in common that could be applied to the teaching and practice of management.

All the statements about art that I have gathered come out something like this: art is the imposition of a pattern, a vision of a whole, on many disparate parts so as to create a representation of that vision; art is an imposition of order on chaos. The artist has to have not only the vision that he or she wants to communicate but also the skills or craft with which to present the vision. This process entails choosing the correct art form and, within that art form, the correct technique. In good art, the result is a blending of vision and craft that involves the viewer, reader, or listener without requiring that he separate the parts in order to appreciate the whole.

We all know people who have vision but no skill in implementing it; we call them dreamers. In the arts they are the habitués of cafés who constantly talk about "work in progress" that is never completed. Others we know possess highly honed skills but no visions to work on. Their melancholy lament identifies them: "If only I had an idea, what a story I could write!" or "If only I knew what top management really wants me to do!" Those without ideas are hacks who grind out potboilers according to worn-out formulas. We can learn nothing from them except what to avoid. In any enterprise both dreamers and technicians, regardless of their level, are condemned to ineffectiveness.

To see how this distinction relates to management, we shall examine two qualities good artists have—competence (technical skill) and imagination (the facility of mind to arrive at visions). By combining these qualities, a leader, like an artist, can communicate his visions and create a response in those around him.

"Criticism Comes Easier than Craftsmanship"
—*Pliny the Elder*

Surgical instruments, brushes, chisels, swords, reins, spatulas, or ballet shoes are never used properly when given to a true novice, even if he has great talent. Intuition alone is insufficient for even amateur performance. In the arts, the proper use of tools evolves after years of innumerable mistakes and a few precious successes. Artists create instruments to meet needs as they arise and perfect methods of use by trial and error. These methods are handed down from teacher to pupil and are virtually never arrived at instinctively or without practice. There are no short cuts to developing a skill. It is not exaggerating to say that professional techniques are nearly always anti-instinctive and that every master once had his instincts broken in for disciplined service.

In the management of complex affairs like politics and government, unprepared practitioners often intervene and cause misdirected, though well-intentioned, results. This may account for Jay Forrester's law: "Any intuitive alteration of a complex system will cause it to become worse off."[1] Most of us would not be comfortable using intuition to operate an atomic reactor, a submarine, or an airplane. We might tremble if asked to remove a brain tumor, direct a symphony, jump a horse, or prepare a state dinner.

All these activities are, however, far less complicated than successfully launching a new economic policy, introducing new technology to an entire industry, or properly restructuring an institution's organization to meet new markets and demands. Yet these are things that managers are expected to be able to do well, rapidly, and almost immediately. Are companies making sure that their managers are masters of the best available techniques before they are called on to carry out tasks that are fraught with grave human, political, and social consequences? I doubt it. Acquiring technique is essential to having competence.

MANAGEMENT'S MATERIALS

Most artists use materials whose nature must be known in depth to produce the best work. Musical instruments, for example, are complex in their construction and difficult to manipulate. Each material has its own strengths and weaknesses, and the true craftsman knows its limitations and how to work with it so that it does not resist his efforts. The manager's materials are human talents, including his own. The core of his job is to accompish grand purposes through human efforts. The French author and politician Jean-Jacques Servan-Schreiber sums up the idea: "Management is the art of arts because it is the organizer of talent."

Organizing others' talents

We may ask how a manager acquires a master's knowledge of his materials. Like an architect wishing to transcend the limits of previous construction methods, he must study the nature of his materials and experiment with their possibilities. If a manager believes all people in his charge to be homogeneous

1. Jay Forrester, *Urban Dynamics* (Cambridge, Mass., MIT Press, 1969), p. 9.

material that can be shaped into any form by the chisels of marketplace pressures, he has a very primitive outlook on motivation. With nineteenth-century overseers and captains of shanghaied crews, he shares a policy based on the knout.

No doubt some managers can deal with people in this way, but the techniques of their management art are as unperfected as their philosophy is barbaric. Today, managers with such an outlook are akin to architects designing houses without knowing the stress limits of their materials. They can survive only in relatively isolated enclaves of society. Those who manage others need a knowledge and appreciation of motivation, which requires a far deeper understanding of human beings as individuals than brandishing the lash does.

But how does a business teach a manager to deal with subordinates, particularly with seasoned veterans, whose activity is essential to the organization's growth? At the very least, he should be instructed to avoid antagonizing them unnecessarily, as political leaders new to office so often do. An organization's management is like a knife whose cutting edge is imagination but whose momentum is derived from the mass of experience and effort of the personnel behind that edge. Both edge and mass are needed to make the knife cut. The adjectives "dull" and "sharp" are not unknown in appraising overall managerial effectiveness.

A manager must understand not only the persons in his own organization but also the drives, anxieties, and reactions of those beyond the perimeter of his control—stockholders, customers, competitors, and government officials. Our knowledge of management "material" is both tentative and limited. This lack of knowledge is one reason why waves of fashion in new manipulation and motivation methods sweep over us from time to time.

In other arts, the masters of skill assign a large role to learning from error and practice. Fencing and riding masters physically punish their pupils for deviating from proper form and often use ridicule to correct lapses in concentration. One master believes that skill in these two arts can only be developed to the highest level under the harshest conditions of military discipline. He said, "It's remarkable how a few days of reflection on his errors in the guardhouse can cause someone to keep his heels down and his elbows in."

We certainly cannot use military discipline in management, but errors could be seen as opportunities for the teacher to direct future practice and training. In the arts, such training progresses in gradual steps, from simple elements to more complex maneuvers, each to be thoroughly learned before going on to new levels. All masters know that if an area of fundamental skill is neglected, it will ultimately plague all future work and cause serious flaws in performance. A fencer whose disengage riposte is never developed is as limited in the way he can maneuver in a match as a manager is who realizes he does not know how to deal with people. His energies go into protecting that weakness rather than into developing a better strategy.

Companies' management training schemes, however, seldom leave room for the gradual process of learning. Consequently, there are many people, some in high positions, who are deficient in even an elementary understanding of the importance of human relations. And when ill-prepared persons have to deal with areas in which they are weak—for instance, accounting methods and sophisticated management information systems—their lack of human skills is even more crucial than their lack of quantitative ones. The gaps in their training place continual stress on their subordinates.

It need not be this way. Few persons can learn anything faster than managers faced with real problems. But they must be willing to suspend their status as hierarchs and to assume the humbler status of students under competent teachers. For insecure, second-rate people, this produces a social problem of which first-rate people are, happily, not even aware. A company wishing to give a good education in management always provides ways to minimize this potentially neurotic friction.

One final point relative to training in competence in the arts is that only someone who can actually perform in an art is qualified to teach it. There is no question that constructive criticism from an informed bystander is helpful; actors, for instance, can learn a great deal about human motivation from psychiatrists. Nevertheless, this kind of procedure is different from the one an actor goes through to show another how to express human feelings.

This kind of apprenticeship in the art of management is more difficult to complete than is apprenticeship in the other arts. Dancers, actors, painters, and musicians usually arrive at the master's studio at a tender age and have high motivation to keep presenting themselves for the harsh selection process.

Not so in management. Few managers have had childhood visions of becoming managers, and usually it is not until later in life after preparing for other professions that they discover a talent or interest in management.

The "late-blooming" managers suffer because of the general attitude companies have toward taking responsibility for management training. Not one member of the New York Philharmonic Orchestra expects the management of the orchestra to help him develop his skills on his instrument. That is entirely up to him, and he knows his reputation as a musician is totally dependent on his performance ability. Intention, potential, and aspiration have no place or weight in his appraisal. How well he can play is what counts, not how well he might play with further training. In the music world, a chasm separates the first-rate from the second-rate, and everyone not only knows it but accepts it.

The difference between the orchestra and the corporation is that the individual musician has had a teacher, and probably will have one, all his life. The teacher has responsibility for the performance. In a corporation, the student manager has to learn his art in an environment where the goals are always changing and from a hierarchy that sees his development as his own affair.

To learn the art of management entirely on one's own is impossible, even in a master-student relationship. Higher managers must, therefore, assume some responsibility for the training of those who will succeed them and who are currently subordinate to them. There is an apparent perversity in the obligation to assist others to destroy, or at least to make obsolete, one's current operational vision, and yet that is the noble imperative for the best teachers of management.

To make one's subordinates into mere carbon copies of oneself and to embrace selection methods which make that easy betrays the future growth of any enterprise or institution. When asked by a bright pupil, "When should I discontinue my lessons from you?," a wise painting master replied, "When your pictures begin to look like copies of mine." We all know of leaders so dominant that their subordinates try to emulate their every act. Lacking the master's genius, they succeed only in copying his faults and producing parodies of his accomplishments. This is why the history of art is marked by great break-throughs of genius that become worn-out or stylized by the school they have created. This stagnation sets up conditions for the emergence of a new vision of greatness to arrest the previous decline. The aphorism "Nothing fails like success," coined by William Inge, dean of St. Paul's, finds it roots in situations like these.

Lord Ragland, that unfortunate military leader during the Crimean War, said that when faced with a problem he always asked himself, "What would the Duke of Wellington have done?" I submit that the thought of imitating someone else never crossed the duke's mind. Instead, he asked himself, "What will my enemy do?" That is the approach of a great leader to all conflict situations, from battles to competition for markets. The leader uses his imagination for strokes of genius geared to the present; the imitator perverts his imagination by trying to find the right action for conditions long consigned to the dustbin of history. The results of both attitudes are predictable and deserved.

I submit two propositions:

☐ When the tools and materials of an art are inanimate, as in sculpture, or symbolic, as in accounting and music, development is a personal resonsibility.

☐ When the materials of an art are others' personalities, talents, and efforts, as in military, government, and business management, personal development depends to some extent on those in overall charge. The education of its members becomes a social responsibility of the institution itself, which it must assume to assure its own survival. Skills that good managers ought to possess fall into this category.

Organizing one's own talents

Written and oral expression, two skills a modern manager must command so as to be fully effective, can be improved by proper training. In large organizations, reliance on discussion alone is extremely risky because each step in transmission degrades the message. As a message passes through a hierarchy, rebounding from the prejudices, anxieties, and vested interests of each receiver, it can become unrecognizable to its originator. The ability to speak before groups of varied size, from 3 to 3,000 is also needed. It is scandalous that there are managers inept at this most ancient tool of leadership. Part of this skill is the ability to engage in conference dialogue and to present ideas and programs. By saving time and clarifying issues, making even slight progress in articulating ideas in the echelons below top management could amplify the decisiveness of an organization.

What do business leaders do now to remedy such deficiencies? Very little. They seem to assume that managers can pick up these skills quickly and easily or that specialists in writing and presentations can be hired whenever needed. A few managers *do* have natural gifts in these areas, but most do not. The idea that hired hands can express a manager's true thinking in his own style is a trap executives of every level fall into. It is akin to having a hireling turn what Mozart hums into musical notation and orchestration. It might sound like music, but it would not be Mozart.

In any truly creative work, both the concept and the striving for its expression interact with and amplify each other. If a manager does not undergo the discipline necessary to express his vision in clear prose or persuasive speech, the realization of the vision could suffer. Fuzzy expression hides loose thinking, which can be disastrous when coupled with authority and responsibility.

"The painter's brush consumes his dreams"
—William Butler Yeats

Visions spring from contemplation of problems, events, and possibilities; the realization of visions requires passion and action. A manager may take either of two attitudes toward his problems: he can see them as isolated puzzles to be solved independently of each other, or he can see them as connected puzzles to be solved by redesigning.

The management sciences necessarily adopt the first of these approaches, but the management arts require the second. This leads us to inquire about what we may learn from the arts in arriving at those "good" visions that are the sine qua non of every masterwork of art—or of management.

MANAGEMENT'S VISIONS

In his *Holism and Evolution,* Jan Christiaan Smuts, the South African statesman and philosopher, wrote, "A whole, which is more than the sum of its parts, has something internal, some inwardness of structure and function, some specific inner relation, some internality of character or nature that constitutes that *more.*"[2] This is obvious in things like poetry, painting, or music, where single units of words, pigments, or tones are combined to produce a pattern that does not exist in the units themselves. In Smuts's terms, that pattern is something more, and it is more vital than any assembly of units, however large, that lacks such a pattern.

Much as a curious child disassembles a clock into its constituent gears, spindles, and springs, analysis breaks wholes into smaller and smaller pieces for examination in isolation. Most of the great advances in science have followed this procedure—elucidation of finer and finer detail with more and more powerful instruments of observation. But analysis can be done only on something that already exists, and for it to exist, there has to be some relation among the parts, almost as if someone had designed it. For instance, a truly creative scientist is one who has a vision of what the separate things he observes might constitute. His "science" is a way of proving his "art."

Every artist attempts to produce cohesive patterns by selecting, rejecting, and relating the various components available to him to express his vision. Every manager also deals with such designs; some he has inherited, some he struggles to express, some he loathes, and others are still unknown and appear only as early tremors of imagination.

Without recognition of the central role of imagination and individual performance in the management art, the subject of management as an academic discipline would become mere elementary science pedagogy—all analysis and no synthesis. Unfortunately, minds trained to carry out effective syntheses and to make the necessary judgments for general management are still in short supply.

Without that clear vision that underlies all good art, the manager's components are merely isolated bits and pieces. As with the other arts, there are no objective criteria by which the manager can judge whether one arrangement is superior to another. The criteria he uses to select a configuration are subjective.

2. New York, Viking Press, 1961, p. xii.

Each criterion is weighted by his personal prejudice, belief, tradition, and temperament. He builds and destroys every time he makes rearrangements of his possibilities, much as any artist does in composing, painting, or sculpting.

A conference of top executives selecting personnel to head a set of lower units is akin to a crew of fresco painters, each of whom adds his stroke to finish the picture that will be viewed as a whole. As it is for the artist, every move the executive makes is a compromise between the vision he has and the limits of the materials available to him. This constant tension between vision and possibility accounts for the maxim "Great works of art are never finished; they are abandoned." Later, when their project cuts its way through the tangle of disasters and successes to a conclusion, others can analyze whether or not the right actions were initiated, the best people selected, or the correct information used.

By placing this emphasis on vision as a product of the imagination, I do not mean to imply that the process is totally uninfluenced by experience. The ability to form visions can be nurtured by the sort of education that encourages audacity and experimentation yet provides constructive criticism and models to follow.

Learning from experience

Managers can learn from critiques of success and failure, but such criticism is useful only to the extent that it helps them produce a better vision the next time around. Sometimes a leader's awareness of tactics that fail makes it difficult for him to tolerate any design other than one that will maintain a state of equilibrium. This pursuit of the status quo can either mark a consolidation stage in which many radical changes are finally digested or signal the beginning of an institution's decline.

If a manager loses heart and does not follow any dream or vision, the organization is doomed. But it often takes courage and an audacious self-confidence to maintain one's course. At the onset of his deafness, Beethoven said, "I will take fate by the throat." While not given to such vivid metaphors, every manager worth his salt must sometimes embrace the same attitude when he faces an overwhelming problem or opportunity.

I once asked a ballet teacher if she could tell which students would become expert performers. "Yes, and usually after a few sessions," she answered. "Most all who come here have fine bodies and good coordination, and they quickly learn the positions in the book sense. But first-class work can only be done by those who can shed their inhibitions. Those who constantly worry about how they look and what people will think or who hold themselves back out of fear of appearing ridiculous will never make it. I try to help those who are merely timid, and I have a little success, but inhibition is the most difficult obstacle of all. Some have 'it'; some don't. I don't pretend to understand it, even though I can recognize it quickly."

The ballet mistress articulated what most of us recognize as the debilitating effects of self-consciousness. Experienced managers know the same phenomenon; men and women of superb credentials turn in mediocre work, and others far less equipped, on paper, produce results of surprisingly high quality. Audacity and self-confidence are not the same as rashness; a healthy self-confidence is based on developed and tested powers of thought and action, not on nervous compulsion to do anything at all except think. Audacity builds on previous challenges and successes, in which confidence has been reinforced by every step forward and each problem addressed is one of increased difficulty.

This kind of reinforced experience constitutes the value of veterans in military units. Confident and seasoned, the veterans stiffen the resolve of green troops and furnish nuclei around which the troops' confidence can build. Using the veterans as models, the young troops learn how to respond in action. Without such models, the first noises of combat can trigger uncontrollable panic.

Learning from models

In the arts, teachers draw their students' attention to models, to great works by master artists. In fact, the urge to join such pantheons motivates the highly talented to their greatest efforts far more than does the prospect of economic gain. The memoirs of successful practitioners nearly always indicate that they were influenced, usually at an early age, by great men and women who advanced their field and by examples of masterpieces encountered in museums or libraries.

Following the maxim that youth needs models far more than it does critics is sound advice for attracting talent. One almost searches in vain, however, for good biographies of great managers. I believe there is an unworked mine of profound inspirational value in the stories of those who have made great contributions to the art of management. How else can our young people be attracted by worthy motives to this calling? Statesmen are nurtured on Plutarch; soldiers study the great captains; painters, poets, musicians, and writers follow the lofty standards set by their idols.

In comparison, neophytes to the art of management are badly served. Most histories of enterprise are dreary chronicles that carry a whiff of official committee approval and are more likely to repel than attract the nascent manager in search of the romance that abounds in the art of management. Every enterprise worth anything has begun as an adventure, and every one in the future will do the same. Books and articles that let us rediscover purpose will not only inspire the young but will also invigorate the cynical, who feel that their jobs have lost meaning.

Example is still the best teacher, and the only way to learn to see things as wholes (to attempt the art of design) and acquire the requisite audacity is to watch how others do it or read about how they did it.

One of the most remarkable enterprises in history, by any standard, was the East India Company. The story of how merchant adventurers fought for and gained tenuous footholds in trade and, through a series of advances led by men of genius, governed the subcontinent as it took its place as a modern nation is hard to beat in fiction. Phillip Woodruff's two volumes *The Men Who Ruled India*[3] set it all down in a compelling narrative. Every page is rich in lessons for modern managers. I am still astonished to know that, at its peak, the Indian civil service consisted of only 1,000 members; what a colorful and bold collection they were! The incredibly early ages at which they were given enormous responsibilities and the unbounded energy they applied to their shared vision make one humble when comparing current business practice in these matters.

I do not intend to develop this theme of the men who ruled India except in two regards: their attitudes toward training and their quest for excellence in performance. In the early days of the Indian civil service, the tutelage of new members (most of them in their late teens) was that of associating with an elder brother who instructed them in their duties. The mentor gave them progressively difficult missions, extricated them when they were over their heads, wrote confidential reports on their progress, and made recommendations for new assignments designed to develop strengths and eliminate weaknesses. As a tribal leader might see to the survival of his tribe by ensuring that the training of its young men is adequate, the governor-general himself examined the progress reports on the young members of the civil service.

By 1800, the scope and depth of the company's responsibilities called for nothing less than the creation and management of an entire government apparatus. In 1806, the directors established what I believe to be the first institutions dedicated solely to teaching the art of management—one at Fort William in India, another at Haileybury in England. The English school had a distinguished faculty covering a broad curriculum, including Oriental languages, political economy, mathematics, science, philosophy, history, and Asiatic literature. The school lasted until 1858, when it closed after transfer of the company's responsibilities to the Crown.

It is not surprising that the managers of the East India Company became leaders and governors of India. The minute-in-council of Lord Wellesley,[4] who set up the Fort William school, contains lessons for all managers and leaders.

3. New York, St. Martin's Press, 1954.
4. *Asiatic Annual Register*, 1802.

According to him, the school's purpose was "to establish a just conformity between their personal considerations and the dignity and importance of their public stations, and a sufficient correspondence between their qualifications and their duties" for those men recruited in the company's service. The school's founders knew that the art of government could not be taught in a lecture hall, but they also knew that turning a young man unprepared for the burdens of management into the chaos of raw experience was not sensible. To them, education was necessary in order to benefit from experience.

The managers they trained therefore had skills and vision. But they also had the desire to communicate their purpose. And here is the final parallel between management and art. An artist is judged by how well he communicates his purposes to the viewer by reflecting his visions in his works of art. Similarly, in business the manager must be a leader who can communicate his vision to his subordinates. Given a leader they can respect, even the old veterans will put backbone into a program of action.

"Genuine poetry can communicate before it is understood"
—*T. S. Eliot*

A vision, however arrived at, demands realization in some concrete form. If the vision or its realization is faulty, we call the result bad art—or bad management; if the realization is congruent with a good vision, we call it a masterpiece—or effective management. The point is an obvious one: the source of good management is found in the imagination of leaders, persons who form new visions and manifest them with a high degree of craft. The blending of vision and craft communicates the purpose. In the arts, people who do that well are masters. In business, they are leaders.

Another contrast between the arts and the sciences is that they are apprehended in different ways. Whereas the benefits of science can come to people secondhand, almost by report, the appreciation of art always personally involves the spectator. The artist, then, must engage and involve the viewer, listener, or reader in the work of art itself. For science to be understood, there is no such condition.

At every level of management, from shop floor to board room, across the spectrum of our institutions, whether government, business, education, armed forces, or the church, we need a rediscovery of the value of the individual imagination and a rekindling of that passion for humane purposes which is the authentic light of leadership. To manage is to lead, and to lead others requires that one enlist the emotions of others to share a vision as their own. If *that* is not an art, then nothing is.

14. Everyone Who Makes It Has a Mentor

Interviews with F. J. Lunding, G. L. Clements, and D. S. Perkins*

In 1931 John Hancock, chairman of Jewel Tea Company, hired a young lawyer, Franklin J. Lunding, to negotiate the acquisition of some food stores in Chicago. By 1942, Lunding was president of Jewel Tea Co. Inc. He was only 36 years old. Like Hancock, Lunding also needed help running the food stores, so he appointed the young office manager, George L. Clements, to be assistant to the president. By 1951, Clements was president, and he was 41 years old. In 1953, in an effort to bring new blood into the organization, Lunding hired Donald S. Perkins as a trainee. With the farsighted guidance of both Lunding and Clements, Perkins became president of the Jewel Companies in 1965, when he was 37 years old. Perkins is now chairman and chief executive officer. That simple fact epitomizes what is now a Jewel tradition; young people shall be given their heads, to challenge the organization to grow. These young people will also have an older person in the organization to look after them in their early years to ensure that their careers get off to a good start. Out of these relationships it is hoped that young people learn to take risks, accept a philosophical commitment to sharing, and learn to relate to people in an intuitive empathetic way. These mentor relationships develop leaders. In the interviews that follow, Messrs. Lunding, Clements, and Perkins discuss these issues, how they affected each other's lives, and ultimately how the imprints of their personalities and relationships can be seen in the strategies and policies of the Jewel Companies.

Franklin J. Lunding

HBR: Was there anyone in your background who gave you the idea that to give young people responsibility early is the way to help them grow in a business? For instance, did John Hancock [chairman of Jewel Tea, 1924–1954] do anything for you when you were a young man?

*These interviews were conducted and edited by Eliza G. C. Collins, senior editor, and Patricia Scott, manuscript editor, HBR.

Yes he did. He recommended me as general counsel of this company in 1931 when I was only 25 years old. I came out here to Chicago, and the first thing I had to do was buy a group of food stores. I handled that negotiation, the contract, and the whole works myself.

How did Hancock know you?

I knew Hancock because his daughter was in my class at the University of North Dakota. He was always interested in young people. Maybe that's one of the reasons I developed somewhat the same interest. Although we were very different people, we got along fine. He stayed on in the business, as chairman of the board. That was fine with me; I was still running it.

Did you feel that you got a sense of confidence from Hancock's choosing you?

No, I never thought about it. I didn't have any feeling that I couldn't do things. I was brought up in the country, in North Dakota, where my father was a farm implement dealer. My parents were both immigrants, one from Norway, one from Sweden. My four sisters and I, immigrants' children, all got through college and some professional schools. But we did it on our own.

Between my freshman and sophomore years, that would be 1924, I went as an immigrant with a bicycle and about three dollars in my pocket to Mossbank, Saskatchewan to sell books to farmers. I started riding on my bike from farm to farm on those country roads selling books—"12 courses on agriculture, 11,200 simple practical ideas all indexed." You get used to doing things for yourself.

So by the time you got to Jewel Tea with Hancock and Maurice Karker [president 1924–1942], you had nothing to lose by accepting the challenge and running the business?

No, in fact I liked it. By 1934 I was assistant to the president, Karker, and then in 1937, merchandise manager, in effect running things in our Food Stores.

Did Hancock leave you alone or was there a lot of coaching in your relationship?

I did things my way. Of course, that might have been his way for all I knew. I would call him up and tell him I was going to do something, and he'd usually say, "That's fine."

You felt you could challenge Hancock and Karker's judgment and experience?

There was no need. I was responsible for the business. I used my own judgment and they understood that. For instance, in 1938 the Food Stores were failing and the meat markets were really losing money. I had an experienced meat man, but every time I'd reduce prices to get more sales, he'd go out and reduce the quality. You can't run markets like that, so I said to him, "As a company we aren't going to be here much longer if things go on this way," and he said, "You're just going to have an awful time without me." I said, "Do you mean we'd lose money?" He said, "Yes." So I said, "How much are we making now? I'm going to lose it my way."

So, you had a sense of your own responsibility; you weren't saying, "Oh well, Karker's the president, and if the stores go bust, it's in his lap."

No, I was desperate because I was responsible for running those stores. And, eventually, I offered to quit because of them. Karker had said I could have only eight new meat markets, when I knew meat markets were the key to survival. So I said, "If I'm going to fail, I'll fail based on my judgment. I'm not going to risk my reputation on someone else's judgment. I'll take my lumps on my own, but not on someone else's if I think they're wrong." Karker approved an unlimited number of markets.

Say a subordinate of yours felt exactly the same way about a decision you'd made.

If someone felt that way, I'd be glad to have him come and tell me I was wrong. This is connected to the idea I was interested in more than any other, and that is to have a philosophy people can believe in and that will last. The way you hear Perkins talking these days, I guess it's lasted. And that's what I called the first assistant philosophy.

What was the philosophy?

Simply that executive responsibility involves assisting the people down the line to be successful. The boss in any department is the first assistant to those who report to him. You've got to live your life in a worthwhile way. This is a worthwhile philosophy. It doesn't hurt people, it helps them; and after it helps them, it helps the business.

But it was unique for the time. People weren't used to thinking in terms of an upside down organization in those days. The typical executive was more like a king, saying, "I make all the decisions, and all you little gnomes do my bidding, or else."

In any event, in the 1950s, I finally got my thoughts down on paper and put out a little book called *Sharing a Business,* which tells how I felt about whose responsibility was what.[1]

Would you say that Hancock had any direct influence on the philosophy that you thought up for Jewel Tea?

No, that was all my own thinking. It's a much harder job to be a first assistant to people working for you than to tell them what to do. It makes doing your job the same thing as trying to bring people along. If you *can't* do it, and

1. Franklin J. Lunding, "Sharing a Business," Chicago: Updegraff Press Ltd., 1954.

they don't fit, then first try to help them, but if that doesn't work get them out . . . don't let them be dead on the job.

Did you choose George Clements the way Hancock chose you?

George was already in the company. He started out in the Expense Section as a very young kid. When I became president of the company, in 1942, there was a war on and there were a lot of problems. Previously I was running the Food Stores, but then I had to go look out for all of the business.

George was the office manager and did some accounting work. But it seemed to me that he had an adminstrative ability and some talents that the two older, more experienced people there didn't have, so I just pulled him out and made him vice president. I had to have someone good to get some of these things done.

Did you feel like his first assistant?

Yes. George needed help. But he sure could take it, and run with it.

Could he have done it without your sponsorship?

I guess not, but . . . I couldn't have done it without him either; remember, I needed him more than he needed me. What I loved was that all you had to do was give him a go. I just worked hell out of him. He's one of the great operating doers.

When you picked George Clements out over the heads of these other two fellows, were you consciously choosing him to be a successor to yourself?

No, I just wanted to make sure someone was looking after the Food Stores. But I had a feeling he had it.

Isn't it true that you actually brought Donald Perkins to Jewel?

Yes. In 1951 he married a girl whose name was Phyllis Babb, and her father was with Lever Brothers, where I was chairman of the Executive Committee. I was able to get a good look at Don.

What was it about Donald Perkins that made you think he was someone who ought to be in your company?

Well, his school record was very good. He was a poor kid, and had a widowed mother. Somewhat accidentally he happened to end up at Yale; he hadn't thought about it, in fact, until someone came along with a scholarship. When he was graduated, his mother came down on a bus to New Haven and they went home to St. Louis on a bus together. That's pretty good.

Did you plan that Perkins would advance in the company?

Consider what this business looked like in those days. We didn't have a very high social standing. Mothers would rather have their boys and girls be bankers or lawyers. When you're in the chain store business, people kind of assume that you have a weak mind and a strong back. So we had to figure out ways of getting brains into the business. That's another way the first assistant philosophy helps the business; it attracts the smart ones.

Most young people fear that they'll get out someplace and no one will notice them. So you ask, how did I get Don Perkins? Well, I think he was willing to believe me. I said to him, "If you have it, you'll make it, and if you don't, you won't. And you can make it early. Look at my record—I'm not going to deny anyone the same chance."

Did you spend a considerable amount of your time handpicking people?

I'm looking for them all the time. Still am. Can't stop. Perkins wasn't as hard to get as Walter Elisha, who is president of our Jewel Food Stores. He took me a few years and three martinis.

Once, I wrote to the secretary of the Alumni Association at the University of North Dakota, Lloyd Stone, whom I knew, and said, "Lloyd, if you see a really unique, unusual person, send him to me, but don't bother me with anyone else." He only sent me one, Wes Christopherson, who's now president of Jewel Companies, of course.

What is it you look for?

I think anyone who can get through college with a good record must have some brains. Don Perkins was a Baker Scholar. We didn't insist that all be Phi Beta Kappas or MBAs or anything like that, but you have a much better chance with people with brains than with dimwits. There aren't many like Christopherson, Perkins, or Clements . . .you have to locate them.

Did you actively encourage George Clements to look out for the young Don Perkins?

No, Clements' job was to take care of everyone in the business. He did a first-class job of it, too. However, I think there was a direct mentor relationship between George and Don. But Don wasn't the fair-haired boy; he earned everything he got. I wouldn't have pushed for him to be what he is if he didn't have it, in my judgment. I knew what he was doing, but I wasn't paying any unusual attention to Perkins, any more than to anyone else.

It seems as if you think that the way to encourage young people to produce is to let them alone on a day-to-day level.

Sure, and you put them into a program. We sent Don out to California for several months to travel door-to-door for our Routes Department, in which we sell directly to the homemaker.

So you actually manage their careers?

Of course, and the Routes is a great way to find out a lot about the public.

You can't sell in 35 or 40 kitchens a day for months and not find out about what goes on in the kitchens of America. Young people hate it while they do it, but they all say afterward that it is great. You see, you're face to face with the customer and the hard business of selling. In top management, you can get too sophisticated, whereas the Routes put you up against people of all kinds. It's the greatest training ground there is.

Like you riding your bicycle in Canada, going door to door?

That's right, I learned a lot. The guy who is going to go out and knock on cold doors is a pretty strong individual.

George L. Clements

Do you feel that mentor relationships have played a strong part in shaping Jewel leadership?

Absolutely. The first thing that was important for Jewel in forming mentor relationships, which I never thought of before, is that John Hancock, who was president of Jewel right after World War I, brought in Franklin Lunding. Hancock placed the young Lunding in Jewel. To my knowledge that began the sponsorship of young people, and Lunding followed that by bringing in young men. I don't know what Lunding would say to this, but I think that's what started it.

Another important thing that happened, and he may not be conscious of this, is that along the way Lunding went to the Harvard Business School for one of those Advanced Management courses, and he came back with an increased awareness that business has a social responsibility—that it isn't just there to make money and sell people, take a profit and use people, but it has to give people something. This, I think, was important to what happened.

The next important thing is that Lunding gave me my first leg-up in the business.

How did you feel when he did that?

I was more than a little floored. I was the office manager at the time and the youngest of the lot. He had men who knew merchandising and operating a hell of a lot better than I did. I remember saying to him, "I don't know. You jumped me over these guys. I don't know how I'm going to make it and I don't know what to do." He said, "Well, why don't you go to work for them?" That was all I needed.

So I got the fellows in, heads of parts of the business, and said, "Look, I'm it . . . he made me the executive vice president. But, here's the business, and these are your responsibilities. Now my job, as I look at it, is to work for you, not you for me. I'm going to keep you off each other's throats; I'm going to pull you together when I have to. There may be times when there's a difference of opinion, and I'll have to make a decision. But, fundamentally, I'm going to work for you."

Did you feel that Lunding was working for you?

Lunding was a leader. Lunding was the one that gave me, gave the others, the philosophy by which to live. In other words, he gave us that first assistant philosophy—that's what he did.

We were visiting one day and he said, "George, your aim in life is to make Jewel a better place to trade, a better place to work." I don't think he realized what he said, but I took it and ran with it. And all the way through our relationship it was like that. He'd say it and I'd run with it.

Would you say that your relationship with him changed you?

Oh yes, oh yes. I would say he gave me a direction, a personal philosophy, I'd been missing. When he brought up the idea that to run a business is to share it, I could convert that immediately to care and share, and I could take that out and sell it to the organization—the more you care, the more you share.

If something was not going the way you thought it ought to, did you feel that you could challenge him openly?

You've got to understand Lunding. There are ways, if you think somebody's wrong, to manage the situation so that egos are not hurt or punctured and, sometimes, you can get around it. Sure there were times when I could give him the hard sell, and he'd take it. He was great; he'd give me something to work with and leave me alone.

Lunding left the Food Stores office early and moved his office down to the Loop, and sat there all by himself. He was that kind of a man. He could work from that office with a secretary all alone; I could never do that. He would read things, then telephone, make suggestions, ask questions, or go to conventions and make speeches. Me, I had to be involved in the organization, be involved with people, involved in the problems. I'm the type of guy that somebody always had to put something in my head and heart for me to really go.

How would you describe your relationship with Perkins?

Perkins was brought in by Lunding, around 1953. Don Booz was the first MBA; Perkins was the second or third. But he hadn't been here too long before I knew he was my successor. He had such tremendous ability; with numbers and with people, his peers, bosses, and subordinates. In fact, I remember one job he was on; the person who ran the department said, "You know, he's really good. This is the first time I've ever had someone working for me that I know I'm eventually going to work for."

What do you think most characterized him?

He was very mature. Like myself and Lunding he had a background of hard work, and he could work with people. If he had a question about somebody, he'd keep it to himself. He wouldn't run that person down; he'd just forget it and work around it. When I realized that he had it—and that was early in his career—he was still in his 20s—I never said anything, never told him, never told anybody. But I felt it was my job to give him experience around the organization, to do it carefully, and try to teach him patience and take some of the Harvard influence out of him.

What was particularly bothersome?

I don't know that Don agrees with me—but I think that the case study method teaches people that there is *a* problem and there is *an* answer. And once you find that answer, then you're all through. Business isn't like that . . . it's not all black and white; it's gray. It's not simple; it's very grand. Sometimes problems are never solved. You have to keep going with them. You struggle with them; you work with them and it takes time, years sometimes. Don had to learn to be patient and not say, "I did that; what do you have for me now."

How did you help him do that?

I just sat on him. I'd let him make a mistake, and he'd never make the same mistake twice. For instance, after he'd been on his first real assignment as merchandising manager of the Routes for a while, he felt he'd been there long enough. So I said to him, "Do you have a replacement?" He said, "Oh, sure, so and so. . . ." Well, I didn't think the person was qualified, but as far as Don was concerned, he was, enough for Don to be able to move to another job, which was uppermost in his mind.

What happened?

The man wasn't right for the job.

And guessing the person wasn't right, you were able to sit back and let Perkins do this?

Oh sure, sure. Maybe I was wrong about the man. I've been wrong many times, and young people absolutely have to have the freedom to make mistakes. Just so they aren't too big. What was more important, me being right or Don learning?

With that kind of incident, would the two of you discuss it afterward?

I mentioned it and he admitted he was wrong, but he didn't want to talk about it. If you're trying to develop a person, you don't hammer into him again and again that he made a mistake. He knows he made a mistake. The question then is—what are you going to do about it?

Would it have been difficult for you if Perkins had challenged you?

Not really, though it's very difficult for some executives to give young people their heads and accept their challenges, and there were a lot of young people who had no sound basis for what they were saying, but Perkins wasn't one of them. Another important thing in developing young people is to let them know what is going on so that they can challenge you.

How did you do that?

Way early in the game, I heard that a pretty smart young guy had said, "I wonder what the secret six are up to now." That was me and my Food Stores staff. Very obviously we weren't communicating what went on in our meetings. I decided we had to let people know what we were doing. They needed that. Any young person needs that. And out of this came, we gave it a fancy name, the Management Development Council.

When was this?

That was after 1960 when we started annual recruiting of MBAs. That council is still operating because I talked to them this year. It was an attempt to bring together young people with potential from every part of the business to communicate what was going on in their parts of the business.

The council also brings in a Perkins, a Clements, a Dick Cline of Osco, or a Jim Hensen of Star Markets, and the young people ask them point-blank questions. They are really encouraged to challenge top management as to what it is doing. The Osco person on the Council might not ask Dick Cline a touchy question, but some Food Stores person might.

Were you consciously trying to develop Perkins?

Oh, sure, but it wasn't hard, he was so ambitious. The only other thing I had to do besides give him experience was to get him—you know "the bright boy right out of the Harvard Business School"—accepted in the organization. I knew he had to have a success. So the idea was to expose him to many parts of the business—first, so that he knew the business; and second, so people like the one I mentioned earlier who said, "I never had somebody work for me whom I'm going to work for," would know him.

The best place to put him at one point early on was in Jewel Food Stores, so we made him chief of staff, Store Operating. That was the best way to slip him in there. And it wasn't long before his tremendous talent showed itself: he was always writing speeches for the boss, working out all sorts of problems. He became, very obviously, a guy that people respected. Those that didn't probably weren't worth a damn anyway.

Was that enough of a success for him?

No, he needed a real tough baby. So after he was in charge of growth planning, and development, I made him vice president of the Routes department. And he squealed. He really didn't want to go there, but it wasn't going to be easy. We were starting to franchise the Routes, and if he could help make that work, he'd have a success in store operating, merchandising, and management.

Would his chances to advance have been affected if he'd failed?

It would have been too bad. But it never came to my mind that it was a make-or-break thing because it never occurred to me that he couldn't do it. I just knew he had to have a success, and was confident he would.

Is an ingredient of success the superior's confidence?

Absolutely. A boss has to have every bit of confidence in a person. The minute the boss loses confidence, the person will feel it, and he's going to go downhill. But remember, I don't think that there was a real personal relationship with Perkins before he was executive vice president. He was just working for the company. He was one individual. After all, I was trying to do the same thing with a lot of individuals. I tried to see what I could put into them rather than what they could do for me.

Did Lunding share your feelings about Perkins, as early on as you did?

Lunding felt strongly about Perkins. He certainly pushed him at me.

He pushed him at you?

Perkins had an ear with Lunding. Well, there were times that I suspected he did, though I'm not sure. I didn't raise the question. I don't give a damn. But there were times when it seemed to me that something would come from Lunding that would indicate that Perkins had said something. But I can't ever remember a situation where Lunding said, "Now, look, Perkins talked to me about this and don't you think you ought to do something?" I can't ever remember a situation like that.

If Perkins had run around me all the time, he wouldn't have been the man I thought he was.

What was your relationship like when he was executive vice president and you were president?

It was a much closer relationship then because he and I were running the company. He could take the ball, or I could take the ball. I wouldn't worry about who had the ball or who was doing what. I'd support what he did. He'd support what I did. When there were disagreements, if I felt strongly about it, we did it, and if he felt strongly about it, I let him do it. Well . . . sometimes I'd let him think about it for a while. You know, if your relationship is right as it was with us, you can work that out. It's not a problem.

Do you feel Perkins is a leader in the same way Franklin Lunding was?

Not the same. No. And of course, he isn't quite as stubborn as Lunding. But I think Perkins is both a leader and a manager.

How did you feel when you saw him come along and you said to yourself, "OK, there's my successor?" You're talking as if you had great delight in bringing this person along.

I did. It was a joy to me to work with someone like that. I could use his brains, his ability, strengths, and youthfulness. Our relationship was a great pleasure for me; our personalities matched so well.

You never felt threatened by his success?

John Hancock told me something once I'll never forget. He said, "There's always enough credit to go around." Perkins's success meant that I was doing my job.

Sometimes with close mentor relationships there comes a point where there's a split, where a younger person has made it and needs the older person to let go. Did you feel that way about Lunding?

No. I was too indebted to Lunding to take that attitude. With Perkins I was very anxious to get off his back if that was necessary. It's hard to lose the daily involvement, but when you realize that someone else can do it better, it's time to go.

What were the things you were most concerned to pass on to Perkins?

Social consciousness, first assistant philosophy, willingness to dare to do things. These were strengths we had in this business. Oh gosh, the years I spent with Perkins, you know, starting out together when he was executive vice president ending with him as chairman of the board, those were some of the best times of my life.

Donald S. Perkins

We'd like to discuss whether your relationships with Mr. Clements and Mr. Lunding helped you develop leadership qualities and what you feel each contributed.

I came to work for Jewel because Frank Lunding heard about me from my mother-in-law and invited me to come in for an interview. I was very impressed with the fact that the chairman would spend time with me; you won't be surprised that I try to do that today with prospective MBAs.

Frank found out that I drank tea instead of coffee, and when I got back to Wright Patterson Air Force Base in Ohio where I was stationed, a package of Jewel tea and one of these old-fashioned teapots that Jewel had been giving away in the Routes business for years arrived in the mail with a note saying, "Thought you ought to have some good tea," or something like that. It's pretty hard not to be impressed with someone that thoughtful.

What about George Clements?

I did not meet George Clements until I came back from my Routes training, and he debriefed me to find out what I'd learned. At that time I began to realize that the real challenge for someone like me at Jewel was to prove myself to George Clements. By the nature of what Frank thought the business needed, I felt I was more or less acceptable early, but in terms of what George felt might be needed, I had to do a lot of proving. I said to myself early in the game that I would succeed at Jewel when I got George Clements's acceptance and support.

What was it about Clements that you recognized was different?

I can be more comfortable about saying this now, because at a recent retirement dinner for Frank Lunding, the subject of Abraham Zaleznik's article, "Leaders and Managers: Are They Different?" came up.[2] Frank and George agreed that Frank was the leader and George was the manager. If that discussion had not been held, I couldn't be this candid. George is a tough-minded excellent manager and, as such, believes you aren't worth anything just because you have a good education, did well in school, or for any other reason, except that you get things done through people and do them well and honorably and are successful.

Were you aware at the beginning that you were, in a sense, chosen?

I never felt as though I was chosen within Jewel. I grew up in St. Louis, was raised by a working mother, and knew that the way out of a less-than-affluent neighborhood was through education. After a couple of academic exeriences that were reasonably successful, I did have some confidence in myself as you would, I think, expect me to have. So if you ask me what was most important in terms of my attitude in my first few years at Jewel—my self-confidence was significantly more important than any thought that I had a special relationship with anybody in the business, because I didn't.

When would you say you were first aware of Clements taking an interest in you?

2. Abraham Zaleznik, "Leaders and Managers: Are They Different?" HBR May-June 1977, p. 67.

For the first five or six years at Jewel, I was always aware that George was very helpful in a management sense—always asking about the problems in the business, and how we might solve them. When I'd been in the business six years or so, I had a major change from being the merchandise manager of the Routes to being the assistant to the operating head of the Food Stores. That's when I realized that George was taking more than a general interest in me.

When you came to Jewel, were you aware of wanting a mentor or of needing something, or that there was something lacking?

Absolutely. I knew I needed to be developed. In typical business school fashion, I wanted to join a company that met certain criteria. First, it had to be in the consumer goods business, because that's what I consider to be fun. Second, it had to be a well-managed business because I didn't think that I'd learned how to actually manage anything at the Harvard Business School. Third, it had to be a company that was financially strong. Jewel met all of those very well.

I didn't use the word *mentor,* but since one of my important yardsticks was to work for a well-managed business, I knew I needed to learn.

Did Clements and Lunding spend time with you in your early years?

My relationship with Frank Lunding and George Clements wasn't so close then that I could really discuss how the business was working or why they didn't do things the way I would. But I could discuss things with Don Booz, who's now running his own consulting firm. He was the personnel manager at the time I was hired. I had known him at the Business School and then, of course, knew him while he was at Jewel.

Don Booz was a great help in the early years. We lived near each other and commuted together. I seldom saw him in the personnel department, but we had a lot of conversations driving in an automobile. Young people in our business sometimes blush when I say to them, "Well, have you reorganized the business recently?" but I am just remembering those conversations we had driving to and from work.

But once I began to have enough success in the business to make it reasonable for me to have more contact with them, the mentor relationships with Clements and Lunding became very real.

One of the things that often characterizes successful mentor relationships is a strong emotional interchange between the younger and older person, where the younger person feels encouraged to challenge directly the older person's ideas, and the older person has enough confidence in himself to take it. Did that characterize your relationship with Clements later on?

Very much so with George. I think the best way to characterize the relationship that developed was that though in many ways we had different backgrounds, George and I admired each other so much and came at problems from different angles so that when we agreed on something, we stopped worrying about it and went ahead and did it.

But if you thought he was wrong, did you feel even though you were considerably younger—19 years difference—you could say, "I don't think you're right"?

Yes, we had a relationship like that. It didn't start the first time I came in to tell him about my experience on the Routes, I'll assure you of that. Exactly when it started, I'm not sure. Who knows where close human relationships start? I don't.

It was all a very businesslike relationship at first, but from the time I moved to the office next to him and he asked me to be responsible for growth planning and development, he had time to talk about anything that I thought was important. But I never had to say, "I think you're wrong." Anything that I thought was worth talking about, he thought was worth listening to. Needless to say, anything that he thought was worth talking about, I thought was worth listening to.

We had respect for each other's contributions. He knew the business needed to be changed, and I think that the role I played for him was as a suggester of possible changes. He could tap whatever creativity I had and bounce it off of his experience; that made a pretty good working relationship.

Did he ever have to override your decisions or pull rank on you?

No, we never had a conversation that ever came close to his saying, "I'm the chairman."

You may not know this, but Clements said he knew you were his successor from the beginning.

I didn't know that. He has a very kind memory. In a way I'm sure George saw me as one potential successor. George was enough of a manager and enough of an outstanding developer of people that I believe he must have known that had he made that very obvious to me, whenever it was, it would have done me and our relationship more harm than good. So there were times early in my career when I wasn't sure that anybody was looking at me or was particularly interested in me.

Did your early experiences at Jewel affect you personally?

The greatest change, I think, came from learning how to relate to people, how to make sure that everyone knows that you want to get something done, without applying pressure or demanding something be done. When I was the number two person in the advertising department in the Routes, I was picked to be the successor to the general merchandise manager. I'd never been a buyer and all the key people in that department were buyers.

So I sat down with each person and said, "You know, I don't know anything about the buying business, so why don't you tell me what you'd do if you had my job?" They suggested more things than I had time to do. I suppose that's an illustration of being a first assistant, particularly when you aren't sure about what you're supposed to do.

What do you think was the most important thing you learned from the Routes?

First I learned the business. When I was running a Route, it was a lonesome job. I remember one night at 6 o'clock it was raining, I had a number of back calls to make to customers who hadn't been home earlier. I looked up in the truck mirror and said, "What am I doing here?"

But when I came back and talked to the people in the office who were responsible for making decisions for the Routes business, I realized that even with that brief experience, I had an up-to-date knowledge about what was really going on in the field. That didn't hurt my confidence about suggesting what might be done differently.

Were you aware that when Clements sent you back to the Routes after you were in the Food Stores that he was presenting you with a challenge so that you would be accepted by the rest of the company?

No, I didn't think of it that way . . . I thought he was giving me a job I didn't want. I was having fun working on the future of the business, and he was sending me to its past. But he did that because that's George Clements the manager. As much as he was a supporter, he was still going to find out at each level what I could do. That was 1961. I'd been with Jewel for eight years.

The first six years, other than a brief training relationship with the Food Stores, were spent in the Routes business, I'd just got away for a year or a year and a half, had great fun doing what I was doing . . . and he wanted me to go back. I tried my best to talk him out of it.

You've said your early experiences at Jewel influenced your ways of relating to people. Mentors often help people develop other leadership qualities as well, such as their philosophic attitudes and their ability to take risks. Would you say this was true for you?

I had had enough of a struggle before coming to Jewel that I wasn't sure that the world was full of people who were out to help me. Phyllis, my wife, began to change my thinking when I first met her. Then I had a chance to observe Frank Lunding and George Clements, and to realize that success at Jewel was based on human concern.

At Jewel, I saw it not only acceptable but necessary to be yourself, to be honest and straightforward, ideals that are fundamental to the idea of sharing. To observe such a pattern, and then to feel comfortable in being able to develop your own business style against that framework—that was really important.

Have these concepts had a real influence in the company?

Yes. The changes Jewel had gone through in the 1960s were significant. That was when I asked George, Frank, and a wonderful man named Robert Updegraff, a Jewel director for 25 years, to agree to come to try to put on paper the concepts and influences that have been important to our business.

Instead of rewriting Frank's book *Sharing a Business,* we wrote *The Jewel Concepts.* I'm delighted to find that these concepts of the book are referred to throughout the business by, in many cases, relatively new people and often in speeches made by the officers of our operating companies. It's a way of thinking that is comfortable and appropriate for Jewel. Even a summer MBA finds out what a first assistant is.

In your daily working with Clements, were you aware of his taking risks with you, of him letting you go ahead down a path?

Absolutely. When I was in the Routes department, most of the action was in the Stores. We had a Routes catalog, very much like the one that we still have today, and I persuaded George to let us put some catalog desks in stores to sell merchandise. I remember that we lost $50,000 on the venture, but I suppose that isn't as expensive as a training cost. But, yes, George let me spend the $50,000 on an idea, and never said, "I told you so." He said, "OK, what do we do next?"

Did you find that the relationship you had with Clements and Lunding affected strategy decisions you might make?

I can't imagine a major decision could be made at Jewel that wouldn't consider the people involved. Formalizing the concept of autonomous companies in 1966 was a good example. Decentralization was natural to the Routes business even though the Food Stores were highly centralized.

In this matter of autonomy I give George Clements great credit. I remember a conversation that we had when we were talking about how to organize the business as we were acquiring Star Markets and Osco Drugs. He remembered that when he was operating the Food Stores in Chicago, an attractive location would become available and he could analyze it and approve it while another company was waiting to hear from corporate headquarters. He understood the value of being independent and being on the spot when he was in the leadership position at Jewel, and he didn't want to lose that as the business got more complicated. That thinking dictated our approach to the development of autonomous operating companies.

We understand that at Jewel each MBA trainee is assigned an officer as a sponsor to act as a mentor. Is that true?

Yes, just as Don Booz was a sponsor for me. I remember writing him letters about the rigors of operating Routes, and I would receive both sympathetic and unsympathetic replies, but at least feel good about the communication.

How did this program start?

Our MBA recruiting program started in answer to a request from George in the late 1950s or early 1960s to add some more talented people to our business. And I said, "Develop a recruiting program that offers them what you offered me," which meant a chance to find out what happens in our business for a period of time before settling down in a more typical regular job. Then we merchandized that idea and the idea of a sponsorship so that the trainee would have someone to relate to during the training period.

How far do you expect the sponsors to be responsible for these people?

If the individual trainee does a poor job, and if no one else will tell him or her about it, the sponsor should do it. If the trainee is doing a good job, I would expect the sponsor to tell him or her that. I would expect the sponsor to know enough about that trainee to have discussions during the training period, to be very influential in deciding where and what kind of more permanent job that trainee takes. A sponsor should know more about his or her trainee than anyone else in Jewel.

And he or she actually helps the trainee plan his career and talks to other people about him?

Exactly, but then we cut the apron strings, because the individual typically goes to work for somebody else. However, the friendships that have developed during that sponsorship period probably never end. You can cut the apron strings, but you don't cut the friendship. One of the wonderful things that happens to a trainee as he or she touches base with all parts of Jewel, is getting to know people throughout the company. Walter Elisha, president of the Jewel Food Stores, who went through this kind of training program, is delighted to have as his top operating officer a man who was the manager of a store in which he trained.

So the sponsor is usually somebody who does not become the person's direct boss?

Only rarely would it turn out that he would be. It's not ruled out, but it isn't likely to happen. Also I don't think it's fair to overemphasize the sponsor relationship to MBA recruiting. We try to give every person that comes into this business—MBA or high school student—sponsorship. Sometimes we do this well and sometimes we do it poorly. But we do try to encourage all of our people to empathize with the new employee's concerns.

Is this part of the first assistant philosophy?

It's consistent with it. Let's put it another way. There are a lot of people at Jewel who understand systems and know how to operate a group of stores. The people that Wes Christopherson and I look for to become key management people in the business have these abilities, but they also are able to recruit, develop, and motivate outstanding people.

Do you expect the vice presidents who act as sponsors to get emotionally involved with these people if they have to? To get to know them well . . . to become to them what Clements was to you?

If you are asking me if you can work with people without love, the answer is no. On the other hand, if you are asking if it is possible to help people grow by expressing love only in terms of permissiveness, by never hurting them and never being candid with them, the answer is also no. So sponsorship is somewhat like parenthood.

I think George and I had a relationship that we would have been proud to have had we been father and son, but one we could not likely have had if we *had* been father and son. So many of the good elements were there without other complicating problems such as the son having to prove his independence of the father.

Over the years have you noticed a qualitative difference between managers who were brought up with the sponsor approach and those who were not?

I don't know that anyone has ever succeeded in any business without having some unselfish sponsorship or mentorship, whatever it might have been called. Everyone who succeeds has had a mentor or mentors. We've all been helped. For some the help comes with more warmth than for others, and with some it's done with more forethought, but most people who succeed in a business will remember fondly individuals who helped them in their early days.

Do you see a real difference at Jewel, for instance?

No, but I see great difference in the ability of people to be sponsors.

When you became CEO in 1970, five of your division presidents were under 45, so that those five today would still be under 55. How do you make room for motivated, trained MBAs?

Room is made in two ways. One is through the attrition of those who are not the most outstanding.

But secondly, and probably more important numerically, our retirement program supports and perhaps even encourages early retirement. This retirement program is not only important to the retiree but is important in terms of opening up new opportunities. We have 170 or so operating company officers. I believe that right now only 2 of those are over 60.

Are the top men and women able to accept this rush of young, talented people? Doesn't that create tension for some of them?

Beginning with Frank Lunding's presidency at the age of 36 and his successful stewardship of the business at that time, there's been a degree of pride and expectation in the business that Jewel would have youthful leaders.

When Wes Christopherson became assistant sales manager in the Routes, Ed Johnson, an absolutely marvelous person now retired, and I agreed that in working with Christopherson, Johnson was probably developing his boss.

This training probably wouldn't exist in organizations that you acquire such as Turnstyle or Star Markets. How do you change the thinking of people who are already there?

With tender, loving care, and over time. When we've acquired businesses, we've always thought that we were acquiring good management. If we were to help those managers continue to be successful, they would need to continue to do things in their own way. That's part of the idea of decentralization; it's also part of being the first assistant to the group of managers that we may have or acquire. We don't demand that they do many things in one certain fashion. Some things they adopt and adapt, and some they don't like.

One of the other risks often associated with mentor relationships is that the younger person at some point might become overly dependent on the older person. Did you feel at any time that if you didn't have these strong people around, you might not be able to make it?

Was I as cocky and confident when I became president as when I was a trainee? Absolutely not. But I don't think that this was a matter of being dependent. Rather I had matured enough to understand realistically what the problems might be, that there was no easy answer to many of the questions of the business, and that many goals can't be reached in a year. If I'd understood what the problems turned out to be, I'd have been even less confident.

Clearly, Clements and Lunding were confident you could do it.

Frank Lunding gave up the job of chairman at, I believe, the age of 58, because he and George had decided I was ready to be president. And George Clements made basically the same decision at the age of 61 because he decided Wes Christopherson was ready to be president.

These decisions were based on when people were ready, rather than on chronology. For that reason I said in 1970 that the right tenure for the CEO of Jewel should be 10 years. And my 10 years will be up in 1980. If we want to have a vibrant questioning management that's looking out for changing customers' wants today, we should operate in a way that ensures top management change from time to time.

Do you feel now that being a mentor is part of your responsibility?

Yes, I'm proud to be a sponsor. Yes, I'm proud when I find myself able to be a good first assistant. Wes Christopherson and I try to know the young talent in Jewel. But the organization is not going to let someone succeed just because either of us takes an interest in that person. We must have thousands of sponsors. Every manager must be a sponsor.

Some people think that the main values to mentor relationships occur after they've ended. Have you been aware since your day-to-day contact with Clements and Lunding has broken that there is something that reveals itself that you weren't aware of before?

I've developed a frame of reference over the years that I use as I consider the problems of the business—I mentally ask myself in dealing with a tough problem how I might explain our action to Frank, or George, or Phyllis or my children—Betsy, Jerry, and Susan—in such a way that they'd say, "Yes, that makes sense. You're not just being a hard-driving, thoughtless businessman who's forgotten the human lessons that were there in Jewel to be learned."

15. The Abrasive Personality

Harry Levinson

Not everyone who rises quickly in a company and has good analytical skills and a lot of energy is abrasive, nor are all abrasive people in high management levels, but when the two do coincide, top management has a real problem. The problem is simply how to keep the extraordinarily talented person in a position where he or she can be most effective, and at the same time not sacrifice the feelings and aspirations of the people who work with and for this person. According to this author, managers can cope with this dilemma by helping their abrasive subordinates to understand the negative consequences of their personalities. This method takes time and patience, but it is most likely the only way managers can save such people for the organization.

The corporate president stared out the window of his skyscraper office. His forehead was furrowed in anger and puzzlement. His fingers drummed the arm of his chair with a speed that signified intense frustration. The other executives in the room waited expectantly. Each had said his piece. Each had come to his and her own conclusion about the problem.

Darrel Sandstrom, vice president of one of the corporation's major divisions, was the problem. Sandstrom was one of those rare young men who had rocketed to the division vice presidency at an age when most of his peers were still in lower-middle management. "He is sharp," his peers said, "but watch out for his afterburn. You'll get singed as he goes by." And that, in a phrase, was the problem.

There was no question that Sandstrom was well on his way to the top. Others were already vying for a handhold on his coattails. He had a reputation for being a self-starter. Give him a tough problem, like a failing division, and he would turn it around almost before anyone knew what had happened. He was an executive who could quickly take charge, unerringly get to the heart of a problem, lay out the steps for overcoming it, bulldoze his way through corporate red tape, and reorganize to get the job done. All that was well and good. Unfortunately, that was not all there was to it.

In staff discussions and meetings with his peers Sandstrom would ask pointed questions and make incisive comments. However, he would also brush his peers' superfluous words aside with little tact, making them fearful to offer their thoughts in his presence. Often he would get his way in meetings because of the persuasiveness of his arguments and his commanding presentations, but just as often those who were responsible for following up the conclusions of a meeting would not do so.

In meetings with his superiors, his questions were appropriate, his conclusions correct, and his insights important assets in examining problems. But he would antagonize his superiors by showing little patience with points and questions that to him seemed irrelevant or elementary. Unwilling to compromise, Sandstrom was an intellectual bully with little regard for those of his colleagues who could not keep up with him.

There were complaints from subordinates too. Some resented his controlling manner. Fearing his wrath, they spoke up at meetings only when they knew it to be safe. They knew he would not accept mediocrity and so they strived to attain the perfection he demanded of them. When he said they had done a good job, they knew they had earned his compliments, though many felt he did not really mean what he said.

His meetings were not noted for their liveliness; in fact hê did not have much of a sense of humor. On the golf course and tennis courts he was equally humorless and competitive. Playing as intensely as he worked, he did not know what a game was.

And now here he was. The division presidency was open and the corporate president was in a dilemma. To promote Sandstrom was to perpetuate in a more responsible position what seemed to many a combination of Moshe Dayan, General George Patton, and Admiral Hyman Rickover. Sandstrom would produce; no question about that. But at what cost? Could the corporation afford it? If Sandstrom did not get the job, the likelihood was that he would quit. The company could ill afford that either, for his division's bottom line was a significant portion of its bottom line.

Around the table the opinion was divided. "Fire him now," some said; "you'll have to do it sooner or later." "Be gentle with him," others said; "if you hurt him, he'll lose his momentum." "He'll mature with age," said others. Still others commented, "When he gets to be president, he'll relax." And there were those who said, "What difference does it make? He's bringing in the bucks." The corporate president faced the dilemma; Sandstrom could not be promoted but neither could he be spared. None of the options presented gave him a way out; none of them could.

Darrel Sandstrom epitomizes people who puzzle, dismay, frustrate, and enrage others in organizations—those who have an abrasive personality. Men and women of high, sometimes brilliant, achievement who stubbornly insist on having their own way, and are contemptuous of others, are the bane of bosses, subordinates, peers, and colleagues.

In the long run, they are a bane to themselves as well; when they fail, their failure is usually due to their abrasive personalities. Because of their value to their organizations, however, their superiors frequently go to great lengths to help them fit in the organization. In fact, top executives probably refer more managers with abrasive personalities to psychologists and psychiatrists, and human relations training programs in order to rescue them, than any other single classification of executives.

In this article I describe the abrasive personality, trace its origins, and suggest what managers might do to both help and cope with such people.

A Profile

Like the proverbial porcupine, an abrasive person seems to have a natural knack for jabbing others in an irritating and sometimes painful way. But that knack masks a desperation worse than that of those who receive the jabs— namely, a need to be perfect. (For a closer look at how a need to be perfect drives a person to the point where he alienates and causes significant stress to most people around him, see "The Need to Be Perfect" on page 238.) The person who becomes a Darrel Sandstrom, however, is not just someone who needs perfection. He has other characteristics which, combined with that need, create the behavior others find so offensive.

Such a person is most usually extremely intelligent. With a passion for perfection, accuracy, and completeness, he pushes himself very hard, and can be counted on to do a job well, often spectacularly. He tends to want to do the job himself, however, finding it difficult to lean on others who he feels will not do it to his standards, on time, or with the required finesse. He has, therefore, great difficulty delegating even $25 decisions. Such complete thoroughness, however, no matter how good for the company as a whole, tends to leave others figuratively breathless, making them feel that they cannot compete in the same league.

He is often keenly analytical, capable of cutting through to the nub of a problem, but with his need for constant achievement, he is impatient with those who cannot think as quickly or speak as forthrightly as he can. Thus his capacity for analysis tends not to be matched by equal skill as a leader to implement the answers he has deduced.

On a one-to-one basis he is often genial and helpful to people he is not supervising. But despite what he says, he is usually not a good developer of people for, frequently, they feel too inadequate when they have to compare themselves with him. Also, the abrasive person's intense rivalry with others often leads him to undercut them, even though he himself may not be aware of doing so.

When his competitive instincts overwhelm his judgment, an abrasive person will sometimes crudely raise issues others are reluctant to speak about, leaving himself a scapegoat for his own forthrightness. In groups he tends to dominate others, treating all differences as challenges to be debated and vanquished. At the same time that he is domineering to his subordinates, he is fawning to his superiors. If he feels himself to be exceptionally competent, however, he may try to dominate his superiors also.

Though often in imaginative pursuit of bigger and broader achievements for which he frequently gets many accolades, he may well leave his bosses and those around him with no sense of having any input to the task or project. He moves so fast and ranges so widely that even when he has good ideas, his boss will tend to turn him down, fearing that if he gives an inch, the subordinate will take a mile. The boss feels there will be no catching him, no containing him, and no protecting the stellar subordinate, himself, or higher management from any waves that may be created, the backwash from which might overwhelm them all.

Once reined in by his boss, the abrasive person feels that he has been let down, that his efforts have been in vain. Feeling unjustly treated, he becomes angry because he was asked to do something and it did not end well. Therefore, he reasons, he is being penalized because other people are jealous, rivalrous, or do not want to undertake anything new. Seeing his boss as somebody to be outflanked, rather than as somebody whose step-by-step involvement is necessary for a project's success, he is politically insensitive and often righteously denies the need for such sensitivity.

Although others often perceive him as both grandiose and emotionally cold, the abrasive person has a strong and very intense emotional interest in himself. Needing to see himself as extraordinary, he acts sometimes as if he were a privileged person—indeed, as if he had a right to be different or even inconsiderate.

At times he sees others as mere devices for his self-aggrandizement, existing as extensions of himself, rather than as full-fledged, unique adults with their own wishes, desires, and aspirations. To inflate his always low sense of self-worth, he competes intensely for attention, affection, and applause. At the same time, he seems to expect others to accept his work, decision, or logic just because it is his. When disappointed in these expectations, he becomes enraged.

To such a person, self-control is very important, as is control of others, which he makes total if possible. Thus he overorganizes, and copes with imperfections in others by oversupervising them. To him, losing a little control is the same as losing total control. To prevent that, he is rigid, constricted, and unable to compromise. In fact, for him, making a compromise is the same as giving in to lower standards. He therefore has little capacity for the necessary give and take of organizational political systems. This inflexibility is especially apparent around issues of abstract values which, for him, become specifically concrete.

To others the same control makes him appear emphatically right, self-confident, and self-assured. In contrast, those who are not so sure of what they believe or of the clarity of an issue, feel inadequate and less virtuous.

The abrasive person, appearing to have encyclopedic knowledge, is often well read, and, with already a good academic background, strives for more. While subordinates and even peers may strive as well to meet the high expectations of such a person, and some may reach extraordinary heights, many ultimately give up, especially if he beats them down. Thus the legandary Vince Lombardi drove the Green Bay Packers to great success, but all of its members, recognizing that he was the key to their success, felt that the better and more competent he was the less adequate they were. When such a person dies or leaves an organization, those left behind are demoralized because they have no self-confidence. Usually they will feel that they have not been able to measure up, and indeed, frequently, they cannot.

If they are compelled to retire, abrasive people will have difficulty. If they are not compelled to retire, they tend to hold on to the very end, and with age, their judgment is usually impaired. In their view, they have less and less need to adapt to people and circumstances, or to change their way of doing things. Thus they become more and more tangential to the main thrust of the business. If they are entrepreneurs, they may frequently destroy organizations in an unconscious effort to keep somebody else from taking over their babies. J. Edgar Hoover, a case in point, ultimately corrupted and very nearly destroyed the reputation of the FBI out of his own self-righteousness.

Solving the Dilemma

Given that you, the reader, have a subordinate who fits the profile I have drawn, what can you do? Corrective effort occurs in stages, and takes time and patience on everybody's part.

The following steps can be used with any employee who is having a behavior problem, but they are particularly effective in introducing an abrasive person to the consequences of his or her behavior.

☐ Recognize the psychological axiom that each person is always doing the best he can. Understanding that abrasive, provocative behavior springs from an extremely vulnerable self-image, a hunger for affection, and an eagerness for contact, do not become angry. Instead, initiate frequent discussion with this person.

☐ In such discussions, uncritically report your observations of his abrasive behavior. Describe what you see, especially the more subtle behavior to which people react automatically. Ask how he thinks others feel when he says or does what you describe. How does he think they are likely to respond? Is that the result he wants? If not, what would you do differently to get the response he wants? How would he respond if someone else said or did what he does?

☐ Point out that you recognize his desire to achieve and that you want to help. But tell him that if he wants to advance in the company, he needs to take others into account, and that his progress along these lines has implications for his future. Assure him also that everyone experiences defeats and disappointments along the way.

☐ When, as is likely to be the case, his provocative behavior ultimately irritates you, try to avoid both impulsively attacking back on the one hand and being critical of yourself for not responding in kind on the other. Explain to him that although you understand his need to do or be the best, he made you angry and that others he works with must feel the same. Tell him you get irritated and annoyed, particularly with hostile, depreciating, or controlling tactics. After all, you can say, you are only human, too, even if he thinks he is not. Let him know how frequently such behavior occurs.

☐ If he challenges, philosophizes, defends, or tries to debate your observations, or accuses you of hostility to him, do not counterattack. Tell him you are not interested in arguing. Merely report your observations of what he is doing or misinterpreting *at that moment*. Keep his goal the point of your discussion; does he want to make it or not?

☐ If your relationship is strong enough, you might ask why he must defend or attack in situations that are not combat. Point out that to be part of a critical examination of a problem is one thing; to turn such a situation into a win-lose argument is another.

☐ Expect to have to repeat this process again and again, pointing out legitimate achievements about which he can be proud. Explain that goals are achieved step by step, that compromise is not necessarily second best, that the all-or-none principle usually results in futile disappointment, and that perfection is not attainable.

Much good talent can be saved if managers employ these steps with their abrasive subordinates. Of course, some people are less abrasive than others and may be able to modulate their behavior voluntarily and cope consciously with their abrasive tendencies. For those who cannot, however, more drastic measures may be needed.

FURTHER STEPS

Sometimes people with unconscious drives cannot see reality despite repeated attempts to show them. Perhaps they are too busy thinking up defensive arguments or are preoccupied with their own thoughts. Whatever, if they do not respond to the gentle counseling I have described, then they should be confronted with what their arrogant, hostile, and controlling behavior is costing them.

Such people must be told *very early on* how their behavior undermines them. All too often afraid to do this, their bosses quickly become resentful and withdraw, leaving their subordinates uncomfortable but not knowing why. Feeling anxious, the abrasive subordinate then attempts to win back the regard and esteem of the boss in the only way he knows, by intensifying this behavior. That only makes things worse.

Abrasive persons can make significant contributions to an organization, but managers need to steer them again and again into taking those political steps that will enable them to experience success rather than rejection. Rather than corral such people, who tend to figuratively butt their heads against restrictions, managers do better to act like sheepdogs, gently nudging them back into position when they stray.

Highly conscientious people, who need to demonstrate their own competence by doing things themselves, are likely to have had to prove themselves against considerable odds in the past. Their demonstration of competence has had to be in terms of what they, themselves, could do as individuals. Thus they need political guidance and instruction in teamwork, as well as support from a superior who will tell them the consequences of their behavior in straightforward terms.

These people will often need frequent feedback on each successive step they take in improving their political relationships. As they move slowly in such a process, or at least more slowly than they are accustomed to, they will experience increasing anxiety. While not demonstrating their individual competence, such people may feel that they are not doing well, and get so anxious that they may indeed fail. When they have such feelings, they then tend to revert to their old unilateral way of doing things.

However, if despite the boss's best efforts the subordinate does not respond, the manager must tell him *in no uncertain terms* that his behavior is abrasive and therefore unsatisfactory. Managers should not assume that their subordinates know this, but should tell them and tell them repeatedly, and in written form. Being told once or twice during a performance appraisal should be enough. My experience is, however, that most superiors are very reluctant to tell people, particularly abrasive ones, the effects of their behavior during performance appraisals.

In one instance, when I was asked to see such a manager, he did not know why he had been referred to me. When I told him, he was dismayed. Showing me his performance appraisal, he complained that his boss had not told him. Rather his boss had commented favorably on all his qualities and assets, and in one sentence had written that his behavior with people was improving. In reality, the boss was so enraged with his subordinate's behavior that he was not promoting him as far as he would have wished.

When the steps I have outlined have been followed to no avail, when the subordinate clearly knows, and he or she is unable to respond by changing his or her behavior, when repeated words to the person and even failures to be promoted have produced no significant improvement, there are two likely consequences. First, the abrasive person will feel unfairly treated, unrecognized for his or her skills and competence, and unappreciated for what he or she could bring to the organization. Second, the superior is usually desperate, angry, and at his wit's end.

If by this point the abrasive person has not already been referred to a competent psychologist or psychiatrist for therapy, he should be. *Nothing else will have a significant effect,* and even therapy may not. Whether it does will depend on the severity of the problem and the skill of the therapist. This is not a problem that will be solved in a T-group, or a weekend encounter, or some other form of confrontation.

The manager should make sure the subordinate understands that when a person is referred to a psychologist, there are two implications. The first is that the person is so competent, skilled, or capable in some dimension of his role that his superiors would not only hate to lose him, but also have reason to expect that the person could flower into a mature executive who can assume greater responsibility. The second is that despite his talent, the subordinate is so unable to get along with other people that he cannot be promoted beyond his present role. Both points should be made emphatically.

These same principles apply equally in dealing with any ineffective or dysfunctional behavior on the job. Some people cannot seem to get their work done. Others have a habit of getting in their own way as well as that of others. Still others manage to stumble their way to work late each morning or produce incomplete or inadequate work. Whatever the case, steps in treating them are essentially the same.

Other Problem Situations

What do you do if the abrasive person is your boss, your peer, someone you are interviewing, or, hardest to face of all, yourself? What recourse do you have then?

THE BOSS

Let us assume that you are relatively new or inexperienced in a particular area and need a certain amount of time to achieve your own competence. Chances are that because of his knowledge and competence, your abrasive boss will have much to teach. Since his high standards will ensure that the model he provides will be a good one, there will be sufficient reason for you to tolerate his abrasiveness.

But after two years, or whenever you establish your own competence, you will begin to chafe under the rigid control. As you push for your own freedom, your boss is likely to become threatened with loss of control and feel that you are becoming rivalrous. He is then likely to turn on you, now no longer a disciple, and, in sometimes devious ways, get back at you. Your memos will lie on his desk, unanswered. Information being sent through channels will be delayed. Complaints, suggestions, requests will either be rejected outright or merely tabled. Sometimes he will reorganize the unit around you, which will fence you in and force you to deal with decoys—nominal bosses who have no real power.

If you are in a safe position, you might tell the boss how he appears to you, and his effect on subordinates. If he is at a high level, it will usually do little good to go above his head. Certainly, you should check out how much concern his superiors have about him, how much they are willing to tolerate, and how able they are to face him in a confrontation. Few at higher management levels are willing to take on a bright, combative, seemingly self-confident opponent—especially if he has a record of achievement, and there is little concrete evidence of the negative effects of his behavior.

In short, after you have learned what you can from such a person, it is probably time to get out from under him.

THE PEER

If you are the peer of an abrasive person, do not hesitate to tell him if his behavior intimidates you. Speaking of your irritation and anger and that of others, you might tell him you do not think he wants to deliberately estrange people or be self-defeating. He might become angry, but if approached in a kindly manner, he is more likely to be contrite and may even ask for more feedback on specific occasions.

THE CANDIDATE

What should you look for during an interview to avoid hiring someone who will turn out to be abrasive?

Pay attention to the charming personality. Not all charming persons are self-centered, but many are. Some preen themselves, dress to perfection, and in other ways indicate that they give an inordinate amount of attention to themselves. The more exhibitionistic the person, the more a person needs approval, the less he or she can be thoughtful of others. Also pay special attention to precision in speech or manner. Clarity is a virtue, but a need for exactness indicates a need to control.

Find out how the person gets things done by having him or her describe past projects and activities. How much does he report starting and finishing tasks all by himself, even to the surprise of his superiors? To do so is not necessarily bad; in fact, it may be good for a person to be a self-starter. But repeated singular achievement might indicate a problem in working as part of a team. How often does he use "I"? How closely did he have to check the work of subordinates? How important was it for him to have control of what was happening? How did he talk to people about their mistakes? How did he go about coaching them?

How did he view the limits and inadequacies of others, as human imperfections or as faults? How much better does he think things could have been done? Why were they not done better? Why could he not do better? What did his bosses say about him in performance appraisals?

YOU, YOURSELF

Finally, what if you are abrasive? If you ask yourself the questions that follow and find that you answer three of them in the affirmative, the chances are that your behavior is abrasive to the people around you. If you answer six or more affirmatively, it takes no great insight to recognize that you have more problems than are good for your career. Of course, none of these questions taken by itself is necessarily indicative of anything, but enough affirmative answers may reveal an abrasive profile.

If you are the problem and it troubles you, you can work at self-correction. Most often, however, you need the help of a third person—your spouse, a friend, your boss, or a professional. If your behavior causes you serious problems on the job, then a professional is indicated. Managers and executives with naturally heavy orientations to control need to check themselves carefully for this kind of behavior lest unconsciously they defeat their own ends.

Do You Have an Abrasive Personality?

You might ask yourself these questions. Then ask them of your spouse, your peers, your friends—and even your subordinates:

1. Are you condescendingly critical? When you talk of others in the organization, do you speak of "straightening them out" or "whipping them into shape"?

2. Do you need to be in full control? Does almost everything need to be cleared with you?

3. In meetings, do your comments take a disproportionate amount of time?

4. Are you quick to rise to the attack, to challenge?

5. Do you have a need to debate? Do discussions quickly become arguments?

6. Are people reluctant to discuss things with you? Does no one speak up? When someone does, are his or her statements inane?

7. Are you preoccupied with acquiring symbols of status and power?

8. Do you weasel out of responsibilities?

9. Are you reluctant to let others have the same privileges or perquisites as yourself?

10. When you talk about your activities, do you use the word "I" disproportionately?

11. Do your subordinates admire you because are so strong and capable or because, in your organization, *they* feel so strong and capable—and supported?

12. To your amazement do people speak of you as cold and distant when you really want them to like you?

13. Do you regard yourself as more competent than your peers, than your boss? Does your behavior let them know that?

Appendix to Chapter 15

The Need to Be Perfect

If a person's ultimate aspiration, his ego ideal, is perfection, then he is always going to fall short of it—by astronomical distances. And if this person's self-image is already low, the distance between where he perceives himself to be and the omnipotence he wants to attain will be constantly increasing as the feeling of failure continues. He must, therefore, push himself ever harder—all the time. Others who are or may be viewed as competitors threaten his self-image even further; if they win, by his own definition, he loses. His intense need to be perfect then becomes translated into intense rivalry.

If a person is always pushing himself toward impossible aspirations and is never able to achieve them, there are two consequences for his emotions. The greater the gap between his ego ideal and self-image, the greater will be both his guilt and anger with himself for not achieving the dream. And the angrier a person is with himself, the more likely he is to attack himself or drive himself to narrow the gap between his ideal and his present self-image. Only in narrowing the gap can he reduce his feelings of anger, depression, and inadequacy.

However, as the unconscious drive for perfection is irrational, no degree of conscious effort can possibly achieve the ideal or decrease the self-punishment such a person brings down on himself for not achieving it. The anger and self-hatred are never-ending, therefore, and build up to the point where they spill over in the form of hostile attacks on peers and subordinates, such as treating them with contempt and condescension.

These feelings may also spill over onto spouses, children, and even pets. In fact, the abrasive person's need for self-punishment may be so great that he may take great, albeit neurotic, pleasure in provoking others who will subsequently reject—that is, punish—him. In effect, he acts as if he were his own parent, punishing himself as well as others. In Anna Freud's words, he becomes a good hater.[1]

1. Anna Freud, "Comments on Aggression," *International Journal of Psychoanalysis,* Vol. 53, No. 2 (1972), p. 163.

Part IV
Intuitive Ways of Relating to People

One of the limitations of reason is that it cannot explain enough. How do we account for some people's abilities to invent things never thought of before? Or how do we explain one person's ability to communicate effectively while other people fail? If only reason or analysis were involved, we would have direct access to the process as sequential thinking can be demonstrated. But these acts are not rational and are difficult to measure and quantify. Perhaps because of the difficulty and because qualitative judgments are often regarded as too personal, subjective, and nonuniform, performance appraisal systems in organizations generally do not account for behavior but concentrate on what can be measured, such as achieving goals.

This exclusion would be well and good if the behavioral aspects would just go away, but they don't. As Harry Levinson points out in "Appraisal of What Performance?," although appraisal systems often only measure whether a person reaches his or her goals, managers really judge people not according to what they did but how they did it. So despite managerial attempts to rationalize appraisal systems, such systems just cannot account for all of a person's performance.

The same is true of motivation systems. People are not objects to be manipulated by this or that theoretical approach; they do not respond positively to a rational argument as to why they should perform better. As Thomas Fitzgerald writes in "Why Motivation Theory Doesn't Work," the problems of motivation are rooted in rationality itself.

When a manager, or anyone, appeals only to the rational in a person, he or she appeals to only one portion of that person's intelligence. Also, in doing that, a manager is neglecting the person's emotions, also housed in the part of the brain to which we do not have direct access. The unconscious, or what William C. Schutz calls "The Interpersonal Underworld," determines how a person behaves. Without recognizing its existence and the important role it plays, a manager trying to influence behavior is not likely to succeed. The articles in this section, then, explore the dynamics that underlie the behavior we observe and indicate ways managers can influence their employees through creating a different kind of environment.

16. The Interpersonal Underworld

William C. Schutz

Given that we all have interpersonal problems, how do we begin to go about diagnosing them so we can cure them? So much of what is going on between people is not quantifiable, but is part of what this author calls the interpersonal underworld, or covert ways to resist, oppose, delay, fail, support, or sabotage each other. The author describes examples of interpersonal problems and situations and then presents a theory of behavior that managers can apply in analyzing their own situations. His theory, not the only one extant in psychological literature, is based on the notion that people need people and that each of us has three basic needs in common, namely the needs for inclusion, control, and affection.

Although the businessman must spend a major part of his time dealing with other people, he has in the past had little help in overcoming the difficulties that inevitably arise when people get together. The terms that have been used to describe these problems—terms like *disciplinary problems, human relations troubles,* or the currently popular *communications difficulties*—have served only to hide the real difficulties, for they are descriptions of symptoms. The real causes must be sought at a deeper level; they lie in interpersonal relations.

In every meeting of two or more people two levels of interaction occur. One is the overt—the play that is apparently being played. The other is the covert—like a ballet going on in back of the performance on the interpersonal stage—a subtle struggle for attention and status, for control and influence, and for liking and warmth. This ballet influences the performance by pushing the overt players into unusual postures and making them say and do unusual things. Thus, the objective, hardheaded executive is overtly very resistant to a splendid idea suggested by the brash young fellow who may someday replace him. But

AUTHOR'S NOTE: For a fuller discussion of the points covered here, see my book, *FIRO: A Three-Dimensional Theory of Interpersonal Behavior,* Rinehart & Company, Inc., 1958.

this example is much too obvious. The ballet's effect on the actors is usually more subtle.

The importance of these covert factors can hardly be overestimated. The productivity of any particular group is profoundly influenced by them. One of the main functions of this article is to attempt to dispel the idea that strong interpersonal differences existing within a group setting can be effectively handled by ignoring them—as if by the magic of closing your eyes you could make problems go away. Rather, interpersonal problems must be understood and dealt with. If ignored, they are usually transformed so that they are not expressed directly as open hostility but find their expression through the task behavior of the group. Failure to allow these group processes to work in a direct fashion will decrease the group's productivity.

The types of behavior that result from interpersonal difficulties are various. In many cases it is difficult to recognize their connection with interpersonal relations in the work situation. To illustrate some of these more subtle connections, I shall describe several behaviors resulting from or symptomatic of, interpersonal difficulties, and then present a sampling of situations giving rise to these behaviors.

Behavioral Symptoms

Generally, interpersonal problems lead individuals to resist each other and each other's influence in various overt, but more often covert, ways. Each individual may oppose, delay, fail to support, or sabotage another. The mechanisms to be discussed here are largely covert, or unconscious; the individual does these things without being aware of his intention to resist or obstruct.

COMMUNICATIONS PROBLEMS

These days "communications problems" are greatly emphasized as a source of industrial difficulty. This emphasis, however, seems misplaced. For one thing, problems caused by communications are due not to *inadequate* communication but to *too adequate* communication, since what is transmitted most accurately between people is how they feel rather than what they say. Thus, if the boss really feels his research scientist is not very important, that feeling will be communicated to the scientist much more readily than any words that pass between them. For another thing, communications difficulties are primarily the *result* of interpersonal difficulties; they are seldom themselves a primary *cause* of problems. Resisting another person is often accomplished through the medium of communication. Thus:

☐ A person may find it difficult to understand what is being said, or, sometimes, actually not hear what is said. Often a person feels confused; he just cannot follow all the things that are going on. Another sign of resistance is incoherent speech, mumbling, not bothering to make a point clear, or not making sure that the listener has heard. All of these occurrences impede the process of verbal communication.

☐ Resistance may also take the form of forgetting to pick up a message that was to have been left on one's desk. Or one may forget to mail a memo or leave a message of importance to someone else; or the message may be garbled, ambiguous, or actually contain a factual error. Similarly, misreading and misinterpretation increase greatly in situations of interpersonal strife.

Individually, these behaviors all appear to be simple human failings and, indeed, in many cases may be only that. However, it is always a good bet, especially when the incidents recur, that they are unconsciously motivated by interpersonal differences. In short, interpersonal problems frequently find expression through the obstruction of valid communication. Excessive communications problems can usually be interpreted as a symptom of interpersonal trouble.

LOSS OF MOTIVATION

Another expression of interpersonal problems is the loss of motivation to work on a task. In innumerable ways the individual's work becomes ineffective because he lacks the desire to produce. The accumulation of many minor inefficiencies amounts to the equivalent of losing the services of a group member or a part of one or more members' resources and abilities. For example:

☐ If a group member is supposed to look up some information that is needed for other members of the group to complete their work, he may just miss getting to the company library before Friday night closing time. Therefore he will have to wait over the weekend and, in the meantime, hold up two other people who are waiting for his report. Or perhaps some morning he will oversleep when he should be at the committee meeting.

☐ Another individual does only what is required of him and nothing extra. If he works from nine to five, he will leave promptly at five, for he considers his work a chore, a task to be accomplished and nothing more. If something goes wrong because of someone else's error, he will make no effort to compensate for it. If he is not very busy and someone else needs a hand, he will not lend it. All in all, he will do only the very minimum required to retain his job.

☐ Another manifestation of a man's loss of motivation is a sudden realization that his outside interests and commitments are much stronger than he had thought when the group began. He finds that he has conflicting meetings and other things to do that force him to leave meetings early, to arrive late, or perhaps even to miss one. Or he may have reports to write that prevent him from coming or working for this committee.

☐ Chronic absenteeism or lateness is still another manifestation of an interpersonal difficulty. Perhaps a group member has an actual illness or some commitment at home that prevents his coming; there may be any one of a large number of reasons for his absence or lateness, many of which are rational. But these situations may happen too often to make the whole pattern a rational one. If a man has a meeting and the snow is heavy, it may be that he cannot make the meeting because of the traffic situation; but if it were a meeting which he really wanted to attend, the snow would not be a great enough obstacle to prevent him from going.

☐ Also, a loss of motivation very frequently expresses itself in an actual feeling of physical tiredness. Handling emotional and interpersonal difficulties is hard work, especially if it involves holding back certain strong feelings. This work actually makes the individual so tired that he has great difficulty in bringing himself to work and to persevere on a job once it is begun. It often happens that an individual who feels completely exhausted in one part of his work situation miraculously perks up when a new task comes along or when he goes home to a more enjoyable activity. Again, this is not a case of deliberate malingering. The person actually feels tired. When the conflict-inducing situation is removed, the tiredness lifts.

In general, what is happening is that a person suddenly finds that other groups in which his interpersonal relations are happier are more important than the present group, and hence his motivation to work in the situation is reduced. A man will seek a situation in which he is happiest and will attempt to avoid unpleasant situations as far as possible. In other words, he escapes the situation by withdrawing his involvement.

INDISCRIMINATE OPPOSITION

Another category of responses to interpersonal difficulties involves direct blockage of action. This mechanism is often quite overt and conscious, but it likewise has many covert and unconscious forms.

A symptom of a bad relationship is resistance to suggestions. It may happen that an individual in the group makes suggestions that are opposed by another member regardless of their merit. As soon as the first member begins to talk, the second man—because he feels hostile to the first—feels a surge of resistance or reluctance to accept anything he is going to hear. This is, of course, not beneficial from the standpoint of the group, because a very good suggestion may be rejected for irrelevant personal reasons.

The manner in which such opposition is manifested is often very subtle. If an antagonist makes a suggestion, rather than use direct attack an individual may say smilingly, "That sounds interesting, but perhaps if we tried this other method it would be even more effective." Another technique is to postpone a decision on an opponent's suggestion. The parliamentary procedure of "tabling" is one formal method, as are setting up investigating committees, considering other matters first, offering amendments, or being unavailable for a meeting to decide on the suggestion. Undoubtedly the experienced businessman can extend this list indefinitely. Again, it is important to note that, although the techniques are often deliberately used, they are perhaps used even more often without the user's awareness of his motivation.

OPERATIONAL PROBLEMS

There are several ailments of total group functioning that are symptomatic of interpersonal difficulties. In most cases, difficulty in reaching decisions is a sure indication of interpersonal strife. This usually implies that the group is unable to tell anybody *no,* since to make such a decision involves saying *yes* to the proponents of another view. Compromises are then put through that satisfy neither side and that certainly do not accomplish the task as effectively as the group could under optimal conditions. The compromise is really one between the individuals who are in conflict, and not a compromise, essentially, of the issues of the case.

Another symptom of interpersonal problems in a group is inefficient division of labor. If the relationships among the men are poor, difficulties arise as soon as it comes time to assign different roles and divide the labor so that the group can operate more effectively. Strongly held interpersonal feelings prevent the group from saying *no* to somebody who wants to be in a particular position in the group but whom the other members consider unsuited to that position. This person may, therefore, be put into the role anyway, to the detriment of the functioning of the group. For example:

In one group of marketing personnel there was a man of clearly outstanding abilities regarding ideas for the solution of the group's problem. Because of his strength and dominance in the group he was accepted as the leader. One result of this was that he was not in a very good position to express his ideas, since as the leader he had to assume a conciliator role; thus, his virtue as a member who could contribute to the substance of the group's task was diminished.

A second result was that he could not act as a good administrator—that is, could not effectively coordinate the efforts of the other group members. So, by not being able to say *no* to this person, or by not being able to discuss more openly the best use to be made of his abilities, the group lost in two very important ways.

Another frequent instance of this difficulty is putting a man who is extremely capable in a subordinate role, with the result that his abilities cannot be utilized by the group. Thus:

In a different group the phenomenon opposite to the previous example occurred, resulting in equal injury to the group's performance. Because of personal hostility from several other members the most competent man was relegated to the role of secretary. There his time was consumed taking minutes, and his stellar abilities were wasted.

In general, then, ability to place men properly within a group is one indication of good basic interpersonal relations, while inability is a sign that there must be something wrong among the people that prevents them from using their resources optimally.

TASK DISTORTIONS

Interpersonal difficulties are almost invariably reflected in a group's performance on its task, although at times these effects are more obvious than at others. Here are three examples of interpersonal problems being expressed directly in work behavior, taken from groups of eight graduate students working on actual industrial problems at the Harvard Business School:

One of these groups was working on the problem of bringing out a new product for a major manufacturer. The members developed a marketing strategy for this product in which the big stress was on the image that the product would present to consumers. In fact, they put so much stress on the image that they neglected certain other factors.

My observations of this group in operation indicated the reason for the inefficient emphasis. From the beginning certain men were assigned by the group not to the actual task but to the presentation to be made to the company at the completion of the work. Some of them became very concerned with the impression *they* would make—in fact more concerned with this than with the impression the product would make. Therefore, they unconsciously sought the aspect of their assigned task that would allow them to work on their interpersonal problem and anxiety and concentrated on it to the consequent neglect of other factors that were also important.

Another group evolved a marketing strategy for bringing out a family of products. On examination, it appeared that this product family was not particularly well integrated. In addition, there was reason to believe that a single product would be more effective.

From interviews with the individual members and from observations of their working as a group, it became clear that the family of products was a compromise solution. Certain members of the group had wanted one product; others had wanted a different one. Instead of trying to work out these differences of opinion in terms of marketing considerations, the group decided implicitly to bring out the whole family as a solution to their interpersonal problem.

Still another group devised a marketing solution with a heavy emphasis on a decentralized distribution system. But the company representatives immediately wondered about the wisdom of using such autonomous distributors, since company-hired distributors should lead to more profits. The group was at a loss to justify its own suggestion.

Again, observations of the group throughout the term indicated a possible reason. The group had had a serious interpersonal blowup at one point, and the members had decided to go their separate ways. The result of this decision was autonomous operation by the individual members of the group. Apparently the group members were unconsciously influenced by the fact that their group could operate more effectively as autonomous individuals.

Interpersonal problems are often worked out on some aspect of the task that closely approximates the relationship that is of concern to the group (company to dealer, company to consumer, and so forth). In this way the tensions generated by the interpersonal problems can be relieved by symbolically displacing them into the work situation. The drawback of this phenomenon is that, although it appears that the group is very task-oriented, its work may in fact be quite inappropriate and inefficient at many points.

Common Issues

We have looked at some of the behaviors that may be considered symptomatic of inadequate interpersonal relations. Certain problem situations that occur in group and interpersonal dealings with great frequency generate these symptoms. As an illustration of the nature of the problems and some of their vicissitudes, I shall now discuss three of them.

CONSENSUS FOR DECISION

In every group, sooner or later, a decision-making apparatus must be agreed on. Whether it be consensus, majority rule, unanimity, or any other method, there must be some *modus operandi* for the group to make decisions. By consensus I mean, here, that everyone in the group is agreed that a certain course of action is best for the group, regardless of whether or not he individually agrees with it. Ordinarily, if the group does not have consensus and a decision goes through, the group pays. For instance:

Let us suppose that a group, perhaps a committee, has gotten together with the task of deciding a particular issue. The issue has come to a vote, and the vote is fairly decisive, say six to two. The two people in the minority, however, do not really feel that they have had an opportunity to express their feelings about the issue. Although they are committed to go along with the decision, they have an inner reluctance to do so. This covert reluctance may manifest itself in any of the symptoms already mentioned. Perhaps the most common symptom is a loss of interest, although this situation could be expected to give rise to any of them.

The question of consensus is central in decision making. In a deeper sense, consensus means that everyone in a group feels that the group understands his position and his feelings about it; and he feels, then, that the group should take a particular course of action even though he does not personally agree. If the individual is not allowed to voice his own feelings and reasons for voting against the particular issue, he will, at least unconsciously, resist the efficient functioning of the group from that point on. If consensus is not required, decisions can often be made more quickly (for example, by majority rule or by fiat), but delay will probably result, due to the unacknowledged members having various ways of resisting once the decision has been made and the action is undertaken.

The ability to detect a lack of consensus is, of course, a very important attribute for a group leader. A few rules of thumb might be of help here. The clue is that it is very difficult to find out whether there is a consensus unless each person is allowed to speak; for lack of disagreement does not necessarily indicate that the group has consensus. Frequently people simply are reluctant to raise their objections. However, if each member is asked separately whether or not he assents to the issue, the group leader can usually pick up objections:

He may be able to spot disagreement by noticing such things as changes in tone of voice. In one group the leader asked if everyone agreed on a suggested course of action. As he went around the room he got the following responses: *yes, yes, yes, yes, yes, okay.* This leader, being fairly astute, immediately began to question the man who had said *okay*, because this man apparently could not quite bring himself to be like the other members of the group with regard to this decision. This inability is usually a good indication of an objection. The individual is reluctant to object directly because of the weight of all the other members disagreeing with him.

After this man had been quizzed for a while, it became clear that he did have a strong objection. Once he was allowed to talk it out, he went along with the group and was quite willing to say *yes* and, in fact, to pitch in and work with the decision that was finally made.

Another good indicator of lack of consensus is any attempt by a member to postpone a decision by further discussion or by further action of some kind. Comments like, "What is it we are voting on?" or "Weren't we supposed to discuss something else first?" or "I have no objection to that, but . . ." all indicate that the individual is not yet ready to cast a positive vote for a given decision. He probably has an objection that ought to be brought out into the open and discussed.

Allowing the objector to raise his point for discussion is not just a hollow gesture. The objector will be more likely to go along with the final decision—or he may eventually carry the day because he reflects some objections that other people had but were not aware of. Whether the group actually changes its vote or not, it will be more likely to reach a correct decision. This opportunity for the group to discuss a previously covert factor is very important for its effectiveness.

AUTHORITY PROBLEM

Another group phenomenon that leads to reduced effectiveness concerns the relationship of the group members to the leader of the group. (The term *leader* will be used loosely to mean the person who is, in the eyes of the group members, supposed to head the group—usually a formal leader, a designated person who has a higher title.) It is the nature of such relationships that members of the group have ambivalent feelings toward the authority figure— both positive and negative feelings. The negative feelings can be particularly disturbing, since it usually is hard for people to express such feelings directly, because their jobs may be in jeopardy or because they feel that they should not attack an authority figure.

Since the hostility must be expressed, however, they often transfer it to another member of the group. Some other member, usually one with character- istics similar to those disliked in the leader, will be attacked more than he realistically should be for his behavior in the group. He will be attacked not only for what he does, but also because the attack that the group would like to level toward the leader is displaced onto him. The term *scapegoat* is often used for this person. For example, if the group members are dissatisfied because the leader is not giving sufficient direction to the group, the dissatisfaction may be vented toward a silent or nonparticipating member, the member in the group who comes closest to having the characteristic of the leader which the group members do not like. For example:

In one marketing group the leader offered the group very little direction, far less than most members would have liked. Subsequently, everyone began to get very angry with one group member who did not say much and who occasionally missed meetings because of his other commitments. The group attacked him for his lack of interest and unwillingness to contribute to the group.

A key to what was really happening is found in the fact that he was actually quite interested and was contributing a great deal, thus making the attack somewhat undeserved; but significantly, the characteristics that angered the group members were precisely those that covertly irritated them about the leader. Apparently they displaced their aggression from the leader, whom they felt they could not attack directly, onto a group member who had similar attributes.

This same mechanism operates when the boss is too *authoritarian*. Somebody in the group who has similar tendencies will be severely attacked, again as a displacement of the attack they would like to level at the boss.

With regard to dealing with this phenomenon, perhaps the most useful thing to be said is that there are times when a leader, in order to allow a group to operate more effectively, must himself become the scapegoat. If he can absorb some of the hostility that is really meant for him or perhaps in some cases even absorb some of the hostility meant for other group members, he can be most useful in helping a group to function more effectively. Of course, in order to do this the leader must be aware that the hostility is not necessarily directed at him personally; it is just an inevitable consequence of group activity that hostility does arise. If he can absorb the hostility directly, it does not have to be deflected into the group where it is most destructive to the group and to the group's ability to fulfill its purposes. An important part of a leader's role is to be a scapegoat occasionally in order that the group may proceed and operate more effectively. This situation brings to mind an old saying, "A good king is one whose subjects prosper."

THE PROBLEM MEMBER

Another frequently occurring group difficulty is the presence of a problem member, one of the most difficult of all interpersonal problems for a group to deal with. Problem members are of two main types—the overactive member and the underactive member. Either can disrupt group functioning, and both are usually difficult to handle.

The overactive problem member dominates the group's attention far more than his abilities warrant. The difficulties arise partly because the apparent intensity of his feelings leads to a general reluctance of the group to hurt the individual while at the same time they cannot curtail his destructive activities. To illustrate what can happen in such a situation:

In one five-man group of military personnel working on a series of tactical problems, Mac immediately took over control of the group. Because he was reasonably competent and highly forceful, he went unchallenged for several meetings. The other group members were not very compatible, so they had a difficult time handling Mac. Gradually some members began losing interest in the group until one discussion of a very trivial topic, the postal rates from Washington to Chicago, came up in one of their rest periods. The exchange that followed was amazing in that Mac was attacked severely and at length by the other group members for his dogmatically stated opinion about postal rates. The group used this topic to vent their stored-up feelings toward Mac. By this time, however, the group had no resources to cope with these strong feelings, and it quickly disintegrated after the conflict.

The optimal solution to the problem represented by this member is to handle him in such a way that he can be retained in the group and his resources made use of and still not be allowed to obstruct the group's functioning:

Another group had this problem with Bob. But this group quickly deposed Bob and set up a leader of considerably less intellect but with superior coordinating abilities. For a short time after they had deposed Bob the group made sure he realized he was not going to run the group; then they gradually allowed him back into the group by paying more attention to his ideas. Finally, after about ten meetings, his ideas were highly influential and sought by the group, although he was not allowed to dominate. In this way the group took care of the problem presented by an overactive member and was still able to utilize his abilities. This is an ideal solution and the sign of a strong, compatible group.

Someone who will not become integrated into the group also poses a problem for the group. The lack of commitment of this member, perhaps even a lack of willingness to work, constitutes a serious group problem. One solution is to eject the member from the group. This is a solution only insofar as it removes the source of a difficulty; it does not allow the group to utilize the man's abilities. The problem member often serves a useful function by enabling other members to direct their hostility toward him, so that they do not have to deal with the real differences among themselves. Thus, it is not unusual that if a chronically negative member is absent, the group finds that it still has disagreements.

Framework for Behavior

Now that I have described examples of several interpersonal problem situations and various reactions to them, I shall present a brief outline of a theory of interpersonal behavior. In order to deal with interpersonal behavior it is necessary to have an understanding of the *general* principles of this behavior, since formulas for handling *specific* situations are of limited value at best. The following theory is by no means the only one extant in psychological literature, but it is offered as a possible framework for understanding phenomena of the type under discussion here.

The basis for evolving this theory of interpersonal behavior is the individual's *fundamental interpersonal relations orientation* or, to abbreviate, FIRO. The basic assumption of this approach is that people need people. Every human being, because he lives in a society, must establish an equilibrium between himself and his human environment—just as he must establish an equilibrium between himself and the physical world. This social nature of man gives rise to certain interpersonal needs, which he must satisfy to some degree while avoiding threat to himself. Although each individual has different intensities of need and different mechanisms for handling them, people have three basic interpersonal needs in common:

The Need for Inclusion

This is the need to maintain a satisfactory relation between the self and other people with respect to interaction or belongingness. Some people like to be with other people all the time; they want to belong to organizations, to interact, to mingle. Other people seek much less contact; they prefer to be alone, to interact minimally, to stay out of groups, to maintain privacy.

If a continuum were to be drawn between these two extremes, every person could be placed at a point (or region) at which he feels most comfortable. Thus, to a certain degree each individual is trying to belong to a group, but he is also trying to maintain a certain amount of privacy. From the other point of view he wishes to some degree to have people initiate interaction toward him through invitations and the like, and also wishes to some degree that people would leave him alone. For each dimension these two aspects may be distinguished: (1) the behavior he initiates toward others, his expressed behavior; and (2) the behavior he prefers others to express toward him, his wanted behavior. This distinction will prove valuable in the discussion of compatibility.

The Need for Control

This is the need to maintain a satisfactory relation between oneself and other people with regard to power and influence. In other words, every individual has a need to control his situation to some degree, so that his environment can be predictable for him. Ordinarily this amounts to controlling other people, because other people are the main agents that threaten him and create an unpredictable and uncontrollable situation. This need for control varies from

Exhibit I Extreme types on the three interpersonal dimensions

EXPRESSED BEHAVIOR		DIMENSION	WANTED BEHAVIOR	
EXTREME HIGH	EXTREME LOW		EXTREME HIGH	EXTREME LOW
OVERSOCIAL	UNDERSOCIAL	INCLUSION	SOCIAL–COMPLIANT	COUNTERSOCIAL
AUTOCRAT	ABDICRAT	CONTROL	SUBMISSIVE	REBELLIOUS
OVERPERSONAL	UNDERPERSONAL	AFFECTION	PERSONAL–COMPLIANT	COUNTERPERSONAL

those who want to control their entire environment, including all the people around them, to those who want to control no one in any situation, no matter how appropriate controlling them would be.

Here, again, everyone varies as to the degree to which he wants to control others. In addition, everyone varies with respect to the degree to which he wants to be controlled by other people, from those who want to be completely controlled and are dependent on others for making decisions for them to those who want to be controlled under no conditions.

The Need for Affection

This is the need to maintain a satisfactory relation between the self and other people with regard to love and affection. In the business setting, this need is seldom made overt. It takes the form of friendship. In essence, affection is a relationship between two people only, a dyadic relationship. At one extreme individuals like very close, personal relationships with each individual they meet. At the other extreme are those who like their personal relationships to be quite impersonal and distant, perhaps friendly but not close and intimate.

Again, between these two extremes everyone has a level of intimacy that is most comfortable for him. From the other side, each individual prefers that others make overtures to him in a way that indicates a certain degree of closeness.

To clarify the various orientations in these three areas, *Exhibit I* presents the extreme positions taken on each of the dimensions. Everyone fits somewhere between these two extremes, most of them in the middle.

Group Compatibility

This theory of interpersonal relations can be very useful to businessmen in determining the compatibility of the members of a group. If at the outset we can choose a group of people who can work together harmoniously, we shall go far toward avoiding situations where a group's efforts are wasted in interpersonal conflicts.

Our theoretical framework is designed to handle this problem. Suppose we consider in more detail the two aspects for each one of the three interpersonal dimensions. One aspect is what we *do* with relation to other people; let us call this "e" for *expressed* behavior. The second is what we *want* from other people, how we want them to act toward us; let us call this "w" for *wanted* behavior. Then we can use "e" and "w" to try to find out how people will relate to each other in the *inclusion* dimension ("I"), the *control* dimension ("C"), and the *affection* dimension ("A"), as shown schematically in *Exhibit II*.

If we make a ten-point scale, from zero to nine, and say that in each of the two aspects of the three dimensions everyone has some propensity, some preferred behavior, we can characterize each person by six scores: e^I, w^I, e^C, w^C, e^A, w^A.

In the course of my research I have developed a questionnaire, called FIRO-B (the "B" refers to *behavior*), comprising a check list of 54 statements designed to measure an individual's propensities in each of these six categories; a portion of it is shown in *Exhibit III*. The resulting scores for each need area can be plotted on a diagram, as in *Exhibit IV*.

Exhibit II Schema of interpersonal behaviors

EXPRESSED BEHAVIOR	DIMENSION	WANTED BEHAVIOR
I initiate interaction with people	INCLUSION	I want to be included
I control people	CONTROL	I want people to control me
I act close and personal toward people	AFFECTION	I want people to get close and personal to me

TWO KINDS

Note that in *Exhibit IV* there are two diagonals, which may be used to explain two different kinds of compatibility—"originator compatibility" (oK) and "interchange compatibility" (xK). Individuals can be located on these diagonals from their scores on FIRO-B.

In popular literature there are at least two well-known and apparently contradictory maxims relating to the bases of compatibility: "Opposites attract," and "Birds of a feather flock together." Considering the diagonals on *Exhibit IV* might aid us in coming to a sensible resolution of these maxims, since there seems to be some truth in each of them.

Exhibit III Sample of questionnaire

GROUP......................................

DATE...

MALE.............FEMALE.............

AGE..

NAME...

FIRO-B

	I	C	A
c			
w			

Please place number of the answer that best applies to you in the box at the left of the statement. Please be as honest as you can.

1. I try to be with people.
   1. usually 2. often 3. sometimes 4. occasionally 5. rarely 6. never

2. I let other people decide what to do.
   1. usually 2. often 3. sometimes 4. occasionally 5. rarely 6. never

3. I join social groups.
   1. usually 2. often 3. sometimes 4. occasionally 5. rarely 6. never

4. I try to have close relationships with people.
   1. usually 2. often 3. sometimes 4. occasionally 5. rarely 6. never

5. I tend to join social organizations when I have an opportunity.
   1. usually 2. often 3. sometimes 4. occasionally 5. rarely 6. never

other people strongly influence my actions.
   usually 2. often 3. sometimes 4. occasionally 5. rarely 6. never

23. I try to ... mal social activities.
   1. most people ... 3. sometimes 4. occasionally 5. rarely 6. never
   ...th people.
   ...netimes

24. I let other people control my actions.
   1. most people 2. many people 3. ... people ...ionally 5. rarely 6. never

25. I act cool and distant with people.
   1. most people 2. many people 3. some people 4. a few people 5. ... 6. never

26. I am easily led by people.
   1. most people 2. many people 3. some people 4. a few people 5. one or two people 6. nobody

27. I try to have close, personal relationships with people.
   1. most people 2. many people 3. some people 4. a few people 5. one or two people 6. nobody

© William C. Schutz 1957

Reproduction in whole or part permitted for any purpose of the United States Government

(See other side)

Originator Diagonal

Let us take an example in the control dimension and consider the lower-right to upper-left line. The people who fall in the lower-right quadrant are the ones who want to control others and do not want to be controlled themselves. These people can be called autocrat-rebels; they want to be the bosses and do not want anyone else to tell them what to do. In the upper-left quadrant we have just the opposite. These are abdicrat-submissives; they want to be told what to do, and they do not want to control anyone else.

For smooth functioning it would appear that if we had one autocrat-rebel, we would not want another one, since they would both want to give orders and neither would want to take them. This is called *competitive* incompatibility. Also, if we had two abdicrat-submissives, a situation would be created wherein both people want someone to tell them what to do and neither wants to do the telling. This is called *apathetic* incompatibility. However, if we have one autocrat-rebel and one abdicrat-submissive, the relationship will probably be

Exhibit IV Graphic representation of interpersonal dimensions

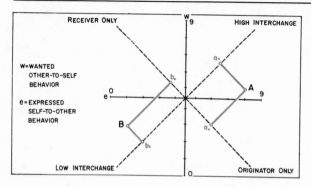

harmonious, since one person wants to give orders and the other wants to take them.

Interchange Diagonal

Now, consider the other diagonal on the diagram. Let us take affection for an example this time. In the upper-right quadrant are the people who express a lot of close personal behavior and want the same expressed to them. These are the people of "high interchange," and they can be called overpersonal-personal-compliants. They like an atmosphere in which there is a lot of affection; so, for instance, they would like a party better than a board of directors meeting. In the lower-left quadrant are people of "low interchange," who like neither to give nor to receive affection. They can be called underpersonal-counterpersonals. They do not want anyone to get very close to them, nor do they want to get very close to anyone. They like their relations rather reserved, cool, and distant.

Here the complementary idea of the originator diagonal—that opposites attract—does not apply; for, if one person likes to be very close and personal and the other person does not, they are going to threaten each other. One who likes to keep his relations reserved is not going to like it when the other makes overtures; and, in the reverse direction, the one who wants very close relations is not going to be very happy if the other does not. So it seems reasonable that the situation would lead to harmony more readily if the people involved were close on this diagonal, unlike the situation on the originator diagonal.

In the inclusion dimension, again, it would be better if both interacting persons were very close to being either very high or very low on this diagonal so that one would not always want to be with people while the other wanted to stay home and read a book. Hence, on the interchange diagonal the "birds of a feather" maxim seems most appropriate; people should be similar in their values along this diagonal.

To exemplify the working of the technique let us consider *Exhibit IV* for the control area:

From FIRO-B we learn that A has a score of 8 on e^C and 5 on w^C, while B has a score of 1 on e^C and 1 on w^C. These points are plotted on the diagram. Each score, for illustrative purposes, may be divided into two components, one on each diagonal. These components are represented by a_x and a_o and b_x and b_o on the diagram.

The measure of interchange compatibility (xK) of A and B is proportional to the distance between a_x and b_x. A smaller distance means a more similar orientation toward the amount of interchange of control that should exist in a relation. In the example, A believes that relations should involve a great deal of influence and control, while B's preference is for less structured, more laissez-faire relations. Their incompatibility in this regard is reflected in the relatively large distance between a_x and b_x.

Originator compatibility (oK) is proportional to the sum of a_o and b_o. Optimal originator compatibility occurs when one score is to the left of the midpoint of the diagonal and the other score is exactly the same distance to the right of the midpoint. In our example this is almost exactly true; thus A and B have high originator compatibility. A wishes to control others but not to be controlled, while B wishes to be controlled but not to control or influence others very much. Hence they complement each other.

Our conclusion then about this pair is the following: they disagree as to the atmosphere they desire regarding mutual influence and control. A likes structured hierarchies while B prefers more permissive relations. However, when there is a situation of a certain structure, they are compatible with regard to the roles they will take in relation to each other. A will take the influential, responsible position, and B will take the subordinate role.

These psychological considerations can very easily be converted into formulas, and in research work and practical applications this is done. There have been several experiments performed that indicate the usefulness of this approach. These experiments demonstrate that groups of from two to eight can be composed—based on FIRO-B scores—in such a way that their productivity, and to some extent their interaction, is predictable. Much research is still to be done to improve the accuracy of these predictions, but the results are highly encouraging.[1]

1. See William C. Schutz, op. cit.

Group Development

Another major point in the theory is that every group, no matter what its function or composition, given enough time, goes through the three interpersonal phases of inclusion, control, and affection in the same sequence. To illustrate:

Recently, I was interviewing a member of a group, which had just completed 30 meetings, to get an idea of her feeling about the experience. In response to the question, "How would you describe what happened in this group?" she replied, "Well, first you're concerned about the problem of where you fit in the group; then you're wondering about what you'll accomplish. Finally, after a while, you learn that people mean something. Your primary concern becomes how people feel about you and about each other."

IN OR OUT

First, *the inclusion phase centers around the question of "in or out."* It begins with the formation of the group. When people are confronted with each other, they must first find the place where they fit in. This involves being in or out of the group, establishing oneself as a specific individual, and seeing if one is going to be paid attention to and not be left behind or ignored. This anxiety area gives rise to individual-centered behavior such as overtalking, extreme withdrawal, exhibitionism, and recitation of biographies and other previous experience.

At the same time the basic problem of commitment to the group is present. Each member is implicitly deciding to what degree he will become a member of the group, how much investment he will withdraw from his other commitments and invest in this new relationship. He is asking, "How much of myself will I devote to this group? How important will I be in this setting? Will they know who I am and what I can do, or will I be indistinguishable from many others?" This is, in short, the problem of identity. He is, in effect, deciding primarily on his preferred amount of inclusion interchange and his preferred amount of inclusion initiation with the other members—just how much actual contact, interaction, and communication he wishes to have.

Hence, the main concerns of the formative process are "boundary problems," problems that have to do with entering into the boundaries of a group and belonging to that group. These are problems of inclusion.

Characteristic of groups in this phase is the occurrence of what have been called "goblet issues." The term is taken from an analogy to a cocktail party where people sometimes pick up their cocktail glass, or goblet, and figuratively peer through it to size up the other people at the party. Hence, they are issues that in themselves are of minor importance to the group members but serve as vehicles for getting to know people, especially in relation to oneself.

Often a goblet issue is made of the first decision confronting a group. In some groups discussions leading to a decision about such an issue continue for an unbelievably long time and then never reach a conclusion. But there has been a great deal of learning in that the members have gained a fairly clear picture of each other. Each member knows who responds favorably to him, who sees things the way he does, how much he knows as compared to the others, how the leader responds to him, and what type of role he can expect to play in the group. Acquiring this knowledge is the unconscious purpose of the goblet issue.

The frustrating experience of having groups endlessly discuss topics of little real interest to anyone is very common. Every group finds its own goblet issues within the framework of its aim. "The weather" is fairly universal; "rules of procedure" is common in formal groups; "Do you know so-and-so?" often characterizes new acquaintances from the same location; relating incidents or telling stories has a goblet element for business gatherings; and "Where are you from?" often serves for military settings. Mark Twain apparently overlooked the fact that nobody really *wants* to "do anything about the weather"—they just want to use it as a topic for sizing up people. These discussions are inevitable, and, contrary to all outward appearances, they do serve an important function. Groups that are not permitted this type of testing out will search for some other method of obtaining the same personal information, perhaps using as a vehicle a decision of more importance to the work of the group.

TOP OR BOTTOM

After the problems of inclusion have been sufficiently resolved, control problems become prominent. *This phase centers around the problem of "top or bottom."* Once members are fairly well established as being together in a group, the issue of decision-making procedures arises. This involves problems of sharing responsibility and its necessary concomitant, distribution of power and control. Characteristic behavior at this stage includes leadership struggles; competition; and discussion of orientation to the task, structuring, rules of procedure, methods of decision making, and sharing the responsibility for the group's work. The primary anxieties at this phase revolve around having too much or too little responsibility and too much or too little influence. Each member is trying to establish himself in the group so that he has the most comfortable amount of interchange and the most comfortable degree of initiation with the other members with regard to control, influence, and responsibility.

NEAR OR FAR

Finally, following a satisfactory resolution of these phases, problems of affection become focal. *This phase centers on the issue of "near or far."* The individuals have come together to form a group; they have differentiated themselves with respect to responsibility and power. Now they must become emotionally integrated. At this stage it is characteristic to see such behavior expressed through positive feelings, direct personal hostility, jealousies, pairing behavior, and, in general, heightened emotional feeling between pairs of people.

The primary anxieties at this stage have to do with not being liked or close enough to people or with being too intimate. Each member is striving to obtain his most favorable amount of affectional interchange and most comfortable position regarding initiating and receiving affection—deciding, like Schopenhauer's porcupines, how to get close enough to receive warmth, yet avoid the pain of sharp quills.

TIGHTENING THE BOLTS

These are not distinct phases. The group development postulate asserts that these problem areas are *emphasized* at certain points in a group's growth, but all three problem areas are always present. Similarly, some people do not always go along with the central issue for the group. For certain individuals a particular problem area will be so personally potent that it will transcend the current group issue. The area of concern for any individual will result from his own problem areas and those of the group's current phase. Perhaps a close approximation to the developmental phenomena is given by the tire-changing model:

When a person changes a tire and replaces the wheel, he first sets the wheel in place and secures it by tightening the bolts one after another just enough so the wheel is in place and the next step can be taken. Then the bolts are tightened further, usually in the same sequence, until the wheel is firmly in place. Finally each bolt is gone over separately to secure it.

In a similar way, the need areas are worked on until they are handled satisfactorily enough to continue with the work at hand. Later on they are returned to and worked over to a more satisfactory degree. If one need area has not been worked out well on the first sequence, it must receive more attention on the next cycle.

Applications of Theory

The next question is: What can we do about these problems so as to utilize this information practically? This is more difficult. The above analysis is derived largely from experience with experimental research on small groups selected for this purpose. Solutions for the problems observed are largely, though not entirely, speculative and can only be offered as suggestions which should be explored carefully in each individual case before being adopted.

More specifically, the interpretations presented here can be looked upon as suggestions for *diagnosis*. The more men in business can become aware of the basic factors underlying their interpersonal difficulties, the better they will be able to meet these difficulties. As in the practice of medicine, if the disease is properly diagnosed, the doctor has a better chance of curing it than if it is improperly or superficially diagnosed, even though a correct diagnosis by no means guarantees a cure.

CLEARING THE AIR

Serious interpersonal difficulties that are left covert only smolder and erupt at the expense of efficiency and productivity. The most effective way covert difficulties can be dealt with is by first making them overt. For example:

In one marketing group, the leader finally told one member that he did not like the way he was acting in the group and that he felt he should contribute more. After a brief but difficult and bitter exchange the two began to tell each other their feelings about the situation. They managed to clear the air, and the situation improved markedly.

When successful, overt discussion is like a cold shower: it is approached with apprehension, the initial impact is very uncomfortable, but the final result justifies the tribulations.

To summarize, "interpersonal problems" include difficulties such as members who are withdrawn from a group; personal hostilities between members; problem members who are either inactive and unintegrated or overactive and destructive; power struggles between group members; members battling for attention; dissatisfaction with the leadership in the group; dissatisfaction with the amount of acknowledgment that an individual's contributions are getting; or dissatisfaction with the amount of affection and warmth exhibited in the group.

If it becomes quite clear to the group members that their difficulties are so severe that their activity is being impaired, then bringing the issues out into the open and talking about them will help. It is somewhat difficult, however, to tell exactly when a problem is so severe that it is holding the group up. Perhaps some of the earlier discussion of symptoms will be useful for assessing the effect of interpersonal factors on the group.

It might be helpful to view groups (including anywhere from two to twenty people) on a continuum—from those that are completely compatible, that is, able to work well together, to those that are completely incompatible, that is, incapable of working together. Any particular group can be placed somewhere along this continuum. To illustrate:

The members of the group at the extreme compatible end of the continuum are able to work well together within a relatively short time with a minimum of difficulty and can operate effectively over a period of time on a wide variety of problems. They need no training or new awareness.

The group at the incompatible end, however, cannot work effectively. The interpersonal problems that cause the task difficulties are so deep-seated in the personalities of the individual members that no amount of outside assistance will be worthwhile. It would take so long before this group could operate effectively that, from a practical standpoint, any kind of training of the group members or any awareness of their problems would be unfruitful.

Between these two extreme types are groups that profit more or less by the kind of awareness that has been discussed. If a group is relatively near the compatible end, with a minimum of awareness and a minimum of discussion of its difficult problems, it will become a smoothly functioning group. If interpersonal problems in a group are very minor, they can usually be ignored without impairing the group seriously; or, if the problems exist between two members, they can often work out their difficulties by themselves outside the group.

With groups near the incompatible end much more intensive work has to be done to get through their problems so that they can function effectively. Such work should probably be guided by someone who is experienced with group process and can help group members to work out their difficulties.

Another advantage of this approach operates more through the individuals than the group. If the individual members can gain the kind of awareness of their own needs in situations as discussed in this article, then this in itself will help them to understand their reactions to other people and, perhaps, to operate more effectively. In addition, it is often helpful to point out to group members that other people have the same basic needs; for, if they understand what other people are trying to do, they may be more tolerant of other people's behavior. Since everyone has these needs, everyone tries to get the same thing from other people, even though each may use different adaptive patterns for achieving his ends. To illustrate such a mechanism:

It generally is felt that if an individual has an excessively strong negative reaction to another individual in the setting of a work group, the individual who is irritated fears deep down within himself that he is like the one who annoys him, that he himself has the trait that is so annoying. It is threatening for him to see it in some other individual, and he must immediately deny it and attack it, almost as if he were trying to deny to himself that he is like this.

Awareness of mechanisms of this type may help in understanding what is happening in the group and one's own reaction in the situation.

Conclusion

The time seems to have come for the businessman to make use of some of the social scientists' more recent findings on the unconscious, or covert, factors in human interaction. Since the businessman does deal so heavily in interpersonal relations, his skill and success are dependent on his ability to understand interpersonal relations and to deal effectively with them. Thus, it becomes important for him to gain a more basic understanding instead of simply trying out panaceas that aim only at the symptoms of the problems and not at the basic problems themselves. He must understand the vast interpersonal underworld that operates beneath the overt, observable behavior.

As I have already pointed out, current interest in what are called "communications problems" provides an example of the symptomatic approach, for these problems are symptoms of poor interpersonal relations rather than primary causes of operational difficulties. It is an error, therefore, to try to attack the problems of communication by building more effective physical lines of communication, when the trouble really lies in the relation between individuals. The way to attack the basic problem would seem to be to investigate what is going on among the individuals themselves and try to improve those relations.

If it is true that the unconscious factors are so all-important to understanding groups, then we ought to find out exactly how these factors do affect what the businessman is usually primarily interested in—namely, effective operation. In this article I have tried to illustrate the inadequacy of attempting to operate by ignoring interpersonal difficulties and attending to the task only, since in reality the interpersonal factors somehow find their way into the task and directly affect the productivity of the group. No matter how much people try to keep interpersonal problems out by ignoring them, they will turn up in subtle forms such as loss of motivation, tiredness, or the group member's preoccupation with outside tasks; or they may get entangled directly with the solution of the task and have to be worked out in the body of the problem.

I have offered a theoretical framework that may be of some help in understanding the structure of these interpersonal problems in an attempt to aid in the diagnosis of interpersonal behavior. Such a diagnosis may then leave the businessman in a better position to deal with what actually occurs. I have tried to suggest possible lines of solution, but these attempts are offered in a much more speculative manner. Although they are based on rather extensive experience with psychological phenomena, they are only suggestions that the individual businessman must try out and adapt to his own needs.

17. Why Motivation Theory Doesn't Work

Thomas H. Fitzgerald

Is it possible that people cannot be "motivated"? This is certainly not a pleasant question to ponder, especially for those managers confronted with mounting problems of high employee turnover, low productivity, and poor morale. The author of this article suggests, however, that the roots of such problems go deeper than is generally recognized, and the major tenets of motivation theory offer solutions that are not quite relevant to what is going on in the workplace. Instead of thinking of employees as objects, to be manipulated by this or that theoretical approach, management must strive to effect fundamental, value-oriented changes in the structure of rationalized work systems.

Rising costs and recessionary pressures have prompted the business community, as well as administrators of public agencies, to seek economies. One potential source of savings is in labor costs, but these have resisted reduction because of the downward rigidity of wage rates and the difficulties of increasing aggregate labor productivity. The growing pressures for economy and productivity also stress other labor problems that increase costs: absenteeism and turnover, idleness and featherbedding, product defects and errors. All this is reflected in one of the more familiar questions one hears at management seminars, "How can I motivate my employees?"

Equally familiar to most of us are the recurring themes concerning the motivation problem developed by perhaps a score of business theorists and commentators. Their speeches and publications, together with a number of widely distributed educational films summarizing their views, have arrived at a common core of midrange theory. What this theory says about employee motivation, both in diagnosis and prescription, is a significant advance from naïve conceptions of "morale" during the World War II era, the discredited industrial engineering approach prior to that, and the casual omniscience of the popular press. But what, really, does it tell us?

Briefly, we are told that the concept of motivation is complex, but can and should be understood. Human beings have basic physiological needs that must be satisfied, but these are supplemented by numerous other biosocial and culturally derived needs. The individual's actual movement to satisfy his needs depends not only on their state of readiness within himself but also on the objective situation in which he moves (i.e., the field containing other actors), together with his perception of the situation, which is in turn influenced by his own past experiences—i.e., successes or failures in finding satisfaction.

Seeds of Doubt

In the business environment, exchanging time for money may take care of a few of the worker's important needs, but it does nothing for those other "higher" needs such as sense of competence, recognition, and so on, that emerge after he has achieved a minimum amount of security. But the work must be performed in any case, and the failure to fill these higher needs results in frustration, antagonism, indolence, and malingering.

When motivation is found thus failing, management's response may not be to throw out the carrot-and-stick theory but to conclude either: (a) that work is inherently irksome and new and more interesting carrots are required, or (b) that workers are a shiftless and lazy lot and stronger sticks are required. The first conclusion, of course, has not solved the problem, while the second is self-validating and defeatist, and leads to more controls, more resentment, more "shiftless" behavior.

What can be done? The advice of the motivator fraternity shows a remarkable unanimity and, with some minor injustice to the subtlety of individual perception and diagnosis, can be summarized in the following three counsels:

1. Enlarge or enrich[1] jobs to make the work more interesting by restoring challenge and the potential for achievement satisfactions. Employees will be motivated to perform well those tasks that are in themselves worth doing.

2. Institute training to modify supervisory style. Supervisors are encouraged to be employee-centered and to assist workers in defining and reaching their job goals. They should act as friendly helpers rather than as policemen.

3. Foster employee "participation" by encouraging workers to take part in the decision process. Participation ranges from such elementary forms as giving employees advance notice of changes or explanations of these changes to more

1. Some theorists distinguish between job enlargement and job enrichment; see, for example, Frederick Herzberg, "One More Time: How Do You Motivate Employees?" HBR January-February 1968, p. 53. I find, however, that little distinction is made between them in actual practice and use enlargement here as a blanket term.

involved forms like stating a problem and requesting employee solutions. The final phase, still largely conceptual, is for the employees themselves to identify the problems, discuss possible solutions, and then arrive at joint decisions. Under these conditions, relationships would no longer be superior/subordinate or master/menial, hence characterized by antagonism and anxiety; instead, they would reflect a refreshing mutuality, trust, honesty, and concern in a climate where organizational goals coalesce with individual goals.

My purpose in this paper is to express doubts about these counsels and to suggest that their general adoption will be more difficult than anyone has recognized publicly. This is not meant to imply that the counselors claim general solutions; they admit difficulties and limitations and the fact that positive motivation in some situations, such as conventional assembly lines, is remote. But their writings, films, and public addresses have an unmistakable hortatory character and require a reasoned demurrer.

My thesis is that the proposed remedies are not adequate because the seriousness of the motivation problem has been underestimated. In what follows, I shall examine some early developments in the organization of rationalized work systems that, from the perspective of contemporary society, reflect assumptions that have become increasingly less valid and at the same time generate extensive tensions and strains. After discussing the advice commonly prescribed to mitigate this distress (the three counsels mentioned earlier), I shall offer some prescriptions of my own.

Roots of Rationality

The problem of employee motivation has its origins in certain fundamental conditions of industrial society, and is magnified by the cumulative effect of historical and cultural trends. The roots of the problem are implicit in three early assumptions in the organization of rationalized work systems and will require more extensive changes in our interdependent, multidimensional systems than most businessmen, motivational theorists, and consultants would like to think.

1. STOPWATCH MEASUREMENT

An early assumption of the factory system involved the choice of a time frame in which certain utilitarian calculations were made. Since workers were paid a daily or hourly wage, the value of their output was computed on the same basis, while the use of the stopwatch made it possible to calculate output-value minute by minute, thereby firmly establishing utility in the short run. Production operations were rationalized to maximize output in this short run through detailed process planning and narrow division of tasks. This system simplified the tabulation of worker outputs and allowed effective control of large quantities of unskilled labor, but let us consider some of its other effects:

□ The imperatives of short-run efficiency disrupted work group solidarities, and, simultaneously, the mass employment system and the extensive size of the plants hindered their formation; thus an important source of day-to-day, small group control of individual deviance was weakened, and the transmission and continuity of those values that make up the workmanship ethic were obstructed.

□ Decisions on the quality of workmanship made by individual workers in the handicraft era were largely replaced by machine process control, which was made necessary in any case by the utilities of standardization and of interchangeability of parts.

□ The vast elaboration of structure, together with the separation and, later, remoteness of ownership from management made it more difficult to identify with, or even see, the patrons of one's efforts.

It is scarcely now disputed that these dysfunctional consequences and the miscalculation of their real costs in a longer time frame are expressed in workplace problems such as employee hostility or indifference and unthinking dependency. What is important here, however, is that a narrow division of labor, churning of labor markets, and large-scale units are intrinsic parts of rationalized production systems where costs are computed in the short run (i.e., "false maximization"). Any attempt to resolve worker and workplace problems must recognize these structural sources.

2. OBJECTIVE DECISION MAKING

Another assumption of rationalized production has to do with what might be called the "spatial" frame; that is, the failure to foresee a widening of rational attitudes to the work force. As rationality became characteristic not only of production operations, but of engineering, investment, marketing, and management generally, calculation of objective inputs and outputs became the habitual basis for decisions. The broader effects of these decisions, however, as well as the cognitive style of the decision makers, could not long go unnoticed within the company. Difficulties arose when the same rational habits of mind infected the work force, displacing existing class and ethnic styles or causing doubts about the continuance of an earlier patrimonial solicitude.

However, the problem becomes more complicated when everyone decides to base the application of his efforts on pleasure-pain, input-output calculations as do utilitarian managers. This is especially true if, as is now the case, schedules of rewards are truncated by single rate pay systems and uniform work standards, while schedules of punishments are partly neutralized by a full employment–welfare system and the protection possible for individuals through combination (unions). Workers are transformed into job itinerants who do not identify with any one employer; the "rational" worker can blandly ask, "What's in it for me?"

But there is a further infection: that is to say, the spread of "competitive" attitudes to the managers and supervisors of the work force. The ethos of competition—of one against all, of individual maximization—belongs, properly speaking, to entrepreneurs and among entrepreneurs. When it spills over into the work force (or is even cultivated there by management that naïvely asserts it as a general good), it leads to a self-perpetuating cycle of suspiciousness, blaming and reprisals, withholding of information—either bad news or necessary facts—errors, defensiveness, and more distrust (although admittedly, one hears less of that competitive bravado with the growth of a systems approach to management).

3. RIGID VALUE SYSTEM

Perhaps the most important assumption concerns the availability of certain *nonrational* elements necessary to the work force, and implicit in the operation of rational organization as we know it. That is to say, the personality traits and values (orderliness, accuracy, neatness, punctuality, specialization of knowledge in a career path, success striving, deference to rank and authority, predictability, impersonality, reliance on rules and procedures, etc.) that "fitted into" the needs of rational bureaucracy so well, were not seen as possible *variables* but as a natural, continuing "given"—as was the society that bred these traits, the culture that was saturated with them.

Clear evidence to the contrary, of course, existed in anthropological reports of other societies in remote places, but now such evidence is widely available here in our own society. The lack of a temperament impelled toward assiduous effort or habitual striving for ever higher goals and the incomplete internalization of certain aesthetic values and normative controls appear not only as an "exception" among ghetto blacks (who explicitly reject them) or the alienated white youth in the street culture, but increasingly in other sectors of society as well.

That there is now a widespread indifference to, or even contempt for, authority, both as "idea" and reality (ascribed status, deference, the legitimacy of externally imposed sanctions, tradition) has been widely reported. A persistent populism and egalitarianism, reinforced by the spread of empirical or "scientific" attitudes and demystification of "divine right," "natural law," and so on, seems to be responsible for the change. Professionalization of knowledge also increasingly strains against the authority of rank.

A further difficulty with this third assumption has been noted by Charles Reich in his book *The Greening of America*.[2] He points out that the rising volume of industrial production, which is the inevitable result of successful, rationally organized enterprises, must be disposed of by means of a pervading and utopian advertising, which in turn is gradually disrupting industry's own foundation, the work force.

Workers, regularly instructed as consumers in a ceaseless acquisition of goods and services, lose their willingness to bear with the common drudgery. The offers of independence, the encouragement to self-aggrandisement, and the persistent flattery they experience as audience all contrast unfavorably with the discipline and the subordination they experience as employees. Work loses its "religious" character, its centrality as the locus for the self. It is replaced by a sort of populist hedonism, ranging from compulsive accumulation to the new connoisseurship.

Even if consumption were not thus stimulated, human beings are not satisfied with constant rewards—unlike Professor Skinner's pigeons, one grain at $T_1 \neq$ one grain at T_n. The escalation of human wants, once satisfaction is achieved, produces a continuing problem. As workers "use up" their material shelter-survival needs, they seek such intangibles and unbuyables as freedom and autonomy (one might add, following Baudelaire: beauty, clarity, luxury, and calm). These, obviously, are incompatible with the life of organized production.

A Realistic Reappraisal

Questions seem to leap from a recognition of the increasing vulnerability of the foregoing assumptions, especially the third assumption. Will it be possible to continue to operate "efficient," closely synchronized, and interdependent organizations if change in the personality-culture system continues in the same direction? Put in another and more value-oriented way: How much personal freedom is *possible* in a hierarchical, bureaucratic authority system? At what point does individual style become incompatible with order?

To push it further, what is the potential for becoming an authentic self in a

2. New York, Random House, 1970.

system characterized by well-defined role behaviors and role expectations that inherently demand reification and internalization?

Other questions, however, are at issue here: Are job enlargement, training, and employee participation realistic approaches to solving the new—as well as the old—motivation problem in industry? Are they practical? Will they work? It is to these counsels that we now turn.

THE ENLARGEMENT COUNSEL

Job enlargement is more modest than participation, less ambitious in its objectives, and apparently easier and less disruptive "to do." This prescription also has more substance than the talk therapies of the training-climate approach to motivation. While there is some empirical validation of the value of job enlargement, I am skeptical over its applicability in a wider variety of work situations and, more important, over a longer period of time.

There is probably little disagreement any more about the desirability of eliminating as much as possible of egregiously repetitive operations, much as we correct poor lighting or dirty lavatories. In fact, in both shops and offices, a really repetitive job is an obvious candidate for automation or computerization. But after the more monotonous jobs are eliminated, we arrive at a wide range of operations where perception, rather than objective reality, is crucial.

Individuals differ vastly in their need for variety, responsibility, and competence, just as they vary in their need for independence or security. The job Jones finds moronic and insufferable is okay with Smith, yet too much for Brown. Restructuring and/or enlarging jobs are brave attempts to fit the job to the man, but *which* man? Do we have different sets and sequences of the same operations for people of varying competence, interest, and drive? Does turnover, then, imply continued rearrangement?

The school solution would reply: it's a matter for employment and placement to select similar people. But, of course, things don't work out that neatly in practice. Additional investments must also be made to broaden employee skills to meet increased responsibilities, although it is not yet clear whether employees will (a) expect greater compensation for this, or (b) be satisfied with increased psychic income.

It is obvious, however, that management's present flexibility in reallocating unskilled labor without loss of training investment would be reduced.

Finally, as time passes, one cannot but wonder how much of the added challenge remains, whether the broadened responsibility persists in its motivational propensity, or the worker merely paraphrases the well-known question

"What have you enlarged for me lately?" (How else to explain the faded motivation of those with amply challenging jobs—say, bored executives, doctors, or college professors?)

THE TRAINING COUNSEL

A second prescription for improved motivation—to enhance supervisory style and the climate of communication through in-house education and training—shares limitations similar to those cited for job enlargement: it does not get at enough of the basic incongruence between individual needs and organizational goals.

The fact that there is *some* congruence can be readily admitted, but this does not change the tension that exists any more than does the recognition of the inconsistency of certain needs within the individual himself. The difficulty is that attention to improving attitudes and undesirable behaviors is usually directed at surface symptoms, without significant attempts to correct the underlying source. If a group of supervisors behave in a bossy, condescending, and insensitive manner, it is rarely because anyone *told* them to act that way, but because of other influences in the organization that are just as real as talk. For example:

☐ The system of selecting supervisors from the work group may make it clear that one type of personality will succeed but others will not.

☐ Supervisory styles are perpetuated by modeling, and by the success of those who learn from the successful models. Attitudes about what is really important are conveyed not only by the official mottoes on posters, but in every conversation, in every inquiry and direction.

☐ An invidious system of monetary and status rewards must of necessity produce relative deprivation for some workers. The resulting competition to achieve rewards (or avoid deprivation) tends to encourage withholding of information and a lack of trust. Blaming, scapegoating, and defensiveness follow.

☐ Punishments and reprisals for deviance or poor performance in themselves provide satisfactions to those who have made the sacrifices necessary to self-discipline.

☐ Dependency is often cultivated at the lower levels because it is thought to ensure predictability of actions.

And so it goes. If we want to change all that, we have to ask (here, in behavioral terminology), "What are those forces in the situation that reinforce specific behaviors while acting to extinguish others?" Even where the supervisory attitudes themselves are found to be a cause of the motivation problem, change may be difficult because these attitudes are linked in with larger value systems—the belief that a supervisor should be dominant, assertive, even truculent, is supported by a more general mythology of masculine authority and prowess, and by a leadership imagery borrowed from athletics or the military.

Structural considerations

The failures of other attempts to change attitudes—as, for example, in efforts to eliminate racism in this country—have led to a reorientation of tactics of change toward more substantive methods; that is, to get inside "the black box" of institutional and organizational process. The lesson of that experience, however, is not necessarily that talk cannot change attitudes for the better, as well as encourage those who are ready to change. Some things are good in themselves, and a management that promotes a decent concern for employees' integrity, growth, and well-being should not have to look to an economic payoff as justification. The point here, however, is that education in itself has limited potential for producing and sustaining improvement unless changes, consistent with officially sponsored values, are also made in process and structure.

THE PARTICIPATION COUNSEL

While participatory management is often urged by corporate liberals these days as the most desirable avenue of change, analysis of its dimensions and their implications for contemporary organizations suggests that it is questionable whether participation can correct pervasive apathy and indifference, let alone provide an unqualified good.

Of course, much of the advice is noble, urging the development of an improved climate of communication, trust, acceptance, mutuality, and so forth; but it is often unclear how, objectively, these attitudes are to be brought about and maintained. Also an open question is whether any significant percentage of the work force even wants to participate, other than perhaps for the novelty of doing so.[3] Although the advocates of this prescription for motivational health have failed to supply many important details of actual implementation, it is not hard to surmise what new difficulties might evolve.

Pressure for more involvement

Participation is not a simple or linear gradation of acts. It means more, for example, than giving accurate information, listening to responses, answering questions, seeking advice or ratification. It may mean interactions with groups

3. See Robert Dahl, "The Case for Worker Control," *New York Review of Books,* November 19, 1970.

of employees, as well as one-over-one relationships. The subjects of participation, moreover, are not necessarily restricted to those few matters that management considers to be of direct, personal interest to employees, or to those plans and decisions that will benefit from employee advice. Neither of these positions can be maintained for long without (a) being recognized by employees as manipulative or (b) leading to expectations for wider and more significant involvement—"Why do they only ask us about plans for painting the office and not about replacing this old equipment and rearranging the layout?"

Once competence is shown (or believed to have been shown) in, say, rearranging the work area, and after participation has become a conscious, officially sponsored activity, participators may very well want to go on to topics of job assignment, the allocation of rewards, or even the selection of leadership. In other words, management's present monopoly—on initiating participation, on the nomination of conferees, and on the limitation of legitimate areas for review—can in itself easily become a source of contention.

Potential for disruption

Another difficulty with participation has to do with organizational effectiveness. The dysfunctions of bureaucratic systems are now well known, while the motivational potential of employee involvement is, if yet unrealized, at least widely anticipated. But the dysfunctional, disruptive effects of participation on rationally organized systems should not be ignored either. Before embarking on participatory management, advocates should consider the following points:

☐ It is not at all clear how the highly variable competence of employee participants can contribute to the solutions of corporate problems that have specific technical constraints, even though these employees are affected by the results. As the store of knowledge expands (and becomes more opaque) along with the need for its accurate application, organizations rely increasingly on experts and professionals, and it may in fact be true that the girls on the carton-folding operation really have nothing to contribute to almost anything important about running a container company. Once again, meritocracy confronts democracy.

☐ The scale of contemporary industry makes the implications of decisions, and the interaction of their effects, hard to foresee, although the need for precision is now greater. At some point the "critical mass" of large organizations is reached where their manageability even by the few—much less the many—becomes questionable. The closely linked, synchronized, interdependent nature of the numerous subsystems that now comprise large organizations would appear to make serious participation questionable not only in its technical aspects but in its goal-directed behavior. Inevitably, participation to any significant degree will cause indeterminacy and delay, loss of consistency and coherence, diluted and compromised objectives.

☐ Although it hasn't been discussed much yet, when blacks and women finally integrate supervisory and mid-management ranks, they may coalesce into identity groupings to seek representation. We already have examples of teachers, college students, welfare recipients, and others who have been demanding the right to participate as groups to help determine not only conditions within the system but its operation and outputs as well. Aside from the real costs in reduced effectiveness (partly balanced, of course, by better motivation, higher output, less waste, and so on) the impact of this new participation on the process and structure of management, though hard to estimate, must be anticipated, because what is really involved is politics, the conscious sharing of control and power. History does not offer many examples of oligarchies that have abdicated with grace and goodwill.

Once again, all this is not to imply that because gross efficiency and productivity may be reduced, we should not proceed toward alternatives. Given the goal of maximizing utility, however, there does seem to be a necessary trade-off between precision, on the one hand, and motivation through participation, on the other hand, and we shouldn't assume that we can have it both ways, just as we now admit that we can't have both full employment and price stability. The amount of each we want (or can tolerate), the location of the best trade-off point, is a matter of experimentation and calculation. Viewed from a wider perspective, it is also entirely possible for organizations to pursue new, multiple, even divergent goals, although the trade-off problem then becomes much tougher, involving basic values, or as they say these days, "priorities."

Conclusion

It may be that the question "How do I motivate my employees?" is not quite relevant to what is going on. Truth is sometimes damaged in the process of analysis and reconstruction, and concepts can easily become more "real" than the reality from which they were cut. When transplanted from the laboratory, the language of motivation may become subtly elitist by suggesting that the employee resembles a captive rodent in a training box equipped with levers, trick doors, food pellets, and electric grids. Talking about a majority (perhaps, in fact, a minority?) of people and how they live as being "motivated" may provide only a pretentious terminology which deflects understanding.

When a man gets up in the morning, we can say this act is a conditioned response to the stimulus of an alarm, but that doesn't *tell* us anything important. To say he is motivated by hunger may be true, but perhaps he is not hungry and thinks instead, "Seven o'clock; *time to get up.*" What he does the rest of the day may have much the same toneless character of going from one thing to another and getting by. This may very well be the way it is for a great many people, at least during the time they spend in the shop or the office, because most of what they really care for is in other places and at other times. A few of them may not even care strongly for much of anything, almost anywhere. Is it just possible that some whom we employ *can't* be motivated?

SOME ALTERNATIVES

I am aware, following a critique such as this, of expectations for suggesting alternatives. They can be offered so as not to deny my wider meliorism; yet their statement should not distract from the main thrust of the argument presented here: the problem of employee motivation is rooted in certain fundamental conditions of industrial society, and its solution will require costly and extensive changes in our interdependent, closely linked systems. Just as most of the signs point to a pervasive consumerism, environmentalism, and governmental surveillance in the market economy, so we should anticipate a persistent alienation of industrial and business manpower in relation to its employers.

What can be done; what is being tried? At very little cost we can avoid giving offense or being intrusive. Merely talking with people also does a lot of good, although it does not seem to be easy for many managers. Here is a brief overview of other possibilities:

☐ Inexpensive means such as emblems, slogans, contests, and sets of monogrammed glasses function as attention getters, but their transference value is always speculative.

☐ Praise and approval can produce temporary improvement of individual effort.

☐ Company-sponsored recreation and house organs are also comparatively cheap and seem to have a positive effect on some of the people part of the time.

☐ Money is recurrently popular as an incentive for more and better woɪk, but the general decline of piecework and profit-sharing plans testifies to the experience that these monetary incentives are not really effective in practice, partly because of intervening variables such as employee perception of an ambiguous means-ends relationship.

☐ Reducing the size of a productive or service unit seems to increase identification and improve motivation, but may introduce inefficiencies (especially as viewed by traditional costing methods) with no assurance of net gain.

☐ Stripping away the baroque elaborations of office may result in loss of the mystique of authority, but it could help create the conditions for unity.

Increasingly more expensive than the foregoing—in original investment as well as in maintenance—are mixes of "training" to improve skills and climate, of job enlargement, and of organizational development and participation. All imply substantial alterations in the way organizations are wired together and in communication and controls. They will eventually involve examination of reward and succession systems, priorities, and ends. Participation especially, as pointed out earlier, not only may start out as an unpleasant ride for those who are accustomed to being fully in charge, but also may become one from which it is increasingly hard to dismount.

What is needed is not merely the "willingness to confront change" (already a safe thought-cliché) but a commitment to go beyond changes in structure and procedures. What may even be required is relinquishing certain behaviors and beliefs, such as an ideology of certitude and constraint, a habit of objectifying people because of ranking or role ascription, or a style of address characterized by cant and bravado—difficult to give up, but not impossible.

We have seen progress in other areas where we once would not have expected it. We look back now at personality testing, slightly incredulous at its colonialist mentality and its banality of concepts, wondering how we could have been taken in by its promises of penetration and mastery. Similarly, perhaps yet in our time, we will be willing to discard the dismal vocabulary of motives, motivators, and motivation and start to think seriously about how to go about becoming a society of persons.

18. Appraisal of *What* Performance?

Harry Levinson

It may be stretching it a bit to argue that the epigram "It's not the winning or losing that counts, but how you play the game" ought to be strictly followed in designing performance appraisal systems. In business, results are important, and few would disagree. What the epigram points out, however, is that some results are not worth the means some take to achieve them. Nonetheless, most performance systems in most companies focus on results of behavior while in reality people are judged just as much on how they get things done. In this article, the author argues that in order for a company to have a performance appraisal system that accounts for the "how" as well as the "what," it will need to establish: job descriptions that are behavior- as well as results-oriented; a critical incident program in which managers write reports regularly on the behavior of their employees; and support mechanisms to help managers honestly appraise the behavior of their employees as well as of their bosses.

A corporate president put a senior executive in charge of a failing operation. His only directive was "Get it in the black." Within two years of that injunction, the new executive moved the operation from a deficit position to one that showed a profit of several million. Fresh from his triumph, the executive announced himself as a candidate for a higher-level position, and indicated that he was already receiving offers from other companies.

The corporate president, however, did not share the executive's positive opinions of his behavior. In fact, the president was not at all pleased with the way the executive had handled things.

Naturally the executive was dismayed, and when he asked what he had done wrong, the corporate president told him that he had indeed accomplished what he had been asked to do, but he had done it singlehandedly, by the sheer force of his own personality. Furthermore, the executive was told, he had replaced people whom the company thought to be good employees with those it regarded as compliant. In effect, by demonstrating his own strength, he had made the organization weaker. Until the executive changed his authoritarian manner, his boss said, it was unlikely that he would be promoted further.

Implicit in this vignette is the major fault in performance appraisal and management by objectives—namely, a fundamental misconception of what is to be appraised.

Performance appraisal has three basic functions: (1) to provide adequate feedback to each person on his or her performance; (2) to serve as a basis for modifying or changing behavior toward more effective working habits; and (3) to provide data to managers with which they may judge future job assignments and compensation. The performance appraisal concept is central to effective management. Much hard and imaginative work has gone into developing and refining it. In fact, there is a great deal of evidence to indicate how useful and effective performance appraisal is. Yet present systems of performance appraisal do not serve any of these functions well.

As it is customarily defined, and used, performance appraisal focuses not on behavior but on outcomes of behavior. But even though the executive in the example achieved his objective, he was evaluated on *how* he attained it. Thus, while the system purports to appraise results, in practice, people are really appraised on how they do things—which is not formally described in the setting of objectives, and for which there are rarely data on record.

In my experience, the crucial aspect of any manager's job and the source of most failures, which is practically never described, is the "how." As long as managers appraise the ends yet actually give greater weight to the means, employ a static job description base which does not describe the "how," and do not have support mechanisms for the appraisal process, widespread dissatisfaction with performance appraisal is bound to continue. In fact, one personnel authority speaks of performance appraisal as "the Achilles heel of our profession."[1]

Just how these inadequacies affect performance appraisal systems and how they can be corrected to provide managers with realistic bases for making judgments about employees' performance is the subject of this article.

Inadequacies of Appraisal Systems

It is widely recognized that there are many things inherently wrong with most of the performance appraisal systems in use. The most obvious drawbacks are:

☐ No matter how well defined the dimensions for appraising performance on

1. Herbert Heneman, "Research Roundup," *The Personnel Administrator*, June 1975, p. 61.

quantitative goals are, judgments on performance are usually subjective and impressionistic.

☐ Because appraisals provide inadequate information about the subtleties of performance, managers using them to compare employees for the purposes of determining salary increases often make arbitrary judgments.

☐ Ratings by different managers, and especially those in different units, are usually incomparable. What is excellent work in one unit may be unacceptable in another in the same company.

☐ When salary increases are allocated on the basis of a curve of normal distribution, which is in turn based on rating of results rather than on behavior, competent employees may not only be denied increases, but may also become demotivated.[2]

☐ Trying to base promotion and layoff decisions on appraisal data leaves the decisions open to acrimonious debate. When employees who have been retired early have complained to federal authorities of age discrimination, defendant companies have discovered that there were inadequate data to support the layoff decisions.

☐ Although managers are urged to give feedback freely and often, there are no built-in mechanisms for ensuring that they do so. Delay in feedback creates both frustration, when good performance is not quickly recognized, and anger, when judgment is rendered for inadequacies long past.

☐ There are few effective established mechanisms to cope with either the sense of inadequacy managers have about appraising subordinates, or the paralysis and procrastination that result from guilt about playing God.

Some people might argue that these problems are deficiencies of managers, not of the system. But even if that were altogether true, managers are part of that system. Performance appraisal needs to be viewed not as a technique but as a process involving both people and data, and as such the whole process is inadequate.

Recognizing that there are many deficiencies in performance appraisals, managers in many companies do not want to do them. In other companies there is a great reluctance to do them straightforwardly. Personnel specialists attribute these problems to the reluctance of managers to adopt new ways and to the fear of irreparably damaging their subordinates' self-esteem. In government, performance appraisal is largely a joke, and in both private and public enterprise, merit ratings are hollow.[3]

2. Paul H. Thompson and Gene W. Dalton, "Performance Appraisal: Managers Beware," HBR January-February 1970, p. 149.

3. Herbert S. Meyer, "The Pay for Performance Dilemma," *Organizational Dynamics,* Winter 1975, p. 39.

One of the main sources of trouble with performance appraisal systems is, as I have already pointed out, that the outcome of behavior rather than the behavior itself is what is evaluated. In fact, most people's jobs are described in terms that are only quantitatively measurable; the job description itself is the root of the problem.

The Static Job Description

When people write their own job descriptions (or make statements from which others will write them), essentially they define their responsibilities and basic functions. Then on performance appraisal forms, managers comment on these functions by describing what an individual is supposed to accomplish. Forms in use in many companies today have such directions as:

1. "List the major objectives of this person's job that can be measured qualitatively or quantitatively."

2. "Define the results expected and the standards of performance—money, quantity, quality, time limits, or completion dates."

3. "Describe the action planned as a result of this appraisal, the next steps to be taken—reevaluation, strategy, tactics, and so on."

4. "List the person's strong points—his assets and accomplishments—and his weak points—areas in which improvement is needed. What are the action plans for improvement?"

In most instances the appraiser is asked to do an overall rating with a five-point scale or some similar device. Finally, he is asked to make a statement about the person's potential for the next step or even for higher-level management.

Nowhere in this set of questions or in any of the performance appraisal systems I have examined is anything asked about *how* the person is to attain the ends he or she is charged with reaching.

While some may assert that the ideal way of managing is to give a person a charge and leave him or her alone to accomplish it, this principle is oversimplified both in theory and practice. People need to know the topography of the land they are expected to cross, and the routes as perceived by those to whom they report.

Every manager has multiple obligations, not the least of which are certain kinds of relationships with peers, subordinates, and various consumer, financial, government, supplier, and other publics. Some of these are more important than others, and some need to be handled with much greater skill and aplomb than others. In some situations a manager may be expected to take a vigorous and firm stand, as in labor negotiations; in others he may have to be conciliative; in still others he may even have to be passive. Unless these varied modes of expected behavior are laid out, the job description is static. Because static job descriptions define behavior in gross terms, crucially important differentiated aspects of behavior are lost when performance appraisals are made.

For example, in one of the more progressive performance appraisal systems, which is used by an innovative company, a manager working out his own job description prepares a mission or role statement of what he is supposed to do according to the guide, which specifically directs him to concentrate on the what and the when, not on the why and the how.[4] The guide instructs him to divide his mission into four general areas: (1) innovation, (2) problem solving, (3) ongoing administration, and (4) personal.

In still another company, a manager appraising a subordinate's performance is asked to describe an employee's accomplishments, neglected areas, goals, and objectives. The manager is told that he is to recognize good work, suggest improvement, get agreement on top-priority elements of the task, clarify responsibility, verify and correct rumors, and talk about personal and long-range goals.

In another company's outstanding performance appraisal guide, which reflects great detail and careful consideration, the categories are: work, effectiveness with others, problem solving, decision making, goal setting, organizing and planning, developing subordinates, attending to self-development, and finding initiatives. Each of these categories is broken down into example statements such as: "exhibits high level of independence in work"; "identifies problems and deals with them"; "appropriately subordinates departmental interest to overall company goal"; or "gives people genuine responsibility, holds them accountable, and allows them freedom to act."

Some personnel researchers have advocated role analysis techniques to cope with static job descriptions, and this is a step in the right direction.[5]

But even these techniques are limited because they lean heavily on what other people—supervisors, subordinates, peers—expect of the manager. These expectations are also generalized; they do not specify behavior.

Nowhere in these examples is an individual told what *behavior* is expected of him in a range of contexts. Who are the sensitive people with whom certain kinds of relationships have to be maintained? What are the specific problems and barriers? What have been the historic manufacturing blunders or frictions?

---

4. John B. Lasagna, "Make Your MBO Pragmatic," HBR November-December 1971, p. 64.
5. Ishwar Dayal, "Role Analysis Techniques in Job Descriptions," *California Management Review*, Summer 1969, p. 47.

How should union relationships and union leaders be dealt with? What are the specific integrative problems to be resolved and what are the historical conflicts? These and many more similar pieces of behavior will be the true bases on which a person will be judged, regardless of the questions an appraisal form asks.

Static job descriptions are catastrophic for managers. Job proficiency and goal achievement usually are necessary but not sufficient conditions for advancement; the key elements in whether one makes it in an organization are political. The collective judgments made about a person, which rarely find their way into performance appraisals, become the social web in which he or she must live. Therefore, when a person is placed in a new situation, whether in a different geographical site, at a different level in the hierarchy, or in a new role, he must be apprised of the subtleties of the relationships he will have with those who will influence his role and his career. Furthermore, he must be helped to differentiate the varied kinds of behavior required to succeed.

Some people develop political diagnostic skill very rapidly; often, however, these are people whose social senses enable them to move beyond their technical and managerial competence. And some may be out-and-out manipulative charlatans who succeed in business without really trying, and whose promotion demoralizes good people. But the great majority of people, those who have concentrated heavily on their professional competence at the expense of acquiring political skill early, will need to have that skill developed, ideally by their own seniors. That development process requires: (1) a dynamic job description, (2) a critical incident process, and (3) a psychological support system.

Dynamic Job Description

If a static job description is at the root of the inadequacies of performance appraisal systems, what is needed is a different kind of job description. What we are looking for is one that amplifies statements of job responsibility and desired outcome by describing the emotional and behavorial topography of the task to be done by the individual in the job.

Psychologists describe behavior in many ways, each having his or her own preferences. I have found four major features of behavior to be fundamentally important in a wide range of managerial settings. These features have to do with how a person characteristically manages what some psychologists call aggression, affection, dependency, and also the nature of the person's ego ideal.[6]

6. Harry Levinson, *The Great Jackass Fallacy* (Cambridge: Harvard University Press, 1973), chap. 3.

Using his preferred system, one can begin formulating a dynamic job description by describing the characteristic behavior required by a job. This is what these terms mean with respect to job descriptions:

1. How does this job require the incumbent to handle his aggression, his attacking capacity?

Must he or she vanquish customers? Must he hold on to his anger in the face of repeated complaints and attacks from others? Will she be the target of hostility and, if so, from whom? Must he give firm direction to others? Must she attack problems vigorously, but handle some areas with great delicacy and finesse? Which problems are to be attacked with vigor and immediacy and which coolly and analytically?

2. How does this job require the incumbent to manage affection, the need to love and to be loved?

Is the person required to be a socially friendly leader of a close-knit work group? Should the person work closely and supportively with subordinates for task accomplishment? Is the task one in which the person will have to be content with the feeling of a job well done, or is it one that involves more public display and recognition? Will he be obscure and unnoticed, or highly visible? Must she lavish attention on the work, a product, a service, or customers? Must he be cold and distant from others and, if so, from whom?

3. How does this job require the incumbent to manage dependency needs?

Will the individual be able to lean on others who have skill and competencies, or will he have to do things himself? How much will she be on her own and in what areas? How much support will there be from superiors and staff functions? How well defined is the nature of the work? What kind of feedback provisions are there? What are the structural and hierarchical relationships? How solid are they and to whom will the person turn and for what? With which people must he interact in order to accomplish what he needs to accomplish, and in what manner?

4. What ego ideal demands does this job fulfill?

If one does the task well, what are the gratifications to be gained? Will the person make a lot of money? Will he achieve considerable organizational and public recognition? Will she be eligible for promotion? Will he feel good about himself and, if so, in what ways? Why? Will she acquire a significant skill, an important element of reputation, or an organizational constituency? Will he acquire power?

Individuals may be described along the same four dynamic dimensions: How does this person characteristically handle aggression? How does he or she characteristically handle affection? How does he or she characteristically handle dependency needs? What is the nature of his or her ego ideal?

Once the subtleties of the task are defined and individuals described, people may be matched to tasks. I am not advocating a return to evaluation of personality traits. I am arguing for a more dynamic conception of the managerial role and a more dynamic assessment of an employee's characteristics. And only when a person's behavior is recognized as basic to how he performs his job will performance appraisal systems be realistic.

Critical Incident Process

Having established a dynamic job description for a person, the next step is to evolve a complementary performance appraisal system that will provide feedback on verifiable behavior, do so in a continuous fashion, and serve coaching-, promotion-, and salary-data needs.

Ideally, a manager and his subordinate will have defined together the objectives to be attained in a certain job, and the criteria by which each will know that those objectives have been attained, including the more qualitative aspects of the job. Then they will have spelled out the subtleties of how various aspects of the job must be performed. They will in this way have elaborated the *behavioral* requirements of the task.

In order for performance appraisal to be effective for coaching, teaching, and changing those aspects of an employee's behavior that are amenable to change, an employee needs to know about each piece of behavior that is good, as well as that which for some reason is not acceptable or needs modification. Such incidents will occur randomly and be judged randomly by his manager.

So that there will be useful data, the manager needs to quickly write down what he has said to the subordinate, describing in a paragraph what the subordinate did or did not do, in what setting, under what circumstances, about what problem. This information forms a *behavioral* record, a critical incident report of which the subordinate already has been informed and which is now in his folder, open to his review. Examples of two incidents can be found in the Appendix on page 293.

This critical incident technique is not new.[7] In the past it has been used largely for case illustrations and, in modified forms, has been suggested as a method for first-level supervisors to evaluate line employees. Supervisors already record negative incidents concerning line employees because warnings and disciplinary steps must be documented. However, efforts to develop scales

7. John C. Flanagan, "The Critical Incident Technique," *Psychological Bulletin,* 51:327, 1954, and John C. Flanagan (coauthor Robert K. Burns), "The Employee Performance Record: A New Appraisal and Development Tool," HBR September-October 1955, p. 95.

from critical incidents for rating behavior have not worked well.[8] Behavior is too complex to be scaled along a few dimensions and then rated.

But instead of scaling behavior, one might directly record the behavior of those being appraised, and evaluate it at a later date. There are other good reasons for adopting this technique as well. At last, here is a process that provides data to help managers perform the basic functions of performance appraisal systems—namely, provide feedback, coaching, and promotion data. Another plus is that recorded data live longer than the manager recording them.

Here is how behavioral data might be put to use in the critical incident process:

1. *Feedback data:* When there is a semiannual or annual review, an employee will have no surprises and the manager will have on paper what he is using as a basis for making his summary feedback and appraisal. Because the data are on record, an employee cannot deny having heard what was said earlier, nor must the manager try to remember all year what have been the bases of his judgments.

Also, as each critical incident is recorded, over time there will be data in an individual's folder to be referred to when and if there are suits alleging discrimination. Critical incidents of behavior, which illustrate behavior patterns, will be the only hard evidence acceptable to adjudicating bodies.

2. *Coaching data:* When employees receive feedback information at the time the incident occurs, they may be able to adapt their behavior more easily. With this technique, the employee will receive indications more often on how he is doing, and will be able to correct small problems before they become large ones. Also, if the employee cannot change his behavior, that fact will become evident to him through the repetitive critical incident notes. If the employee feels unfairly judged or criticized, he may appeal immediately rather than long after the fact. If there are few or no incidents on record, that in itself says something about job behavior, and may be used as a basis for discussion. In any event, both manager and employee will know which behavior is being appraised.

3. *Promotion data:* With such an accumulation of critical incidents, a manager or the personnel department is in a position to evaluate repeatedly how the person characteristically manages aggression, affection, and dependency needs, and the nature of his ego ideal. These successive judgments become cumulative data for better job fit.

When a person is provided continuously with verifiable information, including when he has been passed over for promotion and why, he is able to perceive more accurately the nuances of his behavior and his behavioral patterns. Thus,

---

8. Donald P. Schwab, Herbert G. Heneman III, and Thomas A. DeCotis, "Behaviorally Anchored Rating Scales: A Review of the Literature," *Personnel Psychology,* 28:549, 1975.

when offered other opportunities, the employee is in a better position to weigh his own behavioral configurations against those required by the prospective job. A person who knows himself in this way will be more easily able to say about a given job, "That's not for me." He will see that the next job in the pyramid is not necessarily rightfully his. In recognizing his own behavioral limitations he may save himself much grief as well as avoid painful difficulty for his superiors and the organization.

But the most important reason for having such information is to increase the chances of success of those who are chosen for greater responsibility. In most personnel folders there is practically no information about how a manager is likely to do when placed on his own. Data about dependency are noticeably absent, and many a shining prospect dims when there is no one to support him in a higher-level job. Managements need to know early on who can stand alone, and they cannot know that without behavioral information.

4. *Long-term data:* Frequently, new managers do not know their employees and all too often have little information in the folder with which to appraise them. This problem is compounded when managers move quickly from one area to another. For his part, the employee just as frequently has to prove himself to transient bosses who hold his fate in their hands but know nothing of his past performance. With little information, managers feel unqualified to make judgments. With the critical incident process, however, managers can report incidents, which can be summarized by someone else.

Some may object to "keeping book" on their people or resist a program of constant reviews and endless reports—both extreme views. Some may argue that supervisors will not follow the method. But if managers cannot get raises for or transfer employees without adequate documentation, they will soon learn the need to follow through. The critical incident process compels superiors to face subordinates, a responsibility too many shirk.

While it might seem difficult to analyze performance in terms of aggression, affection, dependency, the ego ideal, or other psychological concepts, to do so is no different from learning to use economic, financial, or accounting concepts. Many managers already talk about these same issues in other words, for example: "taking charge" versus "being a nice guy"; "needing to be stroked" versus the "self-starter"; "fast track" versus the "shelf-sitter." A little practice, together with support mechanisms, can go a long way.

Support Mechanisms

Performance appraisal cannot be limited to a yearly downward reward-punishment judgment. Ideally, appraisal should be a part of a continuing process by which both manager and employee may be guided. In addition, it should enhance an effective superior-subordinate relationship.

To accomplish these aims, performance appraisal must be supported by mechanisms that enable the manager to master his inadequacies and to cope with his feelings of guilt; have a record of that part of his work that occurs outside the purview of his own boss (e.g., task force assignments which require someone to appraise a whole group); and modify those aspects of his superior's behavior that hamper his performance. All of this requires an upward appraisal process.

1. *Managing the guilt:* The manager's guilt about appraising subordinates appears when managers complain about playing God, about destroying people. A great crippler of effective performance appraisal is the feeling of guilt, much of which is irrational, but which most people have when they criticize others.[9] Guilt is what leads to the fear of doing appraisals. It is the root of procrastination, of the failure to appraise honestly, and of the overreaction that can demolish subordinates.

Fortunately, there are group methods for relieving guilt and for helping managers and supervisors understand the critical importance, indeed the necessity, of accurate behavioral evaluations. One way is by having people together at the same peer level discuss their problems in appraisal and talk about their feelings in undertaking the appraisal task. In addition, rehearsals of role playing increase a manager's sense of familiarity and competence and ease his anxiety.

In fact, a five-step process, one step per week for five weeks, can be extremely helpful:

☐ Week one: Group discussion among peers (no more than 12) about their feelings about appraising subordinates.

☐ Week two: Group discussions resulting in advice from each other on the specific problems that each anticipates in appraising individuals.

☐ Week three: Role-playing appraisal interviews.

☐ Week four: Actual appraisals.

☐ Week five: Group discussion to review the appraisals, problems encountered, both anticipated and unanticipated, lessons learned, and skill needs that may have surfaced.

2. *Group appraisal:* By group appraisal, I do not mean peer approval of each other, which usually fails; rather, I mean appraisal of a group's accomplishment. When people work together in a group, whether reporting to the same person or not, they need to establish criteria by which they and those to whom they report will know how well the task force or the group has done—in terms

9. Harry Levinson, "Management by Whose Objectives," HBR July-August 1970, p. 125.

of behavior as well as results. Group appraisals provide information that is helpful both in establishing criteria and in providing each individual with feedback.

At the end of a given task, a group may do a group appraisal or be appraised by the manager to whom they report, and that appraisal may be entered into folders of each of the people who are involved. It will then serve as another basis for managerial- and self-judgment.

3. *Upward appraisal:* Finally, there should be upward appraisal. Some beginning voluntary steps in this direction are being taken in the Sun Oil Company, and by individual executives in other companies. Upward appraisal is a very difficult process because most managers do not want to be evaluated by their subordinates. As a matter of fact, however, most managers *are* evaluated indirectly by their employees, and these evaluations are frequently behavioral.

The employees' work itself is a kind of evaluation. Their work may be done erratically or irresponsibly. Or they may be poorly motivated. Negative behavior is a form of appraisal, and one from which a manager gains little. A manager cannot be quite sure what precipitated the behavior he sees, let alone be sure what to do about it.

If, however, the manager is getting dynamic behavioral appraisal from his employees, then he, too, may correct his course. But if he asks his subordinates for upward appraisal without warning, he is likely to be greeted with dead silence and great caution. A helpful way to deal with this situation is to ask one's employees to define the criteria by which they would appraise the manager's job, not to judge his actual performance.

This process of definition may require a manager to meet with employees weekly for months to define the criteria. By the end of three months, say, the employees should be much more comfortable working with their manager on this issue. And if the manager can be trusted at all, then when he or she finally asks them to evaluate the performance, including specific behaviors, along the dimensions they have worked out together, they are likely to be more willing to do so. Of course, if there is no trust, there is no possibility of upward appraisal. In any event, the upward performance appraisal should go to the manager's superior so that people do not jeopardize themselves by speaking directly.

Under present performance appraisal systems, it is difficult to compensate managers for developing people because the criteria are elusive. With a developing file of upward appraisals, however, executives can judge how well a manager has done in developing his people. The employees cannot evaluate the whole of their manager's job, but they can say a great deal about how well he or she has facilitated their work, increased their proficiency, cleared barriers, protected them against political forces, and raised their level of competence—in short, how the manager has met their ministration, maturation, and mastery needs.[10] A top executive can then quantify such upward evaluations and use the outcome as a basis for compensating a manager for his effectiveness in developing his employees.

When a group of manager peers experiments with upward appraisal and works it out to their own comfort, as well as to that of their employees, then it might be tried at the next lower level. When several successive levels have worked out their own systems, the process might be formalized throughout the organization. Acceptance of the upward appraisal concept is likely to be greater if it has been tested and modeled by the very people who must use it, and if it has not been imposed on them by the personnel department. With appropriate experience, the managers involved in the process would ultimately evolve suitable appraisal forms.

What About Results?

What does adopting the critical incident technique and the dynamic job description mean for judging a person's ability to obtain results? Does quantitative performance lose its importance?

My answer is an unqualified no. There will always be other issues that managers will have to determine, such as level of compensation or promotability—issues that should be dealt with in other sessions after the basic behavioral performance appraisal.[11]

Some of the performance appraisal information may be helpful in making such determinations, but neither of these two functions should contaminate the performance appraisal feedback process. There can still be an annual compensation evaluation, based not only on behavior, which is the basis for coaching, but also on outcome. Did an employee make money? Did he reach quantitative goals? Did she resolve problems in the organization that were her responsibility?

No doubt, there will be some overlapping between behavior and outcome, but the two are qualitatively different. One might behave as it was expected he should, but at the same time not do what had to be done to handle the vagaries of the marketplace. He might not have responded with enough speed or flexibility to a problem, even though his behavior corresponded to all that originally was asked of him in the job description and goal-setting process.

Both behavior and outcome are important, and neither should be overlooked. It is most important, however, that they not be confused.

10. Harry Levinson, *The Exceptional Executive* (Cambridge: Harvard University Press, 1968).
11. Herbert H. Meyer, Emanuel Kay, and John R. P. French, Jr., "Split Roles in Performance Appraisal," HBR January-February 1965, p. 123.

On May 15, the director of manufacturing, together with the president of the union, met with a group of shop stewards and the international business agent who were irate about the temporary 10% cutback in working hours. The cutback had been prematurely announced by corporate personnel without local consultation. The director of manufacturing heard them out, did not get hot under the collar about their tirade, and then explained the need to use up inventories. By reassuring them of the company's true intention, the director of manufacturing reduced tension in the plants.

Executive Vice President

The director of manufacturing and I met today (August 13th) to review his development plans for his subordinates. While these are broadly defined on paper, the director does not hear enough from his subordinates about *their* objectives or ask enough about what *they* are up against. He is impatient with this aspect of his responsibility. I suggested that he allot regular meeting times for such discussions and take more time to listen. He agreed to do so.

Executive Vice President

19. Barriers and Gateways to Communication

Carl R. Rogers and F. J. Roethlisberger

Communication among human beings has always been a problem. How does one know whether what one wants to impart is what someone else hears, or what one might be imparting without even knowing it? These problems cause us all trouble, but with good will, and among friends, we can usually overcome them. In the world of work where often one feels less secure than at home or where there is not the time nor the expectation of good will, solving problems of communications can become very difficult. The following two descriptions of barriers and gateways to communication help to bring the problems down to earth and show some of the simple fundamentals of effective communication. First, Carl R. Rogers analyzes it from the standpoint of human behavior generally (Part I), then F. J. Roethlisberger illustrates it in an industrial context (Part II). Although the article was written 27 years ago, it has meaning and relevance today.

Part I

It may seem curious that a person like myself, whose whole professional effort is devoted to psychotherapy, should be interested in problems of communication. What relationship is there between obstacles to communication and providing therapeutic help to individuals with emotional maladjustments?

Actually the relationship is very close indeed. The whole task of psychotherapy is the task of dealing with a failure in communication. The emotionally maladjusted person, the "neurotic," is in difficulty, first, because communication within himself has broken down and, secondly, because as a result of this his communication with others has been damaged. To put it another way, in the "neurotic" individual parts of himself that have been termed unconscious, or repressed, or denied to awareness, become blocked off so that they no longer communicate themselves to the conscious or managing part of himself; as long as this is true, there are distortions in the way he communicates himself to others, and so he suffers both within himself and in his interpersonal relations.

The task of psychotherapy is to help the person achieve, through a special relationship with a therapist, good communication within himself. Once this is achieved, he can communicate more freely and more effectively with others. We may say then that psychotherapy is good communication, within and between men. We may also turn that statement around and it will still be true. Good communication, free communication, within or between men, is always therapeutic.

It is, then, from a background of experience with communication in counseling and psychotherapy that I want to present two ideas: (1) I wish to state what I believe is one of the major factors in blocking or impeding communication, and then (2) I wish to present what in our experience has proved to be a very important way of improving or facilitating communication.

BARRIER: THE TENDENCY TO EVALUATE

I should like to propose, as a hypothesis for consideration, that the major barrier to mutual interpersonal communication is our very natural tendency to judge, to evaluate, to approve (or disapprove) the statement of the other person or the other group. Let me illustrate my meaning with some very simple examples. Suppose someone, commenting on this discussion, makes the statement, "I didn't like what that man said." What will you respond? Almost invariably your reply will be either approval or disapproval of the attitude expressed. Either you respond, "I didn't either; I thought it was terrible," or else you tend to reply, "Oh, I thought it was really good." In other words, your primary reaction is to evaluate if from *your* point of view, your own frame of reference.

Or take another example. Suppose I say with some feeling, "I think the Republicans are behaving in ways that show a lot of good sound sense these days." What is the response that arises in your mind? The overwhelming likelihood is that it will be evaluative. In other words, you will find yourself agreeing, or disagreeing, or making some judgment about me such as "He must be a conservative," or "He seems solid in his thinking." Or let us take an illustration from the international scene. Russia says vehemently, "The treaty with Japan is a war plot on the part of the United States." We rise as one person to say, "That's a lie!"

This last illustration brings in another element connected with my hypothesis. Although the tendency to make evaluations is common in almost all interchange of language, it is very much heightened in those situations where feelings and emotions are deeply involved. So the stronger our feelings, the more likely it is that there will be no mutual element in the communication. There will be just two ideas, two feelings, two judgments, missing each other in psychological space.

I am sure you recognize this from your own experience. When you have not been emotionally involved yourself and have listened to a heated discussion, you often go away thinking, "Well, they actually weren't talking about the same thing." And they were not. Each was making a judgment, and evaluation, from his own frame of reference. There was really nothing that could be called communication in any genuine sense. This tendency to react to any emotionally meaningful statement by forming an evaluation of it from our own point of view is, I repeat, the major barrier to interpersonal communication.

GATEWAY: LISTENING WITH UNDERSTANDING

Is there any way of solving this problem, of avoiding this barrier? I feel that we are making exciting progress toward this goal, and I should like to present it as simply as I can. Real communication occurs, and this evaluative tendency is avoided, when we listen with understanding. What does that mean? It means to see the expressed idea and attitude from the other person's point of view, to sense how it feels to him, to achieve his frame of reference in regard to the thing he is talking about.

Stated so briefly, this may sound absurdly simple, but it is not. It is an approach that we have found extremely potent in the field of psychotherapy. It is the most effective agent we know for altering the basic personality structure of an individual and for improving his relationships and his communications with others. If I can listen to what he can tell me, if I can understand how it seems to him, if I can see its personal meaning for him, if I can sense the emotional flavor which it has for him, then I will be releasing potent forces of change in him.

Again, if I can really understand how he hates his father, or hates the company, or hates Communists—if I can catch the flavor of his fear of insanity, or his fear of atom bombs, or of Russia—it will be of the greatest help to him in altering those hatreds and fears and in establishing realistic and harmonious relationships with the very people and situations toward which he has felt hatred and fear. We know from our research that such empathic understand-ing—understanding *with* a person, not *about* him—is such an effective ap-proach that it can bring about major changes in personality.

Some of you may be feeling that you listen well to people and yet you have never seen such results. The chances are great indeed that your listening has not been of the type I have described. Fortunately, I can suggest a little laboratory experiment that you can try to test the quality of your understanding. The next time you get into an argument with your wife, or your friend, or with a small group of friends, just stop the discussion for a moment and, for an experiment, institute this rule: "Each person can speak up for himself only *after* he has first restated the ideas and feelings of the previous speaker accurately and to that speaker's satisfaction."

You see what this would mean. It would simply mean that before presenting your own point of view, it would be necessary for you to achieve the other speaker's frame of reference—to understand his thoughts and feelings so well that you could summarize them for him. Sounds simple, doesn't it? But if you try it, you will discover that it is one of the most difficult things you have ever tried to do. However, once you have been able to see the other's point of view, your own comments will have to be drastically revised. You will also find the emotion going out of the discussion, the differences being reduced, and those differences which remain being of a rational and understandable sort.

Can you imagine what this kind of an approach would mean if it were projected in larger areas? What would happen to a labor-management dispute if it were conducted in such a way that labor, without necessarily agreeing, could accurately state management's point of view in a way that management could accept; and management, without approving labor's stand, could state labor's case in a way that labor agreed was accurate? It would mean that real communication was established, and one could practically guarantee that some reasonable solution would be reached.

If, then, this way of approach is an effective avenue to good communication and good relationships, as I am quite sure you will agree if you try the experiment I have mentioned, why is it not more widely tried and used? I will try to list difficulties which keep it from being utilized.

Need for courage

In the first place it takes courage, a quality that is not too widespread. I am indebted to Dr. S. I. Hayakawa, the semanticist, for pointing out that to carry on psychotherapy in this fashion is to take a very real risk, and that courage is required. If you really understand another person in this way, if you are willing to enter his private world and see the way life appears to him, without any attempt to make evaluative judgments, you run the risk of being changed yourself. You might see it his way; you might find yourself influenced in your attitudes or your personality.

This risk of being changed is one of the most frightening prospects many of us can face. If I enter, as fully as I am able, into the private world of a neurotic or psychotic individual, isn't there a risk that I might become lost in that world?

Most of us are afraid to take that risk. Or if we were listening to a Russian Communist, or Senator Joe McCarthy, how many of us would dare to try to see the world from each of their points of view? The great majority of us could not *listen;* we would find ourselves compelled to *evaluate,* because listening would seem too dangerous. So the first requirement is courage, and we do not always have it.

Heightened emotions

But there is a second obstacle. It is just when emotions are strongest that it is most difficult to achieve the frame of reference of the other person or group. Yet it is then that the attitude is most needed if communication is to be established. We have not found this to be an insuperable obstacle in our experience in psychotherapy. A third party, who is able to lay aside his own feelings and evaluations, can assist greatly by listening with understanding to each person or group and clarifying the views and attitudes each holds.

We have found this effective in small groups in which contradictory or antagonistic attitudes exist. When the parties to a dispute realize that they are being understood, that someone sees how the situation seems to them, the statements grow less exaggerated and less defensive, and it is no longer necessary to maintain the attitude, "I am 100% right and you are 100% wrong." The influence of such an understanding catalyst in the group permits the members to come closer and closer to the objective truth involved in the relationship. In this way mutual communication is established, and some type of agreement becomes possible.

So we may say that though heightened emotions make it much more difficult to understand *with* an opponent, our experience makes it clear that a neutral, understanding, catalyst type of leader or therapist can overcome this obstacle in a small group.

Size of group

That last phrase, however, suggests another obstacle to utilizing the approach I have described. Thus far all our experience has been with small face-to-face groups—groups exhibiting industrial tensions, religious tensions, and racial tensions, and therapy groups in which many personal tensions are present. In these small groups our experience, confirmed by a limited amount of research, shows that this basic approach leads to improved communication, to greater acceptance of others and by others, and to attitudes that are more positive and more problem-solving in nature. There is a decrease in defensiveness, in exaggerated statements, in evaluative and critical behavior.

But these findings are from small groups. What about trying to achieve understanding between larger groups that are geographically remote, or between face-to-face groups that are not speaking for themselves but simply as representatives of others, like the delegates at Kaesong? Frankly we do not know the answers to these questions. I believe the situation might be put this way: As social scientists we have a tentative test-tube solution of the problem of breakdown in communicaton. But to confirm the validity of this test-tube solution and to adapt it to the enormous problems of communication breakdown between classes, groups, and nations would involve additional funds, much more research, and creative thinking of a high order.

Yet with our present limited knowledge we can see some steps which might be taken even in large groups to increase the amount of listening *with* and decrease the amount of evaluation *about*. To be imaginative for a moment, let us suppose that a therapeutically oriented international group went to the Russian leaders and said, "We want to achieve a genuine understanding of your views and, even more important, of your attitudes and feelings toward the United States. We will summarize and resummarize these views and feelings if necessary, until you agree that our description represents the situation as it seems to you."

Then suppose they did the same thing with the leaders in our own country. If they then gave the widest possible distribution to these two views, with the feelings clearly described but not expressed in name-calling, might not the effect be very great? It would not guarantee the type of understanding I have been describing, but it would make it much more possible. We can understand the feelings of a person who hates us much more readily when his attitudes are accurately described to us by a neutral third party than we can when he is shaking his fist at us.

Faith in social sciences

But even to describe such a first step is to suggest another obstacle to this approach of understanding. Our civilization does not yet have enough faith in the social sciences to utilize their findings. The opposite is true of the physical sciences. During the war when a test-tube solution was found to the problem of synthetic rubber, millions of dollars and an army of talent were turned loose on the problem of using that finding. If synthetic rubber could be made in milligrams, it could and would be made in thousands of tons. And it was. But in the social science realm, if a way is found of facilitating communication and mutual understanding in small groups, there is no guarantee that the finding will be utilized. It may be a generation or more before the money and the brains will be turned loose to exploit that finding.

Summary

In closing, I should like to summarize this small-scale solution to the problem of barriers in communication, and to point out certain of its characteristics.

I have said that our research and experience to date would make it appear that breakdowns in communication, and the evaluative tendency, which is the major barrier to communication, can be avoided. The solution is provided by creating a situation in which each of the different parties comes to understand the other from the *other's* point of view. This has been achieved, in practice, even when feelings run high, by the influence of a person who is willing to understand each point of view empathically, and who thus acts as a catalyst to precipitate further understanding.

This procedure has important characteristics. It can be initiated by one party, without waiting for the other to be ready. It can even be initiated by a neutral third person, provided he can gain a minimum of cooperation from one of the parties.

This procedure can deal with the insincerities, the defensive exaggerations, the lies, the "false fronts" that characterize almost every failure in communication. These defensive distortions drop away with astonishing speed as people find that the only intent is to understand, not to judge.

This approach leads steadily and rapidly toward the discovery of the truth, toward a realistic appraisal of the objective barriers to communication. The dropping of some defensiveness by one party leads to further dropping of defensiveness by the other party, and truth is thus approached.

This procedure gradually achieves mutual communication. Mutual communication tends to be pointed toward solving a problem rather than toward attacking a person or group. It leads to a situation in which I see how the problem appears to you as well as to me, and you see how it appears to me as well as to you. Thus accurately and realistically defined, the problem is almost certain to yield to intelligent attack; or if it is in part insoluble, it will be comfortably accepted as such.

This then appears to be a test-tube solution to the breakdown of communication as it occurs in small groups. Can we take this small-scale answer, investigate it futher, refine it, develop it, and apply it to the tragic and well-nigh fatal failures of communication which threaten the very existence of our modern world? It seems to me that this is a possibility and a challenge that we should explore.

Part II

In thinking about the many barriers to personal communication, particularly those that are due to differences of background, experience, and motivation, it seems to me extraordinary that any two persons can ever understand each other. Such reflections provoke the question of how communication is possible when people do not see and assume the same things and share the same values.

On this question there are two schools of thought. One school assumes that communication between A and B, for example, has failed when B does not accept what A has to say as being fact, true, or valid; and that the goal of communication is to get B to agree with A's opinions, ideas, facts, or information.

The position of the other school of thought is quite different. It assumes that communication has failed when B does not feel free to express his feelings to A because B fears they will not be accepted by A. Communication is facilitated when on the part of A or B or both there is a willingness to express and accept differences.

As these are quite divergent conceptions, let us explore them further with an example. Bill, an employee, is talking with his boss in the boss's office. The boss says, "I think, Bill, that this is the best way to do your job." Bill says, "Oh yeah!" According to the first school of thought, this reply would be a sign of poor communication. Bill does not understand the best way of doing his work. To improve communication, therefore, it is up to the boss to explain to Bill why his way is the best.

From the point of view of the second school of thought, Bill's reply is a sign neither of good nor of bad communication. Bill's response is indeterminate. But the boss has an opportunity to find out what Bill means if he so desires. Let us assume that this is what he chooses to do, i.e., find out what Bill means. So this boss tries to get Bill to talk more about his job while he (the boss) listens.

For purposes of simplification, I shall call the boss representing the first school of thought *"Smith"* and the boss representing the second school of thought *"Jones."* In the presence of the so-called same stimulus each behaves

AUTHOR'S NOTE: For the concepts I use to present my material I am greatly indebted to some very interesting conversations I have had with my friend, Irving Lee—F. J. R.

differently. Smith chooses to *explain;* Jones chooses to *listen.* In my experience Jones's response works better than Smith's. It works better because Jones is making a more proper evaluation of what is taking place between him and Bill than Smith is. Let us test this hypothesis by continuing with our example.

WHAT SMITH ASSUMES, SEES, AND FEELS

Smith assumes that he understands what Bill means when Bill says, "Oh yeah!," so there is no need to find out. Smith is sure that Bill does not understand why this is the best way to do his job, so Smith has to tell him. In this process let us assume Smith is logical, lucid, and clear. He presents his facts and evidence well. But, alas, Bill remains unconvinced. What does Smith do? Operating under the assumption that what is taking place between him and Bill is something essentially logical, Smith can draw only one of two conclusions: either (1) he has not been clear enough, or (2) Bill is too damned stupid to understand. So he either has to "spell out" his case in words of fewer and fewer syllables or give up. Smith is reluctant to do the latter, so he continues to explain. What happens?

If Bill still does not accept Smith's explanation of why this is the best way for him to do his job, a pattern of interacting feelings is produced of which Smith is often unaware. The more Smith cannot get Bill to understand him, the more frustrated Smith becomes and the more Bill becomes a threat to his logical capacity. Since Smith sees himself as a fairly reasonable and logical chap, this is a difficult feeling to accept. It is much easier for him to perceive Bill as uncooperative or stupid. This perception, however, will affect what Smith says and does. Under these pressures Bill comes to be evaluated more and more in terms of Smith's values. By this process Smith tends to treat Bill's values as unimportant. He tends to deny Bill's uniqueness and difference. He treats Bill as if he had little capacity for self-direction.

Let us be clear. Smith does not see that he is doing these things. When he is feverishly scratching hieroglyphics on the back of an envelope, trying to explain to Bill why this is the best way to do his job, Smith is trying to be helpful. He is a man of goodwill, and he wants to set Bill straight. This is the way Smith sees himself and his behavior. But it is for this very reason that Bill's "Oh yeah!" is getting under Smith's skin.

"How dumb can a guy be?" is Smith's attitude, and unfortunately Bill will hear that more than Smith's good intentions. Bill will feel misunderstood. He will not see Smith as a man of goodwill trying to be helpful. Rather he will perceive him as a threat to his self-esteem and personal integrity. Against this threat Bill will feel the need to defend himself at all cost. Not being so logically articulate as Smith, Bill expresses this need, again, by saying, "Oh yeah!"

WHAT JONES ASSUMES, SEES, AND FEELS

Let us leave this sad scene between Smith and Bill, which I fear is going to terminate by Bill's either leaving in a huff or being kicked out of Smith's office. Let us turn for a moment to Jones and see what he is assuming, seeing, hearing, feeling, doing, and saying when he interacts with Bill.

Jones, it will be remembered, does not assume that he knows what Bill means when he says, "Oh yeah!" so he has to find out. Moreover, he assumes that when Bill said this, he had not exhausted his vocabulary or his feelings. Bill may not necessarily mean one thing; he may mean several different things. So Jones decides to listen.

In this process Jones is not under any illusion that what will take place will be eventually logical. Rather he is assuming that what will take place will be primarily an interaction of feelings. Therefore, he cannot ignore the feelings of Bill, the effect of Bill's feelings on him, or the effect of his feelings on Bill. In other words, he cannot ignore his relationship to Bill; he cannot assume that it will make no difference to what Bill will hear or accept.

Therefore, Jones will be paying strict attention to all of the things Smith has ignored. He will be addressing himself to Bill's feelings, his own, and the interactions between them.

Jones will therefore realize that he has ruffled Bill's feelings with his comment, "I think, Bill, this is the best way to do your job." So instead of trying to get Bill to understand him, he decides to try to understand Bill. He does this by encouraging Bill to speak. Instead of telling Bill how he should feel or think, he asks Bill such questions as, "Is this what you feel?" "Is this what you see?" "Is this what you assume?" Instead of ignoring Bill's evaluations as irrelevant, not valid, inconsequential, or false, he tries to understand Bill's reality as he feels it, perceives it, and assumes it to be. As Bill begins to open up, Jones's curiosity is piqued by this process.

"Bill isn't so dumb; he's quite an interesting guy" becomes Jones's attitude. And that is what Bill hears. Therefore Bill feels understood and accepted as a person. He becomes less defensive. He is in a better frame of mind to explore and reexamine his own perceptions, feelings, and assumptions. In this process he perceives Jones as a source of help. Bill feels free to express his differences. He feels that Jones has some respect for his capacity for self-direction. These positive feelings toward Jones make Bill more inclined to say, "Well, Jones, I don't quite agree with you that this is the best way to do my job, but I'll tell you what I'll do. I'll try to do it that way for a few days, and then I'll tell you what I think."

I grant that my two orientations do not work themselves out in practice in quite so simple or neat a fashion as I have been able to work them out on paper. There are many other ways in which Bill could have responded to Smith in the first place. He might even have said, "O.K., boss, I agree that your way of doing my job is better." But Smith still would not have known how Bill felt when he made this statement or whether Bill was actually going to do his job differently. Likewise, Bill could have responded to Jones in a way different from my example. In spite of Jones's attitude, Bill might still be reluctant to express himself freely to his boss.

The purpose of my examples has not been to demonstrate the right or wrong way of communicating. My purpose has been simply to provide something concrete to point to when I make the following generalizations:

1. Smith represents to me a very common pattern of misunderstanding. The misunderstanding does not arise because Smith is not clear enough in expressing himself. It arises because of Smith's misevaluation of what is taking place when two people are talking together.

2. Smith's misevaluation of the process of personal communication consists of certain very common assumptions, e.g., (a) that what is taking place is something essentially logical; (b) that words in themselves apart from the people involved mean something; and (c) that the purpose of the interaction is to get Bill to see things from Smith's point of view.

3. Because of these assumptions, a chain reaction of perceptions and negative feelings is engendered, which blocks communication. By ignoring Bill's feelings and by rationalizing his own, Smith ignores his relationship to Bill as one of the most important determinants of the communication. As a result, Bill hears Smith's attitude more clearly than the logical content of Smith's words. Bill feels that his individual uniqueness is being denied. His personal integrity being at stake, he becomes defensive and belligerent. As a result, Smith feels frustrated. He perceives Bill as stupid. So he says and does things which only provoke more defensiveness on the part of Bill.

4. In the case of Jones, I have tried to show what might possibly happen if we made a different evaluation of what is taking place when two people are talking together. Jones makes a different set of assumptions. He assumes (a) that what is taking place between him and Bill is an interaction of sentiments;

(b) that Bill—not his words in themselves—means something; (c) that the object of the interaction is to give Bill an opportunity to express freely his differences.

5. Because of these assumptions, a psychological chain reaction of reinforcing feelings and perceptions is set up, which facilitates communication between Bill and him. When Jones addresses himself to Bill's feelings and perceptions from Bill's point of view, Bill feels understood and accepted as a person; he feels free to express his differences. Bill sees Jones as a source of help; Jones sees Bill as an interesting person. Bill in turn becomes more cooperative.

6. If I have identified correctly these very common patterns of personal communication, then some interesting hypotheses can be stated:

a. Jones's method works better than Smith's, not because of any magic, but because Jones has a better map than Smith of the process of personal communication.

b. The practice of Jones's method, however, is not merely an intellectual exercise. It depends on Jones's capacity and willingness to see and accept points of view different from his own, and to practice this orientation in a face-to-face relationship. This practice involves an emotional as well as an intellectual achievement. It depends in part on Jones's awareness of himself, in part on the practice of a skill.

c. Although our colleges and universities try to get students to appreciate intellectually points of view different from their own, very little is done to help them to implement this general intellectual appreciation in a simple face-to-face relationship—at the level of a skill. Most educational institutions train their students to be logical, lucid, and clear. Very little is done to help them to listen more skillfully. As a result, our educated world contains too many Smiths and too few Joneses.

d. The biggest block to personal communication is man's inability to listen intelligently, understandingly, and skillfully to another person. This deficiency in the modern world is widespread and appalling. In our universities as well as elsewhere, too little is being done about it.

7. In conclusion, let me apologize for acting toward you the way Smith did. But who am I to violate a long-standing academic tradition!

20. What Killed Bob Lyons?

Harry Levinson

"What killed Bob Lyons?" is in a sense a psychological mystery story. In this story, however, there is no identifiable killer, merely the events of his life and the too-late attempts of others to help. What can managers do with their Bob Lyonses? Should all managers be counselors and sophisticated in the ways of psychotherapy? The author, a well-known industrial psychologist, says no, of course not. What managers can be, however, is aware of the enormous complexity of the human psyche and on the lookout for behavior patterns that might indicate that someone is in trouble. He also asserts that maintaining emotional balance is an ongoing struggle for everyone, no one is excluded, and that there is a little of Bob Lyons in all of us.

Those who knew Bob Lyons thought extremely well of him. He was a highly successful executive who held an important position in a large company. As his superiors saw him, he was aggressive, with a knack for getting things done through other people. He worked hard and set a vigorous pace. He drove himself relentlessly. In less than ten years with his company, he had moved through several positions of responsibility.

Lyons had always been a good athlete. He was proud of his skill in swimming, hunting, golf, and tennis. In his college days he had lettered in football and baseball. On weekends he preferred to undertake rebuilding and repairing projects around the house, or to hunt, interspersing other sports for a change of pace. He was usually engaged, it seemed, in hard, physical work.

His life was not all work, however. He was active in his church and in the Boy Scouts. His wife delighted in entertaining and in being with other people, so their social life was a round of many parties and social activities. They shared much of their life with their three children.

Early in the spring of his ninth year with the company, Bob Lyons spoke

AUTHOR'S NOTE: I wish to express my appreciation to Mrs. Helen Friend, Dr. Roy W. Menninger, and Dr. Joseph Satten, for critical reading of the manuscript and many useful suggestions.

with the vice president to whom he reported. "Things are a little quiet around here," he said. "Most of the big projects are over. The new building is finished, and we have a lot of things on the ball which four years ago were all fouled up. I don't like this idea of just riding a desk and looking out the window. I like action."

About a month later, Lyons was assigned additional responsibilities. He rushed into them with his usual vigor. Once again he seemed to be buoyant and cheerful. After six months on the assignment, Lyons had the project rolling smoothly. Again he spoke to his vice president, reporting that he was out of projects. The vice president, pleased with Lyons' performance, told him that he had earned the right to do a little dreaming and planning; and, furthermore, dreaming and planning were a necessary part of the position he now held, toward which he had aspired for so long. Bob Lyons listened as his boss spoke, but it was plain to the vice president that the answer did not satisfy him.

About three months after this meeting, the vice president began to notice that replies to his memos and inquiries were not coming back from Lyons with their usual rapidity. He noticed also that Lyons was developing a tendency to put things off, a most unusual behavior pattern for him. He observed that Lyons became easily angered and disturbed over minor difficulties that previously had not irritated him at all.

Bob Lyons then became involved in a conflict with two other executives over a policy issue. Such conflicts were not unusual in the organization, since, inevitably, there were varying points of view on many issues. The conflict was not a personal one, but it did require intervention from higher management before a solution could be reached. In the process of resolving the conflict, Lyons' point of view prevailed on some questions, but not on others.

A few weeks after this conflict had been resolved, Lyons went to the vice president's office. He wanted to have a long private talk, he said. His first words were, "I'm losing my grip. The old steam is gone. I've had diarrhea for four weeks and several times in the past three weeks I've lost my breakfast. I'm worried and yet I don't know what about. I feel that some people have lost confidence in me."

He talked with his boss for an hour and a half. The vice president recounted his achievements in the company to reassure him. He then asked if Lyons thought he should see a doctor. Lyons agreed that he should and, in the presence of the vice president, called his family doctor for an appointment. By this time the vice president was very much concerned. He called Mrs. Lyons and arranged to meet her for lunch the next day. She reported that, in addition to his other symptoms, her husband had difficulty sleeping. She was relieved that the vice president had called her because she was beginning to become worried and had herself planned to call the vice president. Both were now alarmed. They decided that they should get Lyons into a hospital rather than wait for the doctor's appointment, which was still a week off.

The next day Lyons was taken to the hospital. Meanwhile, with Mrs. Lyons' permission, the vice president reported to the family doctor Lyons' recent job behavior and the nature of their conversations. When the vice president had finished, the doctor concluded, "All he needs is a good rest. We don't want to tell him that it may be mental or nervous." The vice president replied that he didn't know what the cause was, but he knew Bob Lyons needed help quickly.

During five days in the hospital, Lyons was subjected to extensive laboratory tests. The vice president visited him daily. He seemed to welcome the rest and the sedation at night. He said he was eating and sleeping much better. He talked about company problems, though he did not speak spontaneously without encouragement. While Lyons was out of the room, another executive who shared his hospital room confided to the vice president that he was worried about Lyons. "He seems to be so morose and depressed that I'm afraid he's losing his mind," the executive said.

By this time the president of the company, who had been kept informed, was also becoming concerned. He had talked to a psychiatrist and planned to talk to Lyons about psychiatric treatment if his doctor did not suggest it. Meanwhile, Lyons was discharged from the hospital as being without physical illness, and his doctor recommended a vacation. Lyons then remained at home for several days where he was again visited by the vice president. He and his wife took a trip to visit friends. He was then ready to come back to work, but the president suggested that he take another week off. The president also suggested that they visit together when Lyons returned.

A few days later, the president telephoned Lyons' home. Mrs. Lyons could not find him to answer the telephone. After 15 minutes she still had not found him and called the vice president about her concern. By the time the vice president arrived at the Lyons home, the police were already there. Bob Lyons had committed suicide.

Why Did It Happen?

This tragic story is not an unusual one. Probably no other single emotional problem is as disturbing to those who must live with it as is suicide. No doubt Bob Lyons' colleagues and superiors suffered almost as much anguish as his family did. The president and vice president were concerned long afterward. They wondered if, despite their conscientious efforts, they had in some way been at fault or if they could have prevented it. Neither his family nor his colleagues could understand why it happened. It made no sense to them that a successful man in the prime of his life, like Lyons, should destroy himself.

Lyons' problem may have been extreme, but similar problems are not rare in business and industry. Executives, managers, supervisors, industrial physicians, and—to a lesser extent—all employees frequently must cope with emotional problems on the job. Many problems are of lesser proportion than Lyons' was, but all have four factors in common:

☐ They are painful both for the person who suffers from them and for those who must deal with him.

☐ They are usually destructive to both the sufferer and the organization.

☐ The origins of the problem are almost always more complex than either of the parties realizes; and only infrequently are even the precipitating events clear.

☐ Rarely does the person responsible for dealing with the on-the-job problem know what he should do about it.

As a result, few businesses have ways of dealing with these matters even reasonably well, and management actions tend to range from abrupt firing to hostile discipline to, in some instances, procrastination that goes on for years. Often there is a vacillating series of management efforts, accompanied by feelings of guilt, failure, and anger on the part of those who must make the managerial decisions. Emotional problems, then, are contagious. The disturbance suffered by one person has its effects on the emotions of others.

WAS IT HEREDITARY?

How can we understand what happened to Bob Lyons and the ways his problem relates to problems with which all of us must deal? The customary commonsense reasons fail us. He had no serious illness. He did not fail in his business activity. There was no indication of difficulty in his family life. The course of the story told by the vice president is too consistent to attribute his death to an accident or to chance. Then, what was responsible?

Heredity? Can we say he inherited a tendency to suicide? Man inherits certain capacities and traits, but these are essentially physiological. He inherits the color of his eyes, the size of his nose, and other physical features. He inherits certain sensory and motor capacities. That is, he will be able to see, hear, or feel physical stimuli—color, sound, warmth—more or less keenly. Newborn infants in a hospital nursery will vary widely in their response to such stimuli. Some are calm and placid; an attendant could drop a metal tray with a clang, but these children would continue to sleep. Others, however, would be startled and awake crying.

The reasons for these differences in reaction are obscure. We have some clues from recent experiments with white rats. When pregnant rats are placed in crowded cages or in other situations where they experience stress, this stress apparently produces biochemical imbalances in the mothers that affect the rat fetuses. When the baby rats are born, they have greater anxiety and greater difficulty in adapting to the external world than rats whose mothers were not subjected to such stress. Among human beings, the mother's diet, the illnesses she has during pregnancy, and her general physical condition have their effects on the human fetus.

SOMETHING PHYSICAL?

Apparently man also inherits the capacity to coordinate his muscles with greater or lesser efficiency. If a person inherits excellent coordination potential and develops it, he may ultimately become a good athlete or a good musician. If he inherits a better than usual capacity for abstracting sights and sounds, he may have the makings of an artist. Man does not inherit athletic or artistic skill, but some men and women inherit such a high level of sensitivity and physiological harmony that they seem to have a "natural bent" toward certain talents.

Some apparently are born with greater general intelligence; therefore, they have the potential for dealing with their environments with better reasoning power and more effective judgment. Others have more specialized capacities: the ability to abstract ideas readily, the ability to remember well, and so on. Such differences, which in some instances appear at birth, bring about different kinds of interactions with the environment. The irritable infant will have quite a different relationship with his mother than will the placid child. The child who walks and talks early comes into contact sooner with a wider range of experiences than does another child in the same general environment, in whom these skills develop later.

Heredity, then, to a large extent determines what a person will be, in the sense that all of us have to be two-armed, ten-fingered, two-legged men or women, short or tall, intelligent or unintelligent, and with different thresholds of our various senses. Each person is different in the combination of endowments that he has and in the degree to which they enable him to cope with life's stresses.

While hereditary factors predispose man to behave in gross, or general, ways, they have little direct effect on his specific behavior. Because of the high level of development of the frontal lobes of his brain, man is capable of both abstract and reflective thinking. He is also capable of a wide range of emotions, particularly feelings about himself in relation to other people. These capacities for thought and feeling make man extremely responsive to many nuances of environmental stimulation. They also make it possible for him to initiate a wide range of actions in keeping with his thoughts and feelings, as well as in response to his environment, particularly to the other people in it.

Another environmental factor that has an important influence on behavior is the extremely long period, particularly in Western cultures, during which the human child is dependent upon his parents. The intimacy of these relationships and the many social pressures that are transmitted through the parents to the children make family influences extremely important in guiding and controlling behavior. The extended period of dependency also presents a psychological problem because each person must then resolve the conflict between his wishes to retain the pleasures of dependency and his desire to become an independent adult. No one ever completely gives up the former or completely obtains the latter.

Each seeks some way of being interdependent with others that enables him to depend on others without losing his pride—because they in turn depend on him. Each person has dependency needs to varying degrees, the extent depending on how well each one has resolved this problem for himself. Some who have not resolved it well will always be more dependent than others. Some have resolved it reasonably well and can accept whatever dependency needs they have. Some have rejected or denied such needs and will have nothing to do with situations in which they might have to depend on others.

So, too, different companies will require different degrees of dependency in their employees. People who remain in a stable public utility company for a long time will be more dependent on their company for their security than will itinerant salesmen who sell magazines on commission. The fact that such a range of possibilities is available for fulfilling such needs at work is one of the health-giving aspects of work in business organizations.

Something Inside Him

Thus, we cannot, after this, very well say that Bob Lyons committed suicide because of heredity. We might be able to say hereditary factors, interacting with environmental factors, led to his death, but in our present state of knowledge it would be extremely difficult to demonstrate a hereditary predisposition that contributed to his self-destruction. Of necessity, we must call on more purely psychological factors for an explanation. In a way, when people, in despair over accounting for why someone like Bob Lyons would kill himself, cry out, "There must have been something odd inside of him that drove him into doing it," they are partially right. Inside all of us are many emotional drives that seem odd when we do not understand them.

For an approach toward understanding, let us return for a moment to the first paragraph of his superiors' description of Lyons. There we find these phrases: "highly successful," "aggressive," "a knack for getting things done through other people," "worked hard," "set a vigorous pace," and "drove himself relentlessly." These phrases speak of drive or energy. The subsequent two paragraphs describe other ways in which he discharged his energy. Some of these ways were highly useful to himself, his company, his family, and his friends. Others had a destructive potential: "He drove himself relentlessly." In fact, his difficulties seemed to begin when he could no longer drive himself on his job.

WARRING DRIVES

The theories of Sigmund Freud help us understand the importance of such drives. According to Freud, there are two constantly operating psychological drives in the personality. One is a *constructive drive* and the other a *destructive drive*. Just as there are always processes of growth and destruction in all biological matter, anabolism and catabolism, so there are similar processes in the personality. These drives constitute the basic, primitive, energy sources for the personality.

The constructive drive (sometimes referred to as the *libido*) is the source of feelings of love, creativity, and psychological growth. The destructive drive gives rise to feelings of anger and hostility to others. The twin forces are variously referred to as Love and Hate, in terms of Greek mythology as Eros and Thanatos, or Sex and Aggression. (When used in this way, both the terms sex and aggression have a far broader meaning than they do in ordinary usage.)

A major psychological task for every human being is to so fuse these drives that the constructive drive tempers, guides, and controls the destructive drive and that the energy from both sources may thus be used in his own self-interest and that of society. If we speak of the destructive drive as the aggressive drive (recognizing that we are using the word aggressive according to its dictionary meaning and not as synonymous with assertion as in ordinary usage), we can say that it is far better for a person to use his aggressive drive, tempered by larger amounts of the constructive drive, in the pursuit of a career, the creation of a family, and business competition than in destroying others, as might be the case if the drives were not adequately fused.

Perhaps an analogy will help. Think of an automobile engine. A mixture of gasoline and air serves as the energy source. If there is too much gasoline, the engine will flood. If there is too much air, then it will sputter and die. With the right blend or fusion of fuel, and particularly with considerably more gasoline than air, which is then channeled through a mechanical structure, the automobile engine can serve a useful purpose.

CHANNELING THE DRIVES

In Bob Lyons' case we saw that much of his constructive and aggressive energy, and more of the former than the latter, was well fused and channeled into his work, his relationships with his family, and service to his community. In some ways his constructive drive was less dominant, for he drove himself, as the vice president put it, "relentlessly."

The two drives are included in a part of the personality (a set of functions, not a physical thing) to which Freud gave the name "id," the Latin neuter for "it." In addition to the two basic drives, the id also includes many memories and experiences that the person can no longer recall.

The brain acts as a vast tape recorder. Theoretically, a person should be able to recall all of the experiences and feelings about those experiences he has had. We know that under hypnosis, in psychoanalysis, and under the influence of some drugs, a person can recall many of them. He could not do so before, no matter how hard he tried. Many of these memories, feelings, and impulses (impulses are derivatives of drives) are *repressed* or buried in the id, but they are still "alive," because they would be expressed, as we shall see later, if there were not adequate controls. For the id cares little about restraint; it operates on the pleasure principle: "I want what I want when I want it."

Repression, incidentally, is the process of "forgetting" or of making unconscious certain kinds of experiences and information which may be too troublesome or painful to handle on a conscious level. Here is how repression may have worked in Bob Lyons' case:

> To judge from his behavior, he may have learned in his childhood that the only way to obtain love from his parents was by good performance. If high performance was the price of love, Lyons may well have resented his parents' attitude. But since such a conscious feeling of anger toward his parents would have been painful to live with, it was repressed. Lyons was no longer aware of his anger toward them, but it remained with him. The id, being unconscious, has no sense of time; it is inconsistent, contradictory, and not amenable to logic or persuasion. Thus, the early experiences that caused Bob Lyons' feelings of resentment were still "alive" and painful in his id.

In speaking of the drives, we have said that psychological growth and survival require more of the constructive drive, implying that there are differences in the amount of drive energy. We assume that there are differences among people in how much drive energy they have. We don't know how these differences come about, nor do we have any satisfactory way of specifying amount other than grossly and comparatively. We do know, however, that warm, affectionate relationships, especially those between mother and child, give added strength to the constructive drive, while those in which the child experiences severe frustration and hostility from others stimulate more aggression in the child. In a general way, the same is true of adults: the relationships and experiences which provide affection and gratification bring out the good side of people, while those which precipitate frustration and anger bring out the bad side of people.

Something Outside Him

Not only did Bob Lyons (as do all of us) have the major psychological task of balancing or fusing his constructive and aggressive drives, but he also had to discharge these drives in socially acceptable ways only. It might have been permissible in more primitive times to hit a man on the head and take his wife, but it is no longer so. There are stringent cultural controls on how love and aggression may be expressed.

These controls on how we may express our basic drives vary from culture to culture, even from one social class to another; but they are transmitted through parents and other authority figures to children. Early in the child's development, the parents control and direct him. They permit some forms of behavior but prohibit others. As the child grows older, he incorporates into his own personality what his parents have taught him. He will incorporate these rules and values most effectively if he feels an affectionate bond with the parents and wants to be like them. This is one of the reasons the parent-child relationship is so important and why it should be one that enables the child to feel happy and secure.

Various values and rules can be "pounded into" the child, but these tend not to be genuinely his. He lives by them only as long as external pressures require him to, and abandons them when the external pressures diminish. Some parents who try to force piety and goodness into their children are dismayed to find them neither pious nor good when they grow up.

STILL, SMALL VOICE

When the child develops a conscience, he becomes self-governing. In Freudian terms, he has developed a *superego*. The superego is made up of four parts: (1)

the values of the culture as transmitted through parents, teachers, friends, scoutmasters, ministers, and so on; (2) rules, prohibitions, and taboos; (3) an ego ideal—the image of ourselves at our future best, which we never fully attain and as a result of which we are perennially discontented with ourselves; and (4) a police-judging or self-critical function.

Some theorists separate the superego and the conscience. They limit the superego to the values and the ego ideal (Parts 1 and 3 above), and refer to the rules (Part 2) and the self-critical function (Part 4) as the conscience. While that distinction is important scientifically, for our purposes we can ignore it. We will consider the conscience to be a part of the superego and include all four factors in the superego, as above.

The superego begins to develop in the child the first time the words "no" or "don't" enter his small world. Its general form tends to be established by the time the child enters elementary school, although it becomes further refined and expanded as a person grows up. Some features of the superego, developed early in life, are not conscious. The person is no longer aware of why he must live by certain rules and values; he knows only that if he does not do so, he feels uncomfortable or experiences anxiety. Some children, for example, feel that they must be the best in their class. They may not know why they feel they must, but if they are not always successful, they feel they are no good.

CONSCIENCE AND CULTURE

Because the superego is acquired from the culture in which a person lives (principally through the medium of his parents and later by incorporating the values, rules, and ideals of others he respects), it is reinforced by the culture. One's superego may keep him from stealing, for example, but there are also social penalties for stealing. Cultural changes may, in turn, bring about some changes in the superego, particularly in those aspects of the superego that are conscious. Thus, every older generation contends that every younger generation is going to the dogs. While certain basic values and rules endure, others change with time. This is also why many parents are so concerned about where the family lives and about the beliefs and attitudes of their children's teachers and friends.

Among the directions that the superego provides are those that have to do with how the constructive and aggressive drives may be directed, how a person may love and how he may hate (and under what circumstances), and what kind of an adult person he should be. A man may love his parents but in a way different from the way he loves his wife. He may not, in Western cultures, love another woman as he loves his wife. In Italy and Spain he may express affection to other men by embracing them, but not in the United States. He may express his anger verbally, but not in physical attack. He may direct some of his aggressive drive in work, sports, and community activities, but not comfortably in those areas that are commonly regarded as feminine.

There are many variations among families and subcultures that become part of the superegos of people in those groups. Among middle-class American families there is a heavy emphasis on achievement, on cleanliness, on good manners, on hard work, and on the avoidance of open expressions of hostility. Lower-class families, particularly those at the lowest socioeconomic levels, are not particularly concerned about these values. Some fundamentalist religious groups prohibit drinking and dancing. Some groups teach their children they are sinful by nature, others that almost anything they want to do is acceptable.

"KNOW THEN THYSELF"

How one looks upon himself, or his self-image, is related to the superego. One measure of self-evaluation is the disparity between the ego ideal and how one perceives himself at present. When one is depreciated by people who are important to him, this reinforces the critical aspects of the superego and lowers self-esteem. When self-esteem is enhanced, however, this counteracts the criticism of the superego and neutralizes some of the aggressive drive, thus stimulating the person to an expanded, more confident view of himself and his capacities.

It has been said that no wound is as painful as that inflicted by the superego. When a man behaves in ways not in keeping with the values and rules he has made a part of himself or when, in his judgment, he falls too short of his ego ideal, the superego induces a feeling of guilt. For most of us guilt feelings are so strong and so painful that we try to make up for violations of the superego by some form of atonement. The religious concept of penance is a recognition of this phenomenon. Restitution is another way to relieve guilt feelings. It is not unusual to see newspaper articles about people who have anonymously sent money to the government because they cheated on their taxes years before. Government officials speak of this as "conscience money."

Because the development of the superego begins early and the child is not in a position to judge rationally the relative importance of some of the rules he is taught, it is easy for the child to learn to judge himself more harshly than he should. With his limited capacity to reason, he may hold himself to blame for events he had nothing to do with. For example, suppose a two-year-old child is severely hurt in a fall. His four-year-old brother, who must inevitably have some feelings of hostility and rivalry toward the younger child, may come to feel he is responsible for the fall. As a matter of fact, he had nothing to do with the fall, but for a small child the wish is often tantamount to the act. To wish the younger child to be destroyed may be the same to a four-year-old as actually having pushed him. He may then harbor irrational guilt feelings for many years thereafter, completely unaware that he has such feelings or how they came about.

Since there is love and hate in every relationship, children have considerable hostility toward, as well as affection for, their parents. Usually young children do not understand that their hostile feelings are not "bad" and that parents will not be destroyed merely because their children have such feelings. As a result, most of us carry a considerable load of irrational guilt feelings. One of the major tasks in some forms of psychological treatment for people who are emotionally disturbed is to make such irrational unconscious feelings conscious so their irrationality may be recognized and they will no longer plague the person.

THE BALANCE WHEEL

The superego, then, becomes a built-in governor, as it were. It is the internalized civilizing agent. Without it, there would be no continuing self-guide to behavior. The superego is an automatic protective device. Because of it some issues are never raised; we never even ask: "Should I or should I not steal?" As a guide to behavior it makes for stability and consistency of performance.

If, however, the values and rules that the child is taught are inconsistent, then the superego will be inconsistent. If there are too many, too strict rules, then the superego becomes a harsh taskmaster, either constricting too narrowly the way a person can behave or burdening him excessively with feelings of guilt and demanding constant atonement. But even without punishment or strict rules, a tyrannical superego can develop—if performance is the basis for obtaining love and there are unrealistic expectations of extremely high performance. In such a case, there tends to be a quality of drivenness to much of the person's behavior. He has a feeling that there is so much that he ought to do or must do as contrasted with so much he would enjoy doing. Unless he is constantly doing what he feels he ought to do, then he feels uncomfortable, not knowing either why he ought to be doing or why he feels uncomfortable if he is not doing. Lyons, for example, not only drove himself relentlessly, but also usually had to be working hard.

We have seen so far that the constructive and aggressive drives, which continuously seek discharge, are major motivating forces in the personality. The superego, with its capacity to induce guilt feelings, not only defines acceptable ways in which the drives may be discharged but also serves as a motivating force.

Not everything we do, of course, is completely influenced by our emotional drives. Our environment plays its part and should be considered in our attempt to understand Bob Lyons' suicide. For, in addition to the task of balancing or fusing our drives in keeping with the strictures of the superego, we do have to deal with our external environment. At times, this environment is a source of affection, support, and security. The infant in his mother's arms, a woman in a happy marriage, a man enjoying himself among his friends, a man building a business, a minister serving his congregation, all draw emotional nourishment from the environment. Such nourishment strengthens the constructive forces of the personality.

Looked at closely, *needs for status and esteem are essentially needs for love and affection.* Each person, no matter how old or jaded, wants to be held in esteem by some others. Few can survive long without giving and receiving love, though often these expressions are thoroughly disguised, even from the self. Status needs have to do with the constructive forces of the personality as we have described them here. When one seeks symbols of status, he simply searches for concrete indications that some others do or will hold him in esteem. One way to describe status needs is to say that the person needs infusions of love and of gratification to foster his own strength.

However, the environment may also stimulate aggression: anger and jealousy, exploitation, competition for various advantages, economic reverses, wars, and so on. Every person has to deal with the realities of his environment—whether with the necessities of earning a living, the frustration of an unsolved problem, the achievement of personal goals, the development of satisfying relationships with other people, or something else. We saw that Lyons was actively involved with all of these things in his environment.

Ego and Reality

Now we have spoken of three sets of forces—id drives, the superego, and the environment—each interacting with the others, which must be kept in sufficient balance or equilibrium so that a person can function effectively. Some mechanism is required to do the balancing task, to serve as the executive part of the personality. Such a component of personality must fuse the drives, control their discharge in keeping with the conditions set by the superego, and act upon the environment. Freud gave the name *ego* to this set of functions. We tend to speak of the ego as a thing; actually, the term is merely a short way of describing *the organized executive functions of the personality, those functions that have to do with self-control and with testing reality.*

The ego includes such mental functions as recall, perception, judgment, attention, and conceptual or abstract thinking—those aspects of the personality which enable the individual to receive, organize, interpret, and act upon stimuli or psychological and physiological data. The ego develops (except in those who are mentally retarded) as the person grows. Like a computer, the ego acquires and stores information in the form of memory images, particularly information and experiences that previously have led to successful solution of problems. When an impulse arises from one of the drives, the ego contains the impulse until, in effect, it has checked with the superego and has determined what the consequences of acting on the impulse will be.

The impulse may have to be fully contained, or expressed in some modified fashion to meet both the conditions of the superego and the demands of the environment. The ego presumably checks its memory images to find acceptable ways of refining and discharging the impulse. When the ego can do this well, we speak of a strong ego or of psychological maturity. When it cannot do so adequately, we say a person does not have adequate strength or that he is immature. *The ego acts on the basis of what is called the reality principle:* "What are the long-run consequences of this behavior?"

The process of checking the memory images and organizing a response is what we know as thinking. Thinking is trial action or "dry run," as it were. Sometimes it goes on consciously, but much of the time it is an unconscious process. Thinking serves to delay impulses until they can be discharged in the most satisfactory way the person knows how. When a person acts impulsively in minor ways, for instance, in being inconsiderate of another person, we commonly speak of such behavior as "thoughtless."

The ego, operating on the reality principle and obeying the superego, must contain, refine, or redirect id impulses so that the integrity of the personality is preserved. The ego is constantly concerned with the cost and consequences of any action. In other words, the ego is concerned with psychological economy.

BELEAGUERED EGO

This task puts the ego in a difficult position. This system of psychological functions is always a buffer between the other systems, the id and the superego, and also between them and the forces of the environment. The ego, then, is always under psychological pressure. To carry on its integrating function well requires considerable strength. Strength comes from several sources: the basic inherited capacities, experiences of love and gratification that enhance the constructive forces, the development of skills and abilities that help it master the environment, and the physical health of the person. The ego may be weakened through physical injury or illness—a brain tumor, a debilitating sickness—or by having to devote too much of its energy to repressing or otherwise coping with severe multiple or chronic emotional pressures.

The ego cannot deal with all the stimuli that impinge upon it. It is constantly being bombarded with all kinds of data. It would be swamped if it tried to deal with all the information it had, in the form of both past experiences and present ones. It must be selective in what it will deal with. Some data are therefore passed directly on to the id. The ego is never consciously aware of them. Furthermore, it has not been able to resolve successfully all its psychological problems, some of which are extremely painful. With these it acts on the thesis "If you can't lick it, forget it." These problems are repressed, or pushed down into the id. The little boy who erroneously thought he hurt his brother, then repressed his guilt feelings, is a case in point.

Perhaps some other examples will help us to understand these processes better:

Suppose someone walking along the street sees a new car parked at the curb. He has an impulse to take the car and, acting on the impulse, drives it off. We say he acted impulsively, by which we mean he was governed by an impulse from the id and not by rational considerations. To put it another way, we might say that the ego was weak, that it did not anticipate the consequences of the act and control the impulse. The price paid for acting on the impulse, perhaps a jail term, is a high one for what little momentary pleasure might have been gained. We say such a person is immature, meaning that his ego is not sufficiently developed to enable him to act in a wiser and less costly way.

A store manager might also be said not to have good judgment if he bought items without thinking through their marketing possibilities or merely because he liked the salesman who sold them. This is another form of impulsiveness or immaturity. Marketing men count on the irrational impulsiveness in all of us by creating in supermarkets such a vast array of stimuli to our desires for pleasure that the ego does not function quite as well as it might. Impulse buying results—unless the ego is bolstered by additional support in the form of a shopping list and a budget.

Here is a more personal example. If you observe young children, you see that they live extremely active lives. They have many pleasant moments and some painful ones. They remember experiences from day to day and recall exciting events like a trip to the zoo with great relish. Now try to remember your own early childhood experiences, especially those that occurred before you were four or five. Probably you will be able to recall few in any detail, if you can recall any at all. Many other experiences of childhood, adolescence, and even adulthood are beyond voluntary recall. Yet under hypnosis they could be recalled. This information, much of it not immediately necessary to solve today's problems, is stored in the id.

Memory traces of some of these experiences, which might help us solve problems, are stored in the ego, though even they are usually not conscious. A person may be surprised to find himself at home, having driven from work while preoccupied with a problem, without ever having noticed the turns, stop lights, or other cars. Obviously, he used many cues and did many specific things to get home safely, though he did so without being aware of what he was doing.

A final example illustrates the way the ego deals with impulses from the id. Suppose an attractive secretary comes to work in a new dress whose lines are calculated to stimulate the interest of men—in short, to stimulate the sexual impulse. When this impulse reaches the ego of one of the men in the office, the ego, acting within the limits set by the superego ("Look, but don't touch"), and its judgment of the consequences of giving vent to the impulse ("You'll destroy your reputation"), will control and refine the impulse. The man may then comment, "That's a pretty dress"—a highly attenuated derivative of the original impulse. Another man with a more rigid superego might never notice the dress. His superego would protect him by automatically prohibiting the ego from being sensitive to such a stimulus.

Ego's Assistants

If the ego has the job of first balancing the forces from the id, the superego, and the environment, and then of mediating and synchronizing them into a system that operates relatively smoothly, it requires the assistance of two kinds of psychological devices to make its work possible. Thus:

1. It needs *anxiety* to serve as an alarm system to alert it to possible dangers to its equilibrium.

2. It must have *defense mechanisms,* which can be called into play, triggered by the alarm system; these will help it either to fend off the possible threats or to counteract them.

ANXIETY'S PURPOSE

The alarm-triggering system called anxiety is what we are conscious of whenever we are afraid of something. It is a feeling of unease or tension. But there is a much more subtle and complex phenomenon of anxiety, which operates spontaneously and unconsciously whenever the ego is threatened. Being unaware of its operation, we may not know consciously why we are restless, tense, or upset. Bob Lyons, we recall, was worried but he did not know why. We have all experienced his anxiety. A feeling of tension and restlessness that one person picks up from another is very common. Sensing that the other person is upset makes us feel uneasy for reasons that are not very clear to us. We do not consciously decide that we are threatened, but we feel we "can't relax," that we must be on guard.

Perhaps the work of unconscious anxiety may be likened to a gyroscope on a ship or an airplane. The gyroscope must sense the imbalance of the ship or plane as a result of waves, currents, or storms. It must then set into motion counteracting forces to regain the vehicle's balance. This analogy highlights something else for us: *There is no state of placid emotional stability, just as there is never a smooth ocean or an atmosphere devoid of air currents. There is no peace of mind short of the grave. Everyone is always engaged in maintaining his psychological equilibrium.* Even when a person is asleep, his dreaming is an effort to resolve psychological problems, to discharge tension, and to maintain sleep. The workings of unconscious anxiety may be seen in a number of different ways:

Suppose a three-year-old child, drinking milk from a glass, bites and shatters the edge of the glass. The glass cuts the child's lip, which bleeds profusely. Striving to remain calm, the mother places a compress under the lip and stops the bleeding. But she does not know whether the child has swallowed any of the glass and, therefore, what she should do next. She asks the child if he has swallowed glass. He says he has not. To be certain, she asks again, saying, "Please tell me if you have, because if you have, you might have a tummyache and we don't want you to have a tummyache." At this point the child says he *has* swallowed some glass. Now the mother does not know whether he has or has not.

Before the mother can decide that she had better take the child to the hospital, he begins to quiver as he might shake from the cold. This shaking is involuntary. Though the child has no conscious concept of the possible fatal danger of swallowing glass, and though the mother has tried to remain calm, unconsciously the child has sensed the inherent threat in the situation. Automatically, emergency physiological and biochemical processes are called into play to cope with the danger. It is the effects of these we see in the shaking. The manner and attitude of the hospital physician assure the child that there is no threat and gradually the shaking subsides.

Adults may have the same experience in many different ways. Suppose you are driving your car down the street and a youngster dashes out from between parked cars into the path of yours. You immediately slam on the brakes. For a moment you do not know whether you have hit the child. When you get out of the car, you see that you have not; but you find yourself shaking, your heart beating rapidly, your skin perspiring. You did not consciously cause any of these things to happen. The threat to your equilibrium, constituting a stress, aroused anxiety, which in turn mobilized your resources for dealing with the emergency. A similar experience is a commonplace among athletes. Some of them experience such psychological tension before competitive events that they cannot eat; if they do, they throw up.

Here we are speaking of conscious anxiety at one level. We are aware of certain threats and react to them. But at another, unconscious level, our reaction is disproportionate to the event. There is no objective reason for the driver to continue to be anxious when he discovers that he has not hit the child. The overt threat is past. Yet he may continue to shake for hours and may even dream about the event to the point of having nightmares. It is understandable that the athlete would want to win the game for conscious reasons. Why the competition should cause him such violent physical reaction is a more complex and obscure problem. He himself does not know why he must go to such extremes of defensive mobilization that his body cannot tolerate food. Unconscious anxiety is at work.

EGO DEFENSES

If we are to penetrate deeply enough into Bob Lyons' reasons for suicide, we must go beyond admitting that he was undoubtedly anxious and under stress. We need to see why his ego was not sufficiently protected from such a completely destructive attack—why the defense mechanisms mentioned earlier as one of the ego's assistants did not enable him to overcome his anxiety.

There are a number of personality mechanisms that operate automatically to help the ego maintain or regain its equilibrium. These mechanisms may be viewed as falling into three broad classes:

1. One group has to do with shaping or forming the personality. Included in this category is *identification,* the process of behaving like someone else. A man identifies himself with his boss when he dresses or speaks as his boss does. Women identify themselves with a leading movie star when they adopt her hair style. Another device, *introjection,* is a stronger form of identification, although the line betweem them is hazy. When one introjects the mannerisms or attitudes of another, he makes these firmly a part of himself. We speak of introjecting the value of the parents and thereby of becoming a "chip off the old block."

2. Another group of mechanisms are universally used devices that are required to control, guide, refine, and channel the basic drives or impulses from the id. We have already talked about *repression.* Another mechanism, *sublimation,* is the process by which basic drives are refined and directed into acceptable channels. Lyons, for example, sublimated much of his aggressive drive in his work.

3. A third group of mechanisms is made up of temporary devices that are called into play automatically when there is some threat to the personality.

Denial, a form of repression, is one of these devices, and can be clarified by an example.

Suppose a plant superintendent has five years to go to retirement and his boss suggests that he pick a successor and train him. But our plant superintendent does not select a successor, despite repreated requests from the boss. He cannot "hear" what the boss is saying. He may be forced to select such a man. When the time for retirement arrives, he may then say to his boss that the boss really did not intend to retire him. He cannot believe the boss will compel him to leave. This behavior reflects a denial of the reality of the situation because the ego has difficulty accepting what it regards to be a loss of love (status, esteem, etc.).

Rationalization is another temporary mechanism that all of us use from time to time. In fact, as the following example shows, it provides the subject matter for comedy!

A man's wife suggests that it is time to get a new car because theirs is already eight years old and getting shabby. At first, acting under the influence of the superego, the man doubts if he needs a new car. He cannot justify it to himself. To buy one without an adequate reason would be a waste of money for him. "You're too mature to be so extravagant and to fall for style," his superego says. The guilt aroused by the thought of buying a new car gives rise to anxiety, and the idea is rejected to appease the superego. The old car still runs well, he says; it gives no trouble, and a new one would be expensive. Soon we see him in an automobile showroom. "Just looking," he tells the salesman. "He thinks he's found a sucker," he chuckles to himself to avoid the condemnation of the superego. Next, however, he begins to complain to his wife and his friends that the old car will soon need repairs, that it will never be worth more on a trade-in. Before long he has developed a complete rationale for buying the new car, and has convinced himself to do so.

Projection, another temporary mechanism, is the process of attributing one's own feelings to someone else. If, for example, one can project hostility onto someone else ("He's mad at me; he's out to get me"), then one can justify to his superego his hostility toward the other person ("It's all right for me to get him first").

Idealization is the process of putting a halo around someone else and thereby being unable to see his faults. This process is seen most vividly in people who are in love or who have identified strongly with political leaders. It enhances the image of the idealized person as a source of strength and gratification.

Reaction formation is a formidable term for the process of doing the opposite of what one wants to do to avoid the threat of giving rein to impulses. Some people become so frightened of their own aggressive impulses that they act in an extremely meek and mild manner, avoiding all suggestion of aggression.

Another important mechanism is *substitution,* or displacement. This is the process in which the ego, unable to direct impulses to the appropriate target, directs them to a substitute target. In a benign way, this is what happens when a person devotes much of his affection to pets or to his work if, for whatever reasons, he does not have satisfactory ways of giving his affection to other people. More destructive displacement occurs when a person seeks substitute targets for his aggression. Unable to express his anger at his boss to the boss, a man may displace it onto the working conditions or wages. He may even unwittingly carry it home and criticize his wife or his children. This is the mechanism behind scapegoating and prejudice. Not only does displacement of this kind hurt others; worse yet, it doesn't contribute to the solution of the real problem.

Compensation is still another mechanism, and often a highly constructive one. This is the process of developing talents and skills to make up for one's deficiencies, or of undertaking activities and relationships to regain lost gratification. In certain respects, compensation and substitution are, of course, closely related.

The Defensive Process

These mechanisms need not be elaborated further here. Our answer to why Bob Lyons killed himself has necessarily been delayed long enough. Now we see the point, however. When the ego is threatened in some fashion, anxiety spontaneously and unconsciously triggers off mechanisms to counteract the threat. If there are too many emergencies for the personality, it may then overuse these mechanisms, and this in turn will seriously distort the person's view of reality, or cripple him psychologically. To identify with those one respects is fine; to imitate them slavishly is to lose one's individuality. It is one thing to rationalize occasionally, as we all do, but another to base judgments consistently on rationalizations. At times all of us project our own feelings, but we would be sick indeed if we felt most of the time that everyone else had it in for us.

By and large, self-fulfillment has to do with the ego's capacity to function as effectively as it can. When emotional conflicts can be diminished, when the need for defensiveness can be decreased, the energy that ordinarily maintained the defenses is freed for more useful activity. In a sense, the effect is to remove some of the brakes from the psychological wheels. Furthermore, when, as threats are removed, the defenses need no longer be used, one perceives reality more accurately. He then can relate to other people more reasonably and can communicate more clearly. A psychological blossoming-out can occur. When such balancing fails to take place, the ego is overwhelmed for the time being. In

Bob Lyons' case, he acted to relieve his emotional pain and killed himself before equilibrium could be restored in a less destructive way. Since this balancing process is the ultimate key to an understanding of Lyons' act, let us make sure we understand how it works and then apply our knowledge directly to Bob Lyons' case:

Fusion of drives toward appropriate target

Suppose a man is called into his boss's office and his boss criticizes him harshly for something he did not do. The ideally healthy man, if he exists, will listen calmly to what his boss has to say and, in good control of his rising aggressive impulse, might well reply, "Boss, I'm sorry that such a mistake has happened. I had nothing to do with that particular activity, but perhaps I can help you figure out a way to keep the same mistake from happening again." His boss, also brimming with good mental health, might then respond, "I'm sorry that I criticized you unfairly. I would appreciate your giving me a hand on this." Together they direct their energies toward the solution of the problem.

Displacement to less appropriate target

But take a similar situation where, however, the man knows his boss will brook no contradiction or is so emotionally overwrought that there is little point in trying to be reasonable with him. This man may fume with anger at the unjust attack but control his impulse to strike back at the boss. His reality-testing ego tells him that such action won't help the situation at all. He takes the criticism, anticipating a better solution when the boss cools off. Nevertheless, he is angry for being unjustly criticized, and there has been no opportunity to discharge his aroused aggressive impulse in an appropriate way toward the solution of the problem.

Because in this situation is seems so rational to control one's impulse (i.e., the boss is upset and there's no point in discussing it with him now), the ego finds this secondary anger an inappropriate feeling to allow into consciousness. The more primitive secondary anger is then repressed. When the employee goes bowling that night, he gets particular pleasure from knocking the pins down, without knowing why. Unconsciously he is using bowling to drain off his excess aggression. Such a displacement is a partially constructive way of discharging aggression: it hurts no one, it provides gratification. However, it does not contribute directly to resolving the problem itself, presuming that some further action toward solution might be required.

Containment of drives

Suppose that another man finds himself in the same situation. This man has learned in the course of growing up that it is not permissible to express one's aggression directly to authority figures. Being human, he has aggressive impulses, but also, having a severe superego, he feels guilty about them and goes to great lengths to repress them. When the boss criticizes him and his aggressive impulse is stimulated, repression automatically sets in and the impulse is controlled without his being aware of it. However, it is so controlled that he can't speak up to contribute to the solution of the problem.

Because this man constantly maintains a high degree of control to meet the demands of his superego, he is already in a potentially more explosive situation, ready to defend himself from the slightest possible threat. If he has to contain more of his anger within himself, we have a situation that is much like rising steam pressure in a boiler. If this situation is repetitive or chronic, the mobilization and remobilization of defenses almost requires of the ego that it be in a steady emergency state. The alarm bells are ringing most of the time. This kind of reaction strains the ego's resources and is particularly wearing physiologically because each psychological response to stress is accompanied by physiological mobilization, too.

The result is psychosomatic symptoms. The body is literally damaged by its own fluids, leading to ulcers, hypertension, and similar phenomena. This experience is commonly recognized in the phrase "stewing in one's own juice." Clinical data seem to show that there are reasons why one particular organ is the site for a psychosomatic symptom, but often these reasons are obscure.

Displacement onto the self

Take still another man. This one also has learned that aggression should not be expressed to others, and he cannot do so without feelings of guilt. In fact, his superego won't tolerate much hostility on his part, so he lives constantly with feelings of guilt. The guilt, in turn, makes him feel inadequate, as his superego repeatedly berates him for his hostility. No matter how nice, by means of reaction formation, he may try to be, he can't satisfy his superego. Somehow, he himself always seems to be at fault. With such a rigid, punitive superego, this man under the same kind of attack may then respond by saying, "I guess you're right. I'm always wrong; it's my fault. I never seem to do things right." He may also then have a mild depression. Depression is always an indication of anger with oneself, originating from anger toward another, and reflects the attack of the superego on the ego. The aggression is displaced from the appropriate target back onto the self and results in a form of self-blame and self-punishment.

Another form of self-attack or self-punishment is seen in many accidents. Most accidents are not actually accidents in the sense that they occur by chance, but are unconscious modes of self-punishment. The "forgetting" to turn the motor switch off before repairing the machine or not seeing or hearing possible threats frequently are indications that denial or repression has been operating in order to permit the person to hurt himself to appease his own superego. In extreme form, this self-directed aggression is the mechanism behind suicide, and now we are prepared to see what happened to Bob Lyons.

The Reason Why

Driven by an extremely severe superego, Bob Lyons sublimated his drives successfully in his work as long as he could work hard. There was an ego-superego-id environment equilibrium, although only a tenuous one. By driving himself, he could appease the relentless pressure of his superego.

Such a superego, however, is never satisfied. Its demands arise from unconscious sources, which, because they are unconscious, probably have existed from early childhood and are to a large extent irrational. If they were not irrational, their terms could be met.

Whenever he reached a goal toward which he had aspired, Lyons got no satisfaction from it, for his superego still drove him. And when he could no longer work as hard as he had, this for him was an environmental deprivation. He could no longer earn love by performing well. His superego became more relentless. The vacation, with no demands on him at all, simply added to his guilt, his feelings of unworthiness and inadequacy. With sublimations and displacements reduced, given the kind of superego he had, his aggressive drive had only his ego as a major target.

And at that moment, the only way that Bob Lyons knew to appease his superego was to kill himself.

Had his superego been developed differently, Lyons might have achieved as he did because of ego reasons (the pleasure and gratification he got from his work), with a mild assist from the superego to do well. When his superego developed so strongly, probably because of a heavy burden of hostility in childhood for which he felt irrationally guilty for a lifetime, there was no real pleasure in what he did and nothing more than temporary gratification. The relentless driving of himself was a form of self-sacrifice, just as are alcoholism, most accidents, repeated failures on the job, presenting the worst side of one's self to others, and some forms of crime.

We should recognize that there is a bit of this phenomenon in all of us, just as we can see something of ourselves at times in each of the preceding three examples. The ancient observation that "man is his own worst enemy" is testimony to the self-destructive potential in each person. Bob Lyons differed from the rest of us only in degree, and only because of a combination of forces at a given point, which precipitated his death. A change in any single force might conceivably have prevented it: more and harder work, psychiatric treatment, no vacation to add to the feelings of guilt and uselessness, or open recognition by his physician of the seriousness of mental illness.

GROPING FOR SHADOWS

But how would his physician or his friends have recognized early symptoms of Bob Lyons' illness? It would not have been easy. We cannot put an ego under a microscope or locate the id in any part of the body. These are simply names given to what seem to be systems of forces operating in the personality. We cannot see repression—it is only a name for the observation that some things are forgotten and can be recalled only under certain circumstances. The same is true when we speak of something being unconscious. It is not relegated to a given physical organ or place. One is merely not able to call it into consciousness.

If the ego has a constant balancing task and calls certain mechanisms into play to carry it out, being concerned with psychological economy, the ego will develop preferred mechanisms, preferred because they work best consistently. These become the established personality traits. As individuals we make our preferred models of adjustment those ways of behaving which are most comfortable (least anxiety-arousing) to us.

The consistent modes of adjustment, the personality traits, become the hallmarks by which we are known to others. Even physical styles of behavior become part of this system. If we hear on the telephone a voice that we recognize, we can place it with a name. If we meet a friend we have not seen in ten years, we will observe that he seems to be the same as he always was—he talks, reacts, thinks in much the same way. Some are hail-fellow-well-met gregarious types, others more diffident and conservative. Each has his own preferred modes of adjustment, his preferred way of consistently maintaining equilibrium.

Given these entrenched modes of adaptation, even clinical psychologists and psychiatrists are unlikely to make *radical* changes in people, although they can often help alter certain forces so that people can behave more healthily than they did previously. The alteration of internal forces (ego-superego-id) is the job of the clinician. The layman often can make a contribution to the alteration of external forces (ego-environment). Even minor changes of the balance of forces can make significant differences in how people feel, think, and behave.

The very fact that people do not radically change their styles of behavior makes it possible to detect signs of emotional stress. Given certain characteristic modes of adaptation in the form of personality traits, once a person experiences some kind of emotional stress, he is likely first to make greater use of those mechanisms that worked best for him before. The first sign of stress is that a person seems to be conspicuously more like he always was. If he ordinarily is a quiet man, under stress he may become withdrawn. If he is like Lyons, his first reaction may well be to try to work harder.

Secondly, if this first line of defense does not work too well (or if the stress is too severe or chronic for that method alone), we will begin to see the appearance of inefficient functioning—vague fears, inability to concentrate, compulsions to do certain things, increasing irritability, and declining work performance. We will also see the results of physiological defensive efforts. We saw in Lyons' case that tension, jitteriness, and inability to hold food or to sleep all accompanied his psychological stress. The whole organism—physiological and psychological— was involved in the struggle.

Psychological and physiological symptoms are ways of "binding" or attempting to control the anxiety. They are ways of trying to do something about a problem, however ineffective they may be. And they are the best ways of dealing with that problem that the person has available to him at the moment, though better ways of coping may be apparent to others who do not have his psychological makeup. That's why it is dangerous to try to remove symptoms. Instead, it is wiser to resolve the underlying problem.

Thirdly, if neither of these types of defenses can contain the anxiety, we may see sharp changes in personality. The person no longer behaves as he did before. Lyons felt himself to be falling apart, unable to work as he did previously. A neat person may become slovenly, an efficient one alcoholic. Radical changes in personality indicate severe illness, which usually requires hospitalization.

Conspicuous change in behavior indicates that the ego is no longer able to maintain effective control. If a person is so upset that he hears voices or sees things that do not exist, previously unconscious thoughts and feelings are breaking through. Obviously irrational behavior indicates the same thing. There is a loss of contact with reality, seriously impaired judgment, and an inability to be responsible for oneself. In such a state, Bob Lyons committed suicide.

Conclusion

Now that we *think* we understand why Bob Lyons killed himself, it is important that two cautions be raised.

ABOUT OURSELVES

First, the reader newly exposed to psychoanalytic theory invariably falls victim to what may be called the freshman medical student's syndrome: he gets every symptom in the book. Everything to which this article refers, the average reader will be able to see in himself. As we were discussing Lyons, we were talking about human beings and human motivation; so it was inevitable that we ended up talking about ourselves. We must recognize this tendency to read ourselves into these pages, and compensate for this by consciously trying to maintain an objective distance from the material.

At the same time, does this very experience not make it clear to us that everyone has the continuing task of maintaining an equilibrium? At any given time any one of us may be listing to starboard a little, or trying to keep from being buffeted about by a sudden storm. Despite these pressures, we must nevertheless move forward, correcting for the list as best we can, or conserving our strength to ride out the storm. Each will defend himself the best way he knows how. As he does so, the more energy he must devote to defense, the less he will have available for forward movement.

Each of us at one time or another, therefore, will be emotionally disturbed or upset. For a few hours, a few days, a few weeks, we may be irritable or angry ("I got up on the wrong side of the bed"), or blue ("I'm feeling low today"), or hypersensitive. When we feel these ways, when we are having difficulty maintaining an equilibrium, for that brief period of time we are emotionally disturbed. We cannot work as well as we usually do. It is more difficult for us to sustain our relationships with other people. We may feel hopeless or helpless. We're just not ourselves.

But just because we are mildly emotionally disturbed does not mean we need professional help or hospitalization. A cold is a minor form of upper respiratory infection, the extreme of which is pneumonia. If one has a cold, that does not mean he will have pneumonia. Even if he does get pneumonia, with present treatment methods most people recover, and the same is true of mental illness. The difference between the mild and the severe is one of degree, not of kind. It is just more of the same thing.

Because each of us is human and no one of us has had either perfect heredity or perfect environment, each of us has his weak spots. When the balance of forces is such that there is stress where we are weak, we will have difficulty. The incidence of mental illness, then, is not one out of twenty or some other proportionate statistic. Rather it is one out of one!

WHAT WE CAN DO

The second caution has to do with the limitations of this exposition and the reader's preparation for understanding it. This necessarily has been a highly condensed version of some aspects of psychoanalytic theory. Many important aspects of the theory have been omitted and others have been presented without the many qualifications a serious scientific presentation would require. The reader should therefore look upon what is presented only as an introduction to better understanding of problems. He should be careful about overgeneralization and should studiously avoid using jargon or interpreting people's behavior to them.

Unless he observes these limitations, the layman will be unable to help anyone. Within these limitations, however, a businessman can render extremely important help to others in his company—and to himself. Specifically, he can recognize that:

☐ *All* behavior is motivated, much of it by thoughts and feelings of which the person himself is not aware. Behavior does not occur by chance.

☐ At any one time each person is doing the best he can, as a result of the multiple forces that bring about any given behavior. A change in the forces is required to bring about a change in behavior.

☐ Love neutralizes aggression and diminishes hostility. "A soft word turneth away wrath," says the old aphorism. This does not mean maudlin expressions, but actions that reflect esteem and regard for the other person as a human being. The most useful demonstration of affection is support which takes the form of:

☐ *Understanding* that the pain of emotional distress is real. It will not go away by wishing it away, by dismissing it as "all in your head," or by urging the person to "forget it," "snap out of it," or to "take a vacation."

☐ *Listening* if the person brings his problem to you, or if it so impairs his work that you must call his work performance to his attention. Listening permits him to define his problem more clearly and thereby to examine courses of action. Acting constructively to solve a problem is the best way the ego has to maintain the fusion of drives in dealing with reality. Listening, by providing some relief for the distressed person, already brings about some alteration in the balance of forces.

If you listen, however, you must clearly recognize your limitations: (1) you can offer only emergency help; (2) you cannot hold yourself *responsible* for other people's personal problems, some of which would defy the most competent specialist.

☐ *Referring* the troubled person to professional sources of help if the problem is more than a temporary one, or if the person is severely upset. Every organization should have channels for referral. If a person who has responsibility for other people has no formal organizational channels for referral, he would do well to establish contact with a psychiatrist, a clinical psychologist, or a community mental health agency. He will then have professional sources of guidance available when problems arise.

Finally, we can maintain a watchful, but not morbid, eye on ourselves. If we find that we are having difficulties that interfere with our work or with gratifying relationships with other people, then we should be wise enough to seek professional help.

Appendix to Chapter 20

Handling the Constructive Drive

In this article, because we are focusing on Bob Lyons' case, we are looking at ways in which the ego deals with the *aggressive* drive by calling into play certain defense mechanisms in order to maintain its equilibrium. But the ego also must deal with the *constructive* drive in order to maintain the proper balance. We see how it might handle sexual stimulation by control and refinement, or even denial, of the impulse. Other examples illustrate how the same mechanisms that are used to cope with the aggressive drive apply themselves to handling constructive drives and, in so doing, often cause us distress as well as relief:

1. *Fusion of Drives.* Fused with the aggressive drive, and dominant over it, the constructive drive is directed toward appropriate targets in intimate relationships with one's family, the solution of work and family problems, citizenship activities, and so on. Idealistic love without an aggressive component might lead to merely fantasied images of a sweetheart rather than marriage, or a person might dream about job success rather than take action toward it.

2. *Displacement to Less Appropriate Targets.* Like the aggressive drive, the constructive drive may be deflected from appropriate targets. Homosexuality is one such phenomenon whose dynamics are too complex for discussion here. In brief, the homosexual cannot establish adequate and satisfying relationships with those of the opposite sex. Instead, he uses the mechanism of substitution and builds up extended rationalizations to appease his superego.

Some people can invest themselves in causes, but not really in other people. Some lavish great affection on animals or houses or hobbies at the expense of personal relationships. Some adults can have affectionate relationships only with young children, but cannot tolerate other adults. These targets provide useful channels for love, but not the fully satisfying wide range of relationships enjoyed by most mature adults.

3. *Containment.* Some people, for complicated reasons, learned that it was psychologically safe not to express affection and have repressed their affection-

ate feelings. These people we know colloquially as "cold fish," people seemingly without emotion. They may be highly intellectual or great professional successes, but they have divorced compassion from judgment and feeling from reasoning. Others are known as ruthlessly efficient. They keep their emotions tightly controlled and their feelings of love deeply buried within themselves.

4. *Displacement onto the Self.* Children rejected by their parents learn bitterly that it is too painful to try to love other people because they will not return love. In adult life, such people become highly self-centered. In conversation they are constantly talking about themselves. They give overmeticulous attention to their appearance, and revel in self-display. They tend to seek out activities that provide public adulation, and become extremely unhappy when they cannot get it. We find such people unpleasant to deal with because they are unable to give anything of themselves to someone else. Often they exploit others for their own gain. Because they cannot love others, they have almost no real friends and often are unable to sustain their marriages.

For these people much of the constructive drive is displaced onto themselves because environmental forces have made identification and introjection difficult, thereby impairing the possibility of relationships with other people. The early conflicts, now repressed, still exist unconsciously for the person. With its memories of early pain, the ego will not open itself again to the possibilities of rejection and narrowly constricts the constructive drive to a limited target to protect itself. Because of the limited range of attachments their egos permit, such people do not really enjoy life, despite what appears to others to be an extremely sparkling series of social adventures.

Each person must have a certain amount of self-love if he is to have self-respect. Overweening egocentricity, however, is ultimately destructive because of the absence of gratification, because of the pain caused other people, and because it diverts energy from social contributions the person could make.

An extreme form of egocentricity is hypochondriasis. Some people invest all of their energy in themselves in an extremely distorted way by being preoccupied with their own bodies. They are never free of aches and pains, often spend years and untold dollars "doctoring." They sacrifice most of life's pleasures to nurse their fancied ills, undeterred by repeated medical reports that show there is no need for surgery or that they do not have cancer, and the like. In some respects, such people commit slow suicide as they cut themselves off more and more from the outside world. In some cases, such persons will even allow one or more limbs to atrophy from disuse because they claim it is too painful to walk or to move.

Part V
Being an Effective Leader

Preface

Perhaps leaders more than any other people in organizations need to develop their intuitive and creative capacities. From numerous studies of leadership, we find that leaders are charismatic, mature, wise, have good judgment, are interpersonally competent, and give their employees, or countrymen, something to believe in. Often these people also move others with words, arousing their emotions in support of a cause, country, or company.

What is being described in fact is an integrated person, someone whose intuitive and rational capacities are both highly developed. Such a person makes a good leader. If he or she is lacking in reason, his or her brilliant ideas and visions will never find expression. If this person lacks imagination, the expression will be no more inspiring that the individual lines a pen scratches on paper.

In this section the articles concern themselves with the intuitive capacities. For instance, in "Power Is the Great Motivator," David McClelland and David Burnham discuss how the most effective managers, the ones who are successful in motivating their employees, are those who have a need to influence others for the good of the company. One of the reasons these people are so respected and influential is because their employees perceive that the manager is not acting for his own aggrandizement but for the good of something outside himself. Good managers, according to McClelland and Burnham, are mature people who perceive value outside themselves.

Leaders, ultimately, believe in something. They perceive a vision that they need to communicate to others. Anthony Athos, in "Is the Corporation Next to Fall?," encourages managers to shift their value systems from the rigidly objective to include more of the subjective aspects of organizational goals and structures, lest younger generations of employees revolt against what they perceive as a rational inhuman system.

Finally, in "Skyhooks," O. A. Ohmann writes that employees have a fine sensitivity to spiritual qualities and want to work for someone who believes in something and in whom they can believe. "Bread alone will not satisfy workers," he maintains. "Man is searching for anchors outside himself. He runs wearily to the periphery of the spider web of his own reason and logic, and looks for new 'skyhooks'—for an abiding faith around which life's experiences can be integrated and given meaning." It is the job of a leader to provide them.

21. Power Is the Great Motivator

David C. McClelland and David H. Burnham

Good managers, ones who get the best out of their subordinates and who thereby produce positive results for their organizations, are the keys to an organization's success. It is not surprising, then, that much research and thought has gone into trying to define just what motivates a good manager and how to describe him so that his characteristics can be objectively measured and identified. In this article, the authors describe a motivation pattern that empirical research has discovered most good managers share. Good managers are not motivated by a need for personal aggrandizement, or by a need to get along with subordinates, but rather by a need to influence others' behavior for the good of the whole organization. In other words, good managers want power. On its own, however, power can lead to authoritarianism, so it needs to be tempered by maturity and a high degree of self-control. The authors maintain that workshops can help a manager discover whether he has the correct motivation profile to be a good manager. If he does, or even if he does not have the correct profile, workshops can help him become a good or better manager.

What makes or motivates a good manager? The question is so enormous in scope that anyone trying to answer it has difficulty knowing where to begin. Some people might say that a good manager is one who is successful, and by now most business researchers and businessmen themselves know what motivates people who successfully run their own small businesses. The key to their success has turned out to be what psychologists call "the need for achievement," the desire to do something better or more efficiently than it has been done before. Any number of books and articles summarize research studies explaining how the achievement motive is necessary for a person to attain success on his own.[1]

But what has achievement motivation got to do with good management?

AUTHOR'S NOTE: All the case material in this article is disguised.

1. For instance, see my books *The Achieving Society* (New York, Van Nostrand, 1961) and (with David Winter) *Motivating Economic Achievement* (New York, Free Press, 1969).— D.C.McC.

There is no reason on theoretical grounds why a person who has a strong need to be more efficient should make a good manager. While it sounds as if everyone ought to have the need to achieve, in fact, as psychologists define and measure achievement motivation, it leads people to behave in very special ways that do not necessarily lead to good management.

For one thing, because they focus on personal improvement, on doing things better by themselves, achievement-motivated people want to do things themselves. For another, they want concrete short-term feedback on their performance so that they can tell how well they are doing. Yet a manager, particularly one of or in a large complex organization, cannot perform all the tasks necessary for success by himself or herself. He must manage others so that they will do things for the organization. Also, feedback on his subordinate's performance may be a lot vaguer and more delayed than it would be if he were doing everything himself.

The manager's job seems to call more for someone who can influence people than for someone who does things better on his own. In motivational terms, then, we might expect the successful manager to have a greater "need for power" than need to achieve. But there must be other qualities beside the need for power that go into the makeup of a good manager. Just what these qualities are and how they interrelate is the subject of this article.

To measure the motivations of managers, good and bad, we studied a number of individual managers from different large U.S. corporations who were participating in management workshops designed to improve their managerial effectiveness. (The workshop techniques and research methods and terms used are described in the Appendix on page 357.)

The general conclusion of these studies is that the top manager of a company must possess a high need for power—that is, a concern for influencing people. However, this need must be disciplined and controlled so that it is directed toward the benefit of the institution as a whole and not toward the manager's personal aggrandizement. Moreover, the top manager's need for power ought to be greater than his need for being liked by people.

Now let us look at what these ideas mean in the context of real individuals in real situations and see what constitutes the profile of the good manager. Finally, we will look at the workshops themselves to determine how they go about changing behavior.

Measuring Managerial Effectiveness

First off, what does it mean when we say that a good manager has a greater need for "power" than for "achievement"? To get a more concrete idea, let us consider the case of Ken Briggs, a sales manager in a large U.S. corporation who joined one of our managerial workshops (see the Appendix). Some six or seven years ago, Ken Briggs was promoted to a managerial position at corporate headquarters, where he had responsibility for salesmen who service his company's largest accounts.

In filling out his questionnaire at the workshop, Ken showed that he correctly perceived what his job required of him, namely, that he should influence others' success more than achieve new goals himself or socialize with his subordinates. However, when asked with other members of the workshop to write a story depicting a managerial situation, Ken unwittingly revealed through his fiction that he did not share those concerns. Indeed, he discovered that his need for achievement was very high—in fact over the 90th percentile—and his need for power was very low, in about the 15th percentile. Ken's high need to achieve was no surprise—after all, he had been a very successful salesman—but obviously his motivation to influence others was much less than his job required. Ken was a little disturbed but thought that perhaps the measuring instruments were not too accurate and that the gap between the ideal and his score was not as great as it seemed.

Then came the real shocker. Ken's subordinates confirmed what his stories revealed: he was a poor manager, having little positive impact on those who worked for him. Ken's subordinates felt that they had little responsibility delegated to them, that he never rewarded but only criticized them, and that the office was not well organized, but confused and chaotic. On all three of these scales, his office rated in the 10th to 15th percentile relative to national norms.

As Ken talked the results over privately with a workshop leader, he became more and more upset. He finally agreed, however, that the results of the survey confirmed feelings he had been afraid to admit to himself or others. For years, he had been miserable in his managerial role. He now knew the reason: he simply did not want to nor had he been able to influence or manage others. As he thought back, he realized that he had failed every time he had tried to influence his staff, and he felt worse than ever.

Ken had responded to failure by setting very high standards—his office scored in the 98th percentile on this scale—and by trying to do most things himself, which was close to impossible; his own activity and lack of delegation consequently left his staff demoralized. Ken's experience is typical of those who have a strong need to achieve but low power motivation. They may become very successful salesmen and, as a consequence, may be promoted into managerial jobs for which they, ironically, are unsuited.

If achievement motivation does not make a good manager, what motive does? It is not enough to suspect that power motivation may be important; one needs hard evidence that people who are better managers than Ken Briggs do in fact

possess stronger power motivation and perhaps score higher in other characteristics as well. But how does one decide who is the better manager?

Real-world performance measures are hard to come by if one is trying to rate
managerial effectiveness in production, marketing, finance, or research and
development. In trying to determine who the better managers were in Ken
Briggs's company, we did not want to rely only on the opinions of their
superiors. For a variety of reasons, superiors' judgments of their subordinates'
real-world performance may be inaccurate. In the absence of some standard
measure of performance, we decided that the next best index of a manager's
effectiveness would be the climate he or she creates in the office, reflected in the
morale of subordinates.

Almost by definition, a good manager is one who, among other things, helps
subordinates feel strong and responsible, who rewards them properly for good
performance, and who sees that things are organized in such a way that
subordinates feel they know what they should be doing. Above all, managers
should foster among subordinates a strong sense of team spirit, of pride in
working as part of a particular team. If a manager creates and encourages this
spirit, his subordinates certainly should perform better.

In the company Ken Briggs works for, we have direct evidence of a
connection between morale and performance in the one area where performance
measures are easy to come by—namely, sales. In April 1973, at least three
employees from this company's 16 sales districts filled out questionnaires that
rated their office for organizational clarity and team spirit (see the Appendix).
Their scores were averaged and totaled to give an overall morale score for each
office. The percentage gains or losses in sales for each district in 1973 were
compared with those for 1972. The difference in sales figures by district ranged
from a gain of nearly 30% to a loss of 8%, with a median gain of around 14%.
Exhibit I shows the average gain in sales performance plotted against the
increasing averages in morale scores.

In *Exhibit I* we can see that the relationship between sales and morale is
surprisingly close. The six districts with the lowest morale early in the year
showed an average sales gain of only around 7% by year's end (although there
was wide variation within this group), whereas the two districts with the
highest morale showed an average gain of 28%. When morale scores rise above
the 50th percentile in terms of national norms, they seem to lead to better sales
performance. In Ken Briggs's company, at least, high morale at the beginning is
a good index of how well the sales division actually performed in the coming
year.

And it seems very likely that the manager who can create high morale among
salesmen can also do the same for employees in other areas (production, design,

Average percent gain in sales by district from 1972 to 1973

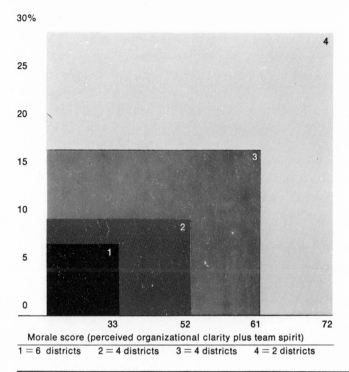

Morale score (perceived organizational clarity plus team spirit)

1 = 6 districts   2 = 4 districts   3 = 4 districts   4 = 2 districts

and so on), leading to better performance. Given that high morale in an office indicates that there is a good manager present, what general characteristics does he possess?

A NEED FOR POWER

In examining the motive scores of over 50 managers of both high and low morale units in all sections of the same large company, we found that most of the managers—over 70%—were high in power motivation compared with men in general. This finding confirms the fact that power motivation is important for management. (Remember that as we use the term *power motivation,* it refers not to dictatorial behavior, but to a desire to have impact, to be strong and influential.) The better managers, as judged by the morale of those working for them, tended to score even higher in power motivation. But the most important determining factor of high morale turned out not to be how their power motivation compared to their need to achieve but whether it was higher than their need to be liked. This relationship existed for 80% of the better sales managers, as compared with only 10% of the poorer managers. And the same held true for other managers in nearly all parts of the company.

In the research, product development, and operations divisions, 73% of the better managers had a stronger need for power than a need to be liked (or what we term "affiliation motive"), as compared with only 22% of the poorer managers. Why should this be so? Sociologists have long argued that, for a bureaucracy to function effectively, those who manage it must be universalistic in applying rules. That is, if they make exceptions for the particular needs of individuals, the whole system will break down.

The manager with a high need for being liked is precisely the one who wants to stay on good terms with everybody, and, therefore, is the one most likely to make exceptions in terms of particular needs. If a male employee asks for time off to stay home with his sick wife to help look after her and the kids, the affiliative manager agrees almost without thinking, because he feels sorry for the man and agrees that his family needs him.

When President Ford remarked in pardoning ex-President Nixon that he had "suffered enough," he was responding as an affiliative manager would, because he was sympathizing primarily with Nixon's needs and feelings. Sociological theory and our data both argue, however, that the person whose need for affiliation is high does not make a good manager. This kind of person creates poor morale because he or she does not understand that other people in the office will tend to regard exceptions to the rules as unfair to themselves, just as many U.S. citizens felt it was unfair to let Richard Nixon off and punish others less involved than he was in the Watergate scandal.

SOCIALIZED POWER

But so far our findings are a little alarming. Do they suggest that the good manager is one who cares for power and is not at all concerned about the needs of other people? Not quite, for the good manager has other characteristics that must still be taken into account.

Above all, the good manager's power motivation is not oriented toward personal aggrandizement but toward the institution that he or she serves. In another major research study, we found that the signs of controlled action or inhibition that appear when a person exercises his or her imagination in writing stories tell a great deal about the kind of power that person needs.[2] We discovered that, if a high power motive score is balanced by high inhibition, stories about power tend to be altruistic. That is, the heroes in the story exercise power on behalf of someone else. This is the "socialized" face of power, as distinguished from the concern for personal power, which is characteristic of individuals whose stories are loaded with power imagery but which show no sign of inhibition or self-control. In our earlier study, we found ample evidence that these latter individuals exercise their power impulsively. They are more rude to other people, they drink too much, they try to exploit others sexually, and they collect symbols of personal prestige such as fancy cars or big offices.

Individuals high in power and in control, on the other hand, are more institution-minded; they tend to get elected to more offices, to control their drinking, and to want to serve others. Not surprisingly, we found in the workshops that the better managers in the corporation also tend to score high on both power and inhibition.

Profile of a Good Manager

Let us recapitulate what we have discussed so far and have illustrated with data from one company. The better managers we studied are high in power motivation, low in affiliation motivation, and high in inhibition. They care about institutional power and use it to stimulate their employees to be more productive. Now let us compare them with affiliative managers—those in whom the need for affiliation is higher than the need for power—and with the personal power managers—those in whom the need for power is higher than for affiliation but whose inhibition score is low.

In the sales division of our illustrative company, there were managers who matched the three types fairly closely. *Exhibit II* shows how their subordinates rated the offices they worked in on responsibility, organizational clarity, and team spirit. There are scores from at least three subordinates for each manager, and several managers are represented for each type, so that the averages shown in the exhibit are quite stable. Note that the manager who is concerned about being liked by people tends to have subordinates who feel that they have very little personal responsibility, that organizational procedures are not clear, and that they have little pride in their work group.

In short, as we expected, affiliative managers make so many ad hominem and

2. David C. McClelland, William N. Davis, Rudolf Kalin, and Erie Warner, *The Drinking Man* (New York, The Free Press, 1972).

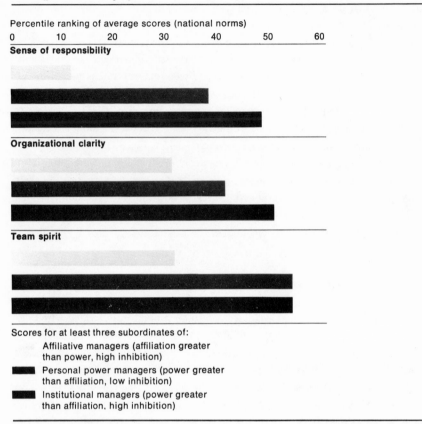

Exhibit II. Average scores on selected climate dimensions by subordinates of managers with different motive profiles

Percentile ranking of average scores (national norms)

| 0 | 10 | 20 | 30 | 40 | 50 | 60 |

Sense of responsibility

Organizational clarity

Team spirit

Scores for at least three subordinates of:

Affiliative managers (affiliation greater than power, high inhibition)

Personal power managers (power greater than affiliation, low inhibition)

Institutional managers (power greater than affiliation, high inhibition)

ad hoc decisions that they almost totally abandon orderly procedures. Their disregard for procedure leaves employees feeling weak, irresponsible, and without a sense of what might happen next, of where they stand in relation to their manager, or even of what they ought to be doing. In this company, the group of affiliative managers portrayed in *Exhibit II* were below the 30th percentile in morale scores.

The managers who are motivated by a need for personal power are somewhat more effective. They are able to create a greater sense of responsibility in their divisions and, above all, a greater team spirit. They can be thought of as managerial equivalents of successful tank commanders such as General Patton, whose own daring inspired admiration in his troops. But notice how in *Exhibit II* these men are still only in the 40th percentile in the amount of organizational clarity they create, as compared to the high-power, low-affiliation, high-inhibition managers, whom we shall term "institutional."

Managers motivated by personal power are not disciplined enough to be good institution builders, and often their subordinates are loyal to them as individuals rather than to the institution they both serve. When a personal-power manager leaves, disorganization often follows. His subordinates' strong group spirit, which the manager has personally inspired, deflates. The subordinates do not know what to do for themselves.

Of the managerial types, the "institutional" manager is the most successful in creating an effective work climate. *Exhibit II* shows that his subordinates feel that they have more responsibility. Also, this kind of manager creates high morale because he produces the greatest sense of organizational clarity and team spirit. If such a manager leaves, he or she can be more readily replaced by another manager, because the employees have been encouraged to be loyal to the institution rather than to a particular person.

MANAGERIAL STYLES

Since it seems undeniable from *Exhibit II* that either kind of power orientation creates better morale in subordinates than a "people" orientation, we must consider that a concern for power is essential to good management. Our findings seem to fly in the face of a long and influential tradition of organizational psychology, which insists that authoritarian management is what is wrong with most businesses in this country. Let us say frankly that we think the bogeyman of authoritarianism has in fact been wrongly used to downplay the importance of power in management. After all, management is an influence game. Some proponents of democratic management seem to have forgotten this fact, urging managers to be primarily concerned with people's human needs rather than with helping them to get things done.

But a good deal of the apparent conflict between our findings and those of other behavioral scientists in this area arises from the fact that we are talking about *motives,* and behaviorists are often talking about *actions.* What we are saying is that managers must be interested in playing the influence game in a controlled way. That does not necessarily mean that they are or should be authoritarian in action. On the contrary, it appears that power-motivated managers make their subordinates feel strong rather than weak. The true authoritarian in action would have the reverse effect, making people feel weak and powerless.

Thus another important ingredient in the profile of a manager is his or her managerial style. In the illustrative company, 63% of the better managers (those whose subordinates had higher morale) scored higher on the democratic or coaching styles of management as compared with only 22% of the poorer managers, a statistically significant difference. By contrast, the latter scored higher on authoritarian or coercive management styles. Since the better managers were also higher in power motivation, it seems that, in action, they express their power motivation in a democratic way, which is more likely to be effective.

To see how motivation and style interact, let us consider the case of George Prentice, a manager in the sales division of another company. George had exactly the right motive combination to be an institutional manager. He was high in the need for power, low in the need for affiliation, and high in inhibition. He exercised his power in a controlled organized way. His stories reflected this fact. In one, for instance, he wrote, "The men sitting around the table were feeling pretty good; they had just finished plans for reorganizing the company; the company has been beset with a number of organizational problems. This group, headed by a hard-driving, brilliant young executive, has completely reorganized the company structurally with new jobs and responsibilities."

This described how George himself was perceived by the company, and shortly after the workshop he was promoted to vice president in charge of all sales. But George was also known to his colleagues as a monster, a tough guy who would "walk over his grandmother" if she stood in the way of his advancement. He had the right motive combination and, in fact, was more interested in institutional growth than in personal power, but his managerial style was all wrong. Taking his cue from some of the top executives in the corporation, he told people what they had to do and threatened them with dire consequences if they didn't do it.

When George was confronted with his authoritarianism in a workshop, he recognized that this style was counterproductive—in fact, in another part of the study we found that it was associated with low morale—and he subsequently changed to acting more like a coach, which was the scale on which he scored the lowest initially. George saw more clearly that his job was not to force other people to do things but to help them to figure out ways of getting their job done better for the company.

THE INSTITUTIONAL MANAGER

One reason it was easy for George Prentice to change his managerial style was that in his imaginative stories he was already having thoughts about helping others, characteristic of men with the institution-building motivational pattern.

In further examining institution builders' thoughts and actions, we found they have four major characteristics:

1. They are more organization-minded; that is, they tend to join more organizations and to feel responsible for building up these organizations. Furthermore, they believe strongly in the importance of centralized authority.

2. They report that they like to work. This finding is particularly interesting, because our research on achievement motivation has led many commentators to argue that achievement motivation promotes the "Protestant work ethic." Almost the precise opposite is true. People who have a high need to achieve like to get out of work by becoming more efficient. They would like to see the same result obtained in less time or with less effort. But managers who have a need for institutional power actually seem to like the discipline of work. It satisfies their need for getting things done in an orderly way.

3. They seem quite willing to sacrifice some of their own self-interest for the welfare of the organization they serve. For example, they are more willing to make contributions to charities.

4. They have a keen sense of justice. It is almost as if they feel that if a person works hard and sacrifices for the good of the organization, he should and will get a just reward for his effort.

It is easy to see how each of these four concerns helps a person become a good manager, concerned about what the institution can achieve.

Maturity

Before we go on to look at how the workshops can help managers to improve their managerial style and recognize their own motivations, let us consider one more fact we discovered in studying the better managers at George Prentice's company. They were more mature (see Appendix, p. 357). Mature people can be most simply described as less egotistic. Somehow their positive self-image is not at stake in what they are doing. They are less defensive, more willing to seek advice from experts, and have a longer range view. They accumulate fewer personal possessions and seem older and wiser. It is as if they have awakened to the fact that they are not going to live forever and have lost some of the feeling that their own personal future is all that important.

Many U.S. businessmen fear this kind of maturity. They suspect that it will make them less hard driving, less expansion-minded, and less committed to organizational effectiveness. Our data do not support their fears. These fears are exactly the ones George Prentice had before he went to the workshop. Afterward he was a more effective manager, not despite his loss of some of the sense of his own importance, but because of it. The reason is simple: his subordinates believed afterward that he genuinely was more concerned about the company than about himself. Where once they respected his confidence but feared him, they now trust him. Once he supported their image of him as a "big man" by talking about the new Porsche and the new Honda he had bought; when we saw him recently he said, almost as an aside, "I don't buy things any more."

Changing Managerial Style

George Prentice was able to change his managerial style after learning more about himself in a workshop. But does self-knowledge generally improve managerial behavior?

Some people might ask, "What good does it do to know, if I am a manager, that I should have a strong power motive, not too great a concern about being liked, a sense of discipline, a high level of maturity, and a coaching managerial style? What can I do about it?" The answer is that workshops for managers that give information to them in a supportive setting enable them to change.

Consider the results shown in *Exhibit III,* where "before" and "after" scores are compared. Once again we use the responses of subordinates to give some measure of the effectiveness of managers. To judge by their subordinates' responses, the managers were clearly more effective afterward. The subordinates felt that they were given more responsibility, that they received more rewards, that the organizational procedures were clearer, and that morale was higher. These differences are all statistically significant.

But what do these differences mean in human terms? How did the managers change? Sometimes they decided they should get into another line of work. This happened to Ken Briggs, for example, who found that the reason he was doing so poorly as a manager was because he had almost no interest in influencing others. He understood how he would have to change if he were to do well in his present job, but in the end decided, with the help of management, that he would prefer to work back into his first love, sales.

Ken Briggs moved into "remaindering," to help retail outlets for his company's products get rid of last year's stock so that they could take on each year's new styles. He is very successful in this new role; he has cut costs, increased dollar volume, and in time has worked himself into an independent role selling some of the old stock on his own in a way that is quite satisfactory to the business. And he does not have to manage anybody any more.

In George Prentice's case, less change was needed. He was obviously a very competent person with the right motive profile for a top managerial position. When he was promoted, he performed even more successfully than before

Exhibit III. Average scores on selected climate dimensions by over 50 salesmen before and after their managers were trained

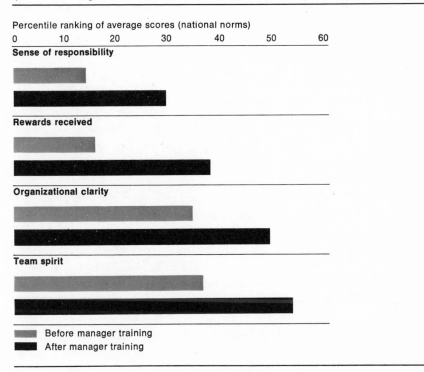

Percentile ranking of average scores (national norms)

| 0 | 10 | 20 | 30 | 40 | 50 | 60 |

Sense of responsibility

Rewards received

Organizational clarity

Team spirit

■ Before manager training
■ After manager training

because he realized the need to become more positive in his approach and less coercive in his managerial style.

But what about a person who does not want to change his job and discovers that he does not have the right motive profile to be a manager?

The case of Charlie Blake is instructive. Charlie was as low in power motivation as Ken Briggs, his need to achieve was about average, and his affiliation motivation was above average. Thus he had the affiliative manager profile, and, as expected, the morale among his subordinates was very low. When Charlie learned that his subordinates' sense of responsibility and perception of a reward system were in the 10th percentile and that team spirit was in the 30th, he was shocked. When shown a film depicting three managerial climates, Charlie said he preferred what turned out to be the authoritarian climate. He became angry when the workshop trainer and other members in the group pointed out the limitations of this managerial style. He became obstructive in the group process and objected strenuously to what was being taught.

In an interview conducted much later, Charlie said, "I blew my cool. When I started yelling at you for being all wrong, I got even madder when you pointed out that, according to my style questionnaire, you bet that that was just what I did to my salesmen. Down underneath I knew something must be wrong. The sales performance for my division wasn't so good. Most of it was due to me anyway and not to my salesmen. Obviously their reports that they felt very little responsibility was delegated to them and that I didn't reward them at all had to mean something. So I finally decided to sit down and try to figure what I could do about it. I knew I had to start being a manager instead of trying to do everything myself and blowing my cool at others because they didn't do what I thought they should. In the end, after I calmed down on the way back from the workshop, I realized that it is not so bad to make a mistake; it's bad not to learn from it."

After the course, Charlie put his plans into effect. Six months later, his subordinates were asked to rate him again. He attended a second workshop to study these results and reported, "On the way home I was very nervous. I knew I had been working with those guys and not selling so much myself, but I was very much afraid of what they were going to say about how things were going in the office. When I found out that the team spirit and some of those other low scores had jumped from around 30th to the 55th percentile, I was so delighted and relieved that I couldn't say anything all day long."

When he was asked how he acted differently from before, he said, "In previous years when the corporate headquarters said we had to make 110% of our original goal, I had called the salesmen in and said, in effect, 'This is ridiculous; we are not going to make it, but you know perfectly well what will happen if we don't. So get out there and work your tail off.' The result was that I worked 20 hours a day and they did nothing.

"This time I approached it differently. I told them three things. First, they were going to have to do some sacrificing for the company. Second, working harder is not going to do much good because we are already working about as hard as we can. What will be required are special deals and promotions. You are going to have to figure out some new angles if we are to make it. Third, I'm going to back you up. I'm going to set a realistic goal with each of you. If you make that goal but don't make the company goal, I'll see to it that you are not punished. But if you do make the company goal, I'll see to it that you will get some kind of special rewards."

When the salesmen challenged Charlie, saying he did not have enough influence to give them rewards, rather than becoming angry Charlie promised rewards that were in his power to give—such as longer vacations.

Note that Charlie has now begun to behave in a number of ways that we found to be characteristic of the good institutional manager. He is, above all, higher in power motivation, the desire to influence his salesmen, and lower in his tendency to try to do everything himself. He asks the men to sacrifice for the company. He does not defensively chew them out when they challenge him but tries to figure out what their needs are so that he can influence them. He realizes that his job is more one of strengthening and supporting his subordinates than of criticizing them. And he is keenly interested in giving them just rewards for their efforts.

The changes in his approach to his job have certainly paid off. The sales figures for his office in 1973 were up more than 16% over 1972 and up still further in 1974 over 1973. In 1973 his gain over the previous year ranked seventh in the nation; in 1974 it ranked third. And he wasn't the only one in his company to change managerial styles. Overall sales at his company were up substantially in 1973 as compared with 1972, an increase that played a large part in turning the overall company performance around from a $15 million loss in 1972 to a $3 million profit in 1973. The company continued to improve its performance in 1974 with an 11% further gain in sales and a 38% increase in profits.

Of course not everyone can be reached by a workshop. Henry Carter managed a sales office for a company that had very low morale (around the 20th percentile) before he went for training. When morale was checked some six months later, it had not improved. Overall sales gain subsequently reflected this fact since it was only 2% above the previous year's figures.

Oddly enough, Henry's problem was that he was so well liked by everybody that he felt little pressure to change. Always the life of the party, he is particularly popular because he supplies other managers with special hard-to-get brands of cigars and wines at a discount. He uses his close ties with everyone to bolster his position in the company, even though it is known that his office does not perform well compared with others.

His great interpersonal skills became evident at the workshop when he did very poorly at one of the business games. When the discussion turned to why he had done so badly and whether he acted that way on the job, two prestigious participants immediately sprang to his defense, explaining away Henry's failure by arguing that the way he did things was often a real help to others and the company. As a result, Henry did not have to cope with such questions at all. He had so successfully developed his role as a likable, helpful friend to everyone in management that, even though his salesmen performed badly, he did not feel under any pressure to change.

Checks and Balances

What have we learned from Ken Briggs, George Prentice, Charlie Blake, and Henry Carter? Principally, we have discovered what motive combination makes an effective manager. We have also seen that change is possible if a person has the right combination of qualities.

Oddly enough, the good manager in a large company does not have a high need for achievement, as we define and measure that motive, although there must be plenty of that motive somewhere in his organization. The top managers shown here have a high need for power and an interest in influencing others, both greater than their interest in being liked by people. The manager's concern for power should be socialized—controlled so that the institution as a whole, not only the individual, benefits. Men and nations with this motive profile are empire builders; they tend to create high morale and to expand the organizations they head.

But there is also danger in this motive profile; empire building can lead to imperialism and authoritarianism in companies and in countries.

The same motive pattern that produces good power management can also lead a company or a country to try to dominate others, ostensibly in the interests of organizational expansion. Thus it is not surprising that big business has had to be regulated from time to time by federal agencies. And it is most likely that international agencies will perform the same regulative function for empire-building countries.

For an individual, the regulative function is performed by two characteristics that are part of the profile of the very best managers—a greater emotional maturity, where there is little egotism, and a democratic, coaching managerial style. If an institutional power motivation is checked by maturity, it does not lead to an aggressive, egotistic expansiveness.

For countries, this checking means that they can control their destinies beyond their borders without being aggressive and hostile. For individuals, it means they can control their subordinates and influence others around them without resorting to coercion or to an authoritarian management style. Real disinterested statesmanship has a vital role to play at the top of both countries and companies.

Summarized in this way, what we have found out through empirical and statistical investigations may just sound like good common sense. But the improvement over common sense is that now the characteristics of the good manager are objectively known. Managers of corporations can select those who are likely to be good managers and train those already in managerial positions to be more effective with more confidence.

Appendix to Chapter 21

Workshop Techniques

The case studies and data on companies used in this article were derived from a number of workshops we conducted where executives came to learn about their managerial styles and abilities as well as how to change them. The workshops had a dual purpose, however. They provided an opportunity for us to study which motivation pattern—whether it be a concern for achievement, power, people, or a combination thereof—makes the best managers.

When the managers first arrived at the workshops, they were asked to fill out a questionnaire about their job. Each participant analyzed his job, explaining what he or she thought it required of him. The managers were asked to write a number of stories to pictures of various work situations. The stories were coded for the extent to which an individual was concerned about achievement, affiliation, or power, as well as for the amount of inhibition or self-control they revealed. The results were then matched against national norms. The differences between a person's job requirements and his or her motivational patterns can often help assess whether the person is in the right job, whether he is a candidate for promotion to another job, or whether he is likely to be able to adjust to fit his present position.

At the workshops and in this article, we use the technical terms *need for achievement, need for power,* and *need for affiliation* as defined in the books *The Achieving Society* and *Power: The Inner Experience.* The terms refer to measurable factors in groups and individuals. Briefly, these characteristics are measured by coding an individual's spontaneous thoughts for the frequency with which he thinks about doing something better or more efficiently than before (need for achievement), about establishing or maintaining friendly relations with others (need for affiliation), or about having impact on others (need for power). (When we talk about power, we are not talking about dictatorial power, but about the need to be strong and influential.) As used here, therefore, the motive labels are precise terms, referring to a particular method of defining and measuring, much as "gravity" is used in physics, or "gross national product" is used in economics.

To find out what kind of managerial style the participants had, we gave them a questionnaire in which they had to choose how they would handle various realistic work situations in office settings. Their answers were coded for six different management styles or ways of dealing with work situations. The styles depicted were democratic, affiliative, pace-setting, coaching, coercive, and authoritarian. The managers were asked to comment on the effectiveness of each style and to name the style that they prefer.

One way to determine how effective managers are is to ask the people who work for them. Thus, to isolate the characteristics that good managers have, we surveyed at least three subordinates of each manager at the workshop to see how they answered questions about their work situations that revealed characteristics of their supervisors along several dimensions, namely: (1) the amount of conformity to rules required, (2) the responsibility they feel they are given, (3) the emphasis the department places on standards of performance, (4) the degree to which they feel rewards are given for good work as opposed to punishment for something that goes wrong, (5) the degree of organizational clarity in the office, and (6) its team spirit.[1] The managers who received the highest morale scores (organizational clarity plus team spirit) from their subordinates were determined to be the best managers, possessing the most desirable motive patterns.

The subordinates were also surveyed six months after the managers returned to their offices to see if the morale scores rose after the workshop.

One other measure was obtained from the participants to find out which managers had another characteristic deemed important for good management: maturity. Scores were obtained for four stages in the progress toward maturity by coding the stories that the managers had written for such matters as their attitudes toward authority and the kinds of emotions displayed over specific issues.

People in Stage I are dependent on others for guidance and strength. Those in Stage II are interested primarily in autonomy, in controlling themselves. In Stage III, people want to manipulate others; in Stage IV, they lose their egotistic desires and wish to selflessly serve others.[2]

The conclusions presented in this article are based on workshops attended by over 500 managers from over 25 different U.S. corporations. However, the data in the exhibits are drawn from just one of these companies for illustrative purposes.

---

1. Based on G. H. Litwin and R. A. Stringer's *Motivation and Organizational Climate* (Boston, Division of Research, Harvard Business School, 1966).
2. Based on work by Abigail Stewart reported in David C. McClelland's *Power: The Inner Experience* (New York, Irvington Publishers, 1975).

22. Power, Dependence, and Effective Management

John P. Kotter

Americans have probably always been suspicious of power—the United States was born out of a rebellion against it, and our political processes seem to confirm that distrust. We have equated power with exploitation and corruption. But, the author of this article asserts, the negative aspects of power have blinded people to its positive points, to its uses, and to the fact that, without it, people cannot accomplish very much anywhere. And that is especially true in management. The author maintains that, as organizations have grown more complex, it has become more difficult, if not impossible, for managers to achieve their ends either independently or through persuasion and formal authority alone. They increasingly need power to influence other people on whom they are dependent. Furthermore, he says, effective managers tend to be very successful at developing four different types of power, which they use along with persuasion to influence others. And they do so, the author concludes, with maturity, great skill, and a sensitivity to the obligations and risks involved.

Americans, as a rule, are not very comfortable with power or with its dynamics. We often distrust and question the motives of people who we think actively seek power. We have a certain fear of being manipulated. Even those people who think the dynamics of power are inevitable and needed often feel somewhat guilty when they themselves mobilize and use power. Simply put, the overall attitude and feeling toward power, which can easily be traced to the nation's very birth, is negative. In his enormously popular *Greening of America*, Charles Reich reflects the views of many when he writes, "It is not the misuse of power that is evil; the very existence of power is evil."[1]

AUTHOR'S NOTE: This article is based on data from a clinical study of a highly diverse group of 26 organizations including large and small, public and private, manufacturing and service organizations. The study was funded by the Division of Research at the Harvard Business School. As part of the study process, the author interviewed about 250 managers.

1. Charles A. Reich, *The Greening of America: How the Youth Revolution Is Trying to Make America Liveable* (New York, Random House, 1970).

One of the many consequences of this attitude is that power as a topic for rational study and dialogue has not received much attention, even in managerial circles. If the reader doubts this, all he or she need do is flip through some textbooks, journals, or advanced management course descriptions. The word *power* rarely appears.

This lack of attention to the subject of power merely adds to the already enormous confusion and misunderstanding surrounding the topic of power and management. And this misunderstanding is becoming increasingly burdensome because in today's large and complex organizations the effective performance of most managerial jobs requires one to be skilled at the acquisition and use of power.

From my own observations, I suspect that a large number of managers— especially the young, well-educated ones—perform significantly below their potential because they do not understand the dynamics of power and because they have not nurtured and developed the instincts needed to effectively acquire and use power.

In this article I hope to clear up some of the confusion regarding power and managerial work by providing tentative answers to three questions:

1. Why are the dynamics of power necessarily an important part of managerial processes?

2. How do effective managers acquire power?

3. How and for what purposes do effective managers use power?

I will not address questions related to the misuse of power, but not because I think they are unimportant. The fact that some managers, some of the time, acquire and use power mostly for their own aggrandizement is obviously a very important issue that deserves attention and careful study. But that is a complex topic unto itself and one that has already received more attention than the subject of this article.

Recognizing Dependence in the Manager's Job

One of the distinguishing characteristics of a typical manager is how dependent he is on the activities of a variety of other people to perform his job effectively.[2] Unlike doctors and mathematicians, whose performance is more directly dependent on their own talents and efforts, a manager can be dependent in varying degrees on superiors, subordinates, peers in other parts of the organization, the

2. See Leonard R. Sayles, *Managerial Behavior: Administration in Complex Organization* (New York, McGraw-Hill, 1964), as well as Rosemary Stewart, *Managers and Their Jobs* (London, Macmillan, 1967), and *Contrasts in Management* (London, McGraw-Hill, 1976).

subordinates of peers, outside suppliers, customers, competitors, unions, regulating agencies, and many others.

These dependency relationships are an inherent part of managerial jobs because of two organizational facts of life: division of labor and limited resources. Because the work in organizations is divided into specialized divisions, departments, and jobs, managers are made directly or indirectly dependent on many others for information, staff services, and cooperation in general. Because of their organization's limited resources, managers are also dependent on their external environments for support. Without some minimal cooperation from suppliers, competitors, unions, regulatory agencies, and customers, managers cannot help their organizations survive and achieve their objectives.

Dealing with these dependencies and the manager's subsequent vulnerability is an important and difficult part of a manager's job because, while it is theoretically possible that all of these people and organizations would automatically act in just the manner that a manager wants and needs, such is almost never the case in reality. All the people on whom a manager is dependent have limited time, energy, and talent, for which there are competing demands.

Some people may be uncooperative because they are too busy elsewhere, and some because they are not really capable of helping. Others may well have goals, values, and beliefs that are quite different and in conflict with the manager's and may therefore have no desire whatsoever to help or cooperate. This is obviously true of a competing company and sometimes of a union, but it can also apply to a boss who is feeling threatened by a manager's career progress or to a peer whose objectives clash with the manager's.

Indeed, managers often find themselves dependent on many people (and things) whom they do not directly control and who are not "cooperating." This is the key to one of the biggest frustrations managers feel in their jobs, even in the top ones, which the following example illustrates:

After nearly a year of rumors, it was finally announced in May 1974 that the president of ABC Corporation had been elected chairman of the board and that Jim Franklin, the vice president of finance, would replace him as president. While everyone at ABC was aware that a shift would take place soon, it was not at all clear before the announcement who would be the next president. Most people had guessed it would be Phil Cook, the marketing vice president.

Nine months into his job as chief executive officer, Franklin found that Phil Cook (still the marketing vice president) seemed to be fighting him in small and subtle ways. There was never anything blatant, but Cook just did not cooperate with Franklin as the other vice presidents did. Shortly after being elected, Franklin had tried to bypass what he saw as a potential conflict with Cook by telling him that he would understand if Cook would prefer to move somewhere else where he could be a CEO also. Franklin said that it would be a big loss to the company but that he would be willing to help Cook in a number of ways if he wanted to look for a presidential opportunity elsewhere. Cook had thanked him but had said that family and community commitments would prevent him from relocating and all CEO opportunities were bound to be in a different city.

Since the situation did not improve after the tenth and eleventh months, Franklin seriously considered forcing Cook out. When he thought about the consequences of such a move, Franklin became more and more aware of just how dependent he was on Cook. Marketing and sales were generally the keys to success in their industry, and the company's sales force was one of the best, if not the best, in the industry. Cook had been with the company for 25 years. He had built a strong personal relationship with many of the people in the sales force and was universally popular. A mass exodus just might occur if Cook were fired. The loss of a large number of salesmen, or even a lot of turmoil in the department, could have a serious effect on the company's performance.

After one year as chief executive officer, Franklin found that the situation between Cook and himself had not improved and had become a constant source of frustration.

As a person gains more formal authority in an organization, the areas in which he or she is vulnerable increase and become more complex rather than the reverse. As the previous example suggests, it is not at all unusual for the president of an organization to be in a highly dependent position, a fact often not apparent to either the outsider or to the lower-level manager who covets the president's job.

A considerable amount of the behavior of highly successful managers that seems inexplicable in light of what management texts usually tell us managers do become understandable when one considers a manager's need for, and efforts at, managing his or her relationships with others.[3] To be able to plan, organize, budget, staff, control, and evaluate, managers need some control over the many people on whom they are dependent. Trying to control others solely by directing them and on the basis of the power associated with one's position simply will not work—first, because managers are always dependent on some people over whom they have no formal authority, and second, because virtually no one in modern organizations will passively accept and completely obey a constant stream of orders from someone just because he or she is the "boss."

Trying to influence others by means of persuasion alone will not work either. Although it is very powerful and possibly the single most important method of influence, persuasion has some serious drawbacks too. To make it work requires time (often lots of it), skill, and information on the part of the persuader. And persuasion can fail simply because the other person chooses not to listen or does not listen carefully.

---

3. I am talking about the type of inexplicable differences that Henry Mintzberg has found; see his article "The Manager's Job: Folklore and Fact," HBR July-August 1975, p. 49.

This is not to say that directing people on the basis of the formal power of one's position and persuasion are not important means by which successful managers cope. They obviously are. But, even taken together, they are not usually enough.

Successful managers cope with their dependence on others by being sensitive to it, by eliminating or avoiding unnecessary dependence, and by establishing power over those others. Good managers then use that power to help them plan, organize, staff, budget, evaluate, and so on. *In other words, it is primarily because of the dependence inherent in managerial jobs that the dynamics of power necessarily form an important part of a manager's processes.*

An argument that took place during a middle management training seminar I participated in a few years ago helps illustrate further this important relationship between a manager's need for power and the degree of his or her dependence on others:

Two participants, both managers in their thirties, got into a heated disagreement regarding the acquisition and use of power by managers. One took the position that power was absolutely central to managerial work, while the other argued that it was virtually irrelevant. In support of their positions, each described a very "successful" manager with whom he worked. In one of these examples, the manager seemed to be constantly developing and using power, while in the other, such behavior was rare. Subsequently, both seminar participants were asked to describe their successful managers' jobs in terms of the dependence *inherent* in those jobs.

The young manager who felt power was unimportant described a staff vice president in a small company who was dependent only on his immediate subordinates, his peers, and his boss. This person, Joe Phillips, had to depend on his subordinates to do their jobs appropriately, but, if necessary, he could fill in for any of them or secure replacement for them rather easily. He also had considerable formal authority over them; that is, he could give them raises and new assignments, recommend promotions, and fire them. He was moderately dependent on the other four vice presidents in the company for information and cooperation. They were likewise dependent on him. The president had considerable formal authority over Phillips but was also moderately dependent on him for help, expert advice, the service his staff performed, other information, and general cooperation.

The second young manager—the one who felt power was very important—described a service department manager, Sam Weller, in a large, complex, and growing company who was in quite a different position. Weller was dependent not only on his boss for rewards and information, but also on 30 other individuals who made up the divisional and corporate top management. And while his boss, like Phillip's was moderately dependent on him too, most of the top managers were not. Because Weller's subordinates, unlike Phillips's, had people reporting to them, Weller was dependent not only on his subordinates but also on his subordinates' subordinates. Because he could not himself easily replace or do most of their technical jobs, unlike Phillips, he was very dependent on all these people.

In addition, for critical supplies, Weller was dependent on two other department managers in the division. Without their timely help, it was impossible for his department to do its job. These departments, however, did not have similar needs for Weller's help and cooperation. Weller was also dependent on local labor union officials and on a federal agency that regulated the division's industry. Both could shut his division down if they wanted.

Finally, Weller was dependent on two outside suppliers of key materials. Because of the volume of his department's purchase relative to the size of these two companies, he had little power over them.

Under these circumstances, it is hardly surprising that Sam Weller had to spend considerable time and effort acquiring and using power to manage his many dependencies, while Joe Phillips did not.

As this example also illustrates, not all management jobs require an incumbent to be able to provide the same amount of successful power-oriented behavior. But most management jobs today are more like Weller's than Phillips's. And, perhaps more important, the trend over the past two or three decades is away from jobs like Phillips's and toward jobs like Weller's. So long as our technologies continue to become more complex, the average organization continues to grow larger, and the average industry continues to become more competitive and regulated, that trend will continue; as it does so, the effective acquisition and use of power by managers will become even more important.

Establishing Power in Relationships

To help cope with the dependency relationships inherent in their jobs, effective managers create, increase, or maintain four different types of power over others.[4] Having power based in these areas puts the manager in a position both to influence those people on whom he or she is dependent when necessary and to avoid being hurt by any of them.

SENSE OF OBLIGATION

One of the ways that successful managers generate power in their relationships with others is to create a sense of obligation in those others. When the manager is successful, the others feel that they should—rightly—allow the manager to influence them within certain limits.

4. These categories closely resemble the five developed by John R. P. French and Bertram Raven; see "The Base of Social Power" in *Group Dynamics: Research and Theory*, Dorwin Cartwright and Alvin Zandler, eds. (New York, Harper & Row, 1968), chap. 20. Three of the categories are similar to the types of "authority"-based power described by Max Weber in *The Theory of Social and Economic Organization* (New York, Free Press, 1947).

Successful managers often go out of their way to do favors for people who they expect will feel an obligation to return those favors. As can be seen in the following description of a manager by one of his subordinates, some people are very skilled at identifying opportunities for doing favors that cost them very little but that others appreciate very much:

Most of the people here would walk over hot coals in their bare feet if my boss asked them to. He has an incredible capacity to do little things that mean a lot to people. Today, for example, in his junk mail he came across an advertisement for something that one of my subordinates had in passing once mentioned that he was shopping for. So my boss routed it to him. That probably took 15 seconds of his time, and yet my subordinate really appreciated it. To give you another example, two weeks ago he somehow learned that the purchasing manager's mother had died. On his way home that night, he stopped off at the funeral parlor. Our purchasing manager was, of course, there at the time. I bet he'll remember that brief visit for quite a while.

Recognizing that most people believe that friendship carries with it certain obligations ("A friend in need . . ."), successful managers often try to develop true friendships with those on whom they are dependent. They will also make formal and informal deals in which they give something up in exchange for certain future obligations.

BELIEF IN A MANAGER'S EXPERTISE

A second way successful managers gain power is by building reputations as "experts" in certain matters. Believing in the manager's expertise, others will often defer to the manager on those matters. Managers usually establish this type of power through visible achievement. The larger the achievement and the more visible it is, the more power the manager tends to develop.

One of the reasons that managers display concern about their "professional reputations" and their "track records" is that they have an impact on others' beliefs about their expertise. These factors become particularly important in large settings, where most people have only secondhand information about most other people's professional competence, as the following shows:

Herb Randley and Bert Kline are both 35-year-old vice presidents in a large research-and-development organization. According to their closest associates, they are equally bright and competent in their technical fields and as managers. Yet Randley has a much stronger professional reputation in most parts of the company, and his ideas generally carry much more weight. Close friends and associates claim the reason that Randley is so much more powerful is related to a number of tactics that he has used more than Kline has.

Randley has published more scientific papers and managerial articles than Kline. Randley has been more selective in the assignments he has worked on, choosing those that are visible and that require his strong suits. He has given more speeches and presentations on projects that are his own achievements. And in meetings in general, he is allegedly forceful in areas where he has expertise and silent in those where he does not.

IDENTIFICATION WITH A MANAGER

A third method by which managers gain power is by fostering others' unconscious identification with them or with ideas they "stand for." Sigmund Freud was the first to describe this phenomenon, which is most clearly seen in the way people look up to "charismatic" leaders. Generally, the more a person finds a manager both consciously and (more important) unconsciously an ideal person, the more he or she will defer to that manager.

Managers develop power based on others' idealized views of them in a number of ways. They try to look and behave in ways that others respect. They go out of their way to be visible to their employees and to give speeches about their organizational goals, values, and ideals. They even consider, while making hiring and promotion decisions, whether they will be able to develop this type of power over the candidates:

One vice president of sales in a moderate-size manufacturing company was reputed to be so much in control of his sales force that he could get them to respond to new and different marketing programs in a third of the time taken by the company's best competitors. His power over his employees was based primarily on their strong identification with him and what he stood for. Emigrating to the United States at age 17, this person worked his way up "from nothing." When made a sales manager in 1965, he began recruiting other young immigrants and sons of immigrants from his former country. When made vice president of sales in 1970, he continued to do so. In 1975, 85% of his sales force was made up of people whom he hired directly or who were hired by others he brought in.

PERCEIVED DEPENDENCE ON A MANAGER

The final way that an effective manager often gains power is by feeding others' beliefs that they are dependent on the manager either for help or for not being hurt. The more they perceive they are dependent, the more most people will be inclined to cooperate with such a manager.

There are two methods that successful managers often use to create perceived dependence.

Finding and acquiring resources

In the first, the manager identifies and secures (if necessary) resources that another person requires to perform his job, that he does not possess, and that are not readily available elsewhere. These resources include such things as authority to make certain decisions; control of money, equipment, and office space; access to important people; information and control of information channels; and subordinates. Then the manager takes action so that the other person correctly perceives that the manager has such resources and is willing and ready to use them to help (or hinder) the other person. Consider the following extreme—but true—example.

When young Tim Babcock was put in charge of a division of a large manufacturing company and told to "turn it around," he spent the first few weeks studying it from afar. He decided that the division was in disastrous shape and that he would need to take many large steps quickly to save it. To be able to do that, he realized he needed to develop considerable power fast over most of the division's management and staff. He did the following:

☐ He gave the division's management two hours' notice of his arrival.

☐ He arrived in a limousine with six assistants.

☐ He immediately called a meeting of the 40 top managers.

☐ He outlined briefly his assessment of the situation, his commitment to turn things around, and the basic direction he wanted things to move in.

☐ He then fired the four top managers in the room and told them that they had to be out of the building in two hours.

☐ He then said he would personally dedicate himself to sabotaging the career of anyone who tried to block his efforts to save the division.

☐ He ended the 60-minute meeting by announcing that his assistants would set up appointments for him with each of them starting at 7:00 A.M. the next morning.

Throughout the critical six-month period that followed, those who remained at the division generally cooperated energetically with Mr. Babcock.

Affecting perceptions of resources

A second way effective managers gain these types of power is by influencing other persons' perceptions of the manager's resources.[5] In settings where many people are involved and where the manager does not interact continuously with those he or she is dependent on, those people will seldom possess "hard facts"

5. For an excellent discussion of this method, see Richard E. Neustadt, *Presidential Power* (New York, John Wiley, 1960).

regarding what relevant resources the manager commands directly or indirectly (through others), what resources he will command in the future, or how prepared he is to use those resources to help or hinder them. They will be forced to make their own judgments.

Insofar as a manager can influence people's judgments, he can generate much more power than one would generally ascribe to him in light of the reality of his resources.

In trying to influence people's judgments, managers pay considerable attention to the "trappings" of power and to their own reputations and images. Among other actions, they sometimes carefully select, decorate, and arrange their offices in ways that give signs of power. They associate with people or organizations that are known to be powerful or that others perceive as powerful. Managers selectively foster rumors concerning their own power. Indeed, those who are particularly skilled at creating power in this way tend to be very sensitive to the impressions that all their actions might have on others.

FORMAL AUTHORITY

Before discussing how managers use their power to influence others, it is useful to see how formal authority relates to power. By *formal authority,* I mean those elements that automatically come with a managerial job—perhaps a title, an office, a budget, the right to make certain decisions, a set of subordinates, a reporting relationship, and so on.

Effective managers use the elements of formal authority as resources to help them develop any or all of the four types of power previously discussed, just as they use other resources (such as their education). Two managers with the same formal authority can have very different amounts of power entirely because of the way they have used that authority. For example:

☐ By sitting down with employees who are new or with people who are starting new projects and clearly specifying who has the formal authority to do what, one manager creates a strong sense of obligation in others to defer to his authority later.

☐ By selectively withholding or giving the high-quality service his department can provide other departments, one manager makes other managers clearly perceive that they are dependent on him.

On its own, then, formal authority does not guarantee a certain amount of power; it is only a resource that managers can use to generate power in their relationships.

Exercising Power to Influence Others

Successful managers use the power they develop in their relationships, along with persuasion, to influence people on whom they are dependent to behave in ways that make it possible for the managers to get their jobs done effectively. They use their power to influence others directly, face to face, and in more indirect ways.

FACE-TO-FACE INFLUENCE

The chief advantage of influencing others directly by exercising any of the types of power is speed. If the power exists and the manager correctly understands the nature and strength of it, he can influence the other person with nothing more than a brief request or command:

☐ Jones thinks Smith feels obliged to him for past favors. Furthermore, Jones thinks that his request to speed up a project by two days probably falls within a zone that Smith would consider legitimate in light of his own definition of his obligation to Jones. So Jones simply calls Smith and makes his request. Smith pauses for only a second and says yes, he'll do it.

☐ Manager Johnson has some power based on perceived dependence over manager Baker. When Johnson tells Baker that he wants a report done in 24 hours, Baker grudgingly considers the costs of compliance, of noncompliance, and of complaining to higher authorities. He decides that doing the report is the least costly action and tells Johnson he will do it.

☐ Young Porter identifies strongly with Marquette, an older manager who is not his boss. Porter thinks Marquette is the epitome of a great manager and tries to model himself after him. When Marquette asks Porter to work on a special project "that could be very valuable in improving the company's ability to meet new competitive products," Porter agrees without hesitation and works 15 hours per week above and beyond his normal hours to get the project done and done well.

When used to influence others, each of the four types of power has different advantages and drawbacks. For example, power based on perceived expertise or on identification with a manager can often be used to influence attitudes as well as someone's immediate behavior and thus can have a lasting impact. It is very difficult to influence attitudes by using power based on perceived dependence, but if it can be done, it usually has the advantage of being able to influence a much broader range of behavior than the other methods do. When exercising power based on perceived expertise, for example, one can only influence attitudes and behavior within that narrow zone defined by the "expertise."

The drawbacks associated with the use of power based on perceived dependence are particularly important to recognize. A person who feels dependent on a manager for rewards (or lack of punishments) might quickly agree to a request from the manager but then not follow through—especially if the manager cannot easily find out if the person has obeyed or not. Repeated influence attempts based on perceived dependence also seem to encourage the other person to try to gain some power to balance the manager's. And perhaps most important, using power based on perceived dependence in a coercive way is very risky. Coercion invites retaliation.

For instance, in the example in which Tim Babcock took such extreme steps to save the division he was assigned to "turn around," his development and use of power based on perceived dependence could have led to mass resignation and the collapse of the division. Babcock fully recognized this risk, however, and behaved as he did because he felt there was simply *no other way* that he could gain the very large amount of quick cooperation needed to save the division.

Effective managers will often draw on more than one form of power to influence someone, or they will combine power with persuasion. In general, they do so because a combination can be more potent and less risky than any single method, as the following description shows:

> One of the best managers we have in the company has lots of power based on one thing or another over most people. But he seldom if ever just tells or asks someone to do something. He almost always takes a few minutes to try to persuade them. The power he has over people generally induces them to listen carefully and certainly disposes them to be influenced. That, of course, makes the persuasion process go quickly and easily. And he never risks getting the other person mad or upset by making what that person thinks is an unfair request or command.

It is also common for managers not to coercively exercise power based on perceived dependence by itself, but to combine it with other methods to reduce the risk of retaliation. In this way, managers are able to have a large impact without leaving the bitter aftertaste of punishment alone.

INDIRECT INFLUENCE METHODS

Effective managers also rely on two types of less direct methods to influence those on whom they are dependent. In the first way, they use any or all of the face-to-face methods to influence other people, who in turn have some specific impact on a desired person.

Product manager Stein needed plant manager Billings to "sign off" on a new product idea (Product X), which Billings thought was terrible. Stein decided that there was no way he could logically persuade Billings because Billings just

Exhibit: Methods of influence

Face-to-face methods	What they can influence	Advantages	Drawbacks
Exercise obligation-based power.	Behavior within zone that the other perceives as legitimate in light of the obligation.	Quick. Requires no outlay of tangible resources.	If the request is outside the acceptable zone, it will fail; if it is too far outside, others might see it as illegitimate.
Exercise power based on perceived expertise.	Attitudes and behavior within the zone of perceived expertise.	Quick. Requires no outlay of tangible resources.	If the request is outside the acceptable zone, it will fail; if it is too far outside, others might see it as illegitimate.
Exercise power based on identification with a manager.	Attitudes and behavior that are not in conflict with the ideals that underlie the identification.	Quick. Requires no expenditure of limited resources.	Restricted to influence attempts that are not in conflict with the ideals that underlie the identification.
Exercise power based on perceived dependence.	Wide range of behavior that can be monitored.	Quick. Can often succeed when other methods fail.	Repeated influence attempts encourage the other to gain power over the influencer.
Coercively exercise power based on perceived dependence.	Wide range of behavior that can be easily monitored.	Quick. Can often succeed when other methods fail.	Invites retaliation. Very risky.
Use persuasion.	Very wide range of attitudes and behavior.	Can produce internalized motivation that does not require monitoring. Requires no power or outlay of scarce material resources.	Can be very time-consuming. Requires other person to listen.
Combine these methods.	Depends on the exact combination.	Can be more potent and less risky than using a single method.	More costly than using a single method.

Indirect methods	What they can influence	Advantages	Drawbacks
Manipulate the other's environment by using any or all of the face-to-face methods.	Wide range of behavior and attitudes.	Can succeed when face-to-face methods fail.	Can be time-consuming. Is complex to implement. Is very risky, especially if used frequently.
Change the forces that continuously act on the individual: Formal organizational arrangements. Informal social arrangements. Technology. Resources available. Statement of organizational goals.	Wide range of behavior and attitudes on a continuous basis.	Has continuous influence, not just a one-shot effect. Can have a very powerful impact.	Often requires a considerable power outlay to achieve.

would not listen to him. With time, Stein felt, he could have broken through that barrier. But he did not have that time. Stein also realized that Billings would never, just because of some deal or favor, sign off on a product he did not believe in. Stein also felt it not worth the risk of trying to force Billings to sign off, so here is what he did:

☐ On Monday, Stein got Reynolds, a person Billings respected, to send Billings two market research studies that were very favorable to Product X, with a note attached saying, "Have you seen this? I found them rather surprising. I am not sure if I entirely believe them, but still . . ."

☐ On Tuesday, Stein got a representative of one of the company's biggest customers to mention casually to Billings on the phone that he had heard a rumor about Product X being introduced soon and was "glad to see you guys are on your toes as usual."

☐ On Wednesday, Stein had two industrial engineers stand about three feet away from Billings as they were waiting for a meeting to begin and talk about the favorable test results on Product X.

☐ On Thursday, Stein set up a meeting to talk about Product X with Billings and invited only people whom Billings liked or respected and who also felt favorably about Product X.

☐ On Friday, Stein went to see Billings and asked him if he was willing to sign off on Product X. He was.

This type of manipulation of the environments of others can influence both behavior and attitudes and can often succeed when other influence methods fail. But it has a number of serious drawbacks. It takes considerable time and energy, and it is quite risky. Many people think it is wrong to try to influence others in this way, even people who, without consciously recognizing it, use this technique themselves. If they think someone is trying, or has tried, to manipulate them, they may retaliate. Furthermore, people who gain the reputation of being manipulators seriously undermine their own capacities for developing power and for influencing others. Almost no one, for example, will want to identify with a manipulator. And virtually no one accepts, at face value, a manipulator's sincere attempts at persuasion. In extreme cases, a reputation as a manipulator can completely ruin a manager's career.

A second way in which managers indirectly influence others is by making permanent changes in an individual's or a group's environment. They change job descriptions, the formal systems that measure performance, the extrinsic incentives available, the tools, people, and other resources that the people or groups work with, the architecture, the norms or values of work groups, and so on. If the manager is successful in making the changes, and the changes have the desired effect on the individual or group, that effect will be sustained over time.

Effective managers recognize that changes in the forces that surround a person can have great impact on that person's behavior. Unlike many of the other influence methods, this one doesn't require a large expenditure of limited resources or effort on the part of the manager on an ongoing basis. Once such a change has been successfully made, it works independently of the manager.

This method of influence is used by all managers to some degree. Many, however, use it sparingly simply because they do not have the power to change the forces acting on the person they wish to influence. In many organizations, only the top managers have the power to change the formal measurement systems, the extrinsic incentives available, the architecture, and so on.

Generating and Using Power Successfully

Managers who are successful at acquiring considerable power and using it to manage their dependence on others tend to share a number of common characteristics:

1. They are sensitive to what others consider to be legitimate behavior in acquiring and using power. They recognize that the four types of power carry with them certain "obligations" regarding their acquisition and use. A person who gains a considerable amount of power based on his perceived expertise is generally expected to be an expert in certain areas. If it ever becomes publicly known that the person is clearly not an expert in those areas, such a person will probably be labeled a "fraud" and will not only lose his power but will suffer other reprimands too.

A person with whom a number of people identify is expected to act like an ideal leader. If he clearly lets people down, he will not only lose that power, he will also suffer the righteous anger of his ex-followers. Many managers who have created or used power based on perceived dependence in ways that their employees have felt unfair, such as in requesting overtime work, have ended up with unions.

2. They have good intuitive understanding of the various types of power and methods of influence. They are sensitive to what types of power are easiest to develop with different types of people. They recognize, for example, that professionals tend to be more influenced by perceived expertise than by other forms of power. They also have a grasp of all the various methods of influence and what each can accomplish, at what costs, and with what risks. (See the *Exhibit* on page 371.) They are good at recognizing the specific conditions in any situation and then at selecting an influence method that is compatible with those conditions.

3. They tend to develop all the types of power, to some degree, and they use all the influence methods mentioned in the exhibit. Unlike managers who are

not very good at influencing people, effective managers usually do not think that only some of the methods are useful or that only some of the methods are moral. They recognize that any of the methods, used under the right circumstances, can help contribute to organizational effectiveness with few dysfunctional consequences. At the same time, they generally try to avoid those methods that are more risky than others and those that may have dysfunctional consequences. For example, they manipulate the environment of others only when absolutely necessary.

4. They establish career goals and seek out managerial positions that allow them to successfully develop and use power. They look for jobs, for example, that use their backgrounds and skills to control or manage some critically important problem or environmental contingency that an organization faces. They recognize that success in that type of job makes others dependent on them and increases their own perceived expertise. They also seek jobs that do not demand a type or a volume of power that is inconsistent with their own skills.

5. They use all of their resources, formal authority, and power to develop still more power. To borrow Edward Banfield's metaphor, they actually look for ways to "invest" their power where they might secure a high positive return.[6] For example, by asking a person to do him two important favors, a manager might be able to finish his construction program one day ahead of schedule. That request may cost him most of the obligation-based power he has over that person, but in return he may significantly increase his perceived expertise as a manager of construction projects in the eyes of everyone in his organization.

Just as in investing money, there is always some risk involved in using power this way; it is possible to get a zero return for a sizable investment, even for the most powerful manager. Effective managers do not try to avoid risks. Instead, they look for prudent risks, just as they do when investing capital.

6. Effective managers engage in power-oriented behavior in ways that are tempered by maturity and self-control.[7] They seldom, if ever, develop and use power in impulsive ways or for their own aggrandizement.

7. Finally, they also recognize and accept as legitimate that, in using these methods, they clearly influence other people's behavior and lives. Unlike many less effective managers, they are reasonably comfortable in using power to influence people. They recognize, often only intuitively, what this article is all about—that their attempts to establish power and use it are an absolutely necessary part of the successful fulfillment of their difficult managerial role.

6. See Edward C. Banfield, *Political Influence* (New York, Free Press, 1965), chap. 11.
7. See David C. McClelland and David H. Burnham, "Power Is the Great Motivator," HBR March-April 1976, p. 100.

23. Power and Politics in Organizational Life

Abraham Zaleznik

The competition for power is characteristic of all political structures. And, whatever else they may be, business organizations are political structures in that they provide both a base for the development of executive careers and a platform for the expression of individual interests and motives. People in positions of authority, however, "differ from 'ordinary' humans," says this author, "in that they have the capacity to impose their personal defenses onto the stage of corporate life. Fortunately, the relationships are susceptible to intelligent management," and it is to the nature of this intelligence that the discussion is devoted.

There are few business activities more prone to a credibility gap than the way in which executives approach organizational life. A sense of disbelief occurs when managers purport to make decisions in rationalistic terms while most observers and participants know that personalities and politics play a significant if not an overriding role. Where does the error lie? In the theory which insists that decisions should be rationalistic and nonpersonal? Or in the practice which treats business organizations as political structures?

Whatever else organizations may be (problem-solving instruments, sociotechnical systems, reward systems, and so on), they are political structures. This means that organizations operate by distributing authority and setting a stage for the exercise of power. It is no wonder, therefore, that individuals who are highly motivated to secure and use power find a familiar and hospitable environment in business.

At the same time, executives are reluctant to acknowledge the place of power both in individual motivation and in organizational relationships. Somehow, power and politics are dirty words. And in linking these words to the play of personalities in organizations, some managers withdraw into the safety of organizational logics.

As I shall suggest in this article, frank recognition of the importance of personality factors and a sensitive use of the strengths and limitations of people in decisions on power distributions can improve the quality of organizational life.

Political Pyramid

Organizations provide a power base for individuals. From a purely economic standpoint, organizations exist to create a surplus of income over costs by meeting needs in the marketplace. But organizations also are political structures which provide opportunities for people to develop careers and therefore provide platforms for the expression of individual interests and motives. The development of careers, particularly at high managerial and professional levels depends on accumulation of power as the vehicle for transforming individual interests into activities that influence other people.

SCARCITY AND COMPETITION

A political pyramid exists when people compete for power in an economy of scarcity. In other words, people cannot get the power they want just for the asking. Instead, they have to enter into the decisions on how to distribute authority in a particular formal organization structure. Scarcity of power arises under two sets of conditions:

1. Where individuals gain power in absolute terms at someone else's expense.

2. Where there is a gain comparatively—not literally at someone else's expense—resulting in a relative shift in the distribution of power.

In either case, the psychology of scarcity and comparison takes over. The human being tends to make comparisons as a basis for his sense of self-esteem. He may compare himself with other people and decide that his absolute loss or the shift in proportional shares of authority reflects an attrition in his power base. He may also compare his position relative to others against a personal standard and feel a sense of loss. This tendency to compare is deeply ingrained in people, especially since they experience early in life the effects of comparisons in the family where—in an absolute sense—time and attention, if not love and affection, go to the most dependent member.

Corporate acquisitions and mergers illustrate the effects of both types of comparisons. In the case of one merger, the president of the acquired company resigned rather than accept the relative displacement in rank that occurred when he no longer could act as a chief executive officer. Two vice presidents vied for the position of executive vice president. Because of their conflicting ambitions, the expedient of making them equals drove the competition underground, but not for long. The vice president with the weaker power base soon resigned in the face of his inability to consolidate a workable definition of his responsibilities. His departure resulted in increased power for the remaining vice president and the gradual elimination of "rival camps," which had been covertly identified with the main contenders for power.

The fact that organizations are pyramids produces a scarcity of positions the higher one moves in the hierarchy. This scarcity, coupled with inequalities, certainly needs to be recognized. While it may be humane and socially desirable to say that people are different rather than unequal in their potential, nevertheless executive talent is in short supply. The end result should be to move the more able people into the top positions and to accord them the pay, responsibility, and authority to match their potential.

On the other side, the strong desires of equally able people for the few top positions available means that someone will either have to face the realization of unfulfilled ambition or have to shift his interest to another organization.[1]

CONSTITUENTS AND CLIENTS

Besides the conditions of scarcity and competition, politics in organizations grows out of the existence of constituencies. A superior may be content himself with shifts in the allocation of resources and consequently power, but he represents subordinates who, for their own reasons, may be unhappy with the changes. These subordinates affirm and support their boss. They can also withdraw affirmation and support, and consequently isolate the superior with all the painful consequences this entails.

While appointments to positions come from above, affirmation of position comes from below. The only difference between party and organizational politics is in the subtlety of the voting procedure. Consider:

☐ In a large consumer products corporation, one division received almost no capital funds for expansion while another division, which had developed a new marketing approach for products common to both, expanded dramatically. The head of the static division found his power diminished considerably, as reflected in how seriously his subordinates took his efforts at influence (e.g., in programs to increase the profit return from existing volume).

He initiated one program after another with little support from subordinates

1. See my article, "The Management of Disappointment," HBR November-December 1967, p. 59.

because he could not make a claim for capital funds. The flow of capital funds in this corporation provided a measure of power gains and losses in both an absolute and a relative sense.

Still another factor that heightens the competition for power that is characteristic of all political structures is the incessant need to use whatever power one possesses. Corporations have an implicit "banking" system in power transactions. The initial "capitalization" that makes up an individual's power base consists of three elements:

1. The quantity of formal authority vested in his position relative to other positions.

2. The authority vested in his expertise and reputation for competence (a factor weighted by how important the expertise is for the growth areas of the corporation as against the historically stable areas of its business).

3. The attractiveness of his personality to others (a combination of respect for him as well as liking, although these two sources of attraction are often in conflict).

This capitalization of power reflects the total esteem with which others regard the individual. By a process that is still not too clear, the individual internalizes all the sources of power capital in a manner parallel to the way he develops a sense of self-esteem. The individual knows he has power, assesses it realistically, and is willing to risk his personal esteem to influence others.

A critical element here is the risk in the uses of power. The individual must perform *and* get results. If he fails to do either, an attrition occurs in his power base in direct proportion to the doubts other people entertained in their earlier appraisals of him.

What occurs here is an erosion of confidence, which ultimately leads the individual to doubt himself and undermines the psychological work which led him in the first place to internalize authority as a prelude to action. (While, as I have suggested, the psychological work that an individual goes through to consolidate his esteem capital is a crucial aspect of power relations, I shall have to reserve careful examination of this problem until a later date. The objective now is to examine from a political framework the problems of organizational life.)

What distinguishes alterations in the authority structure from other types of organizational change is their direct confrontation with the political character of corporate life. Such confrontations are real manipulations of power as compared with the indirect approaches that play on ideologies and attitudes. In the first case, the potency and reality of shifts in authority have an instantaneous effect on what people do, how they interact, and how they think about themselves. In the second case, the shifts in attitude are often based on the willingness of people to respond the way authority figures want them to; ordinarily, however, these shifts in attitude are but temporary expressions of compliance.

One of the most common errors executives make is to confuse compliance with commitment. Compliance is an attitude of acceptance when a directive from an authority figure asks for a change in an individual's position, activities, or ideas. The individual complies or "goes along" usually because he is indifferent to the scope of the directive and the changes it proposes. If compliance occurs out of indifference, then one can predict little difficulty in translating the intent of directives into actual implementation.[2]

Commitment, on the other hand, represents a strong motivation on the part of an individual to adopt or resist the intent of a directive. If the individual commits himself to a change, then he will use his ingenuity to interpret and implement the change in such a way as to assure its success. If he decides to fight or block the change, the individual may act as if he complies but reserve other times and places to negate the effects of directives. For example:

☐ In one large company, the top management met regularly for purposes of organizational planning. The executives responsible for implementing planning decisions could usually be counted on to carry them out when they had fought hard and openly in the course of reaching such decisions. When they seemed to accept a decision, giving all signs of compliance, the decision usually ended up as a notation in the minutes. Surface compliance occurred most frequently when problems involved loyalties to subordinates.

In one instance, a division head agreed to accept a highly regarded executive from another division to meet a serious manpower shortage in his organization. When the time came to effect the transfer, however, this division general manager refused, with some justification, on the grounds that bringing someone in from outside would demoralize his staff. He used compliance initially to respond to the problem of "family" loyalties to which he felt committed. Needless to say, the existence of these loyalties was the major problem to be faced in carrying out organizational planning.

Compliance as a tactic to avoid changes and commitment as an expression of strong motivation in dealing with organizational problems are in turn related to how individuals define their interests. In the power relations among executives, the so-called areas of common interest are usually reserved for the banalities of

2. See Chester Barnard, *The Function of the Executive* (Cambridge, Harvard University Press, 1938), p. 167.

human relationships. The more significant areas of attention usually force conflicts of interest, especially competition for power, to the surface.

Interest Conflicts

Organizations demand, on the one hand, cooperative endeavor and commitment to common purpose. The realities of experience in organizations, on the other hand, show that conflicts of interest exist among people who ultimately share a common fate and are supposed to work together. What makes business more political and less ideological and rationalistic is the overriding importance of conflicts of interest.

If an individual (or group) is told that his job scope is reduced in either absolute or proportional terms for *the good of the corporation,* he faces a conflict. Should he acquiesce for the idea of common good or fight in the service of his self-interest? Any rational man will fight (how constructively depends on the absence of neurotic conflicts and on ego strength). His willingness to fight increases as he comes to realize the intangible nature of what people think is good for the organization. And, in point of fact, his willingness may serve the interests of corporate purpose by highlighting issues and stimulating careful thinking before the reaching of final decisions.

SECONDARY EFFECTS

Conflicts of interest in the competition for resources are easily recognized, as for example, in capital budgeting or in allocating money for research and development. But these conflicts can be subjected to bargaining procedures, which all parties to the competition validate by their participation.

The secondary effects of bargaining do involve organizational and power issues. However, the fact that these power issues *follow* debate on economic problems rather than *lead* it creates a manifest content that can be objectified much more readily than in areas where the primary considerations are the distributions of authority.

In such cases, which include developing a new formal organization structure, management succession, promotions, corporate mergers, and entry of new executives, the conflicts of interest are severe and direct simply because there are no objective measures of right or wrong courses of action. The critical question which has to be answered in specific actions is: Who gets power and position? This involves particular people with their strengths and weaknesses and a specific historical context in which actions are understood in symbolic as well as rational terms. To illustrate:

☐ A large corporation, General Motors in fact, inadvertently confirmed what every seasoned executive knows: that coalitions of power to overcome feelings of rivalry and the play of personal ambitions are fragile solutions. The appointment of Edward Cole to the presidency followed by Semon Knudsen's resignation shattered the illusion that the rational processes in business stand apart or even dominate the human emotions and ties that bind men to one another. If any corporation prides itself on rationality, General Motors is it. To have to experience so publicly the inference that major corporate life, particularly at the executive levels, is not so rational after all, can be damaging to the sense of security people get from belief in an idea as it is embodied in a corporate image.

The fact that Knudsen subsequently was discharged from the presidency of Ford (an event I shall discuss later in this article) suggests that personalities and the politics of corporations are less aberrations and more conditions of life in large organizations.

But just as General Motors wants to maintain an image, many executives prefer to ignore what this illustration suggests: that organizations are political structures that feed on the psychology of comparison. To know something about the psychology of comparison takes us into the theory of self-esteem in both its conscious manifestations and its unconscious origins. Besides possibly enlightening us in general and giving a more realistic picture of people and organizations, there are some practical benefits in such knowledge. These benefits include:

☐ Increased freedom to act more directly; instead of trying to "get around" a problem, one can meet it.

☐ Greater objectivity about people's strengths and limitations, and, therefore, the ability to use them more honestly as well as effectively.

☐ More effective planning in organizational design and in distribution of authority; instead of searching for the "one best solution" in organization structure, one accepts a range of alternatives and then gives priority to the personal or emotional concerns that inhibit action.

Power Relations

Organizational life within a political frame is a series of contradictions. It is an exercise in rationality, but its energy comes from the ideas in the minds of power figures the content of which, as well as their origins, are only dimly perceived. It deals with sources of authority and their distribution; yet it depends in the first place on the existence of a balance of power in the hands of an individual who initiates actions and gets results. It has many rituals associated with it, such as participation, democratization, and the sharing of power; yet the real outcome is the consolidation of power around a central figure to whom other individuals make emotional attachments.

FAULTY COALITIONS

The formal organization structure implements a coalition among key executives. The forms differ, and the psychological significance of various coalitions also differs. But no organization can function without a consolidation of power in the relationship of a central figure with his select group. The coalition need not exist between the chief executive and his immediate subordinates or staff. It may indeed bypass the second level, as in the case of Presidents of the United States who do not build confident relationships within their cabinets but instead rely on members of the executive staff or on selected individuals outside the formal apparatus.

The failure to establish a coalition within the executive structure of an organization can result in severe problems, such as paralysis in the form of inability to make decisions and to evaluate performance, and in-fighting and overt rivalry within the executive group.

When a coalition fails to develop, the first place to look for causes is the chief executive and his problems in creating confident relationships. The causes are many and complex, but they usually hinge around the nature of the chief executive's defenses and what he needs to avoid as a means of alleviating stress. For example:

☐ The "palace revolt" that led to Semon Knudsen's departure from Ford Motor Company, is an illustration of the failure in the formation of a coalition. While it is true that Henry Ford II named Knudsen president of the company, Knudsen's ultimate power as a newcomer to an established power structure depended on forming an alliance. The particular individual with whom an alliance seemed crucial was Lee Iacocca. For some reason, Knudsen and Iacocca competed for power and influence instead of using cooperatively a power base to which both contributed as is the case with most workable coalitions. In the absence of a coalition, the alternate postures of rivalry and battle for control erupted. Ford ultimately responded by weighing his power with one side over the other.

As I have indicated, it is not at all clear why in Knudsen's case the coalition failed to develop. But in any failure the place to look is in the personalities of the main actors and in the nature of their defenses, which make certain coalitions improbable no matter how strongly other realities indicate their necessity.

But defensiveness on the part of a chief executive can also result in building an unrealistic and unworkable coalition, with the self-enforced isolation which is its consequence. One of the most frequently encountered defensive maneuvers which leads to the formation of unrealistic coalitions or to the isolation of the chief executive is the fear of rivalry.

A realistic coalition matches formal authority and competence with the emotional commitments necessary to establish and maintain the coalition. The fear of rivals on the part of chief executives, or the jealousy on the part of subordinates of the chief executive's power, can at the extreme result in paranoid distortions. People become suspicious of one another, and through selective perceptions and projections of their own fantasies create a world of plots and counterplots.

The displacement of personal concerns onto substantive material in decision making is potentially the most dangerous form of defensiveness. The need for defenses arises because people become anxious about the significance of evaluations within existing power coalitions. But perhaps even more basic is the fear and the rivalry to which all coalitions are susceptible given the nature of investments people make in power relations. While it is easy to dismiss emotional reactions like these as neurotic distortions, their prevalence and impact deserve careful attention in all phases of organizational life.

UNCONSCIOUS COLLUSIONS

All individuals and consequently groups experience areas of stress that mobilize defenses. The fact that coalitions embody defensive maneuvers on those occasions where stress goes beyond the usual level of tolerance is not surprising. An even more serious problem, however, occurs when the main force that binds men in a structure is the need to defend against or to act out the conflicts that individuals cannot tolerate alone.

Where coalitions represent the aggregation of power with conscious intention of using the abilities of members for constructive purposes, collusions represent predominance of unconscious conflict and defensive behavior. In organizational life, the presence of collusions and their causes often becomes the knot that has to be unraveled before any changes can be implemented.

The collusion of latent interests among executives can become the central theme and sustaining force of an organization structure of top management. For a collusion to take hold, the conflicts of the "power figure" have to be communicated and sensed by others as an overriding need that seeks active expression in the form of a theme. The themes vary just as do the structures which make a collusion. Thus one common theme is the need to control; another is the need to be admired and idealized; and still another is the need to find a scapegoat to attack in response to frustrations in solving problems.

If people could hold on to and keep within themselves areas of personal conflict, there would be far fewer collusions in organizational life. But it is part of the human condition for conflicts and needs to take over life situations. As a result, we find numerous instances of collusions controlling the behavior of executives. To illustrate:

A multidivisional corporation found itself with a revolution on its hands. The president was sensitive to the opinions of a few outside board members representing important stockholder interests. He was so concerned that he would be criticized by these board members, he demanded from vice presidents full information on their activities and complete loyalty to him. Over a period of years, he moved divisional chief executives to corporate headquarters so he could assure himself of their loyalty. Other executives joined in to gratify the president's need for control and loyalty.

The result of this collusion, however, was to create a schism between headquarters and field operations. Some of the staff members in the field managed to inform the board members of the lack of attention to and understanding of field problems. Discontent grew to such an extent that the board placed the president on early retirement.

Subsequently, the new president, with the support of the board, decentralized authority and appointed new division heads who were to make their offices in divisional headquarters with full authority to manage their respective organizations. One of the lingering problems of the new president was to dissolve the collusion at headquarters without wholesale firing of vice presidents.

Just as power distributions are central to the tasks of organizational planning, so the conservation of power is often the underlying function of collusions. Thus:

A manufacturing vice president of a medium-sized company witnessed over a period of 15 years a procession of changes in top management and ownership. He had managed to retain his job because he made himself indispensable in the management of the factory.

To each new top management, he stressed the importance of "home rule" as a means of assuring loyalty and performance in the plant. He also tacitly encouraged each supervisor to go along with whatever cliques happened to form and dominate the shop floor.

However, over time a gradual loss of competitive position, coupled with open conflict among cliques in the form of union disputes, led to the dismissal of the vice president. None of his successors could reassert control over the shop, and the company eventually moved or liquidated many of the operations in this plant.

"Life Dramas"

Faulty coalitions and unconscious collusions, as I have illustrated, can result from the defensive needs of a chief executive. These needs, which often appear as a demand on others to bolster the self-esteem of the chief executive, are tolerated to a remarkable degree and persist for a long time before harmful effects become apparent to outside stockholders, bankers, or boards of directors, which ultimately control the distributions of power in organizations. Occasionally, corporations undergo critical conflicts in organizational politics, which cannot be ignored in the conscious deliberations that affect how power gets distributed or used.

Intertwined with the various expressions of power conflicts in organizations are three underlying "life dramas" deserving careful attention:

The *first* portrays stripping the powers of a *parental figure*.

The *second* portrays the predominance of *paranoid thinking*, where distortions of reality result from the surfacing of conflicts that formerly had been contained in collusions.

The *third* portrays a *ritualistic ceremonial* in which real power issues are submerged or isolated in compulsive behavior but at the cost of real problem solving and work.

PARENTAL FIGURE

The chief executive in a business, along with the heads of states, religious bodies, and social movements, becomes an object for other people. The term "object" should be understood, in a psychological sense, as a person who is the recipient of strong emotional attachments from others. It is obvious that a chief executive is the *object* because he controls so many of the levers that ultimately direct the flow of rewards and punishments. But there is something to say beyond this obvious calculation of rewards and punishments as the basis for the emotional attachments between leader and led as *object* and *subject*.

Where a leader displays unusual attributes in his intuitive gifts, cultivated abilities, or deeper personal qualities, his fate as the *object* is governed by powerful emotions. I hesitate to use the word "charismatic" to describe such a leader, partially because it suggests a mystique but also because, in its reference to the "great" man as charismatic leader, it expands to superhuman proportions what really belongs to the psychology of everyday life.

What makes for strong emotional attachments is as much in the need of the *subject* as in the qualities of the *object*. In other words, the personalities of leaders take on proportions that meet what subordinates need and even demand. If leaders in fact respond with the special charisma that is often invested in them at the outset, then they are parties to a self-fulfilling prophecy. Of course, the qualities demanded have to be present in some nascent form, ready to emerge as soon as the emotional currents become real in authority relationships.

The emotional attachments I am referring to usually contain mixtures of positive and negative feelings. If the current were only of one kind, such as either admiration or hostility, then the authority relationship would be simpler to describe as well as to manage. All too often, the way positive feelings blend into the negative sets off secondary currents of emotion that intensify the relationships.

On the one side, subordinates cannot help but have fantasies of what they would do if they held the No. I position. Such fantasies, besides providing fleeting pleasures and helping one to regulate his ambitions, also provide channels for imaginative and constructive approaches to solving problems. It is only a short step from imagining what one would do as chief executive to explaining to the real chief executive the ideas which have been distilled from this flight into fantasy. If the chief executive senses envy in back of the thoughts, he may become frightened and choke off ideas which can be used quite constructively.

Critical Episode

But suppose a situation arises where not one but several subordinates enjoy the same fantasy of being No. I? Suppose also that subordinates feel deprived in their relationship with the chief executive? Suppose finally that facing the organization there are substantive problems that are more or less out of control. With these three conditions, and depending on the severity of the real problems besetting the enterprise, the stage is set for a collusion which, when acted out, becomes a critical episode of displacing the parental figure. To demonstrate:

In November 1967, the directors of the Interpublic Group, a $700 million complex in advertising and public relations, moved for the resignation of the leader and chief executive officer, Marion Harper, Jr. Briefly, Harper had managed over a period of 18 years to build the world's largest conglomerate in market services, advertising, and information on the base of a personally successful agency career. In expanding from this base, Harper made acquisitions, started new companies, and widened his orbit into international branches and companies.

As often happens, the innovator and creative person is careless in controlling what he has built, so that financial problems become evident. In Harper's case, he appeared either unwilling or unable to recognize the seriousness of his financial problems and, in particular, the significance of allowing cash balances to go below the minimum required in agreements with lending institutions.

Harper seemed careless in another, even more telling, way. Instead of developing a strong coalition among his executive group, he relied on individual ties to him in which he clearly dominated the relationship. If any of the executives "crossed" him, Harper would exile the offender to one of the "remote" branches or place him on partial retirement.

When the financial problems became critical, the aggrieved executives who had once been dependent on Harper and then cast out, formed their own coalition, and managed to garner the votes necessary to, in effect, fire the head man. Although little information is available on the aftermath of this palace revolution, the new coalition had its own problems—which, one would reasonably judge, included contentions for power.

A cynic viewing this illustration of the demise of a parental figure could conclude that if one seeks to maintain power by dominance, then one had best go all the way. This means that to take some but not all of the power away from rebellious sons sets the stage for a cabal among the deprived. With a score to settle, they await only the right circumstances to move in and depose the aggressor.

While this cynical view has its own appeal, it ignores the deeper issues of why otherwise brilliant men fail to recognize the realistic needs for coalitions in the relationships of superior and subordinates. To answer this question, we would need to understand how powerful people operate with massive blind spots which limit vision and the ability to maneuver in the face of realistic problems.

The one purpose that coalitions serve is to guard against the effects of blind spots, since it is seldom the case that two people have identical limitations in their vision and ability to respond. The need to control and dominate in a personalistic sense is perhaps the most serious of all possible blind spots that can affect a chief executive, because he makes it difficult for people to help him, while creating grievances that sooner or later lead to attacks on him.

The unseating of a chief executive by a coalition of subordinates seldom reduces the emotional charge built up in the uncertain attachments to the ousted leader. A new head man has to emerge and establish a confident coalition. Until the contentions for power subside and the guilt reactions attached to deposing the leader dissolve, individuals remain vulnerable to their own blind spots and unconscious reactions to striving for power.

The references to a parental figure in the preceding discussion may appear to exaggerate the meaning of power conflicts. In whatever ways it exaggerates, it also condenses a variety of truths about coalitions among executives. The chief executive is the central *object* in a coalition because he occupies a position analogous to parents in the family. He is at the nucleus of a political structure whose prototype is the family, in which jealousy, envy, love, and hate find original impetus and expression.

It would be a gross error to assume that in making an analogy between the family and formal organizations the parental role is strictly paternal. There are also characteristics of the mother figure in certain types of chief executives and combinations of mother-father in the formation of executive coalitions.

Chief executives can also suffer from depersonalization in their roles and as a result become emotionally cold and detached. The causes of depersonalization are complex but, in brief, have some connections to the narrow definitions of rationality that exclude the importance of emotions in guiding communication as well as thought.

For the purpose of interpreting how defensive styles affect the behavior of leaders, there is some truth to the suggestion that the neutrality and lack of warmth characteristic of some leaders is a result of an ingrained fear of becoming the *object* for other people—for to become the *object* arouses fears that subordinates will become envious and compete for power.

PARANOID THINKING

This is a form of distortion in ideas and perception to which all human beings are susceptible from time to time. For those individuals who are concerned in their work with the consolidation and uses of power, the experience with suspiciousness, the attribution of bad motives to others, jealousy, and anxiety (characteristics of paranoid thinking) may be more than a passing state of mind.

In fact, such ideas and fantasies may indeed be communicated to others and may even be the main force that binds men into collusions. Organizational life is particularly vulnerable to the effects of paranoid thinking because it stimulates comparisons while it evokes anticipations of added power or fears of diminished power.

To complicate matters even more and to suggest just how ambiguous organizational decisions become, there may be some truth and substance in back of the suspicions, distrust, and jealousies that enflame thinking. Personality conflicts do affect decisions in allocating authority and responsibility, and an individual may not be distorting at all to sense that he had been excluded or denied an ambition based on some undercurrents in his relationships with others. To call these sensitivities paranoid thinking may itself be a gross distortion. But no matter how real the events, the paranoid potential is still high as a fallout of organizational life.

Paranoid thinking goes beyond suspiciousness, distrust, and jealousy. It may take the form of grandiose ideas and overestimation of one's power and control. This form of distortion leads to swings in mood from elation to despair, from a sense of omnipotence to helplessness. Again, when acted out, the search for complete control produces the tragedies that the initial distortions attempt to overcome. The tragedy of Jimmy Hoffa is a good case in point. Consider:

From all indications, Hoffa performed brilliantly as president of the teamsters' union. He was a superb organizer and bargainer, and in many ways a highly moral and even prudish man. There is little evidence to support allegations that he used his office to enrich himself.

Hoffa's troubles stemmed from his angry reactions when he could not get his way in managing the union's pension fund and from his relations with the government. In overestimating his power, Hoffa fell victim to the illusion that no controls outside himself could channel his actions. At this writing, Hoffa is serving a sentence in Lewisburg Penitentiary, having been found guilty of tampering with a jury.

It is interesting to note that Hoffa's successor delegated considerable authority to regional officers, a step that removed him from direct comparisons with Hoffa and served to cement a coalition of top officers in the teamsters.

Executives, too, can be victims of their successes just as much as of their failures. If past successes lead to the false sense of omnipotence that goes unchecked in, say, the executive's control of the board of directors, then he and his organization become the victims of changing times and competitive pressures along with the weakening in perception and reasoning that often accompanies aging.

One could speculate with some reason that paranoid distortions are the direct result of senility and the inability to accept the fact of death. While intellectually aware of the inevitability of death, gifted executives can sometimes not accept emotionally the ultimate in the limitations of power. The disintegration of personality in the conflict between the head and the heart is what we come to recognize as the paranoid potential in all forms of our collective relations.

RITUALISTIC CEREMONIAL

Any collective experience—such as organizational life, with its capacity for charging the atmosphere in the imagery of power conflicts—can fall victim to rigidities. The rigidities I have in mind consist mainly of the formation and elaboration of structures, procedures, and other ceremonials that create the illusion of solving problems but in reality only give people something to act on to discharge valuable energies.

The best example of a ritualistic approach to real problems is the ever-ready solution of bringing people together in a committee on the naïve grounds that the exchange of ideas is bound to produce a solution. There are even fads and fashions to ritualism, as in the sudden appearance of favorite words like *brainstorming* or *synergism*.

It is not that bringing people together to discuss problems is bad. Instead, it is the naïve faith that accompanies such proposals, ultimately deflecting attention from where it properly belongs. Thus:

In one research organization, professionals faced severe problems arising from personal jealousies as well as differences of opinion on the correct goals and content for the research program. Someone would periodically suggest that the problems could not be solved unless people came together, preferably for a weekend away from the job, to share ideas and really get down to the "nitty-gritty" of the problem. (It is interesting to note that no one ever defines the "nitty-gritty.") The group would indeed follow such suggestions and typically end the weekend with a feeling of euphoria brought on by considerable drinking and a sumptuous meal.

The most concrete proposal for action was in the idea that the basic problem stemmed from the organization's increased size so that people no longer knew one another and their work. The solution that appeared, only shortly to disappear, was to publish a laboratory newsletter that would keep people abreast of their colleagues' newest ideas.

In a more general vein, ritualism can be invoked to deal with any real or fancied danger, with uncertainty, ambivalent attitudes, or a sense of personal helplessness. Rituals are used even in the attempt to manipulate people. That power relations in organizations should become a fertile field for ritualism should not surprise anyone.

As I have tried to indicate, the problems of organizational life involve the dangers associated with losses of power; the uncertainties are legion, especially in the recognition that there is no one best way to organize and distribute power, and yet any individual must make a commitment to some form of organization.

Ambivalent attitudes, such as the simultaneous experience of love and hate, are also associated with authority relationships, particularly in how superior-subordinate become the subject and object for the expression of dependency reactions. In addition, the sense of helplessness is particularly sensitized in the events that project gains and losses in power and status.

Finally, superior and subordinate in any power structure are constantly tempted to manipulate each other as a way of gaining control over one's environment, and the more so when there is a lack of confidence and credibility in the organization's efforts to solve problems in realistic ways.

The negative effects of ritualism are precisely in the expenditure of energy to carry out the rituals and also in the childlike expectation that the magic formulas of organizational life substitute for diagnosing and solving real problems. When the heads of organizations are unsure of the bases for the exercise of power and become defensive, the easy solution is to play for time by invoking rituals that may temporarily relieve anxiety.

Similarly, when executives fail to understand the structure and potential of the power coalitions they establish (either consciously or unconsciously), they increasingly rely on rituals to deflect attention away from their responsibilities. And, when leaders are timid men incapable of initiating or responding, the spontaneous reaction is to use people to act out rituals. Usually, the content and symbolism in the rituals provide important clues about the underlying defensiveness of the executive.

Obsessional leaders

The gravitational pull to ceremonials and magic is irresistible. In positions of power, obsessional leaders use in their public performances the mechanisms of defense that originate in their private conflicts. These defenses include hyper-rationality, the isolation of thought and feeling, reactive behavior in turning anger into moral righteousness, and passive control of other people as well as their own thought processes.

Very frequently, particularly in this day and age of psychologizing conflict, obsessive leaders "get religion" and try to convert others into some new state of mind. The use of sensitivity training, with its attachment to "openness" and "leveling" in power relations, seems to be the current favorite.

What these leaders do not readily understand is the fallacy of imposing a total solution for the problem of power relations where reality dictates at best the possibility of only partial and transient solutions. To force openness through the use of group pressure in T-groups and to expect to sustain this pressure in everyday life is to be supremely ritualistic. People intelligently resist saying everything they think to other people because they somehow have a deep recognition that this route leads to becoming overextended emotionally and, ultimately, to sadistic relationships.

Intelligent uses of power

The choice fortunately is not between ritualistic civility and naïve openness in human relationships, particularly where power is concerned. In between is the choice of defining those partial problems which can be solved and through which bright people can learn something about the intelligent uses of power.

We should not lose sight of the basic lesson that people in positions of power differ from "ordinary" human beings mainly in their capacity to impose their personal defenses onto the stage of corporate life. Fortunately, the relationships are susceptible to intelligent management, and it is to the nature of this intelligence that I wish to address the conclusion of this article.

Coming Full Circle

The main job of organizational life, whether it concerns developing a new political pyramid, making new appointments to executive positions, or undergo-ing management succession at top levels, is to bring talented individuals into location for the legitimate uses of power. This is bound to be a highly charged event in corporate relationships because of the real changes in power distributions and the emotional reactions people experience along with the incremental gains and losses of power.

The demand, on the one hand, is for objectivity in assessing people and needs (as opposed to pseudorationality and rationalizing). This objectivity, on the other hand, has to be salvaged from the impact of psychological stresses that impel people to act out fantasies associated with power conflicts. The stresses of change in power relations tend to increase defensiveness, to which counterreactions of rationalizing and of mythmaking serve no enduring purpose except perhaps to drive underground the concerns that make people react defensively in the first place.

STYLISTIC BIASES

Thought and action in the politics of organizational life are subject to the two kinds of errors commonly found in practical life: the errors of omission and those of commission. It is both what people do and what they neglect to do that result in the negative effects of action outweighing the positive. But besides the specific errors of omission and commission (the tactical aspects of action), there are also the more strategic aspects that have to be evaluated. The strategic aspects deal both with the corporate aims and objectives and with the style of the leaders who initiate change.

In general, leaders approach change with certain stylistic biases over which they may not have too much control. There is a preferred approach to power problems that derives from the personality of the leader and his defenses as well as from the realities of the situation. Of particular importance as stylistic biases are the preferences for partial, as contrasted with total, approaches and the preferences for substance over form.

Partial vs. total

The partial approaches attempt to define and segregate problems that become amenable to solution by directive, negotiation, consensus, and compromise.

The total approaches usually escalate the issues in power relations so that implicitly people act as though it were necessary to undergo major conversions. The conversions can be directed toward personality structure, ideals, and beliefs, or toward values that are themselves connected to important aspects of personal experience.

When conversions become the end products of change, then one usually finds the sensitization of concerns over such matters as who dominates and who submits, who controls and who is being controlled, who is accepted and who is rejected. The aftermath of these concerns is the heightening of fantasy and defense at the expense of reality.

It may come as something of a disappointment to readers who are favorably disposed to psychology to consider the possibility that while organizations do have an impact on the attitudes of their constituent members, they cannot change personality structures or carry out therapeutic procedures. People may become more effective while working in certain kinds of organizations, but only when effectiveness is not dependent on the solution of neurotic conflict.

The advocates of total approaches seem to miss this point in their eagerness to convert people and organizations from one set of ideals to another. It becomes a good deal wiser, if these propositions are true, to scale down and make concrete the objectives that one is seeking to achieve.

A good illustration is in the attention given to decentralization of authority. Decentralization can be viewed in the image of conversion to certain ideals about who should have power and how this power should be used responsibly, or through an analytical approach to decide selectively where power is ill-placed and ill-used and to work on change at these locations. In other words, the theory of the partial approach to organizations asserts priorities and depends on good diagnostic observation and thought.

Substance vs. form

Leaders can also present a stylistic bias in their preference for substance or form. Substance, in the language of organizations, is the detail of goals and performance—that is, who has to do what with whom to meet specific objectives. Form directs attention to the relationship of "who to whom" and attempts to achieve goals by specifying how the people should act in relation to each other.

There is no way in which matters of form can be divorced from substance. But students of organization should at least be clear that attention to form *ahead of* substance threatens a person's sense of what is reasonable in undertaking actions. Attention to form may also present an implicit attack on one's conception of his independence and freedom from constraint.

Making form secondary to substance has another virtue: it can secure agreement on priorities without the need of predetermining who will have to give way in the ultimate give-and-take of the negotiations that must precede decisions on organization structure.

Exhibit I. Cognitive management styles in organizational life

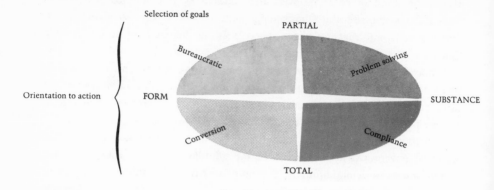

The two dimensions of bias, shown in the *Exhibit I* matrix, along with the four cells that result, clarify different executive approaches to power. The two dimensions define the executive's cognitive biases in: (1) selection of goals (partial vs. total), and (2) orientation toward action (form vs. substance).

In the *bureaucratic* approach—that is, partial goals and attachment to form as a mode of acting—the emphasis is on procedure and the establishment of precedent and rule to control the uses of power.

The appeal of this approach is its promise of certainty in corporate relationships and in the depersonalization of power. The weaknesses of the bureaucratic approach are too familiar to need detailing here. Its major defect, however, is its inability to separate the vital from the trivial. It more easily commands energy over irrelevant issues because the latent function of the bureaucratic approach is to bypass conflict.

My contention here is that few important problems can be attended to without conflict of ideas and interests. Eventually organizations become stagnant because the bureaucratic approaches seldom bring together power and the vital issues that together make organizations dynamic.

The *conversion* approach (total-form) is notable through the human relations and sensitivity training movements as well as ideological programs, such as the Scanlon Plan and other forms of participative management. The popularity of "management by objectives" bears some scrutiny as a conversion movement directed toward power figures.

Another "total" approach that differs from conversion in its emphasis on substance is *compliance* with the directives of the powerful leader. This is the arena of the authoritarian personality (in both the leader, who has the power, and in the led, who seek submission), for whom personal power gets expressed in some higher goal that makes it possible for ends to justify means. The ideals may, for example, be race, as with dictator Adolf Hitler, or religion, as with Father Charles Coughlin, a dictator-type of the depression. In business, the illustrations are of a technological variety, as with Frederick Winslow Taylor's "scientific management" and Henry Ford's automobile and assembly line.

Almost any technology can assume the proportions of the total approach if it is advanced by a charismatic leader and has deep emotional appeal. This explains the popularity of "management information systems," "value analysis," and "program planning and budgeting," which lead to a belief that the system itself is based on order, rationality, and control; therefore, the belief in turn helps to counteract the fears of chaos and lack of control, which make people willing to demand total dependence and compliance in power relations. The effects of this fear on how people seek to arrange power relations in business, government, and the community cannot be overestimated.

PROBLEM-SOLVING APPROACH

It should be perfectly obvious by now that my favored approach to organizational life combines the biases in *Exhibit I* of the partial substantive quadrant which I have designated "problem solving." From observation of competent business executives, we know it is precisely their ability to define problems worthy of thought and action and to use their organization to evolve solutions that characterizes their style.

The contrary notion that executives are primarily caretakers, mediators, and seekers of consensus is more a myth than an accurate portrayal of how the competent ones attach themselves to power. To have power and not direct it to some substantive end that can be attained in the real world is to waste energy. The difficulties with the problem-solving approach are in risking power in favor of a substantive goal.

While there are no absolute right answers in problem solving, there are ways of evaluating the correctness of a program and plan. With a favorable average, the executive finds his power base enhanced and his ability to take risks increased.

The problem-solving approach to organization structure operates according to certain premises:

1. That organization structure is an instrument rather than an end. This means that a structure should be established or modified quickly instead of stringing out deliberations as though there actually exists a best and single solution for the problem of allocating power.

2. That organization structure can be changed but should not be tinkered with. This means that members of an executive organization can rely on a

structure and can implement it without the uncertainty that comes from the constant modification of the organization chart.

3. That organization structure expresses the working coalition attached to the chief executive. In other words, the coalition has to be established de facto for the structure to mean anything. If the structure is out of line with the coalition, there will be an erosion of power and effectiveness. If no coalition exists in the minds of participants, putting it on paper in the form of an organization chart is nothing more than an academic exercise and a confusing one at that.

4. That organization structure represents a blend of people and job definitions, but the priority is in describing the structure to accommodate competent people. The reason for this priority lies in the fact that competent executives are hard to find. Therefore, as an action principle, one should ensure the effective uses of the scarcest resources rather than conform to some ideal version of power relations.

5. That organization structure is a product of negotiation and compromise among executives who hold semiautonomous power bases. The more the power base of an executive is his demonstrated competence, the greater his autonomy of power and therefore capacity to determine the outcome in the allocations of power.

The basic criticism of the problem-solving approach is in the danger of defining issues narrowly and ultimately undermining the moral-ethical basis of leadership. This criticism is valid, but as with so many problems in practical affairs, it can be overcome only by leaders who can see beyond the limits of immediate contingencies. In fact, I have tried to show throughout this article how the limitations of leaders, in both their cognitive and their emotional capacities, become the causes of power problems.

We have therefore come full circle in this analysis: because power problems are the effects of personality on structure, the solutions demand thinking which is free from the disabilities of emotional conflicts. This insight is often the margin between enduring with what exists or taking those modest steps that align competence with institutional authority in the service of human needs.

24. Is the Corporation Next to Fall?

Anthony G. Athos

Although this article was written at a time of great student unrest, conditions which aren't so much a problem today, the author's observations about the subjectivity of organizations are as relevant today as they were then. While economic and political fluctuations may affect the seeming willingness of young people to accept the strictures of large organizations, buried deep in their values systems is still a belief in the ethic of "meaningful human relationships," which will as deeply affect the organizations in which they work.

"Within five years, a president of a major corporation will be locked out of his office by his junior executives," remarked George Koch, president of the Grocery Manufacturers Association, not long ago. The very idea would have seemed outrageous and impossible only a few years ago. But recent experience in other large organizations, notably in universities, makes it clear that the cigars of any chief executive could become public property before long.

This prediction of internal revolt gains credence when considered in the light of the present situation. There is the much-discussed antipathy of the young for all large organizations, and allegedly for large corporations in particular. This loss of acceptance and the potential long-run loss of power have been of concern to business—a concern heightened by recruiters' reports that it is already more difficult to attract sufficient numbers of highly qualified young men to corporate life, even from the graduate schools of business administration.

Then, the rapidly increasing attacks on the products and practices of corporations by individuals and groups (for instance, Ralph Nader and his raiders) have become such a serious problem that companies have undertaken vigorous joint efforts to contend with what has become known as "consumerism." Of course, the deep suspicion of the military-industrial-educational complex focuses on corporations as a prime target.

Finally, the hints from recruiters that even MBAs are harder to hire are supported by impressions gained from professors that such students, like the crusading critics, are more openly questioning the products and practices of corporations and, like the young in general, are more doubtful of the values traditionally implicit in corporate life itself.

In short, the situation is rapidly becoming ripe for the kind of action Koch predicts.

So far, the corporate response seems neither fast enough nor thorough enough, largely because the implications of all the forces affecting business are so confusing that attention is directed toward the few young men who are radical in violent action rather than the many other young (and not so young) men who have become radical in perception. By better understanding these latter men, who are more closely related to the future of corporations, we can get an initial grasp of the problems that require skillful executive response.

Thus those with top responsibility in corporations not only must adjust themselves and their institutions in many ways to potential and present executives with "young" ideas, but must sense where they should *not* do so— rather, insisting and helping these talented men to appreciate better the extent to which they too must adjust. Such an understanding is not easy to come by; no simple conception of cause and effect, no single prescription, can be trusted.

This article is an attempt to provide some understanding. It will consider a number of significant changes of attitude in relatively moderate and very promising young men (whose ideas have already affected many of their seniors). It will explore how these changes are a threat to corporations, and suggest a framework for executive response.

How It Looks from Scarsdale

One of the most intellectually simple, but emotionally difficult, aspects to grasp in understanding these young men relates to the fact that many of them have lived all of their lives politically, socially, and financially secure. They simply have assumed that what they need will be available to them, and frequently that what they want in addition can be easily obtained.

One of the college juniors in the Program for Business Internship run at the Harvard Business School in the summer of 1967 was asked what he had learned from it. He searched the ceiling for a few seconds and said, "Well, I guess I could get at it by saying that I learned the garbage may not always be collected." He, like others, seemed bemused at the amount of resources and effort that goes into providing what he had previously taken for granted. So it is for many students in general.

While their fathers experienced the Depression, the Second World War, and often Korea, most of them were born after World War II, were too young even to have read about Korea, and grew up in the great economic boom of the 1950's in families that achieved relative affluence. Much as their fathers took the radio for granted, they take TV as given.

And, just as their fathers learned from economic and political uncertainty the potential for loss of luxuries and even life, they learned from economic growth and a relatively stable political situation that they could go on to *other* goals. It makes sense that they would assume as given what their fathers had earned, as their fathers had assumed before them; it was all each generation had experienced.

In a brilliantly insightful article, Kenneth Keniston pointed out, among other things, that the achievements of the United States in productivity have realized, for most of those who concern us here, the dreams of affluence and security which have animated much of American life since the country's founding.[1] The rewards of this achievement were savored by the fathers who had wrought it, but were merely taken for granted by the sons who benefited from it. Then the sons discovered that what they had assumed as given was not available to all Americans, and it shocked them.

They were indignant that not everyone was rich enough to live and learn and choose as they were, and secure enough to seek new goals that become possible only when economic and social security exists. (In their suburban innocence they had believed in the American Dream, and it seemed especially flawed by their discovery of racial prejudice.) Not appreciating from personal experience the effort and time it took to achieve "wealth" for many, and the value their elders thus placed on "earning," they demanded that wealth be "given" to the others immediately.

And when the Viet Nam war threatened them with the disrupting and dangerous experience of their fathers, they were furious. A war questionable in conception was not likely to compel them easily to give up their assumption of peace.

Knowing only relative peace, wealth, and social acceptance, they demanded them for all Americans as rights, as bases from which new efforts might be made toward greater goals of human enhancement. And they demanded them NOW.

NEW GOALS AND VALUES

While these young men and women were attending to the nation's unresolved economic, racial, and social problems, and to the threat an unpopular war posed to them and others, they were also searching for those greater goals to replace

1. "You Have to Grow Up in Scarsdale to Know How Bad Things Really Are," *The New York Times Magazine,* April 27, 1969, p. 27.

the ones already largely achieved. These goals related more to what would allow them to be themselves than to doing what others wanted, and to experiencing themselves than achieving what others cared about. The means for accomplishing the goals related more to what has meaning for man as a human being than to efficiency for organizations as economic units.[2]

This search had proceeded far enough for them to begin to view the problems of poverty, race, and war through a looking glass ground by different values from those of their elders. Not valuing "earning" itself, as their parents did (actually *had to,* in order to accumulate wealth), they demanded we "give" wealth to the poor—that is, not sharing our experience and thus our values, they questioned our assumptions about the economic structures we had developed, especially those assumptions about the distribution of wealth.

Being concerned with meaning and man, they increasingly saw blacks as persons rather than vaguely as units of another race, and thus they could identify with the pain of individuals and feel a moral outrage that paralleled the more visceral rage of blacks themselves.

Finally, their developing new values caused them to view the Viet Nam war not only as personally threatening and disruptive but also as a brutal and unjust manifestation of the old values that supported the use of U.S. economic and political power abroad in this century—what President Kennedy harshly called "Pax Americana." In short, they were saying that enough wealth, power, and security was enough. More of the same, ever more of the same, was not just vulgar—it was immoral.

Those affluent students who seek careers in business may feel rather less strongly than many others about some of these points. And they may be likely to proceed differently in their searching. But the differences seem more of degree than of kind, and it would be naïve to assume otherwise.

The impact on corporations of those young men who are even relatively "polite and patient" is thus likely to be significant. They will want their organizations to contribute to "righting the wrongs" (note the accusation implicit in the words) of society, as well as permit—indeed, encourage—within corporations the search for more personally meaningful lives that is associated with the new human values. In their moral indignation and their naïveté about how slowly change comes, they will want action fast and results NOW.

We must explore how we can help them become more aware of what is unrealistic in their demands, as we learn from them something about their developing new values and thus the extent to which we can integrate new goals into our existing framework and act more quickly to achieve them.

---

2. For a more extensive treatment of these ideas, see my article, "The Young and I," *Harvard Business School Bulletin,* September-October 1967, p. 9.

But first it is necessary to dig into the factors that lie behind the demands and counterdemands. What is most visible to us is a surface manifestation of fundamental changes in young people *as persons*. Understanding these basic changes is a prerequisite for intelligent response to them, so it is worth making the effort to understand.

And they are basic changes indeed, involving, among others, a different conception of knowledge. That particular change is relevant to corporations in many ways, and may in part confirm the suspicions of many businessmen that professors have been causing the problems they have to live with. But, as we shall see, it is not as simple as that.

More Frames of Reference

In an intriguing study, William G. Perry, Jr., Director of the Bureau of Study Counsel at Harvard, reports a remarkable shift in the very conception of knowledge since 1900.[3] Perry analyzed the questions given on final examinations at Harvard College in this century.

In 1900, a likely question might have been, "When was the battle of Hastings?" If a student could answer "1066," he was "right." In the late 1960s, a question might have read, "Compare the concepts of authority exemplified by Charles de Gaulle and Mahatma Gandhi." Note that the question does not ask for a comparison of the two men, but for a comparison of the concepts of authority, and these concepts should be ones derived from students' knowledge of the men. Since the ways these concepts are to be compared are not specified, the students must make judgments on the basis of their own values. Their answers could hardly be labeled clearly either "right" or "wrong."

Questions asked of students earlier in this century tended (90% of the time) to require only one frame of reference. Questions more recently tend (80% of the time) to ask students to deal with two or more frames of reference. Consequently, *knowing* means something different for the students of today from what it meant for those of the not very distant past.

To know facts, to remember or memorize them, and be able to produce them on examinations would be regarded by our best students today as a sure sign of a "mickey mouse" course. To Alfred North Whitehead's statement, "Education is the acquisition of the art of the utilization of knowledge," they would probably add, "and thought, and feeling, and values."

Theories, or ways of thinking about phenomena, also seem to have shorter

3. *Forms of Intellectual and Ethical Development in the College Years: A Scheme* (Cambridge, Bureau of Study Counsel, Harvard University, 1968).

and shorter life spans. Believing them, as one might have in 1910, seems pretty silly; using them until something better comes along seems more sensible. As knowledge (in the "fact" sense of the word) and theories (or "ways of thinking") have become more temporary, is it any wonder that feeling has received increased emphasis, and that the younger generation's own value judgments are assumed to be a necessary part of their approach to problems?

Changes in Development

Perry's work led to a complicated conception of the sequences of students' intellectual and ethical development. The detail of his exciting conception is so rich that, to fit my purposes here, I simplify it at the price of considerable distortion, perhaps. (Those responsible for frequent face-to-face interaction with the young may wish to study Perry's report.) To present the essential aspects briefly, I shall collapse his nine sequences of growth to four levels.

While I use the word *level,* it is important at the outset to recognize that I am making no *absolute* value judgment that one is always "better" than another. The fact that they are sequential in the process of development, that each in turn incorporates the ones before, does not mean that a "higher" level of development is necessarily "better" in all situations at all times. The reader no doubt can think of situations where a "Level 1 man" would be better fitted to the circumstances than, say, a "Level 3 man," given certain desired outcomes.

LEVEL 1

At the first level a student might say, "Look, knowledge is absolute. It consists of correct answers, one per problem. The teacher's job is to tell me what the relevant questions are, and what the correct answers are. I write them down." The student with this approach might have done very well indeed at most schools 60 years ago. But no longer.

It assumes a right-wrong position, an either-or conception of knowledge. Persons who see things as black or white tend to follow this approach. In my teaching experience, I often see these men as authoritarian, rigid, and moralistic in their thinking.

I recall a recent incident in which a student attacked something I had said in class so strongly that it made me defensive and angry. But after listening and arguing for a while, I finally saw his point, realized I was wrong, and said so. After class, another student came up to me and said, "It is inconceivable that you would admit you're wrong. You've lost the authority a teacher needs."

Level 1 men are not hard to find in any organization, including corporations. While they are increasingly rare in the graduate schools, they are still being graduated by colleges which function largely at the Level 1 conception of knowledge. Many companies find them reliable at lower levels, but when they reach middle management positions, they may act as a barrier preventing men more promising from rising.

LEVEL 2

Most students proceed to a second level that introduces situationalism and relativism to their conception of knowledge. A student at this level might say, "Knowledge consists of the best answer, one per problem. The teacher's job is to pose the relevant problems and offer a number of possible answers. My job is to figure out which answer is the best one, given the situation—which I don't mind too much if the teacher is fair and doesn't make things too obscure." (A change of the word "teacher" to "boss" is likely to remind the reader of some subordinates.)

My experience in the classroom has led me to view Level 2 students across a spectrum. Let me describe its two ends:

Holistic Group

These students are often unhappy over the excessive absence of personal relevance in the abstractions that were a part of their prior education, and angry at heavy emphasis on analysis, especially when unrelated to what they are experiencing. They want to sense things, to apprehend them rather than comprehend them.

One student who had top grades in all his courses—thereby demonstrating his analytical skills—refused to analyze an interview he had taped and typed up, which was the assignment. He wrote, "This is too beautiful to analyze." In other words, "Thinking is for what does not have deep feeling for me." In a different context, another student looked at me and said, "The only way you can own a butterfly is to kill it or cage it."

In reaction against abstractions, they seek the territory of important personal experiencing and are reluctant to map that territory with ideas. They affect a deliberate inarticulation, a disdain for precise language. "Like, man, it's groovy" is not a very specific communication.

While their cultivation of personal, unique sensation is satisfying to some extent, it frequently leaves them alienated (as others are affected by drugs). They feel a need to be more connected, however, and so one hears them talking earnestly about community, close groups, and shared experiences, and about intimacy and involvement. But the excessive turning-in to the personal, the inability to commit themselves to others, and the refusal to think about what they feel is important—these often preclude satisfaction.

Analytical Group

These students (a larger group) *want* to analyze and comprehend, to be impersonal, objective, distant, and intellectual. They ask, "What is the nature of the game? What are the rules? How do I win?" They like to break things into parts. They enjoy mapping the territory of experience but shy from intense personal experiencing itself. They are uncomfortable with sensing the whole as more than the sum of its parts, and prefer to add up their own conception of parts.

As a result, they often become cynical and see much of life in win-lose terms. They may view others as objects to be manipulated, while others see them as cold and machinelike. I recall one young man in a group, searchingly discussing the existence of God, who suddenly stated, "Let's face it; there is a .5 probability that God exists. Get off it." They frequently act hostilely, though unaware of their feelings. They are the icy-eyed, buttoned-up young men on the make.

Of course, few students are completely at the holistic or the analytical pole. Even the few who are extreme tend to go back and forth from each end, as suggested by the top student who refused to analyze an interview that touched him personally.

Most take positions closer to the center of the spectrum; yet even these tend to separate the two orientations at any one time. A student will either think a certain way about something or someone, or feel a certain way about it or him. He may be uncritical about issues or causes or persons close to him in feeling, and very critical about those he is distant from.

While many students, in my experience, stay at Level 2, more are including in their basic orientation some of the next level of development. And, for increasing numbers of students, it is their main level of orientation.

LEVEL 3

At the third level of development, a student might say:

"Knowledge exists in specific settings. The settings differ, and so do the knowers. Therefore several interpretations are legitimate, depending on the person, his point of view, and his purpose, as well as the setting and the thing being addressed. This leaves me uneasy in a kaleidoscopic world, but I judge my answers, or theories, in terms of how well they fit the data, and predict their behavior, given my purposes in attending to the data.

"So the teacher's job is to pose problems and help me see more ways to view them, as well as help me judge better the fit of my thinking, given my purpose, to the data. My values, as well as the teacher's, are to be used here."

(Try reading this again, substituting "boss" or "father" for "teacher," to see if it fits your experience with your subordinates or teen-age children.)

Students at Level 3 try to experience the whole of something, think about it in several ways, and determine which way of thinking, or combination of ways, best fits the thing, given their persons and their purposes. They refuse to be told what the "right" or the "best" way of thinking is, since that leaves them, their purposes, and their values out of it.

I recently observed an example of this approach in a firm. Its senior men, long priding themselves on their professional orientation, had rejected opportunities that promised great financial rewards whenever such opportunities threatened the values they held as "professional men building a professional firm helping corporations." The firm had achieved unusual status and security as a result of this value orientation and business focus.

Then certain younger members began to question both the value orientation and the client focus. Some wanted the firm to get into the financial world directly to increase the incomes of members, while others wanted the firm to serve clients in the public sector, notably the urban part of society, even if the financial rewards were less.

In response, study teams were set up that included some of the young men pressing for change. The financial study team decided that the firm should not "move to Wall Street" for a number of reasons, one being that the "fundamental character of the firm" would be changed. The public sector team concluded that the firm should devote more resources to urban clients and expand its public sector work.

The many young men who were not involved in the studies found it difficult to accept the recommendations, for they could not be sure that their purposes and their values were the ones used to interpret the findings. Since the reports could not include all the thinking of the study teams, the "outsiders" suspected that too few approaches to the subject had been used. They even doubted the findings technically. In short, they would not give up easily their assumption that they, and only they, could decide such issues for themselves. Their willingness to trust others to represent them was low. Such Level 3 people are indeed difficult to "supervise."

LEVEL 4

At Level 4, a person seems to say: "O.K., I've looked at a great many alternatives, and see the relativism of knowledge and values. Now I've chosen a set of values I intend to live by. I accept these values enough to act on them, and I recognize that my person and my purposes, as well as the settings in which I find myself, have limitations. I also am aware that others will choose to live differently from the way I do, and yet we can accept each other as different."

The basic difference between a Level 3 and a Level 4 man is that the latter is *aware* that his own values, person, purposes, and settings are limited in multiple ways, and he *accepts* the fact that he is relating to others who are different. A Level 4 man "knows" who he is, accepts who others are, and is prepared to live with the differences he finds, in ways he is willing to explore imaginatively.

In the firm I just discussed, there were some young men who found the decision "not to move to Wall Street" possible to understand. Though they did not participate in the study, they were aware of the differing values working on the decision makers and were willing to accept the outcomes as reasonable, if not quite satisfying. So they decided to help achieve many of the goals of the group urging the Wall Street involvement, and were able to create another solution that was sufficiently acceptable to all to be approved.

These Level 4 men, ready to accept others as well as themselves, were imaginative and responsible in dealing with the uncertainty, ambiguity, and imperfection always present in living together in and out of organizations.

If a classroom or a company includes persons at all these levels, the teacher or executive has a complex problem. If he attends to those at Level 1, the others are furious. If he focuses on those at Level 2, the ones at Level 1 are lost and angry ("This guy must be soft or a liberal or something. What's he mean, no clear right or wrong?"); and those at Level 3 are disappointed and bored ("Another incompetent!"). Attending only to those at Level 3 stupefies those at Level 1 and leaves those at Level 2 anxious and resentful. Meanwhile, those at Level 4 may try to help as they can.

Since young men of roughly the same age can be at different levels of development, with each behaving according to where he is and developing from where he is, more than ever before attention is needed to deal with their differences from one another. Unfortunately, corporations, like other large organizations, are accustomed to dealing with what were assumed to be *similarities* among groups of persons who were largely at Levels 1 and 2.

Later, I shall discuss the profound and costly implications of the new stress on differences. But first we must consider three other changes that bear on our ability to respond skillfully: first, the change in young persons' conception of reality; second (one which hits closer to home), in their conception of authority; and third, in their values.

New Conception of Reality

Western man has passed through several phases of his view of reality. J. Samuel Bois[4] has provided a useful interpretation of those stages:

The Age of Primitive Realism (to 650 B.C.)	The world is what I feel it to be.
The Age of Reason (650 B.C.–350 B.C.)	The world is what I say it is.
The Age of Science (1500–1900)	The world is an immense machine, and I can discover how it works.
The Age of Relativism (1900–1966)	The world consists of the probabilities that I create by my way of looking at them.
The Age of Unity (1966–	My world has a structure that no formulation can encompass; I conceive of the world as my own total experience within it, and I play with my own symbolic constructs in a spirit of [uneasy involvement].[5]

The point here is that the changes previously discussed in the conception of knowledge and in the *development* of students have altered something so profound in man as his very conception of reality and his relation to it.

Most executives seem to be in the Age of Science or Relativism, although one still hears of those back at the Age of Reason. When one of the latter encounters a student who is at home in the Age of Unity, the results are not very happy ones—for either, it must be added.

Perhaps even more painful is the situation in which a teacher who talks at the Age of Relativism but behaves at the Age of Reason encounters a student

4. *Explorations in Awareness* (New York, Harper & Row, 1957), chap. 16, as elaborated on by D. Fabun in *The Dynamics of Change* (Englewood Cliffs, N.J., Prentice-Hall, 1967), p. I–25.
5. I have substituted "uneasy involvement" for Bois' actual words, "easy detachment"—a phrase which made sense in 1957 but does not any longer.

functioning in the Age of Unity. The student must see the teacher as not only limited but hypocritical. And of course this "perception," sadly, will prepare him well for life in many corporations.

The "uneasy involvement" of the young tends to emphasize that aspect of the world that is made up of individuals, and thus focuses on relationships as a central aspect of reality. The ways persons relate to others loom large in their awareness as they confront the world. Which brings us to what many executives see as the nub of the problem—authority.

Authority Flows Two Ways

The difficulty of understanding changes in the conception of knowledge, the development of students, and the conception of reality has left us frequently focusing on the all-too-visible challenges to authority in our various institutions. The churches, our political parties, and our universities all have been attacked; and if George Koch is right, our corporations are next.

Hard as it is for most executives to conceive of attacks from within by young executives, imagine if you will this series of events:

The chief executive officer of a large corporation issues a statement affecting employees, on a policy about which he feels strongly.

There is an outcry of protest from some of his first-line supervisors, and the outcry grows as they gain support from various higher-level executives.

The insurgency becomes so troublesome that division managers from all over the country meet in a hotel to determine what action they should take, only to find a large group of young, promising junior executives sitting in the lobby, where they sing songs and demand that the division managers defy the chief executive.

Later a number of plant managers, young executives, and foremen quit, and even a few senior vice presidents begin to question openly their boss's directive.

Sound incredible? Well, in a general way that is what Pope Paul faced after his encyclical on birth control. And if this could happen to the oldest, most successful organization in the history of the Western world, it clearly could happen to corporations.

Taking a look at the problems of this church and its response may be instructive. In Washington, D.C., Cardinal O'Boyle said that the issue was not so much birth control as it was the authority of the Pope and other "executives" within the church. He was, in my view, dead right.

The young priests, and their supportive bishops and even cardinals, were saying, in effect, that the tradition of the past was not sufficient to justify the authority of their leader, that recent custom was just as insufficient, that long acceptance of the role of the leader was no longer solely determining. They were saying that the locus of authority now rests in the *man* in the role, and that their own perception of what was right or true was relevant in judging their superior's view. And they were insisting that the judgments of their superiors be related to the values *they* held.

In short, the critical clerics were expressing the changes I previously discussed (the inclusion of self in the relativistic conceptions of knowledge, development, and reality) in questioning and even denying the authority of a person in the role of pope.

While such a secular view of the Roman Catholic Church and its pontiff obviously leaves much omitted, the illustration remains useful here to the extent that chief executives of many companies have enjoyed internal acceptance of the authority of their role as if they were corporate popes. And the difficulties of the Catholic Church in recruiting young priests, its losses of junior men already on board, the defection of senior men at "middle management" levels, and its internal questioning and attacks by those remaining at all levels are potentially instructive to business leaders as a model of what might come in corporations.

Indeed, some companies already report similar events. The shock of such change to top executives is likely to be painful and seen also as a direct challenge to authority.

THE PERSON, NOT THE ROLE

Our notions of authority long have been rooted in the idea that it flows *down,* and that each level determines how much of it is apportioned to whom below. The top man presumably has all of it. Kings were crowned often by religious leaders, the implication or claim being that they had authority by the grace of God; business executives derived theirs from owners who had rights of property granted by the state. As long as they had the role, everyone assumed they had the power, the right, the authority.

But relatively recently some academics have suggested that authority flows up in organizations, that one has authority only if those below grant it. This view had the initial attraction of an upside-down perception. But while many observers acknowledged the truth in it, more believed that few subordinates had the courage to stand on their heads for long, and so it was decided that most people would be content to have authority continue to flow down from whoever is in the role.

It is this later, rather political, view that is being challenged now. Many young persons of promise are saying that authority, whatever it is, lies mostly in the person, and in his values as a person, and in his actions in a situation, and is not just derived from that person's role. They are saying that authority must be personal, situational, earned, and moral, even if supported by a role, and is thus located in men who belong in power because they meet these measurements.

Naturally, as they have been taught about other things, many of these questioners believe *they* must be the judges of who has authority for them in various situations. This looks suspiciously like accepting authority when one agrees with it and rejecting it when one doesn't. And this abuse is a probable real cost of the new view.

But it is inevitable that the relativism of knowledge, thought, and feeling, and the personal responsibility inherent in such a view, applied to personal development and even to reality, should also result in something other than a rigid, accept-reject posture in relation to authority.

In my own experience with students in classrooms, challenging the "authority" of the teacher has always been a part of every course. In 1958, a new professor at the Harvard Business School was asked in his first class, "What are your qualifications to teach us?" The question pertained to his academic degrees or work experience, while revealing doubts about his adequacy as a teacher.

Last year, no one asked me such an embarrassing question. But I had the feeling within a few class hours that students had tentative answers to a very different and much more discomforting set of questions: "Who are you? Can I trust you? Do you care? Are you aware? Are you mature as a man? Are you knowledgeable and still learning? Are you skillful enough to help me, where I am, to see more options? Where are you going? How will I get there? Why is going there important and worthwhile for me?"

The emphasis is on the person, not on symbols of academic accomplishment or on pounds of knowledge to be dispensed. It is on skill, and insight, and caring, and concern for oneself and for others. It is on a set of values that places the growing of persons, student and teacher—their becoming who they can be as individuals—central to the educational process.

This view is of course applied not only within our educational institutions. Consider the attacks on President Johnson as a person, the continuing suspicion of President Nixon's person, the cartoon ogre that TV made Mayor Daley in the minds of many, the doubts about the intentions of our military teachers. Consider, too, whether the questions I just listed are ones you feel are being asked by your subordinates and children.

Some say with exasperation that you can't run a country this way. You can't run a school, a political party, or a business this way. Well, we possibly can. We probably must. And therefore, in painful time, we will.

Man as Subject

Earlier I mentioned that the relative affluence of many of the young has freed them to explore new but not yet fully articulated goals that relate more to what has meaning for man as a human being than to efficiency for organizations as economic units. The described changes in orientation to knowledge, reality, and authority include a shift in values, with the individual rather than the group in the center. Since every person is to some extent unique, there is emphasis on what is unique for him. And among the things that are unique for him is the meaning he discovers about himself, his world, and the relationship between the two.

This emphasis on what is unique in the individual flies in the face of practice in most large organizations. It is administratively simpler to focus on what is similar among people in groups and have the false comfort of avoiding the uncertainty, ambiguity, and imperfection of the human condition. As we have developed our administrative practices, they have become more rigid and dehumanizing, for both the managers and the managed.

Many writers, especially in this century, have described eloquently the tendency in organizations for those with power to view man as an object rather than a subject.[6] As object, man is the recipient of action, and the focus is on what impinges on him and on his external behavior. The causes of man's behavior are seen as outside him, and anything occurring inside him is discounted. In short, he becomes an "it."

As subject, man is the doer, the one taking action, the one acting on objects. He is seen as having his own unique way of looking at things, his own desired experiences, and his own mode of changing his environment to fit his desires. Accordingly, his behavior is seen as having reasons rather than causes. The subjective view is essential in understanding individuals.

Yet the objective is still essential in dealing with large numbers of persons. I am not arguing that we should discard the objective view but, rather, that we increase our subjective viewing of persons.

A simple example, useful because it is so obvious, if not crucial, is the vari-

6. See, for a recent instance, James F. T. Bugental, "Someone Needs to Worry: The Existential Anxiety of Responsibility and Decision," *Journal of Contemporary Psychotherapy*, Summer 1969, p. 41.

ation increasingly evident in the appearance of the young. When I was a graduate business student in the late 1950s, I was told that we were a colony of penguins indistinguishable to the casual eye. This external uniformity was also prevalent then in corporate settings; apparently men who looked alike could more easily be regarded as interchangeable parts without important internal differences.

Much more diversity in attire, length of hair, and facial adornment seems to exist now in corporations, especially at staff levels, and of course vastly more exists in schools preparing future executives. The young do not see external differentiation as threatening, or disloyal, or necessarily suspect.

But they do see it, incidentally, as a way to identify executives for whom they would *not* want to work. All one has to do is let facial hair grow and, in the job interview, watch for discomfort or an outright complaint. They reason that rejection of what is *on* one's head, in a school setting, is likely to accompany low appreciation for what is *in* it, on the job.

And, like many simple tests, this one works pretty well. If an executive tends to think that a beard identifies the wearer as an artist or hippie, if not an SDS activist, then his capacity to deal with human beings as subjects with important internal differences may indeed be low.

Kenneth Keniston's conclusions give us a broad view of the implications of the central emphasis on the individual. He notes these currents among the young:

☐ "A revulsion against the notion of quantity, particularly economic quantity and materialism, and a turn toward concepts of quality.

☐ "A revolt against uniformity, equalization, standardization and homogenization—not against technology itself, but against the 'technologication of man.'

☐ "A continuing struggle against psychological or institutional closure or rigidity in any form.

☐ "The revolt against centralized power and the complementary demand for participation.

☐ "The new ethic of 'meaningful human relationships,' in which individuals confront each other without masks, pretenses and games."

It is useful at this point, as a kind of summary, to organize the major ideas discussed so far into clusters of spectrums that provide a rough initial framework for executive review and action. They are shown in *Exhibit I.*

It is a fair and useful generalization, I think, to say that most large organizations are closer to the objective end of most of these spectrums (they certainly are in the eyes of the young). If so, we can begin to understand the new tendency to

Exhibit I. "Objective-subjective" value spectrum for organizations

	Objective ←————————→ Subjective	
Organizational goals	Quantity	Quality
Organizational structures	Centralized	Decentralized
Executive style	Closed	Open
	Rigid	Flexible
	Authoritarian	Participative
	Roles	Persons
	Absolute	Relative
Emphasis in decision processes affecting persons	Uniformity	Individuality
	Equalization	Variation
	Similarities	Differences
View of man	Man as it	Man as I
	Know	Think and feel
	Out there	In here
	Causes	Reasons
	External	Internal

swing toward the other end of each spectrum, in reaction against what is perceived as excessive emphasis on the objective.

To Learn the Future

At the risk of sounding preachy, I suggest that, before reading on, the executive should lean back and ask himself whether, and in what ways, he needs and wants to learn more, to grow as a *person* in his role. I suggest it because the notion that just another set of administrative procedures or a new program in the personnel department—another change one makes from time to time—will do in the present circumstances is really worse than doing nothing, for it promises what it cannot deliver.

Acceptance of the idea that one needs to grow personally may not be easy for men who have "arrived" after a long and arduous trip. To be told that one should set out on still another voyage (an uncharted one) may sound disrespectful of past accomplishments, and threatening to boot. And yet, for some executives, the excitement of personally growing and searching may give new meaning to the rest of their lives.

Let me state plainly the reason for my suggestion. The challenge posed to corporations by the ideas that are taking hold can be met only by individuals—men who have executive position and power and who care enough about themselves as persons, about their companies, and about the world around them to invest heavily in their own growing and their organization's renewal.

So, first, executives should set out to learn, before they attempt to teach or initiate some changes, while resisting others. This requires starting with the disturbing awareness that not only have we something to learn, but that we need to learn it from the young.

Robert Frost said it best in his poem, "What Fifty Said":

> When I was young my teachers were the old.
> I gave up fire for form till I was cold.
> I suffered like a metal being cast.
> I went to school to age to learn the past.
>
> Now I am old my teachers are the young.
> What can't be molded must be cracked and sprung.
> I strain at lessons fit to start a suture.
> I go to school to youth to learn the future.[7]

Those executives who are willing to "strain," to "be cracked and sprung," should have little trouble enrolling in the school of youth. There are many ways to proceed.

The easiest and safest (and so perhaps the least useful if no other ways are used) is to read. Ask someone in your organization who seems irritatingly sympathetic with the young to pull together a set of articles and books that he thinks you should read, even books he knows you won't like. If you find the reading not very uncomfortable, tell him that he should not have played it so safe, and if necessary get yourself another man.

Still another route is to visit a local campus and eat in the student cafeteria (not the president's dining room) or attend a movie-lecture series. Or attend any other campus event and look, listen, and ask questions. (Hold off on responding if you can.) Ask your minister or priest or rabbi to arrange for groups of adults and teen-agers, or college students, to talk with each other. See what they have to tell you before you let them know what you have to give to them. Set up small groups of executives and bring some outspoken campus leaders to talk to you, and with you, and focus on what does make sense in what they say.

This learning can be very rewarding in personal terms. A priest I know, disturbed about the apparent lack of meaning to young people in his church's litur-

---

7. *Complete Poems of Robert Frost* (New York, Henry Holt and Company, 1957).

gy, encountered through a young parishioner the rock opera *Tommy*, by a group disconcertingly called "The Who." He found in it some clues to what was wrong in his liturgy and discovered a promising direction for himself to explore.

However you go about it, be sure to get in conversation with young people; do not just learn ways of thinking about them. Try to contain the annoyance of learning from your juniors by reminding yourself of Robert Frost. And ask yourself whether your own children might have a lot to tell you if they thought you would really listen because you want to grow too. Finally, remember that it can hurt to grow. Value the discomfort if you can.

THE SUBJECTIVE ORGANIZATION

Now, take a look at your organization. Try to be tough-minded in gauging the extent to which your company's goals, its means, and its ends are accomplished by overemphasis on the objective. Try to find policies and procedures, rules and regulations that are unnecessarily rigid in design or execution. Experiment with more subjective methods, recognizing that where we are all going is not yet clear, but we must begin to search before we are forced to.

Some examples may help here. The professional firm I discussed before included younger men in its study groups, although only senior partners would have been involved in the past. While the groups still met some resistance from certain other young men, it was mild compared with what would have been the reaction to only senior-men study groups. Furthermore, the response of a few men to the initial negative recommendations of one study group was sufficiently imaginative and reasonable that it stimulated a new activity for the firm.

In short, as the firm included more of what I am calling the subjective (in this instance, wider participation), it retained some of what I am calling the objective (in this instance, what the entire organization had to have to persist *as an organization* of men with varied values).

Some day this firm may decide to include junior men in decisions on who shall become partners and may broaden the criteria for advancement to put even more emphasis on diversity in persons than it now does. For the continued health of the firm, however, the judgments must still be made by means of external measurements of a candidate's fit with the criteria—that is, the person will be measured as object, not subject, though the process of measurement is more subjective.

The inclusion of more of the subjective *cannot* be to the exclusion of the objective, and *should not* go beyond the point where it is useful to all in the organization. A mix of both orientations is needed, tailored to the situation.

This, of course, is already occurring in modest, exploratory ways in many organizations. Staying with promotion procedure and criteria, I recall the instance of an accounting firm whose senior partners found that its young men believed that a single set of promotion criteria, with one order of rank and weighting, was inappropriate because of diversity in the group of younger men. In talking with them, the older men discovered that the firm's perennial problem of developing good administrators (rather than merely good accountants) was caused largely by their promotion of first-rate accountants exclusively, bypassing others who had administrative flair.

After listening to their young men, they decided to design several sets of criteria for promotion that better fitted the talents of the men as well as the needs of the organization. In replacing a single set of criteria with multiple sets, they widened their objective procedure while allowing for a more subjective one. Note that they did not just "pacify" the young, or go further than what made sense for all.

Multiple goals

The kind of searching study I am recommending here must include influence from the top, since the questioning already going on at the bottom creeps up in organizations and results in a malaise, a loss of confidence, that can affect those in the middle unless it is met by the reassuring concern and involvement of the top man, and those close to him.

The time and attention such involvement takes is considerable, and it probably will lead to a question of its impact on profits. Many executives claim that *the* goal of their companies is profit—that is, the goal is singular and quantitative.

But I recently heard the president of a major corporation publicly state that his company's goals were plural, and that the rank order of their importance varied from situation to situation. Sometimes profit was overriding, sometimes not. Sometimes what was right for a person came first, sometimes not. Sometimes growth was most important, sometimes not. And so on. He suggested that corporate leaders who talked *only* profit as a goal seldom actually behaved that way to the degree that they thought they did.

If multiple goals are identified and accepted, and if they are seen as not ranked in one order for all decisions, then it becomes possible to reevaluate virtually every other aspect of corporate life in the light of what I have been trying to say here. Besides organizational structures (especially committees), the actual decision processes currently existing and the policies, rules, and regulations in force can be appraised. And, of course, the range and kind of human beings involved, their informal norms and structures, must be searchingly considered.

It will not take long to find opportunities for change if you mull over the specifics of your situation in terms of the objective-subjective spectrums presented earlier. Having done so, you will be in a position to initiate change rather than react to it. You will be able to see in advance the places where you must stand firm, for now at least; and, having been open yourself to learning, and being one of the sources of exploration and innovation in your organization, you will have earned anew the respect of those who have to live with your *no*.

Better yet, you can help them grow by being more able to explain why your *no* to some things is necessary and useful, if you have your reasons ready, they stand tough questioning, and you are willing to explain and teach.

Let me conclude. Each of us needs to see that:

☐ The overriding conflict between the young and their elders is rooted in the former's excessive emphasis on the subjective and the latter's excessive emphasis on the objective.

☐ Therefore, we are a part of the problem we perceive.

☐ The "solution" to the problem involves our growing and changing as *persons,* so as to integrate more of the views and values of the young.

☐ Our growing can be enhanced by learning from the young.

☐ Such growth can then be expressed in changes in our behavior in our executive roles, as we explore how to renew our organizations skillfully and carefully.

☐ This process will make it possible for us to lead and teach the young more about their own part in the problem we are all having.

Even if you agree with my perception of the problem, you are left with the choice to change. This choice is indeed personal, the effort large, the discomfort great, and the outcome promising if uncertain. Only you can decide—for now, anyway.

25. Business Leadership and a Creative Society

Abram T. Collier

One of the perpetual problems that business leaders face is how to affect the attitudes and morale of employees. Despite the many communications problems involved, the author of this article maintains that business people ought to engage the creative talents of people and articulate creative ideals. A creative society, a business, depends on four concepts. First, a diversity of ideas, to challenge assumptions and encourage change. Second, a process of understanding whereby the different ideas are integrated into the organization without conflict. Third, the belief that human relationships are two-way matters, and that rights are matched by obligations. And fourth, a clear and distinct belief in man's development toward a nonauthoritarian way of life. The ideas expressed in this article, though written in 1953, are as interesting and relevant today as they were then. As the article was an "HBR Classic" in 1968, the author wrote a retrospective commentary at that time, which we include here as well.

High on the list of tasks facing the business administrator are those relating to the basic attitudes, interests, and objectives of his employees. Meeting antagonism and misunderstanding, as he often does, his immediate reaction is to cry out: "How can I get across to my employees some understanding of the objectives I seek?" Well, that question may be important, but perhaps it should not have such priority. It might be better to ask first: "What, in truth, do I seek? What objectives do I have that my employees can also share?"

Some administrators, of course, have not bothered their heads with such intricate problems, feeling that "only results count" or "actions speak louder than words." But advertising and public relations men have demonstrated how inadequate this view is; words and the things they connote are as much a part of our experience as the things that we perceive immediately and directly. And top-rank administrators such as Chester I. Barnard know also that one of the first and greatest functions of leadership is that the leader express for his group the ideals toward which they all, consciously or unconsciously, strive.

Winston Churchill's powerful "blood, sweat, and tears" speech in 1940 has now become a classic model in the political field of the way in which a leader can express the purpose of the people and rally them to common effort. Businessmen, especially those of us concerned with personnel, productivity, and morale, have come to recognize the need for much the same kind of leadership, convinced that only in this way will employees ever have the satisfaction of really feeling they are identified with the enterprise for which they work.

But in seeking to exert such leadership we have already learned that there are some difficult problems of communication in the way. Take the many attempts that have been made, following the example of such companies as Du Pont, General Electric, and Republic Steel, to give supervisors and workers in business some understanding of the economic and political society in which we live. The general experience is that the terms "capitalism," "competition," "American way of life," "land of opportunity," and "free private enterprise," through excessive repetition, abuse, or otherwise, have lost much of their capacity to convey the meaning intended.

Moreover, where new symbols have been introduced for the old, they too have missed the mark. The editors of *Fortune*, for example, have characterized our society as the "permanent revolution," but we do not think of ourselves as revolutionaries—at least not of the bearded and bomb-carrying kind. Other attempts to call our society "open" or "free" have raised the perplexing questions: Open for what? Free for what?

It seems to me that we businessmen ought to aim at articulating an ideology that, in addition to being an accurate expression of management goals, is a little closer to the personal and even religious aspirations of the people than anything we have espoused in the past. Is it not possible that we have been thinking too much in terms of systems, of economics, of products, of laws? Perhaps these approaches should not have failed as they did; perhaps they can be improved. But in any event it seems to me that the fact of their failure (or, at best, their lack of any great success) should be accepted, and that the most profitable line of inquiry is to turn to a different sort of approach altogether.

The Creative Ideal

Accordingly, I put forward this simple proposition: that our society is a creative society; that its prime objective, as well as its great genius, is its creativeness; and that, as creative accomplishment is the actual day-to-day goal of modern business, it is also the keystone of our business philosophy.

I am thinking of creativeness in its widest and deepest sense. Thus, business does not exist merely to produce more goods and services, or better goods and services for more people, though that is no small part of its task. Business also, particularly in these days, affords the principal or the only means whereby individual men may gain the satisfaction of accomplishing something more than merely sustaining their own lives. Pleasure, power, and fame appear to be but by-products of the efforts we make to be useful members of society and to leave it with something more than it had when we arrived. Perhaps we leave only the grain of sand that Robert Frost said he wished to leave on the beach of history; but at least, if we do that, we can feel that we have fulfilled our role in living.

What I am suggesting is that the great goals of happiness, freedom, security—even goodness and truth—are values that should be viewed as subordinate to, and resulting from, a new and positive creative ideal. Our people in business and elsewhere seem to be driven by an urge to build; by a longing to explore and reach out; by a desire to realize, through men and for men, such things and experiences as humanity has never known before. In this light, our vaunted freedoms of thought and action, our sought-for freedoms from worry and want, and even our ethical standards of behavior (products as they are of other places and times) are not ends in themselves; rather, they emerge as important values just because they support and make possible a creative society of men.

This is the modern heresy: that it is not enough to be good, to lead a blameless life; we must also be creative.

THE NEW AND THE OLD

In one sense this ideal is modern in expression only. Wise men in almost every age have been trying to tell us that the greatest individual satisfaction there is comes from a job well done. Samuel Johnson, for example, observed: "Life affords no higher pleasure than that of surmounting difficulties, passing from one step of success to another, forming new wishes and seeing them gratified." And Emerson said: "The *sum* of wisdom is that the time is never lost that is devoted to work."

In another sense, however, this ideal of ours shows some new, significantly new, aspects. Specifically, in American business it is now beginning to be recognized that *everyone* has the capacity for the satisfaction that comes from creative accomplishment. As science unleashes vast new sources of power, it appears possible for the first time in history for men of all types and classes to avoid the toil and suffering of hard labor and to experience the joys of work—a satisfaction that in times past was limited to the few.

Contrast this with the older view. We used to classify as creative only those accomplishments that certain individuals could achieve. The writer, the artist, the composer, the scientist—in other words, the rare people who had the genius to find and express new ideas or new truths—were considered the creative members of our society; the classic examples have been the Newtons, the Beethovens, the Kants, the Michelangelos, the Shakespeares. The magnitude of their work often crushed us by making us feel our own inadequacy.

Today, however, we are beginning to recognize that creative work may be accomplished collectively as well as individually. The great and small organizations that have built and operated our industrial plants, farms, transportation and communication networks, financial systems, and distributive organizations, all are examples of the creative genius that comes from the collective effort of administrators and workers, as well as specialists of all degrees.

DIMENSION OF THE TASK

The first task of business leaders, therefore, is to create an environment in which there can flourish not only individual genius but, more important, the collective capacities of other people in the organization. Some difficult and searching questions must be answered if this task is to be accomplished. What are the basic positive forces operating in a creative business society? What generates their power? What keeps them in balance? What conditions their survival? What controls their direction?

To this end, I should like to submit that the creative ideal depends on these concepts:

1. That the forces in business (and many other types of organization) are nurtured by the existence of *differences between individuals and groups*.

2. That these forces are kept in control and balance by the process of *individuals understanding each other*.

3. That a creative society depends for its survival upon the belief that *rights must be matched by obligations*.

4. That the directing force in a creative society is the *faith* of its members in *individual growth*.

The Power of Difference

In considering the importance of individual difference, it should first be noted that the goal of many societies—including the goal of communist society today and of almost every utopia that has ever been conceived, from Plato to Aldous Huxley—has been to compel men to conform. The theory is that if everyone is induced to accept the same ideas of what is good and proper, conflicts between men and groups of men will disappear and humanity will live happily ever after.

By contrast, one of the cornerstones on which the creative society is built is the incontrovertible fact that men are different, that they cherish these differences, that the joy and fascination of life depend on the existence of differences, and that there are great social values in differences.

DRIVING FORCE

Every great ideal has its own theory of the nature of man. The wholly competitive or acquisitive society, which is gone (if it ever in fact existed), assumed that man was motivated only by his own pleasure, that he was egoistic and greedy, and that his wants were insatiable. By assuming that the average man, the economic man, was moved by animal impulses, it was possible to work out satisfactory theoretical explanations of how men acted in the marketplace.

On the other hand, socialists have assumed, following the notions of Rousseau (and possibly the story of Genesis), that man was essentially good, self-sacrificing, considerate, and loving, but was corrupted by social institutions. On this basis they thought that if institutions were changed or destroyed and if nonconforming individuals and classes were eliminated, then all social problems would cease and the state could and would wither away.

But in a creative society neither of these views is adequate. We observe that men are both egoistic and self-sacrificing—and many things more. While men are, taken as a whole, driven by an urge to create and grow, their characteristics vary with their times, experiences, culture, inheritance, and with all the other circumstances in which they find themselves. To illustrate with a simple example:

In the company with which I am associated we are using, as an aid in selection and placement, a test of personality or temperament in which the results are described not in imprecise words but in graphic form. Taking several major behavior characteristics, it plots with a fair degree of accuracy where a given individual falls on each of several temperament spectra. For instance, there is a spectrum of gregariousness in which the extreme extrovert falls at one end and the extreme introvert at the other; in between are those having various needs for sociability or a capacity to live within themselves.

Thousands upon thousands of tests of this type have been made, and it is fair to say that in no two cases have the results—the combinations of characteristics on the several spectra—been exactly the same. Similarity of types may be observed, but every man and every woman is found to be unique. Furthermore, research into personality shows that men change their personalities, usually extremely slowly but sometimes dramatically. It also shows that behavior is not wholly a matter for the individual alone but depends in large part on the situation in which he finds himself. That is, the set of values according to which he makes his decision may vary with his external circumstances.

The driving force of difference—in individuals and in groups—seems well illustrated by the history of the United States and Canada (in contrast to some other countries). While no doubt we have strong forces in many companies, labor unions, churches, and schools that are trying to enforce a high degree of conformity to some particular viewpoint, practice, or belief, nevertheless those forces have been observably less dominant than the forces of individual integrity. In our business world, if a man has felt that he could do a job better than someone else, he has been free to try; indeed, the fact that he saw things differently has given him both the opportunity and the courage to try.

Moreover, there is good reason to believe that the differences between groups of people in the United States and Canada with respect to cultural, racial, and religious backgrounds have been a factor in the dynamic development of these countries. What does it mean that never before in history have so many diverse religious groups been able to live together with so little disharmony? Has our society progressed *in spite of* differences or *because of* them? Possibly the very existence of differences among various people and groups has given people the courage to disagree with prevailing opinions. Every discovery, every invention, every new industry, every new idea has come about because some person or some group of people has had the courage as well as the insight to disagree with the majority or do what the majority has not thought of doing before.

This is perhaps part of what David McCord Wright had in mind when he pointed out:

"Our dilemma . . . is that if we make man 'free,' they will become creative and from their creations will spring the probability of growth and the certainty of trouble."[1]

DIVERSITY RATHER THAN CONFLICT

Differences do, of course, lead to trouble—to misunderstanding and conflict. Yet conflict is essential to constructive work. More than a generation ago Mary Parker Follett, a woman who has since become recognized for her many profound insights into the nature of business organizations, wrote:

What people often mean by getting rid of conflict is getting rid of diversity, and it is of the utmost importance that these should not be considered the same. We may wish to abolish conflict, but we cannot get rid of diversity. We must face life as it is and

1. *The Impact of the Union* (New York, Harcourt, Brace and Company, 1951), p. 274.

understand that diversity is its most essential feature. . . . Fear of difference is dread of life itself. It is possible to conceive of conflict as not necessarily a wasteful outbreak of incompatibilities but a *normal* process by which socially valuable differences register themselves for the enrichment of all concerned.[2]

Creativeness in an organization depends to a large extent on people who are not too ready to agree. In our own experience, most of us abhor the attitude of "Well, if you're going to argue about it, let's do it your way." We have found that we must have diversity of opinion, firmly as well as fairly expressed, if our business is to make the wise decisions that will enable it to develop and grow.

If we accept difference, it necessarily follows that we are not sure we are right ourselves; we accept the notion that our conclusions about people and society must be treated only as working hypotheses and that there are realities beyond those of our immediate perceptions. It is sometimes forgotten how highly we esteem this concept in the physical sciences. The entire atomic world of neutrons and electrons has never been perceived directly; despite Hiroshima and Nagasaki, it is still a theory or a working hypothesis. The same hypothetical character pertains to all of our knowledge about genes—the transmission of traits from organisms to their offspring.

But if it is necessary to trust to more than our immediate perceptions in the physical sciences, it would seem even more important to do so in social, ethical, and political matters that deal with human beings. The observation of Yale's F.C.S. Northrop, that the ability to live in a world of both immediate perceptions and unperceived hypotheses is the essence of the genius of the West, would apply no less to our industrial and political society than to our scientific progress.

This means that we must subject our old concepts of right and wrong, of good and bad, to a radical change; things are no longer so black and white. Judge Learned Hand, philosopher as well as judge, has described the spirit of liberty as "the spirit that is not too sure that it is right." Tolerance for difference, for the viewpoint that we do not agree with, implies that we are not so sure of our own. We accept our principles of action as working hypotheses, realizing that something may happen to lead us to revise these opinions. While it often sounds as though some of our friends would never change their opinions (particularly on matters of ethics or politics), our great genius lies in the fact that we may talk loudly but, when the chips are down, we seem to act on the basis that all general rules of what is right and wrong must be tempered by common sense.

It can be reasonably contended that the great upheavals of modern history— its wars and its revolutions—are not so much the result of differences between

2. *Creative Experiences* (New York, Longmans, Green & Co., 1924), pp. 300-301.

people as of the feeling of a nation or a class that its capacity for creative expression is in some way threatened or thwarted. This was one cause of the Russian revolt of 1917, although the revolutionaries themselves later made the great and historic blunder of seeking to abolish conflict by abolishing difference rather than by accepting difference and in that way removing the barriers to creative work.

Nations such as ours, that have insisted on the freedom of their people to be different, have had to fight and may well fight again to preserve their right to disagree with one another. Yet, if the principle of difference is one of the cornerstones of creativeness, our society has little to fear *in the long run* from the Stalins who deny the privilege of difference to their own people.

Process of Understanding

If diversity is the first condition of the creative society, then understanding is the second. The Bible's exhortation "with all thy getting, get understanding" is particularly appropriate for modern industry. If for their dynamic creative power our businesses depend on continuing differences in viewpoint, for balance and braking power they must equally depend on understanding, on the felt necessity for securing agreement and cooperation.

In the sense that I am using the term, understanding refers both to self-understanding and understanding of others. Self-awareness as a desirable personal attribute is certainly not newer than the Socratic injunction "Know thyself"; but what is new in our time is the fact that thoughtful social scientists and hardheaded businessmen are coming to see that self-awareness or self-understanding is directly related to an individual's capacity to do creative work with other people. Businessmen are beginning to think not only of the logics of business but also of what Pareto described as the nonlogics or the sentiments of people. They are beginning to see that their own behavior is a factor that influences the behavior of others, and that they are personally involved in more roles than one in every situation in which they play a part.

Let me illustrate from my own personal experience:

For a short time, some years ago, I engaged in the general practice of law. Later I was employed as a lawyer by an insurance company. As a lawyer I found that my clients' problems were not mine; and no matter how hard I tried to solve them, I stood outside of the situation and was not involved in it. But when later I took an administrative position, I found that this detachment was no longer possible, even if I wanted it. I was personally involved in every important decision, and my behavior was affecting others. The shock of being forced to examine my own behavior was by no means small. What I needed to do, however, was no less than what all successful administrators are doing daily in every business.

In addition to self-awareness there is the need for understanding others. What we are learning today is not just that it is a "good thing to see the other fellow's point of view" but also what it is that often makes it difficult to do so. We are learning that we cannot really understand another if we agree with him, nor can we understand him if we disagree! When we feel either love or hate, we lose our power to see the world as others see it. We blur our own perceptions, and we cut off the normal flow of words that help us see into another's mind.

COMMUNICATION GATEWAYS

This conclusion has tremendous significance. If understanding the needs and desires of others is an essential for collective creative effort, it means that we can no longer be quick to evaluate people or their opinions as either good or bad. During the understanding process at least, we must throw our ethical judgments out the window.

Carl R. Rogers and F. J. Roethlisberger made this same point when in essence they said that the great barrier to communication is our tendency to evaluate, to approve or disapprove the statements that other people make.[3] For example:

If you say to me, "I prefer Englishmen to the French," there is almost an overwhelming urge for me to say either "So do I" or "No, I think they are stuffy." We may then talk for hours without a meeting of the minds. If, on the other hand, I want to find out whether we really agree or disagree about this matter, if I want to listen intelligently and to understand what you mean, thus opening the gateway to communication, then I must restrain my natural inclination to presume what you mean and instead make an effort to draw you out. I might ask something like, "Do you mean Englishmen are more to be admired?" You may reply, "Yes, they are really facing up to their economic problems better than the French." And if I continue in that way, rephrasing your comments in question form to test out what you are *trying* to tell me, there is a much better chance that we can have a fruitful discussion.

This brief explanation of a gateway to understanding, of receiving communications, of listening, may sound extremely obvious and somewhat simple. We spend most of our time learning to express ourselves, which is difficult enough but still easier than listening. Indeed, it is fair to say that listening is one of the most difficult things in the world to do. When someone charges into your office and criticizes some action that you have taken, it is not easy to find out what is

3. "Barriers and Gateways to Communication," HBR July-August 1952, p. 46.

really on his mind when your first impulse is to tell him to "go to hell." Or take the case where somebody asks you for your advice because he cannot make up his mind about a personal problem; most of us are inclined to comply with such a request without knowing what the real problem is, or without realizing that the decision will be sound only if it is made by the troubled person himself.

It takes real insight to be able to express in words what someone else is trying to tell us. It also takes great effort and even courage. If we put ourselves in someone else's position, if we try to express adequately his point of view, we may find that our own views become changed in the process. Professor Rogers says, "The risk of being changed is one of the most frightening prospects many of us can face."[4]

There are, of course, many other ways of securing understanding; some of them have been outlined by Stuart Chase in his recent popularization of social science, *Roads to Agreement*.[5] One is particularly worth mentioning:

This way is modeled on the long-established custom of the Quaker business meeting. Quakers as a class are great individualists, but in handling the business affairs of their churches they act only with unanimity. They have no formal voting, no sense of a majority imposing its will on a reluctant minority. If a problem cannot be settled by unanimous agreement, they invoke periods of silence or put over the question until some future meeting. Some solution is usually forthcoming.

This rule of unanimity, it seems, is now being practiced by boards of directors and executive committees in businesses throughout the land. What a far cry this is from deciding what is the greatest good for the greatest number by a mechanical counting of hands! Where difference is accepted, it is possible also to accept the notion that a minority may be right.

INTEGRATION VS. COMPROMISE

The concept of integration as opposed to compromise is also achieving a wider recognition. Integration may be called the means of solving a conflict of opinion in such a way that both sides prevail. The idea behind it is that the basic interests underlying many disputes are not inconsistent. For example:

If two people in an office want to use the same desk, it may appear at first that a major conflict is in the making, which can be solved only if one or the other wins the decision. On investigation, however, it may appear that one of the persons wants the desk in order to have better light, whereas the other wants it in order to be near some friend. If these facts come out, it will be apparent that neither wants the desk as such and that it may well be possible to satisfy the basic interests of both.

4. Ibid, p. 48.
5. New York, Harper & Brothers, 1951, pp. 45 ff.

In order to achieve integration, says Miss Follett, we should "never, if possible, allow an either/or situation to be created. . . . There are almost always more than two alternatives in a situation and our job is to analyze the situation carefully enough for as many as possible to appear. A yes-or-no question is in itself a prejudgment."[6]

May there not be some relationship between these methods of reaching understanding and the spirit that is not too sure that it is right? Is there not some connection between these techniques of agreement and our capacity for collective creativeness? Can it not be said that in a creative society we must have both conflict and agreement?

Rights and Obligations

A third standard of a creative society, and an essential ingredient in our workaday world, has been foreshadowed by the previous discussion of difference and of understanding. It is the belief that human relationships are two-way matters and that rights are matched by obligations.

THE "DOUBLE PLUS"

Karl Marx predicted that in Western society it was inevitable that the rich would become richer and the poor would become poorer. This increasing division between the classes would, as he saw it, accelerate class warfare and the revolution. If our society had indeed been basically competitive and acquisitive, instead of creative and cooperative, Marx might well have been proved right. But the fact is that today, through our collective creativeness, the poor have become richer. Our society has been able to create wealth at a vastly greater rate than it has increased its population.

By and large, we have been able to maintain the viewpoint that our economic and political problem is not so much to redistribute the wealth that exists as to create more wealth for all. As the eminent economist Kenneth Boulding has written, "Economic life is not a 'zero-sum' poker game in which a fixed volume of wealth is circulated among the players, but a 'positive-sum' enterprise in which the accumulation of each person represents something he brings to the 'pot' rather than something he takes out."[7] In other words, we are engaged in a creative task of producing more and better things. We recognize that we share

6. *Dynamic Administration—The Collected Papers of Mary Parker Follett* (New York, Harper & Brothers, 1940), pp. 219-220.

7. "Religious Foundations of Economic Progress," HBR May-June 1952, p. 36.

as we contribute, that no society can long give something for nothing (to the poor *or* the rich), and that we cannot do great work unless *everyone* shares both in the work and in its results.

This concept has been called by many names. Mutuality is one; give-and-take is another. Professor Charles I. Gragg of the Harvard Business School calls it the "double plus." As he sees it, business transactions and other relationships can be described in one of three ways:

1. There is first the kind of a transaction in which the plus is all on my side, leaving a big minus for you. If I take all the profit, however, through my power or my cleverness, then I have really lost the bargain, because you will come to distrust me and will refuse to do business with me for long.

2. The reverse situation is equally disastrous. If I, through an excess of altruism or with misguided notions of humanity, permit you to take the entire profit, with nothing for myself, I put you in the unhappy role of being a recipient of my charity; moreover, I leave myself unable to do further business with anyone.

3. But there is still another and more satisfactory form. Only if you profit moderately and I profit moderately, only if there is a plus for you and a plus for me—a double plus—can we continue to deal with one another steadily and with confidence.

In our business lives we are beginning to see that by consciously fashioning our relationships with our employees, with our suppliers, with our customers—and, indeed, even with our competitors—we are not making suspicious and careful deals so much as common-sense arrangements that are carried on in this spirit of mutual give-and-take. That does not mean anything petty like back-scratching; every service and every kindness is not to be immediately returned, nor is every service to be performed in the hope of return. The correct attitude, rather, is a healthy respect for the well-being and personal integrity of the other fellow.

PROFIT FOR ALL

What does all this imply? Only in an atmosphere of profit (in the broad sense) to all parties can we meet the creative objectives that our society sets. If, in times past, we erred on the side of taking too much for ourselves, it is equally essential that we do not err in the future on the side of trying to do too much for others. A too-literal application of the Sermon on the Mount—the turn of the cheek—does small damage to us but great damage to him who strikes the blow.

Why is it, otherwise, that the problem of providing for the aged worker has once more raised its head, when we thought a few years ago that we had safely tucked it away with compulsory retirement and pensioning at age 65? From the point of view of sympathy for the aged and of convenience in administering our business enterprises, the practice is as desirable today as it was 15 years ago. We have discovered, however, that many individual men who retire are hurt because they lose their sense of being creative, of being useful members of society. Moreover, when we contemplate that 11% of our population will be over 65 in another 20 years, we begin to realize that the real economic cost of compulsory retirement is not the money that goes into pensions but the lost productivity of these older people.

It seems that people, individually and in groups, must continue to be creative; if they are not, the individual or society, or both, will suffer. If we do not intend to keep people over 65 in business, some other way must be found to permit them to continue active membership in the world's work.

The same kind of thinking underlies our concern for other noncontributors to society. Society has been doing an increasingly successful job of minimizing sickness of almost all kinds, not so much out of solicitude for the feelings of persons who are ill as out of its own self-interest in having the benefit of their contribution. Programs undertaken with this motive quickly earn common respect, for the galling part of illness to the sufferer is the necessity of having to depend on others, of not being able to contribute his share.

We are concerned for similar reasons about the criminal and the indolent. It is true that we have not as yet learned enough to be confident of our ability to rehabilitate these people. But we have at least learned that it is no answer to judge them or to punish them; our first task is to understand them. We consider them "cured" only when they join the majority of their fellows, contributing commensurately to what they receive.

Why do businessmen fight against the welfare state? Are businessmen actually heartless and callous? Don't they recognize that the sick and the poor need the aid of the rest who are well and able? Of course they do. But their experience says to them that doctors do not give pills to everyone because a few are sick; that when a man is given something for which he has not worked, he feels degraded; that a man who is well and able wants to earn what he receives.

Businessmen, who have learned from experience that paternalism has failed, hope that government will learn from their mistakes. Businessmen have good reason for believing that government will not really serve the poor and sick until it stops regarding them as "little people" and undertakes instead the harder job of giving them an honest chance to do useful and creative work.

Faith in Men's Growth

The fourth and last condition of maintaining and strengthening a creative society, the force that provides direction and control, is a clear faith in the growth and development of men. The machine age poses a great challenge to our willingness to demonstrate this faith. All of the new wealth we can produce with modern technology is of little avail if in the process men are reduced to the levels of the machines they tend. But fortunately we are not confronted with a Hobson's choice between wealth and men. We have found that the more we are able to train and develop men as individuals, leaving repetitive work to machines, the greater satisfactions they obtain and the more productive (in a material sense) they become.

Take a business with a large content of routine clerical work—e.g., life insurance. In this business we stand on the threshold of a new era in adapting electronics to office workers' problems. When any business reaches this point, to be sure, management is bound to face the problem of securing the cooperation of people who may prefer things as they are. It may even have to face a problem of technological unemployment. But however real and thorny these difficulties are, they are insignificant compared to the human values that are gained. Instead of a business in which, say, 75% of the employees are engaged in routine tasks, the modern machine makes it possible for 75% to be engaged in tasks requiring skill and judgment. The machine eliminates human toil; but, much more important, it also provides opportunities for men to do only those tasks men alone can do.

NEW CONCEPT OF ORGANIZATION

The development of the machine economy has numerous important implications for management. For one thing, it is fast bringing about a new concept of business organization. No longer can the boss know all the details and the intricacies of the operation he supervises. He is being forced more and more to rely on his subordinates, to consult with them, to be guided by their joint conclusions—in short, to permit them to share and to grow in breadth of vision.

This in turn means, of course, a gradual abandonment of authoritarian principles. Administrators have begun to conceive of their role not as manipulators of labor but as coordinators of functions. Reexamining themselves and their jobs, they have discovered that they have no special claim to superior wisdom, no vested authority over the work and lives of others. They have found, rather, that they have a function to perform: to plan ahead, to coordinate the others, to secure their interest and cooperation.

Society will not, as a result, tend to become classless in any Marxian sense. Far from it. We may reasonably anticipate, however, that members of future "elites" will come to occupy positions of status and power less because of wealth, position, or birth and more because of the kind of contributions they make or because of the kind of functions they fulfill. Key positions will tend more and more to be occupied by those who are best able to conceive new ideas and the application of old ones, who are best able to communicate ideas and events, and who are best able to pull together people and things to achieve creative ends. Today's inheritance tax and management's increased interest in personnel development are fast speeding this process along.

ADMINISTRATORS AS TEACHERS

In an important sense the role of the administrator seems destined to become more and more that of the instructor—the kind of teacher who understands his pupils, accepts their differences, commands their respect, and inspires them to creative work of every kind. In such a role, administrators will have less of a problem of discipline to the degree that they are able to develop an environment for creative experience and to lead their students (their workers) to savor the satisfying taste of personal accomplishment. In so doing they will have gone far to eliminate the distinction between "schooling" and "education" that Mark Twain quite properly made when he quipped, "I have never let my schooling interfere with my education."

In their new role as teachers, administrators are learning that attitudes and viewpoints which affect behavior can frequently be communicated effectively only if they are reduced to concrete terms. In their efforts at training and development, particularly, they are recognizing the need to start from real case situations. Witness the growing attention to discussions of actual business problems rather than the oft-repeated clichés on general principles of management.

Abstract ideas, however, are not to be discarded simply because they so often fail to influence behavior. Indeed, as the mark of civilized men they are necessary tools of communication which are quite adequate *if* both writer and reader start from the same premises. They are easily accepted, in other words, if they seem meaningful in relation to one's own experience. Aneurin Bevan's autobiography affords an example of this:

Bevan's life as a young Welsh miner was filled with frustrations. Then he read Karl Marx. This experience "had all the impact of divine revelation. Everything fell in place. The dark places were lighted up and the difficult ways made easy."[8] Marx is most

8. *In Place of Fear* (New York, Simon and Schuster, 1952), p. 19.

abstract, but nevertheless his words have had a great effect on people whose experience has led them to feel like chained and exploited men.

The moral of this fact has not been lost on businessmen and statesmen, who know that the only real and lasting bulwark against Marxism is in the experience of the large body of our workers and our citizens. If that experience is basically creative and satisfying—and it is management's task to see that it is so—the stultifying conformities of the socialist state will always be bitter to their taste.

But businessmen and statesmen, while often seeing what is the best *defense* against Marxism, have not been so quick to see what needs to be done in a *positive* way. Like Marxians, we too must have an appropriate body of abstract ideas—ideas that can constitute a simple article of faith but are also capable of profound extension, ideas that are consistent with experience but are also adaptable to new insights and new truths.

Perhaps this discussion will stimulate others to work out such ideas—each in his own way, as a part of our individual differences, but all toward the same goal, in the spirit of mutuality. What I have written can be no more than a preface.

Conclusion

The problems of production, distribution, and finance are usually foreign to a worker's experience and interests. It is therefore just as silly for top management to hope that workers will be anxious to understand the problems of the business as it would be to fear that they are interested in gaining control of the business. What workers do appear to want is a chance to increase their usefulness and creativeness, a chance to develop their full potential as individuals within the scope of their environment and experience. It has become part of management's function to see not only that they have that chance but that the philosophy behind it is made articulate.

But the creative society is based on more than the relationship between management and workers, indispensable though that is in our industrial age. It depends on close relationships between all fields of human endeavor. Business is not "just business." The Chinese wall between business and the home, the community, the school, and the church has long since been stormed. Business is all people, places, and things; it is physics, economics, politics, sociology, psychology, philosophy, ethics, and aesthetics.

In the same broad sense, business is also religion. One of the recurring themes in most religions is that God is viewed as the Creator and that creativeness is one of His essential attributes. Another recurring theme is that man's spirit, his conscious "self," his unique ability to transcend his material and animal limitations, is the essence of God in man. To suggest that creativeness may be a basic attribute of men in society is thus merely to relate these two ageless insights.

Moreover, it seems that a religious sense of wonder, humility, and faith helps us to see the vision of a boundless future built by the inherent capacities of men from all walks of life and of all races, creeds, natures, and backgrounds. It is a vision of cooperation, togetherness, and sharing the great adventure. It is a vision of independence and courage that explores the far reaches of the universe and probes deep into the essence of what we call man. It is, in short, a vision of a changing, growing, and infinitely exciting world which depends for its existence on the spirit that is not too sure it is right, on a deep-seated desire to open our minds and our hearts to the lives of others, on the practical sense of give-and-take, on our faith in the growth and development of ourselves and our fellow men.

Retrospective Commentary

The author of an article that is exhumed some 15 years after publication has mixed feelings. In some ways he feels as though he were seeing a ghost. In other ways he feels like a father of a foundling who hears that the boy has grown up and won a prize at school: as a father he is proud, but his pride is limited by the knowledge that his own contribution was made in the very distant past.

Reviewing the results of these distant events, I believe I would not write the article much differently if I were to write it today. The events of 15 years, I think, have not proved me wrong.

I still believe that the business of business is discovery, innovation, and creativity. I still believe the job of management is to maintain creativity with order—and order with creativity. I still believe creativity without order breeds chaos, and that order without creativity is a living death.

There is one aspect of the article, however, to which I might want to give greater emphasis if I were writing today—namely, the role of time. As the article suggests, difference, understanding, and mutuality are essential elements in a creative enterprise and should be accorded adequate time so they can be fully operative. Today I am perhaps more aware of the fact that everything has a price in time. Sometimes the price is too high. Sometimes diversity and understanding must be sacrificed to competitive pressures and other dangers.

I continue to believe that most things *can* be done—given sufficient time. The administrator can control, to a considerable extent, the rate of change within his own organization, but he finds it immeasurably more difficult to affect the rate of social change for a society as a whole. This latter rate continues to be agonizingly slow as race riots at home and the war in Viet Nam so amply illustrate.

Nothing I say today, however, can change what I left on the HBR doorstep many years ago. If the foundling has survived, he speaks on his own. And if, gentle reader, you should disagree, please take it up with him, not me. —A.T.C.

26. "Skyhooks": With Special Implications for Monday Through Friday

O. A. Ohmann

Every human being, this observer of organizational behavior asserts, needs "skyhooks"—something that he can believe in and trust and that gives meaning to his activities. (Some say it is God manifesting himself.) In recent years our industrialized society has engendered certain trends that have made the need for skyhooks more important and the possession of skyhooks less accessible: abundance without satisfaction, disillusionment with the notion that science represents the whole truth, and the trend toward bigness. The author calls on managers to meet employees' needs by giving them the maximum opportunity to use their talents and take on responsibility. Originally published in 1955, Ohmann's article was reissued in 1970 as an "HBR Classic," with a retrospective commentary by the author.

During the last several years, while my principal job assignment has been management development, I have become increasingly impressed with the importance of intangibles in the art of administration. With the managerial revolution of the last generation and the transition from owner-manager to professional executive, there has appeared a growing literature on the science and art of administration. A shift in emphasis is noticeable in these writings over the past 30 years.

Following the early engineering approach typified by the work of Frederick Taylor and others, there next developed a search for the basic principles of organization, delegation, supervision, and control. More recently, as labor relations became more critical, the emphasis has shifted to ways of improving human relations. The approach to the problems of supervisory relationships was essentially a manipulative one. Textbooks on the techniques of personnel management mushroomed. Still later it became more and more apparent that the crux of the problem was the supervisor himself, and this resulted in a flood of "how to improve yourself" books. Meanwhile the complexities of the industrial community increased, and the discontents and tensions mounted.

It seems increasingly clear, at least to me, that while some administrative practices and personnel techniques may be better than others, their futility arises from the philosophical assumptions or value judgments on which this superstructure of manipulative procedure rests. We observe again and again that a manager with sound values and a stewardship conception of his role as boss can be a pretty effective leader even though his techniques are quite unorthodox. I am convinced that workers have a fine sensitivity to spiritual qualities and want to work for a boss who believes in something and in whom they can believe.

This observation leads me to suspect that we may have defined the basic purposes and objectives of our industrial enterprise too narrowly, too selfishly, too materialistically. Bread alone will not satisfy workers. There are some indications that our people have lost faith in the basic values of our economic society, and that we need a spiritual rebirth in industrial leadership.

Certainly no people have ever had so much, and enjoyed so little real satisfaction. Our economy has been abundantly productive, our standard of living is at an all-time peak, and yet we are a tense, frustrated, and insecure people full of hostilities and anxieties. Can it be that our *god of production* has feet of clay? Does industry need a new religion—or at least a better one than it has had?

I am convinced that the central problem is not the division of the spoils as organized labor would have us believe. Raising the price of prostitution does not make it the equivalent of love. Is our industrial discontent not in fact the expression of a hunger for a work life that has meaning in terms of higher and more enduring spiritual values? How can we preserve the wholeness of the personality if we are expected to worship God on Sundays and holidays and mammon on Mondays through Fridays?

I do not imply that this search for real meaning in life is or should be limited to the hours on the job, but I do hold that the central values of our industrial society permeate our entire culture. I am sure we do not require a bill of particulars of the spiritual sickness of our time. The evidences of modern man's search for his soul are all about us. Save for the communist countries there has been a worldwide revival of interest in religion. The National Council of Churches reports that 59% of our total population (or 92 million) now claim church affiliation. The November 22, 1954, issue of *Barron's* devoted the entire front page to a review of a book by Barbara Ward, *Faith and Freedom*.[1]

Perhaps even more significant is the renaissance in the quality of religious thought and experience. Quite evidently our religion of materialism, science,

1. New York, W. W. Norton & Company, 1954.

and humanism is not considered adequate. Man is searching for anchors outside himself. He runs wearily to the periphery of the spider web of his own reason and logic, and looks for new "skyhooks"—for an abiding faith around which life's experiences can be integrated and given meaning.

Why "Skyhooks"?

Perhaps we should assume that this need for "skyhooks" is part of man's natural equipment—possibly a function of his intelligence—or, if you prefer, God manifesting Himself in His creatures. It seems to me, however, that the recent intensification of this need (or perhaps the clearer recognition of it) stem in part from certain broad social, economic, political, and philosophical trends. I shall not attempt a comprehensive treatment of these, but shall allude to only a few.

ABUNDANCE WITHOUT SATISFACTION

I have already indicated that on the economic front we have won the battle of production. We have moved from an economy of scarcity to one of abundance. We have become masters of the physical world and have learned how to convert its natural resources to the satisfaction of our material wants. We are no longer so dependent and so intimately bound to the world of nature. In a way we have lost our feeling of being part of nature and with it our humble reverence for God's creation.

While the industrialization of our economy resulted in ever-increasing production, it also made of individual man a production number—an impersonal, de-skilled, interchangeable production unit, measured in so many cents per hour. For most employees, work no longer promotes the growth of personal character by affording opportunities for personal decision, exercise of judgment, and individual responsibility. A recent issue of *Nation's Business* quotes the modern British philosopher, Alexander Lindsay, on this point as follows:

"Industrialism has introduced a new division into society. It is the division between those who manage and take responsibility and those who are managed and have responsibility taken from them. This is a division more important than the division between the rich and poor."[2]

Certainly the modern industrial worker has improved his material standard of living at the cost of becoming more and more dependent on larger and larger

2. John Kord Lagemann, "Job Enlargement Boosts Production," December 1954, p. 36.

groups. Not only his dignity but also his security has suffered. And so he reaches out for new "skyhooks"—for something to believe in, for something that will give meaning to his job.

DISILLUSIONMENT WITH SCIENCE

A second trend that seems to bear some relation to our urgent need for a faith grows out of our disillusionment with science. As a result of the rapid advance of science, the curtains of ignorance and superstition have been pulled wide on all fronts of human curiosity and knowledge. Many of the bonds of our intellectual enslavement have been broken. Reason and scientific method were called on to witness to the truth, the whole truth, and nothing but the truth. We were freed from the past—its traditions, beliefs, philosophies, its mores, morals, and religion. Science became our religion, and reason replaced emotion.

However, even before the atom bomb there was a growing realization that science did not represent the whole truth, that with all its pretensions it could be dead wrong, and, finally and particularly, that without proper moral safeguards the truth did not necessarily make men free. Atomic fission intensified the fear and insecurity of every one of us who contemplated the possibility of the concentration of power in the hands of men without morals. We want science to be in the hands of men who not only recognize their responsibility to man-made ethical standards (which are easily perverted) but have dedicated themselves to the eternal and absolute standards of God. Thus, while the evidence of material science has been welcomed, our own personal experiences will not permit us to believe that life is merely a whirl of atoms without meaning, purpose, beauty, or destiny.

TREND TOWARD BIGNESS

A third factor contributing to our insecurity is the trend toward bigness and the resulting loss of individuality. This is the day of bigger and bigger business—in every aspect of life. The small is being swallowed by the big, and the big by the bigger. This applies to business, to unions, to churches, to education, to research and invention, to newspapers, to our practice of the professions, to government, and to nations. Everything is getting bigger except the individual, and he is getting smaller and more insignificant and more dependent on larger social units. Whether we like it or not, this is becoming an administrative society, a planned and controlled society, with ever-increasing concentration of power. This is the day of collectivism and public-opinion polls. It is the day when the individual must be *adjusted to the group*—when he must above all else be sensitive to the feelings and attitudes of others, must get an idea of how others expect him to act, and then react to this.

This is the insecure world that David Riesman has described so well in his book *The Lonely Crowd*.[3] He pictures man as being no longer "tradition directed" as was primitive man, nor as in Colonial days is he "inner directed" as if by the gyroscope of his own ideals, but today he is "outer directed" as if by radar. He must constantly keep his antenna tuned to the attitudes and reactions of others to him. The shift has been from morals to morale and from self-reliance to dependence on one's peer group. However, the members of one's peer group are each responding to each other. Obviously these shifting sands of public opinion offer no stable values around which life can be consistently integrated and made meaningful. The high-water mark of adjustment in such a society is that the individual be socially accepted and above all else that he appear to be *sincere*.

This is certainly not a favorable environment for the development of steadfast character. It is essentially a neurotic and schizophrenic environment that breeds insecurity.

This socially dependent society also offers an ideal market for the wares of the "huckster," the propagandist, and the demagogue. Lacking a religious interpretation of the divine nature of man, these merchants in mass reaction have sought the least common denominator in human nature and have beamed the movies and newspapers at the ten-year mental level. One wonders if this approach to people does not make them feel that they have been sold short and that they are capable of much better than is expected of them. Has this demoralizing exposure of the cheapness of our values not intensified our search for something better to believe in?

On top of all these disturbing socioeconomic trends came the war. This certainly was materialism, science, and humanism carried to the logical conclusion. The war made us question our values and our direction. It left us less cocksure that we were right, and more fearful of ourselves as well as of others. It made us fearful of the power that we had gained, and led us to search our soul to determine whether we had the moral strength to assume the leadership role that had been given to us. We have been humbled in our efforts to play god and are about ready to give the job back. Note, however, that this is not a characteristic reaction to war. Typically wars have been followed by a noticeable deterioration of moral standards, of traditional values, and of social institutions.

Perhaps none of these rationalizations for our return to religion is entirely

3. New Haven, Yale University Press, 1950.

valid. I suspect that the search for some kind of overarching integrative principle or idea is the expression of a normal human need. Certainly history would indicate that man's need for a god is eternal even though it may be more keenly sensed in times of adversity. A religion gives a point of philosophical orientation around which life's experiences can be organized and digested. Without the equivalent, a personality cannot be whole and healthy. Short-term goals that need to be shifted with the changing tide do not serve the same integrative function as do the "skyhooks" which are fastened to eternal values. I do not personally regard the current religious revival as a cultural hangover, nor as a regression. Being a mystic I prefer instead to view the need for such a faith as the spark of the Creator in us to drive us on to achieve His will and our own divine destiny.

Why Monday Through Friday?

If we may grant for the moment that modern man *is* searching for deeper meanings in life, we may then ask: What has this to do with industry? If he needs "skyhooks," let him get them in church, or work out his own salvation. The business leaders of the past insisted that "business is business" and that it had little bearing on the individual's private life and philosophy.

There are several reasons why "skyhooks" must be a primary concern of the business administrator:

☐ For the individual the job is the center of life, and its values must be in harmony with the rest of life if he is to be a whole and healthy personality.

☐ This is an industrial society, and its values tend to become those of the entire culture.

☐ The public is insisting that business leaders are in fact responsible for the general social welfare—that the manager's responsibilities go far beyond those of running the business. They have delegated this responsibility to the business executive whether he wishes to play this role or not.

☐ Even if the administrator insists on a narrow definition of his function as merely the production of goods and services as efficiently as possible, it is nevertheless essential that he take these intangibles into account, since they are the real secrets of motivating an organization.

☐ Besides all this the administrator needs a better set of "skyhooks" himself if he is to carry his ever-increasing load of responsibility without cracking up. The fact that so many administrators are taking time to rationalize, defend, and justify the private enterprise system is an outward indication of this need for more significant meanings.

Anything Wrong with Capitalism?

We may ask, then: What specifically is wrong with our capitalistic system of private enterprise? What is wrong with production or with trying to improve our present standard of living? What is wrong with a profit, or with private ownership of capital, or with competition? Is this not the true American way of life?

Nothing is necessarily wrong with these values. There are certainly worse motives than the profit motive. A refugee from communism is reported to have observed: "What a delight to be in the United States, where things are produced and sold with such a nice clean motive as making a profit."

I am not an economist, and it is beyond the scope of this article to attempt a revision of our economic theory. I am tempted, however, to make a couple of observations about these traditional economic concepts:

1. That while the values represented by them are not necessarily wrong, they are certainly pretty thin and do not challenge the best in people.

2. That many of the classical economic assumptions are outmoded and are no longer adequate descriptions of the actual operation of our present-day economy.

For example, the concept of economic man as being motivated by self-interest not only is outmoded by the best current facts of the social sciences, but also fails to appeal to the true nobility of spirit of which we are capable.

The concept of the free and competitive market is a far cry from the highly controlled and regulated economy in which business must operate today. General Motors does not appear to want to put Chrysler out of business, and apparently the union also decided to take the heat off Chrysler rather than to press its economic advantage to the logical conclusion. The assumption that everyone is out to destroy his competitors does not explain the sharing of technology through trade associations and journals. No, we also have tremendous capacity for cooperation when challenged by larger visions. We are daily denying the Darwinian notion of the "survival of the fittest"—which, incidentally, William Graham Sumner, one of the nineteenth-century apologists for our economic system, used for justifying unbridled self-interest and competition.

Certainly the traditional concept of private ownership of capital does not quite correspond to the realities of today's control of large blocks of capital by insurance companies and trusteed funds.

The notion of individual security through the accumulation of savings has largely given way to the collectivist means of group insurance, company annuities, and Social Security.

The concept that all profits belong to the stockholders is no longer enthusiastically supported by either the government or the unions, since both are claiming an increasing cut.

And so, while we may argue that the system of private enterprise is self-regulatory and therefore offers maximum individual freedom, the simple, cold fact is that it is in ever-increasing degree a managed or controlled economy—partly at the insistence of the voters, but largely as the result of the inevitable economic pressures and the trend toward bigness.[4]

Regardless of the rightness or wrongness of these changes in our system of enterprise, the changes have been considerable, and I doubt that classical economic theory can be used as an adequate rationale of its virtues. I am therefore not particularly optimistic about the efficacy of the current campaign to have businessmen "save the private enterprise system and the American way of life" by engaging in wholesale economic education, much of which is based on outmoded concepts.

Much as economic theory needs revision, I fear that this is not likely to cure our ills. Nor do I believe that profit-sharing or any other device for increasing the workers' cut (desirable as these efforts may be) will give us what we really want. It is, rather, another type of sharing that is needed, a sharing of more worthy objectives, a sharing of the management function, and a sharing of mutual respect and Christian working relationships.

GOALS AND PURPOSES

What is wrong is more a matter of goals and purposes—of our assumptions about what we are trying to do and how we can dignify and improve ourselves in the doing. There is nothing wrong with production, but we should ask ourselves: *Production for what?* Do we use people for production or production for people? How can production be justified if it destroys personality and human values both in the process of its manufacture and by its end use? Clarence B. Randall of Inland Steel, in his book, *A Creed for Free Enterprise*, says:

We have come to worship production as an end in itself, which of course it is not. It is precisely there that the honest critic of our way of life makes his attack and finds us

4. See John Kenneth Galbraith, *American Capitalism* (Boston, Houghton Mifflin Company, 1952).

vulnerable. Surely there must be for each person some ultimate value, some purpose, some mode of self-expression that makes the experience we call life richer and deeper.[5]

So far, so good, Mr. Randall. But now notice how he visualizes industry making its contribution to this worthy objective:

To produce more and more with less and less effort is merely treading water unless we *thereby release time and energy for the cultivation of the mind and the spirit* and for the achievement of those ends for which Providence placed us on this earth.[6]

Here is the same old dichotomy—work faster and more efficiently so that you can finish your day of drudgery and cultivate your soul on your own time. In fact he says: "A horse with a very evil disposition can nevertheless pull the farmer's plow." No, I am afraid the job *is* the life. *This* is what must be made meaningful. We cannot assume that the end of production justifies the means. What happens to people in the course of producing may be far more important than the end product. Materialism is not a satisfactory "skyhook." People are capable of better and want to do better. (Incidentally, I have the impression that Mr. Randall's practices line up very well with my own point of view even if his words do not.)

Perhaps we should ask: What is the really important difference between Russian communism and our system? Both worship production and are determined to produce more efficiently, and do. Both worship science. Both have tremendously improved the standard of living of their people. Both share the wealth. Both develop considerable loyalties for their system. (In a mere 40 years since Lenin started the communist revolution a third of the world's people have come to accept its allegiance.) True, in Russia capital is controlled by the state, while here it is theoretically controlled by individuals, although in actual practice, through absentee ownership, it is controlled to a considerable extent by central planning agencies and bureaus, both public and private.

No, the real difference is in the philosophy about people and how they may be used as means to ends. It is a difference in the assumptions made about the origin of rights—whether the individual is endowed with rights by his Creator and yields these only voluntarily to civil authority designated by him, or whether rights originate in force and in the will of the government. Is God a myth, or is He the final and absolute judge to whom we are ultimately responsible? Are all standards of conduct merely man-made and relative, or absolute and eternal? Is man a meaningless happenstance of protoplasm, or is he a divine creation with a purpose, with potential for improvement, and with a special destiny in the overall scheme of things? These are some of the

5. Boston, Little, Brown and Company, 1952, p. 16.
6. Ibid.

differences—or at least I hope that they still are. And what a difference these intangible, perhaps mythical "skyhooks" make. They are nevertheless the most real and worthwhile and enduring things in the world. The absence of these values permitted the Nazis to "process" people through the gas chambers in order to recover the gold in their teeth.

The Administrator Contributes

This, then, is part of our general cultural heritage and is passed on to us in many ways. However, it really comes to life in people—in their attitudes, aspirations, and behaviors. And in a managerial society this brings us back to the quality of the individual administrator. He interprets or crystallizes the values and objectives for his group. He sets the climate within which these values either *do* or *do not* become working realities. He must define the goals and purposes of his group in larger and more meaningful perspective. He integrates the smaller, selfish goals of individuals into larger, more social and spiritual, objectives for the group. He provides the vision without which the people perish. Conflicts are resolved by relating the immediate to the long-range and more enduring values. In fact, we might say this *integrative function* is the core of the administrator's contribution.

The good ones have the mental equipment to understand the business and set sound long-term objectives, but the best ones have in addition the philosophical and character values that help them to relate the overall goals of the enterprise to eternal values. This is precisely the point at which deep-seated religious convictions can serve an integrative function, since they represent the most long-range of all possible goals.[7] Most really great leaders in all fields of human endeavor have been peculiarly sensitive to their historic role in human destiny. Their responsibility and loyalty are to some distant vision that gives calm perspective to the hot issues of the day.

This function of the administrator goes far beyond being a likable personality, or applying correct principles of organization, or being skillful in the so-called techniques of human relations. I am convinced that the difficulties which so many executives have with supervisory relationships cannot be remedied by cultivation of the so-called human relations skills. These difficulties spring, rather, from one's conception of his function or role as a boss, his notion about the origin and nature of his authority over others, the assumptions he makes about people and their worth, and his view of what he and his people are trying to accomplish together. To illustrate:

7. For further elaboration, see Gordon W. Allport, *The Individual and His Religion* (New York, The Macmillan Company, 1953).

If, for example, my personal goal is to get ahead in terms of money, position, and power; and if I assume that to achieve this I must best my competitors; that the way to do this is to establish a good production record; that my employees are means to this end; that they are replaceable production units which must be skillfully manipulated; that this can be done by appealing to the lowest form of immediate selfish interest; that the greatest threat to me is that my employees may not fully recognize my authority or accept my leadership—if these are my values, then I am headed for trouble—all supervisory techniques notwithstanding.

I wish I could be quite so positive in painting the picture of the right values and approaches to management. I suspect there are many, many different right answers. No doubt each company or enterprise will have to define its own long-term purposes and develop its own philosophy in terms of its history, traditions, and its real function in our economy. I am also certain that no one philosophy would be equally useful to all managers. The character of an organization is, to a large extent, set by the top man or the top group, and it is inevitable that this be the reflection of the philosophy of these individuals. No one of us can operate with another's philosophy. I have also observed that in most enterprises the basic faith or spirit of the organization is a rather nebulous or undefined something that nevertheless has very profound meaning to the employees.

A SUCCESSFUL EXECUTIVE

Recognizing then the futility of advocating any one pattern of values, I recognize also that it might, however, be suggestive or helpful if I told you something of the philosophy of one extremely successful executive whom I have pumped a good deal on this subject (for he is more inclined to live his values than to talk about them):

As near as I can piece it together, he believes that this world was not an accident but was created by God and that His laws regulate and control the universe and that we are ultimately *responsible to Him*. Man, as God's supreme creation, is in turn endowed with creative ability. Each individual represents a unique combination of talents and potentials. In addition, man is the only animal endowed with freedom of choice and with a high capacity for making value judgments. With these gifts (of heredity and cultural environment) goes an obligation to give the best possible accounting of one's stewardship in terms of maximum self-development and useful service to one's fellows in the hope that one may live a rich life and be a credit to his Creator.

This executive also assumes that each individual possesses certain God-given rights of self-direction which only *the individual* can voluntarily delegate to others in authority over him, and that this is usually done in the interest of achieving some mutual cooperative good. The executive therefore assumes that his *own* authority as boss over others must be exercised with due regard for the attendant obligations to his employees and to the stockholders who have temporarily and voluntarily yielded their rights in the interest of this common undertaking. (Notice that he does not view his authority as originating with or derived from his immediate superior.) This delegated authority must, of course, be used to advance the common good rather than primarily to achieve the selfish ambitions of the leader at the expense of the led.

He further assumes that the voluntary association of employees in industry is for the purpose of increasing the creativity and productivity of all members of the group and thus of bringing about increased benefits to all who may share in the ultimate use of these goods and services. What is equally important, however, is that in the course of this industrial operation each individual should have an opportunity to develop the maximum potential of his skills and that the working relationships should not destroy the individual's ability to achieve his greatest maturity and richness of experience. As supervisor he must set the working conditions and atmosphere that will make it possible for his employees to achieve this dual objective of increasing productivity and maximizing self-development.

These goals can best be achieved by giving employees maximum opportunity to exercise their capacity for decision making and judgment within their assigned area of responsibility. The supervisor is then primarily a coach who must instruct, discipline, and motivate all the members of the group, making it possible for each to exercise his special talent in order to maximize the total team contribution. Profits are regarded as a measure of the group's progress toward these goals, and a loss represents not only an improper but even an immoral use of the talents of the group.

There is nothing "soft" about his operation. He sets high quality standards and welcomes stiff competition as an additional challenge to his group. He therefore expects and gets complete cooperation and dedication on the part of everyone. Incidentally, he views the activity of working together in this manner with others as being one of life's most rewarding experiences. He holds that this way of life is something which we have not yet fully learned, but that its achievement is part of our divine destiny. He is firmly convinced that such conscientious efforts *will* be rewarded with success. He manages with a light touch that releases creativity, yet with complete confidence in the outcome.

This is probably a poor attempt at verbalizing the basic philosophy that this man lives so easily and naturally. I hope, however, that it has revealed something of his conception of his role or function as an executive, and his view of what he and his organization are trying to do together. With this account of his values I am sure that you would have no difficulty completing the description of his administrative practices and operating results. They flow naturally from his underlying faith, without benefit of intensive training in the principles and art of administration.

As you would suspect, people like to work for him—or with him. He attracts good talent (which is one of the real secrets of success). Those with shoddy values, selfish ambitions, or character defects do not survive—the organization is self-pruning. Those who remain develop rapidly because they learn to accept responsibility. He not only advocates but practices decentralization and delegation. His employees will admit that they have made mistakes, but usually add with a grin that they try not to make the same one twice. People respond to his leadership because he has faith in them and expects the best in them rather than the worst. He speaks well of the members of his organization, and they appear to be proud of each other and of their record of performance. He takes a keen interest in developing measurements of performance and in bettering previous records or competitive standards. He feels that no one has a right to "louse up a job"—a point on which he feels the stockholders and the Lord are in complete agreement.

While he does not talk much about "employee communications" or stress formal programs of this type, his practice is to spend a large proportion of his time in the field with his operating people rather than in his office. He is "people oriented," and he does a particularly good job of listening. The union committee members have confidence in his fairness, yet do a workmanlike job of bargaining. In administering salaries he seems to be concerned about helping the individual to improve his contribution so that a pay increase can be justified.

In his general behavior he moves without haste or hysteria. He is typically well organized, relaxed, and confident, even under trying circumstances. There is a high degree of consistency in his behavior and in the quality of his decisions because his basic values do not shift. Since he does not operate by expediency, others can depend on him; and this consistency makes for efficiency in the discharge of delegated responsibility. Those operating problems that do come to him for decision seem to move easily and quickly to a conclusion. His long-term values naturally express themselves in well-defined policies, and it is against this frame of reference that the decisions of the moment easily fall into proper perspective.

In policy-level discussions his contributions have a natural quality of objectivity because "self-concern" does not confuse. Others take him at face value because his motives are not suspect. When differences or conflicts do arise, his approach is not that of compromise; rather, he attempts to integrate the partisan views around mutually acceptable longer-range goals. The issues of the moment then seem to dissolve in a discussion of the best means to the achievement of the objective. I have no doubt that he also has some serious problems, but I have tried to give a faithful account of the impression he creates. There is a *sense of special significance* about his operation, which is shared by his associates.

This Is the Key

It is precisely this "sense of special significance" that is the key to leadership. We all know that there are many different ways of running a successful operation. I am certainly not recommending any particular set of administrative practices—although admittedly some are better than others. Nor am I suggesting that his set of values should be adopted by others, or for that matter could be. What I am saying is that a man's real values have a subtle but inevitable way of being communicated, and they affect the significance of everything he does.

These are the vague intangibles—the "skyhooks"—which are difficult to verbalize but easy to sense and tremendously potent in their influence. They provide a different, invisible, fundamental structure into which the experiences of every day are absorbed and given meaning. They are frequently unverbalized, and in many organizations they defy definition. Yet they are the most real things in the world.

The late Jacob D. Cox, Jr., formerly president of Cleveland Twist Drill Company, told a story that illustrates my point:

Jimmy Green was a new union committee member who stopped in to see Mr. Cox after contract negotiations had been concluded. Jimmy said that every other place he had worked, he had always gone home grouchy; he never wanted to play with the children or take his wife to the movies. And then he said, "But since I have been working here, all that has changed. Now when I come home, the children run to meet me and we have a grand romp together. It is a wonderful difference and I don't know why, but I thought you would like to know."[8] As Mr. Cox observed, there must be a lot of Jimmy Greens in the world who want an opportunity to take part freely in a cooperative effort that has a moral purpose.

8. *Material Human Progress* (Cleveland, Cleveland Twist Drill Company, 1954), p. 104.

Retrospective Commentary

It's time I level with HBR readers about how "Skyhooks" came about. In a very real sense, I did not write it. It came as a stream of consciousness—but only after I had worked very hard for several weeks at putting my ideas together. I wrote the paper mainly to clear my own thinking, and to try it out for criticism on the Cleveland Philosophical Club. After much reading and thinking, I got absolutely nowhere. In desperation I was about to abandon the idea and write on a different subject. Deep inside my consciousness I said in effect to my silent partner within, "Look, if you want me to do this, you better help." About 2 A.M. that morning the ideas flowed in a continuous stream, and I put them down in shorthand notes as fast as I could.

The word "Skyhooks" for the title came in the heat of a discussion with a group of business executives attending the Institute of Humanistic Studies at Aspen, Colorado. As we debated the limits of the rational and scientific approach to life, it occurred to me that science appears rational on the surface, but at its very foundation typically lies a purely intuitive, nonrational assumption made by some scientist. He just hooked himself on a "piece of sky out there" and hung on. It was a complete leap of faith that led him.

In my studies of exceptional executives I had found a mystery not easily explainable by rational elements. These men, too, were hanging on skyhooks of their own—hidden and secret missions that went way beyond their corporate business objectives. Sometimes the mission was a "nutsy" one. Often it had long roots back in the executive's childhood and was emotional, intuitive, beyond rationality, selfless—but it stuck. For example, it might be like John F. Kennedy's determination to become President; reportedly he was doing it for his older brother, who had the ambition to be President but never made it because he was a war casualty.

Or perhaps the mission was like that of the president of one of our largest corporations. When he was 12 years old, his father died. He promised his mother he would help her work the farm in the hills so that his eight younger brothers could go through school. This is what he continued to do all of his life—helping other young men to make something of themselves. He was a great developer of managers.

I could fill a book with such examples. Many great executives I have known have something deep inside that supports them; something they trust when the going gets tough; something ultimate; something personal; something beyond reason—in short, a deep-rooted skyhook that brings them calm and confidence when they stand alone.

There is another interesting aspect to this question. In our rational, analytical, and highly successful Western culture, we have come to place great value on the material gains that represent the end results of our achievements. This is what our kids are complaining about: that we have gone overboard on material values and made a culture of *things*. But the *results* of our strivings are dead works; the life is in the *process* of achieving, in the leap of faith. David was great not when he slew Goliath, but when he decided to try.

So it seems to me that the skyhooks mystique is also characterized by a commitment to value the *process*, the working relationships with others, the spiritual bonds growing out of the faith in the God-potential deep within another person, and the basis of genuine community. The rest is the means, not the end.

In 1955, when my article was published, the generation gap had not been invented, and Marshall McLuhan had not alerted us to the fact that "the medium is the message." Yet a quick look backward reveals the considerable impact of youth and "McLuhanism" on our history and our future. The "McCarthy Kids" have ousted a President and his party, halted the military domination of our foreign policy, radically changed our educational and religious institutions, revised industry's approach to management recruiting, and made the Peace Corps type of job competitive with the "goodies" offered by business. Generalizing about the medium having greater impact than the message, they have pointed out that our values are dictated by our social systems—especially the technological, political, and managerial systems. More important than the things we create in industry, they say, is the *way* we create them—the kind of community we establish in our working together.

Without debating the merits of "pot" versus liquor, or anarchy versus order, I believe their emphasis on social process is introducing a new dimension into our corporate life and values.

"Skyhooks" was written for myself and not for publication. For a while I refused to give anybody a copy, but under pressure I duplicated a small number of copies for my friends, and they wanted copies for their friends. When the Editor of HBR got his copy and asked, "How about publishing it?" I answered,

"Only if you take it as it is; I don't want to revise it." I see little need for revising it now—except perhaps the reference (on page 437) to the increase in membership in the institutional church. The search for ultimate values and meanings is keener than in 1955, but it is apparently no longer satisfied merely by church affiliation.

The Contributors

Anthony G. Athos is Professor of Organizational Behavior at the Harvard Business School. He was cited for excellence in teaching by a vote of students and faculty of the University of Southern California in 1965, and in 1966 was portrayed on the cover of *Time* magazine as one of ten "great college teachers." Among his many publications is his latest book, *Interpersonal Behavior: Communication and Understanding in Relationships* with John J. Gabarro (1978).

Louis B. Barnes is Professor of Organizational Behavior at the Harvard Business School and has been a frequent contributor to *HBR*. He took a leave of absence from 1975 through 1977 in order to serve as President and Professor at the Iran Center for Management Studies in Tehran, Iran.

Herbert Benson is Associate Professor of Medicine at the Harvard Medical School. He is also director of the Hypertension and Behavioral Medicine sections of Beth Israel Hospital in Boston. He is the author of *The Relaxation Response* (1975) and *Mind/Body Effect* (1978).

Henry M. Boettinger was the director of corporate planning at the American Telephone and Telegraph Company at the time he wrote "Is Management Really an Art?" The article was adapted from a lecture delivered to the Oxford Centre for Management Studies, Oxford University, where he was a visiting fellow. He is now retired and living in Cornwall, England, where he is engaged in many varied writing projects.

David H. Burnham is currently Vice President of H. B. Maynard, Inc., in Pittsburgh, Pennsylvania, where he designs human resources programs and materials. Half of his time is spent in doing independent consulting, designing programs for the application of internal behavioral objectives in order to increase productivity. Until 1976, Mr. Burnham was President, Treasurer and

Chief Executive Officer of McBer and Company, a Boston behavioral consulting firm.

Abram T. Collier served as President and as Chairman of New England Mutual Life Insurance Company. Currently semi-retired, he serves as a board member for New England Mutual Life and is the Chairman of its Committee on Finance..

Thomas H. Fitzgerald is the Director of Personnel Research at the Chevrolet Division of General Motors Corporation. While he has published articles on career education and educational planning, he is also active in health care planning and is a member of the board of trustees of his local health services agency.

C. Jackson Grayson, Jr., was Dean of the School of Business Administration at Southern Methodist University from 1968 through 1975. He remained a professor there until 1977, when he left to become Chairman of American Productivity Centers, Inc., in Houston, Texas. From October 1971 to March 1973, he was on a leave of absence from SMU serving as Chairman of the Price Commission in Phase II of President Richard M. Nixon's Economic Stabilization Program.

Larry E. Greiner is Chairman of the Organizational Behavior Department at the University of Southern California Graduate School of Business Administration. He is also the Program Chairman of the Organization Development Division of the Academy of Management.

Pearson Hunt, holder of the Converse Chair at the Harvard Business School, became Professor Emeritus in 1975. He is now a full-time member of the faculty at the University of Massachusetts, Boston, where he is a Professor of Accounting and Finance and served as Chairperson of the University Senate. He is currently conducting many writing projects.

Peter G. W. Keen is Assistant Professor of Organizational Psychology and Management at the Alfred P. Sloan School of Management, Massachusetts Institute of Technology. He is currently a visiting professor at the Wharton School at the University of Pennsylvania.

John P. Kotter is Associate Professor of Business Administration at the Harvard Business School. The winner of the 1977 Exxon Award for innovation in graduate business school curriculum design, he is currently conducting research on managerial careers and general management jobs. His latest books are *Orga-*

nizational Dynamics: Diagnosis and Interventions (1978) and *Self-Assessment and Career Development* with Victor Faux and Charles McArthur (1978).

D. Paul Leitch has been an operations research analyst in the O. R. office at the U. S. Army Natick R & D Command in Natick, Massachusetts, since 1972. Mr. Leitch was formerly Assistant Professor of Behavioral Science, Boston University School of Business Administration. He spent 1971 with Arthur Young & Co. in New York as a manager.

Harry Levinson, a psychologist, is President of the Levinson Institute and Lecturer in the Laboratory of Community Psychiatry, Harvard Medical School. He was previously associated with the Menninger Foundation as Director of the Division of Industrial Mental Health. He also has taught at the Harvard Business School, where from 1968 to 1972 he was the Thomas Henry Carroll Ford Foundation Professor. He is the author of the award-winning book *The Exceptional Executive* (1968) as well as of *Executive Stress* (1970).

J. Sterling Livingston, formerly Professor of Business Administration at the Harvard Business School, is now President of Sterling Institute in Washington, D. C. He has served as chief executive of Management Systems Corporation; Peat, Marwick, Livingston & Co.; Logistics Management Institute; Technology Fund of Puerto Rico; Harbridge House, Inc., and Tamarind Reef Corporation.

David C. McClelland is Professor of Psychology at Harvard University. He is most well-known to *HBR* readers for his work on entrepreneurship and the achievement motive. He is the author of many books, among them *The Achieving Society* (1961) and *Power: The Inner Experience* (1975).

James L. McKenney is Professor of Business Administration at the Harvard Business School, where he teaches and studies management information systems. Among his many published articles and books is *The Management Game* with F. Warren McFarlen and John A. Seiler (1970).

Henry Mintzberg is Professor in the Faculty of Management at McGill University, Montreal, Canada. He has written extensively on the manager and his work and is the author of *The Nature of Managerial Work* (1973) and the McKinsey award-winning article in *HBR* in 1975, "The Manager's Job: Folklore and Fact."

O. A. Ohmann, now retired, was Assistant to the President of Standard Oil of Ohio and worked on problems and programs for management development.

Earlier in his career he was head of the Department of Psychology at the Cleveland College of Western Reserve University.

Richard Tanner Pascale is Associate Professor of Management at the Graduate School of Business, Stanford University. He has been a close student of Japanese managerial practices for many years. He is the author of *Managing the White House* (1974) and has recently compiled a study of the management styles of Harold Geneen (ITT), Roy Ash (Litton Industries) and Edwards Carlson (UAL, Inc.). His book *Zen and the Art of Management* is to be published in 1979.

F. J. Roethlisberger is probably best-known for his pioneering work with W. Dickson and Elton Mayo at the Western Electric Hawthorne plant in the 1920s. In 1950, he was appointed the Wallace Brett Donham Professor of Human Relations at the Harvard Business School, where he taught until his retirement in 1967. He was the author of many articles and books, the last of which, *The Elusive Phenomenon* (1978), was published posthumously and edited by his associate George F. F. Lombard.

Carl. R. Rogers, formerly Professor of Psychology at the University of Chicago (1947–1957) and the University of Wisconsin (1957–1963), and a Resident Fellow, Western Behavioral Sciences Institute, La Jolla, California (1964–1968), now is a Resident Fellow at the Center for Studies of the Person, La Jolla. He is the author of many books and articles, among them *On Becoming A Person* (1961).

William C. Schutz is currently the Director of the Center for Holistic Studies at Antioch University West, San Francisco. He has been a lecturer at the University of California, Berkeley, and at Harvard University as well as an Associate-in-Resident at the Esalen Institute, Big Sur, California. Among Mr. Schutz's many published books are *Elements of Encounter* (1973); *Body Fantasy* (1975), and *Joy* (1967).

H. Edward Wrapp is Professor of Business Policy at the University of Chicago's Graduate School of Business and a board member of eight corporations. He was formerly the Director of the Executive Program and Associate Dean for Management Programs at the University of Chicago's Graduate School of Business. In addition to once having been a corporate executive himself, he has worked on a variety of consulting assignments and has written numerous cases on management.

The Contributors

Abraham Zaleznik is the Cahners-Rabb Professor of Social Psychology of Managment at the Harvard Business School. A director of five corporations, he is also a psychoanalyst and an active member of the American Psychoanalytic Association. Professor Zaleznik is currently doing research in the area of applied psychoanalysis.

Index